THE EVOLUTION OF ANTITRUST IN THE DIGITAL ERA:
Essays on Competition Policy

Volume 1

Editors
David S. Evans
Allan Fels AO
Catherine Tucker

Competition Policy International, 2020

Copyright © 2020 by Competition Policy International
111 Devonshire Street · Boston, MA 02108, USA
www.competitionpolicyinternational.com
contact@competitionpolicyinternational.com

Printed in the United States of America

First Printing, 2020

ISBN 978-1-950769-60-5 (Paperback)
ISBN 978-1-950769-61-2 (Hardcover)
ISBN 978-1-950769-62-9 (Ebook)

Publisher's Cataloging-in-Publication Data
provided by Five Rainbows Cataloging Services

Names: Evans, David S. (David Sparks), 1954- author. | Tucker, Catherine, editor. | Fels, Allan, editor.
Title: The evolution of antitrust in the digital era : essays on competition policy, volume I / David S. Evans ; Catherine Tucker [and] Allan Fels AO, editors.
Description: 1st edition. | Boston : Competition Policy International, 2020.
Identifiers: LCCN 2020945593 (print) | ISBN 978-1-950769-60-5 (paperback) | ISBN 978-1-950769-61-2 (hardcover) | ISBN 978-1-950769-62-9 (ebook)
Subjects: LCSH: Antitrust law. | Competition, Unfair. | Electronic commerce--Law and legislation. | Big data. | Consolidation and merger of corporations. | Commercial law. | BISAC: LAW / Antitrust. | LAW / Commercial / General. | LAW / Mergers & Acquisitions.
Classification: LCC KF1649 .E93 2020 (print) | LCC KF1649 (ebook) | DDC 343.07/21--dc23.

Cover and book design by Inesfera. www.inesfera.com

Editors' Note

The story of antitrust is the story of technology. The essays in this volume tell the latest chapter in this ongoing saga.

In the late 19th century, the disruptive technology of the day was the railroad. In the expanding U.S., local railroads were bought up and consolidated into broad systems by the "trusts" that gave the Sherman Antitrust Act of 1890, and the resulting worldwide body of law, its name. Moving on from transport, various technologies have formed the locus of economic growth, and therefore of antitrust scrutiny, throughout the past hundred years or so.

After the railroads came Standard Oil, and its control over the key input for 20th century economic growth. Again, this was a reflection of technology, both in other industries' need for vast sources of energy, and the improved refining technology that led to scale in the oil industry itself. Antitrust enforcement, famously, split the company up. Then, mid-century, came the telecommunications revolution. In the U.S., concerns crystallized around the role of the Bell System as an incumbent technology provider. Once more, antitrust enforcement split it up. In the 1970s and 80s, IBM's mainframe computing business became the target of enforcement. Following on from that, the banner cases of the 1990s in both the U.S. and Europe were against Microsoft's practices in the desktop computing space. In the latter two instances, however, the consequences were less radical, due, perhaps, to the intervening Chicago School critique of earlier antitrust remedies.

Despite these different outcomes, at each step along the way, antitrust thinking has been defined by the technologies that gave rise to its greatest enforcement challenges. Since the dawn of this century, attention has turned to the current generation of innovators, in what today is termed the "digital economy." The quandaries facing today's legislators, enforcers, and public, are novel and multifaceted. Nonetheless, they bear comparison with the formative struggles that policymakers grappled with throughout the first century of antitrust.

The pieces in this volume draw on the lessons of the past to set out how competition rules might deal with this new set of concerns, in various jurisdictions around the world. Each one draws on general themes, yet nevertheless addresses specific aspects of the contemporary debate.

Much of today's antitrust discussion concerns the businesses run by large companies such as Amazon, Apple, Facebook, Google, and Microsoft. Each has significant share in a given industry, and derives its revenues from what are described as "platforms." But how are such platforms different from the incumbent businesses of the past? The answer to this is not clear. Yet queries surrounding the platforms' alleged dominance, and whether their conduct amounts to an infringement of competition rules, have been a source of controversy for over a decade. The pieces in this volume address this dilemma head-on.

At a fundamental level, there is the definitional threshold of what a "platform" even is, and what rules should apply to such a business. Then there is the question of whether "platforms" have a "special responsibility" towards downstream operators that rely on them to reach customers. In other words, can platform operators favor their own businesses in those related markets? Or do competition laws require them to treat all firms in the same way? What are the risks to competition if platforms are given free rein? In antitrust parlance, these questions are assessed under the rubric of "self-preferencing," which has dominated recent headlines.

Pieces by **Thomas Kramler** and **Robert D. Atkinson** & **Joe Kennedy** report on this controversy from the trenches. The authors draw on their considerable experience in dealing with these issues to ask whether antitrust concerns in the digital economy can effectively be addressed within the confines of existing antitrust law and jurisprudence, or whether new rules are needed.

At the time of publication, this "platform regulation" debate is reaching its crescendo. In 2019, various jurisdictions, including the EU, Germany, Australia, and the Brexiting UK, commissioned detailed reports on whether competition rules need to be updated to deal with "platforms," and "self-preferencing" specifically. The coming months and years will see legislatures take action on these reports. Much is at stake in how these reports' conclusions are interpreted. The pieces in this volume form a vital part of that discourse.

Aside from these (almost existential) concerns, there is the question of how "platforms" interact with other actors in the economy. While it is productive for there to be broad discourse on the role of competition and digital regulatory policy, it is also vital for those rules to stay in their own lane. Otherwise, reforms grounded in the logic of antitrust could unduly expand its role, and counteract other policies. This debate has reached an advanced stage in Australia, where policy efforts have honed in on the media and news industry. Pieces by **Simon Bishop** & **George Siolis**, and **Andrew Low** & **Luke Woodward**, describe these developments, and discuss the risks of focusing on a narrow set of sector-specific concerns to derive broad antitrust solutions.

Then, there are even more specific concerns. Algorithms, anonymously executed in server farms, dominate modern commerce. Aside from mundane operational decisions, algorithms are increasingly used to set pricing and other commercial strategies. This can be pro-competitive and efficient. But algorithms, like people, can also restrict competition and harm consumers. If firms use algorithms that "autonomously" tacitly collude through deep machine learning, can the firms that run them be held liable? The pieces by **Andreas Mundt** and **Gönenç Gürkaynak, Burcu Can**

& **Sinem Uğur** underline the need for further research on how such algorithms operate in real-life settings, before creating a new head of liability.

Technology allows consumers to access and interact with offers in the digital world with remarkable ease. But it has also created the potential for new forms of consumer exploitation, and facilitates highly individualised price discrimination. This creates opportunities for business models based on exploiting incumbents' superior bargaining position, particularly in the business-to-business space. Platforms can make "take-it-or-leave-it" offers that allow the platform to enjoy all the surplus of trade. This notion of an "abuse of a superior bargaining position" is foreign to competition rules in certain jurisdictions, but is known in Japanese competition law, as discussed by **Reiko Aoki** & **Tetsuya Kanda**.

Moore's Law famously predicts that the number of transistors on a microchip will double every two years, though their cost will be halved. These remarkable advances, coupled with parallel developments in mass data gathering and storage, allow today's computers to solve tasks of extraordinary complexity, including innovative, reliable, and lucrative predictive analytics. Yet this possibility raises profound privacy concerns, as reflected in laws such as the California Consumer Privacy Act and the EU's General Data Protection Regulation. Such rules, in turn, raise novel competition issues.

This dynamic has profound implications for competition law, and how it interacts with privacy rules. Although competition and privacy law are separate disciplines, they are in tension with each other. As **Maureen K. Ohlhausen** & **Peter Huston** discuss, this problem came to the forefront in recent U.S. litigation between hiQ and LinkedIn. The latter, invoking the privacy rights of its members, employed technical measures to block hiQ's automated bots from accessing data on LinkedIn's servers. HiQ, in turn, alleged that LinkedIn's actions were in reality an attempt to restrict competition.

As the authors discuss, this case represents the archetypal conflict between data privacy and competition, and will be repeated throughout the world in years to come. The policy dilemma between privacy rules and antitrust cannot be overstated. Protecting privacy by restricting data flows can hinder competition by denying new entrants access to the data they need to compete. On the other hand, ensuring that rivals have easy access to data can diminish privacy by distributing data in ways that consumers may not anticipate or want.

The foregoing should make clear that the story of antitrust in the "digital economy" is but one chapter in a saga that is still being written. Like all sagas, it draws from universal themes, and is self-referential within its canon. Yet it is all the more interesting as a result.

The editors would like to thank Elisa Ramundo, Sam Sadden, and Andrew Leyden for commissioning, compiling, and editing this volume.

Table of Contents

The Antitrust "Challenge" of Digital Platforms: How a Fixation on Size Threatens Productivity and Innovation

By Robert D. Atkinson & Joe Kennedy [1]

Abstract

Over the last several years, much of the debate on antitrust policy has focused on the largest digital platforms, including, Amazon, Apple, Facebook, Google, and Microsoft. Each of these companies is large, has some significant market share in their narrowly defined industry, and most derive much of their revenues from running one or more multi-sided platforms. These factors have generated a backlash by anti-big firm activists and consternation among many European and U.S. competition policy officials. However, a careful review of both the individual markets and the general issues reveals that the challenges these companies pose, while slightly different from previous markets, are not entirely new. Moreover, in most cases legitimate competition policy issues, especially those related to structure, are limited and can be effectively addressed within the confines of existing antitrust law and jurisprudence.

I. INTRODUCTION

Over the last several years, much of the debate on antitrust policy has focused on the largest digital platforms, including, Amazon, Apple, Facebook, Google, and Microsoft. Each of these companies is large, has some significant market share in their narrowly defined industry, and most derive much of their revenues from running one or more multi-sided platforms. These factors have generated a backlash by anti-big firm activists and consternation among many European and U.S. competition policy officials. However, a careful review of both the individual markets and the general issues reveals that the challenges these companies pose, while slightly different from previous markets, are not entirely new. Moreover, in most cases legitimate competition policy issues, especially those related to structure, are

---

1 Dr. Robert D. Atkinson is President of the Information Technology and Innovation Foundation. Joe Kennedy is a Senior Fellow at the Information Technology and Innovation Foundation.

limited and can be effectively addressed within the confines of existing antitrust law and jurisprudence.

These companies, and others like them, add significant value to the economy. Although their size and market share have led to several concerns, regulators should pause before taking action. As with all antitrust cases, any decisions should follow from and be guided by a careful study of all sides of the specific markets involved and be focused on maximizing overall economic welfare. When this is done, regulators will find that many of the "problems" being debated, such as vertical expansion into other markets, accumulation of market power through mergers, and threats to innovation, do not justify a change in either the substance or the enforcement of antitrust law. Where real problems related to conduct, as opposed to presumed ones, do appear, existing tools give agencies sufficient power to deal with them.

It is critical that policymakers and antitrust practitioners get this right. Given the potential transformation of many industries by digital technologies and the importance of both network effects and economies of scale, digitally powered platforms in a range of industries may well become the dominant form of organization going forward, similar to the rise of the large industrial corporation at the turn of the 20th century and large diversified companies in the decades after WWII. In response to the great expansion of economic growth and innovation enabled by those then-new organizational forms, the U.S. federal government interpreted the Sherman and Clayton Acts to let individual companies acquire the size needed to maximize efficiency, but established guardrails against mergers and conduct that conferred clear market power and business practices that limited economic growth or hurt consumers.[2]

The main antitrust laws were passed around the turn of the 19th Century and were originally focused on limiting trusts – formal agreements of cooperation and collusion between separate companies. One key response to banning trusts was to encourage mergers and the emergence of large industrial corporations as a way for companies to take advantage of new technologies which enabled and even required economies of scale. Teddy Roosevelt's Progressive Party platform reflected the common view of the time, "The corporation is an essential part of modern business. The concentration of modern business, in some degree, is both inevitable and necessary for national and international business efficiency."[3] Thirty years later, his cousin Franklin Delano Roosevelt stated, "Nor today should we abandon the principle of strong economic units called corporations, merely because their power is susceptible

---

2 An important influence behind this shift was Robert H. Bork, *The Antitrust Paradox: A Policy at War With Itself*, (New York: Basic Books, 1978).

3 Robert D. Atkinson & Michael Lind, "The Myth of the Roosevelt 'Trustbusters,'" *New Republic*, May 4, 2018, https://newrepublic.com/article/148239/myth-roosevelt-trustbusters.

of easy abuse."[4] This acceptance of large corporations was central to the ability of the United States to become the dominant economic power through the late 1970s. In contrast, Europe continued to allow cartels which reduced the incentives to create large corporations, which meant that Europe developed many fewer large, globally competitive corporations, imposing a structural burden on the EU economy that persists to this day.[5]

If it is true that in the near future large intra-industry digital platforms in industries such as health care, banking, education, and logistics will emerge by combining data analytics, low transactions costs, and global reach with a platform-based business model, it is critical that competition policy evolve to enable, rather than stifle, these new, more productive forms of business organization. Just as antitrust doctrine in the early decades of the 20th century adapted to and indeed embraced the form of the large industrial corporation, antitrust policy needs to do the same today in embracing platform organizations. Applying more restrictive antitrust doctrines and practices to these new models threatens to squash European growth and do to the U.S. economy what Europe did to its economy through the mid-20th century. As such, the stakes of getting this right cannot be overestimated. The first place to start is to focus antitrust policy on what it is supposed to focus on: overall economic welfare.

II.   THE BENEFITS DIGITAL PLATFORMS BRING

The dominant fact about digital platforms is that they deliver significant benefits to a wide range of users, including app developers, sellers of a wide variety of goods and services, advertisers, consumers, and tens of millions of people who use social media to stay in touch with family and friends.

The value of these benefits is hard to measure, in part because many services are offered for free. But even if they were not, the consumer surplus between their value to Internet users and the amount that users actually have to pay is very large. A recent study by MIT economists estimates the median Internet user would require compensation of $17,530 to give up search engines for one year. The equivalent estimates for email and digital maps are $8,414 and $3,648, respectively.[6]

---

4 *Ibid.*

5 Jeffrey Fear, "Cartels and Competition: Neither Markets Nor Hierarchies," (Working Paper, 2006), http://www.hbs.edu/faculty/publication%20files/07-011.pdf.

6 Erik Brynjolfsson, Avinash Collis & Felix Eggers, "Using Massive Online Choice Experiments to Measure Changes in Well-Being," *Proceedings of the National Academy of Sciences*, vol. 116(15), April 9, 2019, https://www.pnas.org/content/116/15/7250, "How Much are Search Engines Worth to You?" MIT Management website, (accessed December 11, 2019), https://mitsloan.mit.edu/ideas-made-to-matter/how-much-are-search-engines-worth-to-you.

A filing by scholars from the Mercatus Center lists five ways Internet platforms create value:[7]

- By allowing people to rent out other people's cars, homes, and other property, they increase the value of underutilized capital.

- By connecting large numbers of buyers and sellers, they make both supply and demand more competitive and allow greater specialization among producers, leading to more choice for consumers.

- By lowering the transaction costs of finding willing partners, negotiating over price, ensuring quality, and monitoring performance, they increase the number of beneficial trades.

- By making it easy for both buyers and sellers to check on the past performance of potential counterparties, they increase the amount of information in the marketplace and reduce the risk to parties.

- By offering an alternative to traditional markets, whose regulators are often captured by existing producers, they create opportunities for new suppliers to satisfy the unmet needs of consumers and force incumbents to become more efficient.

These benefits tend to have progressive effects. The savings from lower prices and free services often benefit low-income consumers the most, because the savings represent a higher proportion of their total income. Moreover, higher-income users are more valuable to platforms because they are more likely to buy advertised goods and services, yet both higher income and lower-income consumers receive the same services.

These companies are also among the most innovative in the world. Amazon and Alphabet led all companies in investment in research and development in 2018.

---

7 Christopher Koopman, Matthew D. Mitchell & Adam Theirer, "The Sharing Economy: Issues Facing Platforms, Participants, and Regulators," (Mercatus Center, Public Interest Comment, May 26, 2005), https://www.mercatus.org/publications/technology-and-innovation/sharing-economy-issues-facing-platforms-participants-and.

Microsoft and Apple came in sixth and seventh, while Facebook was 14th.[8] Each company is constantly innovating its core business in order to respond to competitive threats, including from each other, and attract new users. In addition to their core businesses, they are among the leaders in investing in the next generation of general-purpose technologies, including artificial intelligence, autonomous vehicles, blockchain, quantum computing, and robotics. Development of these technologies will deliver significant economic and social benefits.

III. THE ALLEGED THREAT TO ANTITRUST

Antitrust concerns about the largest digital giants are driven largely by the difficulty for antitrust thinking to effectively adapt to the network age. At the turn of the 19th century, some saw large firms with a significant share of the market as at best suspect; at worst a serious problem. Today, some see platform-based businesses in a similar light.[9] But, in the digital economy, platforms may very well become the dominant form of business organization, for precisely the same reasons large industrial organizations became dominant in the 20th century: they are the most efficient organizational form for the current technology.

Today, antitrust concerns over platforms are driven by two common traits of multi-sided platforms. On the demand side, the push for bigness is caused by network externalities. The network's value to each user is increased by each additional user. One platform that contains everyone is more valuable than two platforms, each of which contains half the users. This is because with one platform every user can reach every other user. For example, Facebook has announced plans to make Facebook Messenger, WhatsApp, and Instagram interoperable, since these services are all owned by Facebook, so that users on one app can message users on the other apps using whichever service they prefer.[10] Internet users would be worse off if the Federal Trade Commission obtained an injunction preventing Facebook from merging these services, or worse, split these companies apart, because then users would have to create and maintain separate accounts on each of these services to communicate with all of their con-

---

8   Statista, "Ranking of the 20 Companies With the Highest Spending on Research and Development in 2018," https://www.statista.com/statistics/265645/ranking-of-the-20-companies-with-the-highest-spending-on-research-and-development/ (accessed November 22, 2019).

9   Tim Wu, *The Curse of Bigness: Antitrust in the New Gilded Age*, (Columbia Global Reports, 2018).

10   Mark Zuckerberg, "A Privacy-Focused Vision for Social Networking," Facebook, March 6, 2019, https://www.facebook.com/notes/mark-zuckerberg/a-privacy-focused-vision-for-social-networking/10156700570096634?mod=article_inline.

tacts.[11] Of course, not every network works this way, and mandating interoperability requirements for social networks could create security risks or create other problems for users, such as spam or harassment.[12] Even the classic example, the telephone, has lost its monopoly on intercommunication; people no longer need a phone to call each other. Internet-protocol standards allow voice packets to be generated and sent on a variety of different platforms. Users also have different interests, so often not everyone needs to communicate with everyone else, in which case the network advantage will fade out at a certain size. The net result is scale. As an Obama administration Council of Economic Advisers' report noted, "Some newer technology markets are also characterized by network effects, with large positive spillovers from having many consumers use the same product. Markets in which network effects are important, such as social media sites, may come to be dominated by one firm…"[13]

On the supply side, firms often grow bigger to benefit from economies of scale. By growing larger, firms can reduce their average total cost of production by spreading their fixed costs over more units. But traditional economic theory also assumes that most firms will eventually face increasing marginal costs because of inefficiencies that come from being too large. These increasing marginal costs limit how large firms can grow, making it difficult for any one firm to capture the entire market. However, digital platforms usually enjoy fixed marginal costs that do not increase with size. This means that their average total cost continues to decline as they add more users, and they do not face the same constraints on their size or market share. These efficiencies benefit society.

Digitally powered business models, including platforms, also have the advantage of being able to have strong offerings along a number of dimensions. Traditional firms normally focus on and gain advantage in one, or possibly two of three aspects: price, quality or customization, in large part because there are significant tradeoffs between each. Customization comes at the expense of low cost, for example. Indeed, much of the business strategy literature is premised on firms identifying which of these market areas they should specialize in. But for many Internet platforms, digital technologies enable them to make strong offerings in all three aspects: low prices, higher quality, and customization.[14]

---

11 John McKinnon & Emily Glazer, "FTC Weighs Seeking Injunction Against Facebook Over How Its Apps Interact," *Wall Street Journal*, December 12, 2019, https://www.wsj.com/articles/ftc-weighs-seeking-injunction-against-facebook-over-how-its-apps-inter-act-11576178055.

12 "Augmenting Compatibility and Competition by Enabling Service Switching Act of 2019," Congress.gov, https://www.congress.gov/bill/116th-congress/senate-bill/2658/all-info.

13 White House, "Benefits of Competition and Indicators of Market Power," May 2, 2016, 3, https://obamawhitehouse.archives.gov/sites/default/files/page/files/20160502_competition_issue_brief_updated_cea.pdf.

14 David Moschella, Seeing Digital: A Visual Guide to the Industries, Organizations, and Careers of the 2020s, (DXC Technology 2018).

These advantages are not likely to be absolute, however. Economists Daniel Spulber & Christopher Yoo point out that market share due to network effects can be interrupted by periodic outbreaks of new competition for the market, raising the possibility that the dominant platform will be replaced.[15] Two of the biggest drivers of this disruption are technology and demographics. Historically, technological innovation played a significant role in companies like IBM (mainframes), Digital Equipment Corporation (minicomputers), AT&T (telephony), Walmart (retail) and FedEx (delivery) losing dominant market shares. Indeed, important transitions such as the move from analog to digital, the rise of the Internet, and the advent of smart phones have been especially challenging for incumbents to spot and respond to.

As antitrust scholars Carl Shapiro & Hal Varian note, "[T]he information economy is populated by temporary, or fragile, monopolies. Hardware and software firms vie for dominance, knowing that today's leading technology or architecture will, more likely than not, be toppled in short order by an upstart with superior technology."[16] And as IT industry expert David Moschella points out, "today's giants are more vulnerable than previous industry leaders in at least one way: the customer switching costs are mostly ones of changing habits, not conversion effort and cost, and this relative ease of transition could be an important factor sometime down the road."[17] Today, rapid advances in technology continue to present platforms with new services and business models. Platforms that do not quickly adapt to these opportunities leave the door open for rivals.

In fact, Spulber & Yoo believe platforms are likely to face even more competition in the future, spurring more innovation.[18] However, in order to enable this dynamic efficiency, regulators may have to allow static inefficiency for a limited period of time. Businesses with large upfront expenses and low marginal costs often need to earn higher rates of return to recoup their investments, and to fund the next big investments in innovation. But even then, their advantages may be temporary, particularly in a globally competitive economy. Similarly, the advantage of efficiencies of scale can be offset if competitors also enjoy zero marginal cost.

The constant entry of new consumers can also present Internet platforms with a challenge. Young consumers have little invested in existing networks, tend to be very comfortable with the latest technology, are more concerned about communi-

---

15   Daniel F. Spulber & Christopher S. Yoo, "Antitrust, the Internet, and the Economics of Networks," in *Oxford Handbook of International Antitrust Economics*, Roger D. Blair & D. Daniel Sokol eds. (Oxford University Press, 2014).

16   Carl Shapiro & Hal R. Varian, *Information Rules: A Strategic Guide to the Network Economy*, 173, (Harvard Business Review Press 1998).

17   David Moschella, *Seeing Digital: A Visual Guide to the Industries, Organizations, and Careers of the 2020s*, 62.

18   Spulber & Yoo, "Antitrust, the Internet, and the Economics of Networks."

cating with a narrow group of friends rather than the whole world, and are less than awed by their parents' technology. Younger users were the main drivers behind instant messaging, WhatsApp, Instagram, and most recently TikTok.

In both cases, antitrust regulators need to balance the benefits of competition for the market with the benefits of scale. However, this tradeoff only needs to be made if there is some harm to the consumer, such as a delay in innovation.

IV. LET ANTITRUST BE ANTITRUST

Nevertheless, the rapid growth of a few large companies that operate digital platforms has produced a lot of anxiety about their effects on society. Purported market dominance has been blamed for a host of ills including reduced privacy, poor data security, censorship, poor moderation of offensive and dangerous content, and excessive political power. These are all important issues, deserving their own policy response. But in most cases antitrust solutions would do nothing to solve them, and indeed may make them worse. Moreover, trying to incorporate them into antitrust policy would replace one widely supported policy goal, the consumer welfare standard, with a jumble of goals that often conflict with each other. Attempts to rank many policy goals on their own would not only give tremendous discretion to unelected regulators. It would threaten the discipline's ability to accomplish the goals it is suited to. Even the best regulators would struggle to find the right balance between these goals. The worst would use the tremendous discretion given to them to reward political supporters.

Moreover, the development of separate policies for privacy and other concerns can have antitrust implications. Rules such as Europe's General Data Protection Regulation impose large, somewhat fixed costs on firms that are subject to them, both in the cost of complying and the risk of punishment for inadvertent breaches. This gives larger firms an advantage because they can spread the fixed costs over a larger user base. Smaller firms therefore find it harder to compete. It can also drive firms from the market, further reducing the amount of competition. As economist Catherine Tucker notes, stringent privacy rules can strengthen advantages larger firms have when it comes to data.[19]

Nobel Laureate economist Jan Tinbergen developed the rule that achieving a desired number of policy targets requires regulators to have an equal number of policy instruments.[20] For this reason, social concerns should remain outside the boundaries of antitrust analysis and practice.

---

19   Catherine Tucker "Digital Data, Platforms and the Usual [Antitrust] Suspects: Network Effects, Switching Costs, Essential Facility," https://ssrn.com/abstract=3326385

20   Huiping Yuan & Stephen M. Miller, "Target Controllability, Time Consistency, and the Tinbergen Rule," October 1, 2013, https://papers.ssrn.com/sol3/papers.cfm?abstract_id=2334342.

V.   HOW ANTITRUST HANDLES CONCERNS ABOUT DATA SCARCITY

As mentioned above, in most cases, a separate policy goal requires a separate policy instrument. Thus, most of the issues raised in the previous section do not involve antitrust issues and deserve non-antitrust solutions. However, data collection does have an antitrust component. Two points are important to keep in mind about data. First, the antitrust aspect is only a small part of this issue and should not get confused with other aspects. Second, current antitrust policy built around the Consumer Welfare Standard works well in dealing with the antitrust issues surrounding data. The confusion comes when proponents of stronger regulation try to use antitrust remedies to fix issues that do not involve antitrust goals.

Proponents of stronger antitrust enforcement for platforms frequently point to data as a strategic asset. It is often said that data is the new oil, implying strategic importance for those who have it and vulnerability for those who do not.[21] But this is simply the wrong metaphor. Unlike oil, data is non-rivalrous (the same data can be used more than once) and is often non-excludable (others may gather the same data that I already own). Even more relevant to its role in antitrust policy, data often has zero marginal costs (the cost of collecting, processing, and storing additional data often approaches zero) but rapidly diminishing returns to scale.

Most important, however, is that much of the most collected personal data often tends to be worth little by itself. Rather, it is the business model and algorithms used to analyze the data that give companies value. Reporting by the *Financial Times* shows that individual pieces of data are often sold cheaply.[22] General information, such as age, gender and location is worth only $0.0005 per person. Information about someone shopping for a car is slightly more valuable at $0.0021 per person. Knowing a woman is in her second trimester of pregnancy bumps it up to $0.11 per person. The total for most individuals is less than a dollar.

Economists Anja Lambrecht and Catherine Tucker argue that data seldom provides a company with a competitive advantage, especially in the face of a superior product offering.[23] Although Amazon Marketplace, for example, benefits from knowing what products users searched for on their website, its large selection, low prices, and superior logistics are far more valuable. Although data makes its business model

---

21   "The World's Most Valuable Resource is No Longer Oil, But Data," *The Economist*, May 6, 2017, https://www.economist.com/leaders/2017/05/06/the-worlds-most-valuable-resource-is-no-longer-oil-but-data.

22   Emily Steel, "Financial Worth of Data Comes in at Under a Penny a Piece," *The Financial Times*, June 12, 2013, https://www.ft.com/content/3cb056c6-d343-11e2-b3ff-00144feab7de.

23   Anja Lambrecht & Catherine E. Tucker, "Can Big Data Protect a Firm from Competition?" *Antitrust Chronicle*, No. 1(1), January 2017), https://www.competitionpolicyinternational.com/can-big-data-protect-a-firm-from-competition/.

better, it is a mistake to think data scarcity is the primary constraint to greater competition. Antitrust law should look at data the same as any other asset that occasionally has strategic value rather than as a unique resource conferring broad market power. In a more recent paper, Tucker cites previous studies to argue that neither network effects nor switching costs are likely to confer market power due to the mere possession of data.[24] One of these showed that the accuracy of Internet searches was not sensitive to the amount of historical data about past searches, implying that Google's market share is due mainly to its present superiority rather than its past dominance.[25] Moreover, because most data is relatively worthless and ubiquitous, government requirements to share it will seldom be justified.

VI.   SHOULD INTERNET COMPANIES BE BANNED FROM COMPETING WITH USERS ON THE PLATFORMS THEY RUN?

Another concern is that companies that run multi-sided platforms often compete with sellers on one or more sides of the market. For example, Amazon offers its own products on Amazon Marketplace, often in direct competition with those of its regular suppliers. Because Amazon can see what products are selling at what prices, critics claim it has an unfair advantage. Similarly, Apple was recently sued by Spotify, which alleged that Apple used unfair tactics in its App Store to suppress its competitors.[26] Senator Elizabeth Warren (D-MA) would prohibit this practice by designating the largest platforms "utilities" and prohibiting companies from both owning the platform and being a seller on the platform.[27]

Of course, digital platforms are not the first, or even the biggest, marketplaces. Large retailers including CVS, Walmart, and Costco, offer shelf space to thousands of manufacturers. They also offer competing products under their own brand names, such as Costco's Kirkland brand. These products usually sit on the same shelf, side-by-side with those of their suppliers, often undercutting them on price. And of course, the retail chains look at sales data when making decisions on what to sell.

The main point to remember when analyzing such cases is that this behavior is usually procompetitive. It may hurt the supplier of a competing good, but it benefits

---

24   Catherine Tucker "Digital Data, Platforms and the Usual [Antitrust] Suspects: Network Effects, Switching Costs, Essential Facility."

25   Leslie Chiou & Catherine Tucker, "Search Engines and Data Retention: Implications for Privacy and Antitrust," (NBER Working paper 23815, September 2017), https://www.nber.org/papers/w23815.

26   Adam Satariano & Jack Nicas, "Spotify Accuses Apple of Anticompetitive Practices in Europe," *The New York Times*, March 13, 2019, https://www.nytimes.com/2019/03/13/business/spotify-apple-complaint.html?searchResultPosition=3.

27   Team Warren, "Here's How We Can Break Up Big Tech," *Medium*, March 8, 2019, https://medium.com/@teamwarren/heres-how-we-can-break-up-big-tech-9ad9e0da324c.

consumers by offering more choice at lower prices. As long as the supplier's intellectual property is not violated and consumers are not confused, government should not dissuade this type of competition. Antitrust policy should protect consumers, not sellers hurt by legitimate competition. While there may be room for general fair-dealing requirements that require platforms to post their policies and enforce them evenly, platforms usually have a strong incentive to engage in fair-dealing: platforms that abuse their suppliers will lose them. This in turn will attract fewer buyers, leading to a downward spiral.

The widespread assumption that platforms' dominant position in a particular market frees them from competition is based on a faulty definition of the relevant market. For platforms providing free services, including Facebook and Google, the relevant market is the total ad market. They derive a significant portion of their revenue from advertisements shown to their users. In many cases, the buyers of these ads are also large sophisticated companies that use analysis by Visual IQ and C3 Metrics to evaluate the return on investment across platforms, including television and radio. The competition for ads leads to a competition for eyeballs as platforms compete for users' limited time and attention. Although YouTube does not offer the same functions as Facebook, users can only pay attention to one or the other at a time.

Platforms that make money from consumers must also compete with off-line firms which still represent the largest part of the economy. Amazon competes with other sellers on its Marketplace, the Internet sites of other retailers and, most significantly, brick and mortar stores. Its cloud-based services compete with those of established companies including Google, Microsoft and Oracle. Apple computers compete with Windows-based systems and its iOS devices, such as the iPhone and iPad, compete with Android-based tablets and smart phones.

Finally, possessing a dominant position in the market does not guarantee a profit. Amazon experienced net cash outlays for many years as it reinvested profits to expand its business. More tellingly, Uber continues to suffer losses with no end in sight. Heavy competition from rival services, including taxis, may prevent it from ever rising out of what is essentially a commodity business.

VII.   FOUR ILLUSTRATIVE CASES OF COMPETITION INVOLVING PLATFORMS

A closer look at some of the more commonly cited instances of market abuse shows that the issues are far more complicated than many observers describe. Although the four instances described below may not be typical, the fact that they are commonly cited as showing the failures of market forces justifies going into more detail.

Amazon's purchase of Quidsi: As mentioned above, the potential for companies to offer competing products on the markets they run is often cited as a threat to competition. The concern, however, seems directed at protecting competing sellers rather than consumer welfare. A frequently mentioned example is Amazon's competition with and eventual purchase of Quidsi. Attorney Lina Khan gives a detailed description of some of the facts in her widely cited article "Amazon's Antitrust Paradox."[28] Quidsi sold a number of household products, including diapers, over Amazon's Marketplace. Khan alleges that, in order to drive Quidsi out of business, Amazon sold diapers at a 30 percent discount from its normal prices. While this tactic may have hurt Quidsi, it clearly helped consumers, at least in the short run. On the surface this tactic was successful because Amazon eventually purchased Quidsi in 2011, eliminating it as a source of competition.

But why was Amazon selling at a loss? For the same reason that Quidsi was. Quidsi's owners saw that Walmart and Target used diapers as loss leaders in order to establish a relationship with new mothers who might then purchase a lot more from the store, generating sufficient profits to make up for the loss on diapers. In the words of their founders:

> [W]e started with selling the loss leader product to basically build a relationship with mom. And once they had the passion for the brand and they were shopping with us on a weekly or a monthly basis that they'd start to fall in love with that brand. We were losing money on every box of diapers that we sold.[29]

After the purchase, Amazon continued to face strong competition in the diaper market. This prevented it from raising prices to recoup the cost of buying Quisdi. In the supply market it had to purchase its product from national brands such as Pampers and Huggies, which were not dependent on Amazon for customers and could therefore negotiate for higher wholesale prices, while in the retail market it faced major chains including Walmart and Target. By 2016 Amazon had acquired 43 percent of the online baby supply market, while Walmart and Target had 23 percent and 18 percent respectively. However, 80 percent of sales occurred off-line.[30] But these sales apparently did not generate much profit. Amazon shut down Quidsi, including diapers.com, in April 2017. Meanwhile the founders of Quidsi used the proceeds from its sale to start a new online retail company, Jet.com, which was eventually purchased

---

28   Lina Khan, "Amazon's Antitrust Paradox," *Yale Law Journal*, vol. 126(3), 2016.

29   Quoted in Kristian Stout and Alec Stapp, "Is Amazon Guilty of Predatory Pricing?" International Center for Law & Economics Blog, May 7, 2019, https://laweconcenter.org/resource/is-amazon-guilty-of-predatory-pricing.

30   Business Insider, "Target, Walmart, Amazon Dominate the Online Baby Goods Market," April 22, 2016, https://www.businessinsider.com/target-walmart-amazon-dominate-the-online-baby-goods-market-2016-4.

by Walmart for $3.3 billion.[31] In perhaps the clearest case of competitive underselling, it is hard to see how Amazon benefited or how consumers were harmed.

Allbirds: Of course, not every case is the same. A more recent example raises some of the same issues in a different context. Allbirds makes environmentally friendly shoes. Rather than sell its product over Amazon's Marketplace and other sites, Allbirds sells direct to the customer. Hence the competition occurs between two websites rather than within Amazon's Marketplace. Once again, Amazon offered a competing product, this time selling similar-looking shoes for less than half the price that Allbirds charges. Its decision to do so is informed by its knowledge of how many customers mistakenly search for Allbirds on its site. However, from here the tale gets more complicated. First, Allbirds is active in the supply market, selling its organic materials to over 100 other brands, some of which may use them to manufacture shoes.[32] Amazon is also not the only company producing a close substitute.[33] But perhaps the most interesting fact is that Allbirds' main objection to Amazon's product is that Amazon achieves its cost advantage by not adhering to Allbirds' stringent environmental and social practices, primarily its use of natural and recycled materials.[34] If consumers are being misled into mistakenly purchasing look-alike shoes when they think they are getting Allbirds, that would present a clear case of consumer harm and probably trademark infringement. But assuming consumers know what they are getting, the entry of close substitutes benefits them.

Google price comparison: The third case looks at Google's price comparison feature on its search engine. In June 2017 the European Commission determined that Google had violated antitrust rules by favoring its own results in searches. The Commission fined Google €2.42 billion ($2.7 billion). Carl Shapiro, who advised Google during the case, recently analyzed its merits.[35] When a person enters a search of "Nikon cameras" into Google's search engine the first several sites that appear on the results screen are sponsored search results accompanied by a photo of one or more

---

31   Jeffrey Eisenach, "Who Should Antitrust Protect? The Case of Diapers.com," American Enterprise Institute Blog, November 5, 2018, https://www.aei.org/technology-and-innovation/who-should-antitrust-protect-the-case-of-diapers-com.

32   Aaron Holmes, "Allbirds' Cofounder Just Slammed Amazon for Selling a Lookalike Shoe: 'Please Steal Our Approach to Sustainability'" *Business Insider*, November 25, 2019, https://www.businessinsider.com/allbirds-slams-amazon-knockoff-shoes-sustainability-approach-2019-11.

33   Kait Hanson, "The Best Allbirds Wool Runner Dupes," Communikate blog, January 29, 2019, https://communikait.com/2019/01/the-best-allbirds-wool-runner-dupes/.

34   Washington Journal of Law, Technology & Arts, "Please Steal Our Business Practices: Allbirds' Novel Approach to Intellectual Property Theft," November 21, 2019, https://wjlta.com/2019/11/21/please-steal-our-business-practices-allbirds-novel-approach-to-intellectual-property-theft/.

35   Carl Shapiro, "Protecting Competition in the American Economy: Merger Control, Tech Titans, Labor Markets," *Journal of Economic Perspectives*, Vol. 33(3), Summer 2019.

cameras that allow users to quickly compare offerings from several sites. These are advertisements paid by online merchants to Google and are clearly marked as sponsored. Next follow sponsored text ads, followed by generic search results generated by the search algorithm. Google does not charge for listing generic results.

The Commission ruled that Google had abused its dominance as a search engine to promote its position in what the Commission determined was a separate market, comparison shopping, by placing its own comparison shopping service above that of rival comparison sites and demoting some of these rival sites in its search results. Although in the fact sheet accompanying its opinion the Commission stated that it "does not object to the design of Google's generic search algorithms, or to demotions as such, nor to the way that Google displays or organizes its search results pages,"[36] the Commission ruled that Google's comparison shopping service gained significant market share at the expense of rivals. The Commission objected "to the fact that Google has leveraged its market dominance in general internet search into a separate market, comparison shopping. Google abused its market dominance as a search engine to promote its own comparison shopping service in search results, whilst demoting those of rivals."[37] The Commission felt that this extension of market power into a new market "deprived European consumers of the benefits of competition on the merits, namely genuine choice and innovation." [38]

The charge that Google actively manipulated the results of the generic search to demote rival comparison sites clearly raises antitrust concerns. The problem with the Commission's analysis is that it also implies Google violated antitrust rules merely by selling new ads with pictures and placing them on top where all of its other ads go. If this is what the Commission believes, it should indicate exactly how consumers, as opposed to rival comparison sites, are hurt merely by placing Google's comparison results on the top. Instead, it only made a broad complaint that there was less competition because Google integrated this new service with its traditional search results, where it is the market leader. While the Commission apparently did not object to Google's *generic* search results, it did apparently object to its overall search results which, according to its definition, includes the paid ads. It apparently thinks that, having shown users a prominent comparison of different ads, Google was required to show similar comparisons by other companies.

The Commission's objection to this type of integration is misguided. Using its strength in regular search results to offer comparison ads that are similar to its tradi-

---

36 European Commission, "Antitrust: Commission Fines Google €2.42 Billion for Abusing Dominance as Search Engine by Giving Illegal Advantage to Own Comparison Shopping Service—Factsheet," European Commission Factsheet, June 27, 2017, https://ec.europa.eu/commission/presscorner/detail/en/MEMO_17_1785.

37 *Ibid.*

38 *Ibid.* The Commission made clear that Google's actions would have been abusive even if comparison shopping sites and merchant platforms were considered to be part of one market.

tional ads does not hurt consumers. While antitrust policy was originally suspicious of efforts to use dominance in one market to enter others, in recent decades courts have become more accepting of such practices, provided there is no harm to consumers. In many cases tying two products together promotes consumer welfare. For example, consumers who purchase a new car usually buy separate items, such as a music console, car loan, and service plan at the same time. Even if they could purchase each of these items separately, they usually prefer to buy them as a package, looking at the total price of the vehicle. In the case of comparison shopping, consumers are better off seeing these results in one search, rather than having to go to multiple ones. Google helped consumers by placing comparisons on top. While it should treat all generic ads equally, it should not be required to give equal prominence to non-paying comparison sites that placed low in its generic results.

Spotify v. Apple: More recently, Spotify filed an antitrust complaint against Apple in the European Union. Although Apple's App Store does not charge for most of the apps downloaded by its users, it does take a percentage of any subscription fees (but not ad revenue or product sales) that apps collect from their users. This percentage is 30 percent in the first year and 15 percent in subsequent years. Spotify alleges Apple has unilaterally changed the rules and interpretations in ways that disadvantage the makers of rival apps in order to favor Apple Music.[39] Specifically, Spotify does not want to pay the subscription fee commission for users who pay for its Premium service through Apple's in-app payment system. (Apple earns no revenue from Spotify users who subscribe through the Spotify website, and existing Spotify users who subscribe through Apple's in-app payment system can cancel their subscription through Apple and re-subscribe through Spotify's website.)

Based on Apple's response, the parties seem to disagree on a lot of the facts.[40] But let's look at the larger picture. Having built an iconic device that can run apps, Apple then decided to allow third parties to write apps for its device. However, it required app developers to sell their apps through its App Store. This gave Apple great control over the apps its users could download but it also allowed the company to ensure that these apps complied with certain standards such as data security and use, the absence of malware, and compatibility with Apple products. For most apps, Apple does not charge a fee, but it does for the type of subscription offered by Spotify's premium service. Which of these business decisions constitute unfair competition?

Spotify is apparently claiming that, having built the device and the store, Apple should be required to make the store available to everyone for free. Users can

---

39 Spotify, "A Timeline: How We Got Here," https://timetoplayfair.com/timeline/.

40 Apple, "Addressing Spotify's Claims," Apple Statement, March 14, 2019, https://www.apple.com/newsroom/2019/03/addressing-spotifys-claims/.

currently download Spotify for free from the App Store. Apple does this because they want their App Store to be appealing to consumers so they will buy Apple devices (e.g. iPhones) What users cannot do is use Apple's in-app payment system to subscribe to Spotify's premium service unless Spotify pays the commission fee. As Apple points out, many Spotify users sign up for its services through mobile carriers, avoiding the App Store completely. It might seem like Apple has an incentive to handicap Spotify so that listeners will use Apple Music instead, or that Apple Music has a natural advantage since it does not have to pay the commission fee to itself for Apple Music. However, every time Apple succeeds in converting a Spotify customer from its site, its gain is offset by the fee Spotify would otherwise have paid it. This reduces the gain from competition. Apple must also compete with Android, which has most of the U.S. and world market. One of the primary methods of competition is the availability of apps for each device. If popular apps such as Spotify are easily available for Android but not on the App Store, Apple could lose phone sales. But perhaps the biggest point is that Apple users can use their phones to sign up for premium service by going to Spotify's mobile website, avoiding the App Store and its commission altogether.

VIII. REMEDIES

The point of the above discussion is not that potential actions will never give platforms unfair market power and therefore should never be stopped. Nor is it to argue that platforms will never engage in anticompetitive behavior. Both are clearly possible. Therefore, we need to continue enforcing antitrust law but focus on maximizing consumer welfare, not protecting competitors. Some supporters of the consumer welfare standard have argued that past enforcement has been too lax and that, going forward, regulators and courts need to err more on the side of ensuring that markets are competitive and less on the side that innovation will be curtailed by excessive government interference.[41]

Whether or not the level of enforcement needs to be adjusted, platforms pose a special challenge for regulators. Because they involve more than one side of a given market, regulators need to conduct a careful empirical study of the effect that a merger or corporate action would have. In particular, they need to examine the effect on all sides of the market before concluding that competition has been harmed. Some practices that normally indicate a threat to competition in most markets can actually increase competition and consumer welfare in platforms. These include pricing below marginal costs, tying, high margins, and exclusive arrangements.[42] For example, revenues from ad markets

---

41 Carl Shapiro, "Protecting Competition in the American Economy: Merger Control, Tech Titans, Labor Markets."

42 Jonathan L. Rubin, "The Systems Approach to Antitrust Analysis," *The Antitrust Bulletin*, vol, 56(1), Spring 2011; Marc Rysman, The Economics of Two-Sided Markets," *Journal of Economic Perspectives*, vol. 23(3), Summer 2009.

may be used to subsidize ad viewers in order to attract a sufficient number to support the ad market. As the above examples show, the details of the market often matter a lot.

Still, some advocate for breaking large platforms up and regulating part of the platform as a utility. Several main problems stand out. The first is that breakups are hard to accomplish. They take several years, regulators are likely to have difficulty separating the various technologies, and regulated industries do not have a history of steady innovation. Second, and partly for these reasons, courts have become much more demanding about proving consumer harm before they will approve an antitrust suit.[43]

Third, past breakups have not led to notable success in the form of increasing competition, raising industry output, or reducing prices.[44] Breaking up the Internet platforms involves separating both integrated working teams and the underlying technology, something regulators are not experienced with. For example, FTC Commissioner Joseph Simons, in speaking about a potential investigation that could force Facebook to divest certain mergers, mentioned that the company's efforts to integrate its three major brands would complicate any effort to break them up.[45] The *Economist* magazine points out that decisions over which part of the business gets access to data, defining the lines between different markets, and anticipating both unintended consequences and the effect of future technology do not have any obvious answers.[46]

Fourth, breakups would require continued regulation to separate the various components from other markets, otherwise the various parts could reestablish their dominance through future mergers or internal growth into related markets. Finally, it is not clear that government-set prices would be better for consumers.

Luckily, existing case law is adequate to deal with the most likely antitrust problems, including mergers, price fixing, and unfair trade practices. But it requires a careful study of the existing markets, a realization of the limits of regulatory action, and a balance between government intervention to preserve market competition and a continued reliance on market forces to drive technology and innovation.

As discussed above, it is possible that the age of digital platforms is just beginning. Many companies, including today's digital leaders, are experimenting with tech-

---

43   Carl Shapiro, "Protecting Competition in the American Economy: Merger Control, Tech Titans, Labor Markets."

44   Robert W. Crandall, "The Failure of Structural Remedies in Sherman Act Monopolization Cases," (AEI-Brookings Joint Center for Regulatory Studies, Working Paper 01-05, March 2001), https://www.brookings.edu/research/the-failure-of-structural-remedies-in-sherman-act-monopolization-cases/.

45   Kadhim Shubber, "Facebook Break-Up Would Be Hard, Says FTC Chief," *Financial Times*, August 19, 2019, https://www.ft.com/content/64e887f6-c2b8-11e9-a8e9-296ca66511c9.

46   "Dismembering Big Tech," *The Economist*, October 24, 2019, https://www.economist.com/business/2019/10/24/dismembering-big-tech.

nology to develop new approaches to some of society's biggest problems. Federal and state policies should encourage this innovation by allowing new arrivals to challenge traditional incumbent firms, even if the result is less direct competition. The reason is that a shift to fewer firms with the winners operating on platforms will likely deliver more benefits to the economy through higher productivity and more benefits to consumers through lower prices. As pointed out above, the combination of massive data, Internet technology, and the right business model could create great value in health care, education, construction, and other industries, many of which have not seen strong productivity growth for several decades. Policies that limit market consolidation or restrict companies from moving into related markets are likely to discourage these efforts.

IX. CONCLUSION

It is true that the largest digital platform companies are different from the traditional corporations that preceded them. Their low marginal costs, global scope, and rapid pace of innovation may make digital platforms a primary source of value creation in the future. But that does not mean that a new platform era requires a major overhaul of existing competition law.[47] A big advantage of current antitrust law is that it is general enough to be applied to new conditions. Thanks to the flexibility of laws enacted over 100 years ago, the Department of Justice and the Federal Trade Administration have the powers they need to address mergers that might result in consumer harm and corporate actions that unfairly disadvantage competitors. If they can identify specific practices regarding the operation of platforms that harm consumers, current laws give them the power to prohibit them. What matters is that the focus of their efforts be firmly fixed on the task of developing clear evidence that the activity would harm economic and consumer welfare.

In the last few years a distinct group of commentators has argued the largest platforms suddenly represent unique threats to competition and innovation.[48] What the critiques do not contain is a careful description of how platforms' behavior harms society as opposed to competitors, and why we should expect a revamped antitrust policy to produce a better result. Much of the analysis is built on speculation about what might happen, coupled with a "neo-Brandeisian" suspicion of bigness.[49] However, the vast number of users and continued innovation demonstrates that a broad section of the population derives great value from existing digital platforms. There is little likelihood that this will change soon.

---

47 Joe Kennedy, "Why Internet Platforms Don't Need Special Regulation, (Information Technology and Innovation Foundation, October 2015), https://itif.org/publications/2015/10/19/why-internet-platforms-dont-need-special-regulation.

48 Lina Khan, "The Separation of Commerce and Platforms," *Columbia Law Review*, Vol. 119, 2019.

49 Robert D. Atkinson & Michael Lind, *Big is Beautiful: Debunking the Myth of Small Business* (MIT Press, 2018).

hiQ v. Linkedin: A Clash Between Privacy and Competition

By Maureen K. Ohlhausen & Peter Huston [1]

Abstract

Advances in data storage, processing power, and system architecture allow today's computers to solve tasks of extraordinary computational complexity, paving the way for innovative, reliable, and lucrative predictive analytics. The implications for both privacy law and antitrust law can be significant. Although competition law and privacy law often coexist peacefully, tension between the two realms can arise, as they have in hiQ v. LinkedIn, a case pending in the Northern District of California. HiQ applies its proprietary algorithms to data scraped from LinkedIn's servers (without LinkedIn's authorization) to provide "people analytics" to its employer customers. One product warns employers if employees' LinkedIn activity suggests they may be considering changing jobs. LinkedIn, invoking the privacy rights of its members, employed technical measures to block hiQ's automated bots from accessing the data on LinkedIn's servers. HiQ alleges that LinkedIn's justification for attempting to block hiQ is pretextual and that it is really seeking to insulate itself from potential competition.

The case demonstrates a legal policy dilemma. Protecting privacy by limiting the spread of data can reduce the benefits of competition by denying upstart rivals access to the data they need to compete and entrenching incumbents (who may already be dominant). Conversely, attempting to bolster competition by insuring that competitive rivals have easy access to personal data can diminish privacy by distributing data in ways that consumers may not anticipate or want.

Noting that hiQ would go bankrupt without access to the data on LinkedIn's platform, the district court gave hiQ an early victory, enjoining LinkedIn from employing its active technical measures to block hiQ's bots. The Ninth Circuit agreed. In reaching their opinions, both the District Court and Ninth Circuit disregarded the concepts of consumer sovereignty about privacy choices and individual control over personal data. This is surprising given the current heightened sensitivity to digital privacy, as reflected in California's Consumer Privacy Act ("CCPA") which, ironically, took effect just months after the Ninth Circuit issued its opinion.

---

1   Partners, Baker Botts, LLP.

I.   INTRODUCTION

Meet Jill. She's not happy at work. Her employer doesn't pay her what she's worth and her boss is a jerk. She decides to start looking for a new job, discretely. As a first step, Jill wants to make sure her profile on LinkedIn, the popular on-line professional network, is sparkling. She updates her list of accomplishments, polishes up the description of her experience, solicits some peer recommendations, and sends out a round of invitations to join her network. To keep her plans private, she double-checks her LinkedIn settings to make sure that each change she makes to her profile is not broadcast to her connections, which include several work colleagues.

Unfortunately, Jill's goal of keeping her job search covert is not shared by hiQ Labs, a data analytics company. HiQ's automated bots scrape data from LinkedIn's servers and run it through the hiQ algorithm. HiQ determines that Jill is a "flight risk." For a fee, and unbeknownst to Jill, hiQ presents this determination to her employer.

At this point, things could veer in a couple of different directions. Maybe Jill's employer, armed with hiQ's "flight risk" conclusion, realizes how valuable she is, offers her a raise and fixes the issues that caused her to be dissatisfied in the first place. On the other hand, maybe Jill's boss demotes her, makes her life even more miserable, and sabotages her chances of finding another job. Either way, she did not consent to hiQ's analysis and use of her LinkedIn data and her life is altered from the course she planned.

Such a scenario is at the heart of litigation now pending between hiQ and LinkedIn. The case raises a number of questions at the intersection of competition and privacy law: Are restrictions on access to data necessary to protect against exploitation of consumers, or are they anticompetitive barriers slowing innovation and insulating incumbents against nascent rivals? Who should be able to access data on digital platforms? What are the rights of consumers, platforms, and competitors, and how should they be balanced?[2]

II.   *hiQ LABS, INC. v. LINKEDIN CORPORATION*

Most people are familiar with LinkedIn, the on-line professional network that allows its 500 million members to share their professional histories and interests. HiQ Labs is younger, much smaller, and less well-known. HiQ's automated bots scrape LinkedIn's servers and apply predictive algorithms to the data. HiQ sells the results of its analysis, which it calls "people analytics," to Fortune 500 clients looking for insights on their workforces. HiQ's business model poses a problem for LinkedIn, which works to preserve the trust and goodwill of its members and informs its members that it prohibits automated bots from scraping the site.

---

2   For a helpful survey of various court approaches to screen-scraping cases, see George H. Fibbe, Screen-Scraping and Harmful Cybertrespass after Intel, 55 Mercer L.Rev. 1011 (2004).

In 2017, LinkedIn sent hiQ a letter demanding that it cease and desist scraping LinkedIn's site or risk legal action under the federal anti-hacking law known as the Computer Fraud and Abuse Act ("CFAA"), California's corollary, the Computer Data Access and Fraud Act ("CDAFA"), codified at California Penal Code section 502, *et seq.*, the Digital Millennium Copyright Act, and the state common law of trespass. LinkedIn also made sure that the various technological systems it employs to thwart automated bots were working against hiQ's incursions. Those systems identify patterns suggesting non-human activity and throttle or block the activity. After receiving LinkedIn's cease and desist letter, hiQ promptly sued LinkedIn in the Northern District of California seeking a declaratory judgment that it was not violating the law. It also accused LinkedIn of violating California's Unfair Competition Law and interfering with hiQ's contracts, among other claims. HiQ moved for a preliminarily injunction to enjoin LinkedIn from employing its blocking technologies against hiQ and asked the court to order LinkedIn to withdraw the cease and desist letter.

Responding to the preliminary injunction motion, LinkedIn pressed the privacy interests of its members. It noted that "hiQ makes no enforceable commitment in a privacy policy or otherwise to LinkedIn's members regarding what it will do with their data or to whom it may sell or transfer it, nor is there any way for LinkedIn members to 'opt out' of hiQ's processing and selling of their data."[3] It also noted,

> [I]f a LinkedIn member decides to delete his or her account, LinkedIn pledges to permanently delete the account and all of the member's information within 30 days. LinkedIn does not keep a copy of that data. The power to remove one's own information from LinkedIn helps ensure that members have control of their own information. hiQ does not claim that it makes any similar pledge, nor could it, as it has no contractual relationship with LinkedIn's members.[4]

Despite this argument, District Court Judge Edward Chen granted hiQ's motion for preliminary injunction.[5] Judge Chen credited hiQ's assertion that it would go bankrupt without access to the data and therefore found that the balance of equities tipped sharply in favor of hiQ. Judge Chen was skeptical of LinkedIn's claim that members opt not to broadcast their profile changes primarily to keep those changes private from their employers. Applying the sliding scale approach to preliminary in-

---

3   LinkedIn Corp's Opposition to Plaintiff's Motion for a Temporary Restraining Order at 3, *HiQ Labs, Inc. v. LinkedIn Corp.*, 273 F. Supp. 3d 1099 (N.D. Cal. 2017), *aff'd*, 938 F.3d 985 (9th Cir. 2019) (Dkt. 31).

4   *Id.* at 6.

5   *HiQ Labs, Inc. v. LinkedIn Corp.*, 273 F. Supp. 3d 1099 (N.D. Cal. 2017), *aff'd*, 938 F.3d 985 (9th Cir. 2019).

junctions, Judge Chen held that because the equities tipped sharply in favor of hiQ, he needed to find only that hiQ had raised serious questions going to the merits to issue a preliminary injunction.

LinkedIn appealed the injunction to the Ninth Circuit. The appeal raised sensitive and highly charged issues — access to data, privacy, competition, innovation, and free speech. The case attracted appellate heavy-weights: Harvard Professor Lawrence Tribe joined the briefing for hiQ and former United States Solicitor General Donald Verrilli, Jr. argued for LinkedIn. The case also attracted numerous *amici*. Interestingly, two non-profit organizations dedicated to digital privacy wound up on opposite sides. The Electronic Frontier Foundation ("EFF") submitted a brief in support of hiQ, while the Electronic Privacy Information Center ("EPIC") supported LinkedIn. At oral argument, the court allowed the parties to argue well-beyond their allotted time.

The Ninth Circuit affirmed the preliminary injunction.[6] The court agreed with Judge Chen's conclusion on irreparable harm and the balance of the equities.[7] As to whether hiQ had raised serious questions on the merits, the court first addressed hiQ's intentional interference with contract claim. HiQ had contracts to supply its "people analytics" product to several clients. The court noted that hiQ would be unable to perform without access to the LinkedIn data. For its part, LinkedIn alleged a "legitimate business purpose" in protecting its members data. It argued that protecting its members privacy was essential to preserving member trust and goodwill. The court, weighing the interest of contractual stability against LinkedIn's interest of protecting its members and its investment in the platform, held that LinkedIn's technical measures to block hiQ had not been recognized as acceptable justifications for contract interference.[8]

Critically, the court cited evidence that LinkedIn had plans to offer services similar to some that hiQ offered, making hiQ a potential competitor:

> LinkedIn's conduct may not be within the realm of fair competition. . . . If companies like LinkedIn, whose servers hold vast amount of public data, are permitted selectively to ban only potential competitors from accessing and using that otherwise public data, the result—complete exclusion of the original innovator in aggregating and analyzing the public information—may well be considered unfair competition under California law.[9]

---

6 *HiQ Labs, Inc. v. LinkedIn Corp.*, 938 F.3d 985 (9th Cir. 2019).

7 *Id.* at 993-995.

8 *Id.* at 997.

9 *Id.* at 998 (citations omitted).

The court also held that LinkedIn's interest in protecting its members' data was relatively weak because members who requested that their profile changes not be broadcast may have made that election merely to avoid annoying their connections with notifications, not to protect their own privacy.[10]

As to LinkedIn's allegation that hiQ is violating the anti-hacking provisions of the CFAA by accessing LinkedIn's servers without authorization, the court held that hiQ had raised a serious question as to whether the CFAA's "without authorization" concept even applied. The court noted that prior to LinkedIn banning hiQ and employing its technological systems to thwart it, hiQ had not needed prior authorization to view LinkedIn member information.[11] For example, the data hiQ scraped was never password protected.[12] LinkedIn has petitioned the Supreme Court for a writ of certiorari on the CFAA issue.[13] The Court had not ruled on that petition as of the writing of this article.

Lastly, the court addressed how granting or denying an injunction would affect the public interest.[14] HiQ had argued that "letting established entities that already have accumulated large user data sets decide who can scrape that data from otherwise public websites gives those entities outsized control over how such data may be put to use."[15] For its part, LinkedIn argued that the preliminary injunction allowed hiQ to freeride and would invite malicious actors to attack its servers, forcing LinkedIn and other companies with public websites "to choose between leaving their servers open to such attacks or protecting their websites with passwords, thereby cutting them off from public view."[16] The court sided with hiQ:

> [G]iving companies like LinkedIn free rein to decide, on any basis, who can collect and use data—data that the companies do not own, that they otherwise make publicly available to viewers, and that the companies themselves collect and use—risks the possible creation of information monopolies that would disserve the public interest.[17]

---

10 *Id.* at 994, 998.

11 *Id.* at 999-1000.

12 *Id.* at 1001.

13 *LinkedIn Corp. v. HiQ Labs, Inc.*, petition for cert. filed (U.S. Mar. 9, 2020) (No. 19-1116).

14 *Id.* at 1004.

15 *Id.* at 1005.

16 *Id.*

17 *Id.*

Notwithstanding the Ninth Circuit's concern over the possible creation of "information monopolies," it bears mentioning that that when the Ninth Circuit wrote its opinion hiQ had not brought a Sherman Act monopolization or attempted monopolization claim against LinkedIn (although it added those claims in an amended complaint filed after the Ninth Circuit's opinion). In its amended complaint, hiQ alleges that LinkedIn possesses monopoly power in the markets for professional social networking platforms and people analytics.[18] Perhaps that is not surprising. Laying aside whether these are properly defined relevant markets, hiQ faces an uphill climb on these claims because there is no generalized duty to aid competitors.[19] Unilaterally refusing to deal with a potential competitor, without more, does not comprise a Sherman Act monopolization violation. Although courts have recognized refusals to deal as a basis for monopolization claims under certain circumstances, the high-water mark for such claims was 35 years ago when the Supreme Court decided that Aspen Skiing Co. engaged in monopolization when it cut off competitor Aspen Highlands Skiing Corporation from a joint all Aspen ski pass.[20] Since then, courts have been skeptical of such claims and have typically required that the refusal not make economic sense but-for its anticompetitive effect, often evidenced by ending a profitable prior course of dealing.

While hiQ did not initially allege a Sherman Act claim, it did allege that LinkedIn violated the California Unfair Competition Law ("UCL"). The UCL is more forgiving than the Sherman Act (how much so is frequently the subject of argument). The UCL supplied the hook for hiQ's argument that LinkedIn's alleged rationale for banning hiQ was pretextual. As the district court noted, the UCL "is not limited to actual antitrust violations, but also includes conduct that threatens an incipient violation of an antitrust law, or violates the policy or spirit of one of those laws because its effects are comparable to or the same as a violation of the law, or otherwise significantly threatens or harms competition."[21] HiQ alleges that LinkedIn's conduct violates the spirit of the antitrust laws because LinkedIn is unfairly leveraging its power in the professional networking market to secure an anticompetitive advantage

---

18 Amended Complaint at ¶ 111 (Dkt 131), *hiQ Labs, Inc. v. LinkedIn Corp.*, No. 3:17-cv-3301 EMC (N.D. Cal. Feb. 14, 2020).

19 *Verizon Comm's, Inc. v. Law Offices of Curtis V. Trinko*, 540 U.S. 398, 411 (2004).

20 *Aspen Skiing Co. v. Aspen Highlands Skiing Corp.*, 472 U.S. 585 (1985).

21 273 F. Supp. 3d at 1117.

in the data analytics market.[22] HiQ also alleges that LinkedIn is unfairly controlling an "essential facility."[23] Neither the monopoly leveraging doctrine nor the essential facilities doctrine have a solid footing at the U.S. Supreme Court, which is perhaps another reason why hiQ did not allege a federal antitrust claim.

III. THE RELATIONSHIP BETWEEN COMPETITION LAW AND PRIVACY LAW

Although both privacy law and competition law share the ultimate goal of protecting consumers, they have different missions. Competition law seeks to ensure that consumers enjoy the benefits of a competitive market — high quality products and services at competitive prices — and that firms who wind up with market power do not extend their power into other markets or use it to exclude competitors. Privacy law, on the other hand, seeks to ensure that consumers have some measure of control over their personal data. The two realms can come into contact in a number of ways. Firms can offer enhanced privacy to distinguish their products and secure a competitive advantage over rivals who offer less protection. In other words, privacy can be a competitive differentiator as an aspect of product quality. Apple, for example, has adopted this strategy, touting its refusal to share its users' data for marketing purposes. LinkedIn, for its part, pledges to its members that it will not rent or sell personal information that members post and, as noted above, informs members that it prohibits automated bots from scraping the site.

Tension between privacy law and competition law arises when a competitor or potential competitor relies on access to consumers' personal information held by a rival. For example, the German competition authority, the Bundeskartellamt, argued that alleged violations of data protection laws by Facebook, which it considers a dominant social network provider, also constituted a violation of German competition law. A German appellate court disagreed, however, holding that merely collecting

---

22 *Id*. The Second Circuit announced in *Berkey Photo, Inc. v. Eastman Kodak Co.*, 603 F.2d 263 (2d Cir. 1979) that "a firm violates § 2 by using its monopoly power in one market to gain competitive advantage in another . . . ." *Id*. at 276. More recently, circuit courts have diminished the monopoly leveraging doctrine as an independent claim under section 2. See, e.g. *In re Microsoft Corp. Antitrust Litig.* 333 F.3d 517 (4th Cir. 2003); *Alaska Airlines, Inc. v. United Airlines, Inc.*, 948 F.2d 536 (9th Cir. 1991). The Supreme Court appeared to take a narrow view of monopoly leveraging in *Trinko*, , noting in a footnote that a party can articulate a successful monopoly leveraging claim only by showing a "dangerous probability of success in monopolizing the second market." 540 U.S. at 415 n. 4 (internal quotes and citations omitted).

23 273 F. Supp. 3d at 1117. The Seventh Circuit articulated the four elements of the essential facilities doctrine in *MCI Communications Corp. v. American Telephone and Telegraph Co.*, 708 F.2d 1081, 1132-33 (7th Cir. 1983): "(1) control of the essential facility by a monopolist; (2) a competitor's inability practically or reasonably to duplicate the essential facility; (3) the denial of the use of the facility to a competitor; and (4) the feasibility of providing the facility." *Id*. at 1132-33. In *Trinko* the Supreme Court pointedly noted that it has never adopted the essential facilities doctrine. 540 U.S. at 410-11.

and processing the data of Facebook users does not constitute an abuse of dominance (Europe's version of monopolization) in violation of competition law without harm to actual or potential competitors.

HiQ v. LinkedIn represents another example of this tension playing out in litigation, and we can expect more. As consumers navigate the modern digital economy, they generate vast amounts of data (now measured in zettabytes (10^{21} bytes) annually). Day-by-day computers, smart phones, digital assistants, social media, wearable technology, home appliances, and cars become more interconnected. Meanwhile, dramatic advances in data storage and retrieval, paired with equally dramatic advances in processing power and system architecture, allow computers to solve tasks of extraordinary computational complexity.

This has paved the way for sophisticated and rapidly deployable predictive analytics and artificial intelligence that is more widely available than ever before. This, in turn, opens the door to groundbreaking innovations — new products and services that can improve the lives of millions. At the same time, however, those with access to such data and analytical tools are often privy to disconcertingly accurate insights into how we are likely to act, where we are likely to go, who we are likely to be with, our state of mind, and what we will likely buy and consume. The privacy implications are significant. The implications for market power, the realm of antitrust law, are equally significant. In short, data can be a very valuable resource and the digital economy prospectors that are digging in these mines are frequently discovering rich new veins of data gold.

This presents a legal policy dilemma. Increasing privacy protections by limiting the spread of data can reduce the benefits of competition by denying rivals access to the data they need to compete, simultaneously entrenching incumbents that hold such data (who may already be dominant). Locking down data, in this view, is considered tantamount to raising a barrier to entry or expansion. Conversely, attempting to bolster competition by ensuring that competitive rivals have access to personal data can diminish privacy by sharing data in ways that consumers may not anticipate or want.

In the tug-of-war between privacy and competition, both the district court and court of appeals in *hiQ v. LinkedIn* have come down firmly on the side of competition, at least so far. That may have something to do with the posture of the case (the opinions were in the context of injunction proceedings, and as of the writing of this article LinkedIn has not even responded to the complaint). Crucially, consumers such as LinkedIn members are not directly represented. To be sure, LinkedIn made privacy-based arguments on their members' behalf. But LinkedIn's credibility on member privacy issues was undermined by hiQ's allegations that LinkedIn was just seeking to protect its market power and that the privacy arguments were just a handy alibi. Both the District Court and the Ninth Circuit rested their decision, in part, on LinkedIn's alleged plans to develop a service competitive to hiQ's (though LinkedIn will obtain users' permission). Given the current heightened sensitivity to digital privacy, however, it is remarkable that both the District Court and Ninth Circuit disregarded the concepts of consumer sovereignty about privacy choices and individual control over their data in their opinions, despite the fact that these principles are wildly popular. According to Pew Research polls, 93 percent of adults say that being in control of who can get information about them is important[24] yet over 8 in 10 say they have very little or no control over the data that companies and the government collects.[25] The U.S. Federal Trade Commission has used its authority over unfair and deceptive practices to challenge harmful uses of consumer data that consumers did not agree to or anticipate. These concepts support LinkedIn's argument that it had a business justification for denying hiQ access. When members post their data on LinkedIn's site, LinkedIn states it does not allow it to be scraped by third parties. Users do not anticipate or consent to companies like hiQ secretly analyzing changes to their profiles for purposes of reporting to their employers. Ironically, just months after the Ninth Circuit issued its opinion, California's Consumer Privacy Act (CCPA) took effect.

Although the CCPA was not in effect when hiQ created its service or when it sued LinkedIn, it is now and it directly affects hiQ's activities. Under the CCPA, businesses that collect a consumer's personal information must inform the consumer what information they are collecting and why. To "collect," under the statute, includes "gathering, obtaining, receiving, or accessing any personal information pertaining to a consumer by any means . . . include[ing] receiving information from the consumer, either actively or passively, or by observing the consumer's behavior."[26] The law defines "personal information" in a way that clearly includes the information hiQ collects. Specifically, it includes information that "relates to, describes, is capable of being associated with, or could reasonably be linked, directly or indirectly, with a particular consumer or household" and "[i]nferences drawn . . . to create a profile about a consumer reflecting the consumer's preferences, characteristics, psychological trends . . . predispositions, behavior, attitudes, intelligence, abilities, and aptitudes."[27] Although "personal information" does not include publicly available information, under CCPA, "publicly available" refers only to information that is lawfully made available from federal, state, or local government records, not information that is publicly posted by the consumer on a private site.[28]

---

24   Mary Madden, Lee Rainie. Pew Research Center, May 20, 2015 "Americans' Attitudes About Privacy, Security and Surveillance." Available at: http://www.pewinternet.org/2015/05/20/americans-attitudes-about-privacy-security-and-surveillance/.

25   Pew Research Center, November 2019, "Americans and Privacy: Concerned, Confused and Feeling Lack of Control Over Their Personal Information."

26   California Consumer Privacy Act, CAL. CIV. CODE § 1798.140(E).

27   Id. §§ 1798.140(o)(1), 1798.140(o)(1)(K).

28   Id. §1798.140(o)(2).

The increasing importance of consumer data to competition coupled with the growing protection of such data in privacy law creates numerous dilemmas. Sharing as a competition remedy has traditionally been invoked where data is difficult or expensive to create, raising an entry barrier that keeps out competitors who need access to such data. By contrast, the concern driving privacy law, like the CCPA, is that consumer data has become too widely available, with a perceived loss of consumer control. The remedy adopted for privacy concerns limits collection and restricts sharing of data, except at the consumer's direction, but attempts to provide these protections and stop a rival from accessing data may trigger antitrust liability, at least under the UCL, or liability for interfering with a rival's contracts.

The case between hiQ and LinkedIn will continue, and the advent of the CCPA may yet get the court's attention. Regardless, this case represents an early clash between the goals of antitrust and privacy law and demonstrates that companies that use consumer data need to be alert to possible threats to their business models from both areas of law.

Vertical Restraints in a Digital World

By David S. Evans [1]

Abstract

The subject of vertical restraints is well-trod territory in antitrust. Most of the cases, and economic literature, have focused, however, on the physical world of manufacturers and distributors. This paper considers what's new and different about the digital world that matters for the antitrust analysis of vertical restraints. Cases and economic learning from the physical world remain highly relevant. What makes the digital world different is the prominence of intermediaries, most of which are multisided platforms, and the implications of the Internet and other information technologies for these intermediaries and the businesses that rely on them. After describing key features — including critical mass, multi-homing, and platform governance regimes — this paper considers important aspects of analyzing vertical restraints in the digital world. It then considers several applications involving platform rules, exclusive contracts, and MFNs for digital intermediaries.

I.   INTRODUCTION

Most cases and economic analyses involving vertical restraints have focused on the physical world of manufacturers and distributors. Commerce, however, is moving rapidly to a digital world populated by firms where the provision of goods and services depends heavily on Internet connections. For the analysis of vertical restraints, this digital world could involve the same principles just different facts. To a large extent that's the case. Certain features of digital businesses, however, are distinct from the physical world and will play a substantial role in matters before competition authorities and courts.

This paper provides a guide to those features and their implications for the analysis of vertical restraints. Section I describes what's new and different about digi-

---

1   Co-Executive Director, Jevons Institute for Competition Law and Economics, and Visiting Professor, University College London, London and Chairman, Global Economics Group, Boston, Mass. This paper is based on my presentation at the Swedish Competition Authority's Pros & Cons 2019 in Stockholm, November 2019. I have worked, and am currently working, as an expert on antitrust cases involving vertical practices by digital platforms for both complainants and defendants and received funding for some of the research on which this article is based. I would like to thank Howard Chang for helpful comments and suggestions and Nicholas Giancarlo for excellent research help.

tal businesses that may matter for antitrust analysis of vertical restraints. Section II provides some general principles for analyzing vertical restraints in the digital world. Section III considers examples of vertical restraints arising from the application of platform rules for participation, exclusive contracts, and MFNs to help illustrate these principles. Section IV concludes briefly.

II.   WHAT'S NEW AND DIFFERENT ABOUT THE DIGITAL WORLD?

The digital economy, as defined here, comprises businesses that rely substantially on the Internet to provide products and services to consumers. The products could be digital, and delivered digitally, such as video (YouTube) or search results (Google). They could be physical products that are delivered physically but are found and bought digitally (Amazon). They could be services that are delivered and consumed physically, such as a ride, but facilitated mainly over the Internet (Uber). They also comprise digital products and services that enable other digital businesses, such as mobile app platforms (Apple). By this definition, the digital economy excludes important digital products that are not provided primarily over the Internet such as payment card networks (Visa). This paper also does not consider businesses that provide the critical physical infrastructure for the digital economy, such as fixed and mobile broadband providers.

The digital economy is substantial and is likely to become an even larger portion of the overall economy. In the U.S., online firms account of almost half of the time people spend on media, 39 percent of total advertising spending, and about 10 percent of total retail commerce.[2] Expectations of future growth are partly responsible for driving up the valuations of digital businesses. As of October 1, 2019, seven of the ten most highly valued publicly traded companies made most of their profits from products and services that depend heavily on the Internet.[3] The growth of online commerce is likely to accelerate with the deployment of 5G technologies that will blanket the physical world with connected devices that can handle vast amounts of data at much greater speeds than today.

Many economically significant digital businesses operate intermediaries. In most cases these intermediaries are multisided platforms that facilitate beneficial interactions, often exchange, between distinct types of participants for which there are usually indirect network effects with other participants. In some cases, these

---

2   Data on time spent consuming media is sourced from Nielsen (2019) "The Nielsen Total Audience Report Q1 2019" at p. 4. Estimates of advertising revenue data is sourced from Interactive Advertising Bureau (2019) "IAB internet advertising revenue report 2018 full year results" at pp. 21-22. Data on e-Commerce's share of total retail sales is sourced from Federal Research Bank of St. Louis, "e-Commerce Retail Sales as a Percent of Total Sales," https://fred.stlouisfed.org/series/ECOMPCTSA#0.

3   Market capitalization data sourced from S&P Capital IQ. The top 10 firms include Microsoft, Apple, Amazon, Alphabet, Berkshire Hathaway, Facebook, Alibaba, Tencent, Visa, and JPMorgan Chase.

intermediaries follow a traditional reseller model in which buyers interact directly with the intermediary rather than with sellers.[4] The main novelties in the analysis of vertical restraints in the digital world involve these digital intermediaries.

A. Significant Digital Businesses Are Usually Multisided Platforms Based on Software

The largest digital businesses earned a substantial part of their revenues from operating multisided platforms. Table 1 lists the seven largest global digital businesses and the intermediaries that drive a large part of their revenues.[5] Many other economically significant digital businesses, such as the various ride-sharing services, operate multisided platforms. And it remains a common model for venture-backed startups.

Digital platforms rely primarily on software to provide core services such as matching, search, discovery, transactions, and communication. They also depend on the Internet to connect participants and to provide those core software-based services. The software for digital platforms typically resides on server farms maintained by "cloud providers" or in proprietary server farms.

Indirect network effects often fuel the growth of multisided platforms. More participants on one side of the platform makes the platform more valuable to participants on the other side of the platform. Rapid growth can occur as more participants join each side and thereby increase the attractiveness of the platform leading to more participants to join.

Table 1: Large Digital Businesses and Their Platforms	
Company	Platforms
Microsoft	Windows, Bing, Azure,
Apple	iOS including App Development Platform and App Store
Amazon.com	Amazon Marketplace, AWS
Alphabet	Android (including Google Play), Google, YouTube
Facebook	Facebook, Messenger, Instagram, WhatsApp
Alibaba	Taobao, Tmall, AliExpress
Tencent	QQ, WeChat, Tencent Games

---

4 See *Matchmakers* at Ch. 7, and Hagiu, Andrei & Julian Wright (2015) "Marketplace or Reseller," *Management Science* 61(1), pp. 184-203, for a discussion of the difference between platforms and resellers. Roughly speaking a shopping mall is platform while a department store is a reseller. This paper refers to "digital multisided platforms" simply as "digital platforms" and digital intermediaries that follow a reseller model as "digital resellers."

5 Amazon also operates a digital platform (Amazon Marketplace) and a digital reseller (Amazon) side-by-side. Buyers see offers from both on its website and app and some sellers participate in both models. Each business model accounts for about half of its e-Commerce revenue.

The Internet as well as other information technologies reduce physical constraints on expanding users and can thereby accelerate these indirect network effects. As a result, digital platforms can prove a concept locally, and then expand to many locations, using similar software and processes. They can do that more quickly than physical businesses that require more local facilities to provide services through broader physical spaces. Digital platforms and resellers now cover most sectors of the economy.

The following discussion focuses on features of digital platforms that are particularly relevant for analyzing antitrust issues involving vertical restraints. These features are the same for digital platforms as they are for physical platforms but are magnified as a result of Internet connectivity, software, and related information technologies. Although the details differ, digital resellers have similar features even though they do not facilitate direct interactions between the various groups of participants.

B. Platforms Need to Reach Critical Mass to Ignite and Grow Profitably

Digital platforms face the same chicken-and-egg problem that physical platforms often face. If they don't offer access to enough of the right participants, they don't have much to offer. This situation is different than traditional businesses which sell products rather than access. To get off the ground, a sliced-bread manufacturer needs a factory and ingredients to make bread. To get off the ground, a heterosexual dating platform must have enough men and women to offer an interesting dating product to either group.

Critical mass refers to the minimum set of members of both sides necessary for the platform to provide a sufficiently valuable service that it can keep those members on board, grow by attracting more users than it loses, and become a profitable enterprise.[6] Economists recognized the importance of critical mass for businesses that had indirect network effects in the 1990s.[7] What that literature missed was the pervasiveness of intermediaries that rely on indirect network effects and how common the critical mass obstacle is in the physical world. The critical mass problem is the same for digital platforms as for traditional ones, although the particulars of solving the challenge may differ.

How the critical mass problem gets solved in practice is a bit outside of the traditional toolkit for economists, as it is fundamentally a disequilibrium phenomenon whose details are highly dependent on the circumstances of the platform. Early adopters and expectation management are often key. Platforms need to get early adopters on board and then get enough momentum to keep them there. Participants

---

6 See *Matchmakers* at Ch. 5.

7 Shapiro, Carl (1999) "Exclusivity in Network Industries," *George Mason Law Review* 7(3), pp. 673-683.

will invest in using the platform if they expect that it will eventually reach critical mass and become valuable to them. Platforms can adopt a variety of strategies to entice more participants on board and shape expectations.[8]

Platforms may try to get "anchor tenants" — a term taken from shopping malls — to create a mass of demand from one type of participants. They can also try to use subsidies to get one or both types of participants on board subject to liquidity constraints. Contingent contracts provide another potential way to crack the chicken-and-egg problem. Participants on each side enter into contracts to join and use the platform that are triggered by other specified participants on the opposite or same side joining. For platforms in which participants on one side provide specific products or services to the other side, the platform can offer those products or services itself — that is, it can vertically integrate into one side of the platform.

Platforms that cannot achieve critical mass relatively quickly often fail. Initially, the platform gets early adopters, and others who stay with it, in expectation that it will become valuable. Some of them may drop off as they become disappointed. For the platform to reach critical mass it needs to attract more participants, on both sides, than it loses. If that doesn't happen quickly enough, the platform will start losing more participants than it gains and eventually fail. Failure is a common result in practice. The fragility of startups can provide an opportunity for established players to maintain their positions as discussed below.

Critical mass isn't just important for startups. Platforms need to maintain critical mass to remain viable. Indirect network effects can work in reverse. If participants on one side leave the platform it becomes less valuable to participants on the other side. This can lead to a death spiral as more participants desert it and it falls below critical mass. Platforms may adopt business practices to reduce the risk of that happening.

C. Consumer Ability to Use Multiple Platforms and Switch Between Them Is Key

Sometimes it is easy for participants to use several similar platforms. They could switch between them depending upon which has more relevant participants for an interaction, has better prices, or for other competitive reasons. That is known as "multihoming." People have several ad-supported media apps on their smartphones

---

8 Microsoft's efforts to launch its X-box video game console, in competition with the dominant PlayStation console, shows the importance of expectation management, driven partly by a commitment to keeping console prices low, and vertical integration, in which Microsoft bought game publishers and produced its own games. See Evans, David & Richard Schmalensee (2007) *Catalyst Code: The Strategies Behind the World's Most Dynamic Companies*, Harvard Business Review Press, at Chapter 6.

and easily switch between them. Advertisers may be able to reach the same people through different media apps.

In other cases, fixed costs, learning costs, and other costs make using several platforms inefficient so that participants standardize on one. That is known as "single-homing." Most people use a single operating system for their personal computers even though in principle they could have several running on the same machine or have desktop and laptops with different operating systems. App developers can reach those users only by writing to that operating system.

When participants on one side single-home, the platform is the only way to get access to those participants at that time. The platform is a bottleneck and an economically material one if it has captured many of those participants. Participants may still be able to switch to another platform, such as from Windows to macOS, even if they need to single-home. Thus, the competitive importance of single-homing depends on the number of participants covered and their ability to switch.

In the digital economy, platforms often sit on top of other platforms.[9] Foundational platforms are most susceptible to single-homing because they are often based on operating systems and hardware platforms that involve material switching costs. The iPhone, which relies on the iOS operating system and the App Store, provides a foundational platform for apps such as Uber. Users may be able to multi-home on app-based platforms — for example, iPhone users could have Uber and Lyft on their phones; app developers can also develop apps for both iOS and Android.

When users can easily switch between apps or websites it is possible that "competition is only a click away." Of course, the ability to click on an alternative is only one aspect of the ability to multi-home which would therefore require deeper consideration in an actual case.

D. Ease of Entry Influenced by Critical Mass and Multihoming

The opportunities and obstacles for entry are influenced by critical mass and multihoming considerations in the same way they are for physical platforms. For our analysis of vertical restraints in the digital economy, however, these considerations are worth calling out because of the importance of platform intermediaries and the role of technologies in fostering indirect network effects and the possibility of multihoming.

To secure critical mass, to ignite and grow, an entrant may be able to tap into a large pool of unaffiliated participants when the market is nascent. The entrant, like the incumbent, still has the challenge of convincing many prospects that the platform service has value. As the market matures, and more prospects have selected platforms,

---

9 See *Matchmakers*, Chapter 3.

the entrant may have to persuade participants on incumbent platforms to consider its platform to build to critical mass.

Entry is easier when multi-homing is possible on both sides. The entrant may be able to get participants on other platforms to try the entrant's platform. Meanwhile, the entrant can perfect its platform and try to build critical mass. Participants on incumbent platforms may be willing to do this because they don't incur any significant switching costs. Even if there are some costs of switching over, they can gain some information on whether the move is worth it.

Entry is harder when there is single-homing on one or both sides. The entrant must convince participants on incumbent platforms to switch, which is hard before it has built critical mass and, even if it has built critical mass, may be hard given the indirect network effect scale advantages possessed by incumbents. The entrant could also tap into participants who haven't committed, which is particularly important in nascent markets where most potential participants haven't joined any platform, or ones who have exited failed platforms.

Vertical restraints, as I discuss below, could be used to convert a market that is naturally prone to multi-homing into single-homing, thereby, making it more difficult for entrants to secure critical mass and for smaller incumbent rivals to maintain it.

E. Platforms Have to Deter Participants from Behaving Badly

Platforms operate communities, in which participants interact with each other and, as in any community, participants may behave badly towards others.[10] Participants can engage in deception, fraud, bullying, hate speech, post porn or other offensive material, breach contracts, and so on. By doing so, these participants impose negative externalities on participants, on the same or other sides, and thereby reduce the value of the platform to its members. These offenses can limit the amount of activity on the platform, the interest of participants to join it, and the amount participants are willing to pay to participate. Platforms have profit incentives to deter these offenses.

Platforms do so by operating governance systems like those run by governments for communities. They have platform rules that prohibit or require certain behavior. They have detection methods, involving software and staff, to ferret out violations of these rules. They impose penalties for breaking the rules as well as screening methods for keeping bad actors off the platform. These governance systems are

---

10   Boudreau, Kevin & Andrei Hagiu (2009) "Platform Rules: Multi-Sided Platforms As Regulators," in *Platforms, Markets and Innovation*, Gawer, ed., Edward Elgar Publishing Inc; Evans, David (2012) "Governing Bad Behavior by Users of Multi-Sided Platforms," *Berkeley Technology Law Journal* 27(2), pp. 1201-1250.

a distinct feature of platforms. Traditional businesses seldom have such elaborate systems. Platforms need them because of the externalities that can arise from the constant interaction of participants.

Governance systems are particularly common and sophisticated for digital platforms.[11] eHarmony, a dating site, prohibits 17 activities including sending annoying communications or providing misleading information. Amazon's marketplace has a seller code of conduct that includes prohibitions against a variety of behaviors such as trying to damage other sellers or improperly influencing consumer ratings. Google's search engine prohibits websites from many efforts to influence ranking unfairly or essentially gaming its algorithms.

Platforms, including digital ones, have more limited options for penalizing bad behavior by their communities than governments do. They typically enforce rules by excluding participants from the platform. The bans could be permanent or temporary. Google, for example, punishes websites that improperly game the system by forcing them far down the search rankings for some period. Amazon permanently bars sellers who engage in fraudulent behavior. The ban could be full or partial. Digital platforms may decide to ban some content, or apps, from a participant, but not all. Facebook may delete some content that a participant has posted but allow the person to continue to use the social network.

These governance systems are controversial now because of allegations that platforms have been too lax, thereby permitting too much bad behavior, or too restrictive, thereby preventing free speech. Most of these complaints lie outside of antitrust.[12] The core antitrust issue concerns situations in which the platform also operates a business on one side of its platform and in which the platform has allegedly used its governance system to raise rivals' costs or exclude competitors on that side.

F. Platforms Use Algorithms to Determine What Users See

To facilitate interactions between participants, platforms provide search and discovery tools for finding possible partners, as well as targeting methods to present themselves to possible partners.[13] The platform may also show connections on its own

---

11 U.S. Congress encouraged platforms to have these systems when it passed Section 230 of the Communications Decency Act. Section 230 essentially immunized platforms from barring participants, or their content, so long as they were doing so as a good-faith application of their rules. For further discussion see Evans, David (2019) "Deterring Bad Behavior on Digital Platforms," available at SSRN: https://ssrn.com/abstract=3455384

12 See Evans, "Deterring Bad Behavior on Digital Platforms," *supra*.

13 Varian, Hal (2019) "Artificial Intelligence, Economics, and Industrial Organization," in *The Economics of Artificial Intelligence: An Agenda*, A. Agrawal, J. Gans & A. Golfarb, eds., University of Chicago Press.

based on its predictions of participants' value from being exposed to those possible trading partners. Digital platforms, more so than others, make heavy use of software-based technologies to perform these functions. These technologies involve algorithms that use data, and statistical methods for learning from that data, to make predictive decisions. Digital platforms also rely on many other techniques. They provide reviews for users and products, tools for participants to display information, and targeted advertising.

Google, for example, uses algorithms to decide which, if any, ads to present on a search-results page following a query. The algorithms predict the likelihood that a consumer who makes that query will find the ad relevant, and useful, and click on the ad. By showing more relevant ads, Google increases the likelihood it will make money from the search engine results page it presents; making the ads more relevant to consumers increases the likelihood they will do more searches.

G. Digital Platforms Are Different from Physical Ones Mainly Because of the Technology

Digital platforms are like physical ones. Getting critical mass is a pervasive problem for platforms. The extent of single-homing is an issue for all. Platform governance systems are common. And they all help participants engage in search and discovery and many try to predict what participants want.

The combination of the Internet, software, data, and information technologies, however, dramatically lowers the cost of starting and scaling a platform, expands the capabilities for matching participants and facilitating exchanges, and increases the ability to collect and deploy data. The combination also makes many new features possible, such as posting feedback.

Of course, digital platforms themselves are highly diverse. Analyzing antitrust, as always, requires a fact-intensive analysis concerning the circumstances surrounding the complaint and the businesses implicated by it.

III. ECONOMIC ANALYSIS OF VERTICAL RESTRAINTS FOR DIGITAL PLATFORMS

There is a vast economic literature on vertical restraints as well as a long history of cases. Most of this work was developed for the physical world. There are many situations in which the literature and precedent applies directly to the digital world. There is no obvious difference between a manufacturer entering into resale price maintenance agreements with digital intermediaries versus physical distributors. Some details may differ, but they always do between matters.

There are, however, situations in which differences involving digital technologies are important. Physical retailers, for example, use data to make decisions on where to place their own and other's products. But the sophistication and power of the algorithms and the ability to vary product placements in virtually real time, over Internet connections, can make digital retail much different from physical retail.

The big difference between the digital and physical world, however, concerns the role of intermediaries and multisided platforms. Given the opportunity to develop large digital distribution platforms, cases involving manufacturers imposing vertical restraints on distributors are likely to be less important than cases involving distributors imposing vertical restraints on participants.

The economic literature on vertical restraints for single-sided firms has insights for multisided ones but one cannot assume that the models and results necessarily apply without modification. That is true for the physical platforms too. The issue becomes more important in the digital world where there are more platforms, and these platforms are powered by Internet and related technologies, and likely more cases in which this issue comes up.

This section runs through some of the key considerations regarding vertical restraints involving digital platforms. Similar factors apply to digital resellers, at least to some degree. These are early days, and as we get more experience with cases this list will surely grow longer and more nuanced.

A. Claims Could Involve Horizontal or Vertical Foreclosure

Digital platforms compete horizontally with other platforms to get both types of participants to join and use them. Apple's iPhone platform and Google's Android platform compete for users, beginning with buying a smartphone, and developers writing apps. A dominant platform could face claims that it has imposed vertical restraints that limit competition between the platforms. In the smartphone case, a claimant might argue that practices that limit interoperability and portability for users and developers are anticompetitive vertical restraints.

Digital platform owners may also compete with some of their participants. Google, for example, offers services on its search engine results page, such as Google Shopping, that compete with services provided by other comparison-shopping platforms which participate in Google's indexing and ranking service. The European Commission claimed that Google engaged in various practices that disadvantaged some of those websites.

There is another dimension of competition for some e-Commerce properties. The property may operate an online marketplace, which is a two-sided platform for buyers and sellers, as well as an online store, which operates under a traditional reseller model. Both, of course, rely on Internet technologies, algorithms, and other innovations involving the digital economy. In addition, e-Commerce properties may offer private-label products in competition with sellers on its online store and marketplace. Amazon and Walmart, which operate the first and third largest e-Commerce platforms in the U.S., both do so.[14]

B. Antitrust Claims Face Usual Issues of Incentive and Ability to Foreclose Competition

Vertical restraints for digital businesses pose the same basic analytical question as for physical ones. Does the business have the ability and the incentive to engage in the practice to foreclose competition? Addressing this question for digital platforms raises the same issues as for physical platforms. The analysis, however, must account for the relevant facts some of which may be particular to the digital world. Market definition, which is not the subject of this paper, should help inform whether the digital business has the ability and incentive to foreclose competition through a vertical practice.[15]

Whether the digital platform can foreclose competition through vertical restraints will typically depend on whether it can limit access to a substantial group of participants on one or both sides of the platform. It usually wouldn't be able to do so if the platform is small relative to the overall market served or if the market is nascent, and most potential participants on both sides haven't joined, so there is plenty of opportunity for entry.[16] A ride-sharing platform may have a small fraction of the drivers and riders who have joined platforms, or it may be operating during a stage of development where there is large untapped pool of both drivers and riders.

The ability of a platform to limit access would depend on the extent to which participants multi-home and, if they single home, how easily they could switch to

---

14 eMarketer, "Digital Investments Pay Off for Walmart in e-Commerce Race," February 14, 2019, https://www.emarketer.com/content/digital-investments-pay-off-for-walmart-in-ecommerce-race.

15 The two-sided platform literature shows that profits, and thus to ability to increase those profits through higher prices, are determined at the platform level as a result of the interdependencies between the two sides and the need to balance their prices. Depending on the jurisdiction and type of platform under consideration the courts may prefer to define markets at the platform or side level. In the U.S. the Supreme Court ruled that the market should be considered at the platform level when indirect network effects are more than minor (the American Express credit card network) for a matter involving vertical restraints (rules that prohibited merchants that accepted the American Express card from then steering consumers who tried to use the card to competing card networks). *Ohio v. American Express Co.*, 138 S.Ct. 2274 (2018).

16 Digital platforms serve diverse sets of customers. Depending on the matter the relevant antitrust market, and the focus of the analysis, could be a segment of the platform rather than its entirety. To simplify the discussion this paper refers to the platform generally.

another platform. This list isn't exhaustive. There may be other factors, including technological ones, that influence whether the platform can prevent access. A ride-sharing platform, for example, could impose an exclusivity provision on drivers but it might be difficult to monitor and enforce compliance.

Whether the digital platform has the incentive to foreclose requires weighing the benefits of foreclosure, including the likelihood of succeeding and securing profits that it wouldn't in the absence of the vertical practice, against the costs, including forgone earnings from participants subsequent to the restraint. The analysis of these issues requires the consideration of the two-sided features of the platform including feedback between the two sides. If a vertical practice results in the loss of some participants on one side, for example, that may reduce the value to the other side, and thereby may increase the costs of engaging in the practice. As with ability, assessing whether there are incentives generally entails fact intensive inquiry, and the details will vary across platforms and practices.

Several features of a digital platform could enhance its ability and incentive to foreclose competition and therefore warrant close examination in cases. A digital platform may capture a substantial portion of potential participants as a result of indirect network effects facilitated by the Internet and related technologies. The platform does not have to be the first mover — just an early mover that got to critical mass early and grew at an accelerating clip after that. The digital platform has at least some control over access to participants on both sides. It therefore has a set of relationships that it could use to foreclose competition for existing or new platforms.

Anticompetitive strategies wouldn't be necessary if indirect network effects made it hopeless for smaller platforms to challenge dominant incumbents. Like all businesses, however, platforms can compete in the face of scale advantages by differentiating themselves. They can try to appeal to particular types of users, on either side, by catering to their different tastes (horizontal differentiation) or focus on particular degrees of quality and price (vertical differentiation). By specializing in these ways, platforms can create value that mitigates their smaller scale. In addition, when consumers can multi-home, or readily switch between digital platforms, the indirect network effects for the leading platform are not necessarily durable. Rivals could pick off participants from the leading platform. Just as indirect network effects accelerated growth for the leading platform, they can also accelerate decline.

As a result, the leading platform cannot just count on its size to keep the market to itself. It therefore may have incentives to foreclose platform rivals despite the advantages it has secured from indirect network effects. The need for rivals to achieve critical mass to attain sustainable growth may provide the leading platform the ability to act on these incentives and foreclose actual or prospective rivals. It can look for strategies that prevent these rivals from securing enough participants on one or both sides. That could include protecting itself from vulnerability arising from the ability of participants to multi-home across and switch between platforms. It could use the standard set of vertical restraints to do so.

Digital platforms could enlist their algorithms for exposing participants on one side of the platform to those on the other. A platform, for example, could condition the extent of exposure of participants on one side to trading partners on the other side based on their degree of loyalty to the platform. It could do this as part of negotiations to get participants to enter into agreements that contain vertical restraints. To obscure its strategy, it could also reduce exposure for participants that refuse to enter vertical restraints rather than refusing them to join the platform. A digital platform that offered a service on its platform that competed with a particular participant could use algorithms to reduce the exposure of that participant to the other side of platform.[17] Doing so could obscure its exclusionary strategy and make it harder to establish than simply refusing to allow the rival participant on the platform.

Digital platforms could enlist their governance systems in vertical restraint strategies. Consider the situation in which the platform also competes with a participant. It could use its governance system to exclude that participant or impose costs on that participant that it doesn't incur. These efforts may be less transparent than a direct denial of access. A platform could also enforce its governance system more strictly for participants who do not agree to vertical restraints that are designed to foreclose competition by rival platforms.

C. Vertical Practices by Digital Platform May Increase the Value of the Platform for Participants and Therefore be Pro-Competitive

The mere prospect that a digital platform could use vertical restraints to harm competition does not mean that it is necessarily doing so. As with vertical restraints generally, the platforms may have imposed the vertical restraints to enhance efficiency, such as by dealing with principal-agent or free-riding issues. The vertical restraint may foreclose competition in the sense that whenever a business offers a better product, or does so more efficiently, it secures an advantage over its rival. The challenge, as with all vertical restraint cases, involves distinguishing the pro-competitive use of vertical restraints from anti-competitive ones.

Digital platforms have profit incentives, for example, to design their algorithms to increase the value that participants on each side can secure from interactions with participants on the other side. That typically means either exposing a participant

---

17   That was the main allegation in the Google Shopping matter. See European Commission, Case AT.39740, Brussels, June 27, 2017, C(2017) 4444 final. Available at http://ec.europa.eu/competition/antitrust/cases/dec_docs/39740/39740_14996_3.pdf.

to the most suitable possible matches or providing information that enables the participant to assess their likely value. In doing so the algorithms necessarily downgrade participants who are likely to be less desirable. That can result in some participants not being presented, in effect, to other participants. Most people do not, for example, look beyond the first search engine results page and are much more likely to engage with organic search results and paid ads that are higher on the first page.

To take another example, as we saw above, digital platforms have profit incentives to deploy governance systems to weed out bad behavior that can degrade the platform. By doing so, they make the platform more desirable for participants. And a more desirable platform is likely to generate more indirect network effects which increases the value to all participants. Some participants may complain about the rules, because they interfere with their business models, and especially if they are expelled from the platform.

Of course, as with anticompetitive effects, assessing whether practices result in pro-competitive efficiencies, generally requires a fact-intensive analysis tailored to the circumstances of the matter. And any pro-competitive benefits need to be weighed against anti-competitive costs when the businesses engaging in the conduct has significant market power.

D. Digital Platforms Require Two-Sided Analysis to Assess Whether Vertical Restraints Result Harm Competition

The economic literature on two-sided platforms shows that the analysis of anticompetitive practices should account for a variety of issues that arise from platforms serving interdependent groups of users. Digital platforms raise the same issues as physical platforms, including the assessment of market definition, market power, and anticompetitive effects.[18]

An important insight of the two-sided literature is that practices that cause harm on one side could benefit the other side so that it doesn't cause an overall decrease in welfare. That is consistent with the platform adopting the practice to increase the value of the platform rather than to foreclose competition. It is also possible that

---

18 Recently, high courts have considered the application of the two-sided analysis to cases. High-court decisions in the United States (*American Express*), the European Union (*Cartes Bancaires*) and China (*Tencent*) have emphasized the importance of accounting for the interdependencies between the two sides, at least in the matters before them. *Ohio v. American Express Co.*, 138 S.Ct. 2274 (2018); *Groupement des Cartes Bancaires (CB) v Commission*, C-67/13 P, EU:C:2014:2204; *Qihoo 360 v. Tencent*, Supreme People's Court of People's Republic of China, Civil Judgment No. Minsanzhongzi 4/2013, October 2014. For a detailed discussion of *American Express* see Evans, David & Richard Schmalensee, *Antitrust Analysis of Platform Markets: Why the Supreme Court Got It Right in American Express* (Boston: CPI, 2019).

the anticompetitive effects of a practice come from the interdependence between the two sides, which might not be detected from looking at each side in isolation. A platform, for example, might be able to impose exclusive contracts that fall below common thresholds used by the courts to assess anticompetitive foreclosure but by imposing these on both sides it makes it hard for an entrant to secure critical mass.

IV. EXCLUSIVE CONTRACTS, GOVERNANCE SYSTEMS, AND MFNS

This section considers three types of matters involving vertical restraints and illustrates them with public information concerning recent cases. Part A considers the use of exclusive contracts by a dominant platform to harm competition with a rival platform. It emphasizes two aspects that are particular to digital platforms: the use of exclusives to prevent rivals from securing or maintaining critical mass or the benefit of indirect network effects; and the role of algorithms in securing loyalty (single-homing) by some participants. Alibaba's use of exclusive contracts for sellers on its Tmall property in China provides an example.

Part B examines the use of governance systems by a dominant platform. It considers the sham use of rules to raise rivals' costs, or exclude, a participant on the side that competes with the platform's own service on that side. Apple's alleged use of its app developer rules to impose limitations on Spotify, which competes with Apple Music, provides an example.

Part C considers the use of MFNs by e-Commerce marketplaces and resellers. It focuses on a common situation for e-Commerce businesses in which they charge sellers a commission and may have MFNs that apply separately to price and commission. The UK's Competition and Markets Authority investigation of the use of price MFNs by price comparison platforms for insurance provides an example.

Throughout this section we assume that the digital platform engaging in the practice has substantial market power in a relevant antitrust market. In practice, of course, that analysis would need to assess the relevant antitrust market, accounting for two-sided considerations, and determine whether the platform has substantial market power (or is dominant) in that market.

A. Exclusive Contracts and the "Cat-and-Dog War" in China

The dominant platform could require some participants on one side, or possibly both, to enter into exclusive contracts for some period. These contracts would deter these participants from multi-homing during that period. That matters in practice mainly in the case in which participants would not find it in their self-interest to single home in the absence of the restraint. The contracts could also deter these participants from switching to a rival platform during that period. The contracts could target all participants on both sides, all participants on one side, or they might target large participants — anchor tenants — on one side. The exclusives could also affect a category of participants, or the platforms that service those participants, that might constitute a relevant antitrust market.

The dominant platform could insist that participants enter into these contracts to operate on the platform. It could provide rewards or penalties for divided loyalties to achieve the same results as an exclusive. The dominant platform could use its algorithms to impose penalties on participants that do not agree to formal exclusives. It could reduce the extent to which non-loyal participants on one side are exposed to participants on the other side or provide loyal participants greater levels of exposure and marketing assistance.

Key considerations for evaluating whether these exclusivity provisions could harm competition include, as is usual, the explicit or *de facto* coverage of the provisions in the relevant antitrust market, the duration of the provisions, and therefore how much of the market is contestable for rivals. This analysis, however, needs to be conducted considering the two-sided features of these platforms. In particular, the analysis should consider the extent to which the exclusivity provisions could prevent: entrants from securing critical mass; smaller incumbents from losing critical mass so that they are no longer viable; and smaller incumbents from capturing indirect network effects that could drive future growth.[19] A further issue is the extent to which participants, forced to single-home, can switch platforms.

Exclusivity agreements could also enhance efficiency. That could be the case for traditional reasons such as preventing free riding on platform efforts, preventing the loss of valuable competitive information to a rival, and aligning platform and participant incentives for mutual gain to name a few. Digital platforms could also raise specific issues that could provide pro-competitive explanations for the practices. The exclusives may help secure and maintain critical mass and thereby provide value to platform participants. Getting key participants on one side to agree to an exclusive could help persuade participants on the other side to join. There could be other reasons why preferential treatment of some participants, in return for loyalty, could increase indirect network effects or reduce negative externalities on the platform. Whether any of these efficiency explanations applies, and the magnitude of the benefits if any, would need to be evaluated.

The Great "Cat-and-Dog War" in China illustrates the potential anticompetitive use of exclusive contracts.[20] Alibaba operates Tmall, whose logo is a cat. Tmall

---

19 A practice that might seem innocuous in a single-sided context could be problematic in a two-sided one because of the role of critical mass in securing ignition.

20 Fox News, "At war with Alibaba: Top brands fight China e-Commerce giant," April 22, 2018," https://www.foxnews.com/world/at-war-with-alibaba-top-brands-fight-china-e-commerce-giant.

is a B2C marketplace of buyers and sellers for consumer products. It competes with JD.com, whose logo is a dog. JD operates both a reseller model and a marketplace model that enable sellers to distribute products to consumers. Tmall is the leading B2C e-Commerce platform in China and twice as large as JD.com: as of 2017 Tmall had a 57 percent share of online retail commerce and JD.com a 28 percent share. Several smaller e-Commerce sites accounted for the remainder. Tmall had about an 80 percent share of apparel sales in China compared to about 8 percent for JD.com in the first half of 2017.[21]

Tmall adopted a policy known as "Choose One of Two." It asks sellers to make a choice between Tmall or other platforms. Tmall acknowledges that it has secured a growing number of exclusives but defends its policy: "Like many e-Commerce platforms, we have exclusive partnerships. The merchant decides to choose such an arrangement because of the attractive services and value Tmall brings to them."[22] It didn't explain the nexus between the exclusive partnerships and the attractive services or whether additional services were provided in exchanged for the exclusives.

Tmall apparently does not make signing an exclusive contract a condition of operating on its platform. Instead, according to numerous merchant interviews reported in the press, and lawsuits filed against the company, Tmall retaliates against sellers that refuse to enter exclusive deals in ways that reduce their visibility and sales. Five large American consumer brands claim that they experienced a sharp drop in traffic to their storefronts on Tmall. According to one article, "Executives said that after they rebuffed Alibaba, their brand's banners vanished from prominent spots in Tmall sales showrooms and products stopped appearing in top search results."[23]

In June 2017, many apparel merchants complained that Tmall requested them to withdraw from other e-Commerce platforms including JD, VIP.com and Dangdang. Some claimed they would lose 30 percent of their sales if they complied. If they refused, however, they would jeopardize the much larger volume of sales on Tmall.[24] Semir, a famous apparel brand in China, shut down its flagship store on JD in September 2017 despite having realized substantial growth on this competing

---

21 Analysys, "Quarterly Reports of China's B2C Online Market from 2016 Q1 to 2017 Q2, https://www.analysys.cn/article/analysis/detail/1000869.

22 Fox News, "At war with Alibaba: Top brands fight China e-Commerce giant," April 22, 2018," https://www.foxnews.com/world/at-war-with-alibaba-top-brands-fight-china-e-commerce-giant.

23 Fox News, "At war with Alibaba: Top brands fight China e-Commerce giant," April 22, 2018," https://www.foxnews.com/world/at-war-with-alibaba-top-brands-fight-china-e-commerce-giant.

24 "Choose One of Two on '6.18': Exclusive Dealing Requested by Tmall Led Big Damage to Online Merchants," Southern Metropolis Daily, July 12, 2017, https://tech.qq.com/a/20170712/020103.htm.

platform. [25] JD.com claimed that as of early 2018 that more than 100 Chinese brands had defected in 2017.

Galanz, which sells home appliances, asserted that during the "6.18" promotional festival in 2019 Tmall attacked six of its core stores through the manipulation of algorithmic results, in retaliation for refusing Tmall's request that Galanz withdraw from the competing Pinduoduo platform. According to Galanz, Tmall excluded its stores from search results and did not display rankings that buyers relied on. [26] As a result, Galanz claims its store sales declined by between 40 to 90 percent compared to the previous year. [27]

Tmall's efforts to secure exclusives have attracted antitrust lawsuits by competing e-Commerce intermediaries. JD, joined by Pinduoduo and VIPshop, have sued Tmall for abuse of dominance in Beijing High People's Court. Galanz, as a platform participant, has also sued Tmall for abuse of dominance in Guangzhou Intellectual Property Court. [28] These cases are interesting because they involve one of the largest e-Commerce properties in the world, Alibaba, and concern the use of algorithmic methods to, according to the complaints, secure explicit or *de facto* exclusives.

While there may be pro-competitive explanations for exclusive contracts, they pose some risks for competition when they are used by dominant digital platforms. Consider the situation in which the dominant platform accounts for the preponderance of buyers in a relevant antitrust market. Sellers could lose access to most customers if they refused to agree to an exclusive. As more sellers enter exclusives, buyers will tend to see the dominant platform even more. As the smaller platform loses sellers it will lose buyers which will make it even less attractive to seller. That could further entrench the dominant platform. The smaller platform may remain viable but limited in its ability to grow and compete. Platforms that haven't reached a critical mass, and are not yet viable, may not be able to do so and, considering that, entrepreneurs and

25 Xie Yunzi, "Overall Increase of Semir Encumbered by its e-Commerce Business, or Due to the Closure of JD Channel," China Entrepreneur, November 7, 2017, http://www.sohu.com/a/202831895_115280.

26 Qian Lina, Shi Dan, "Galanz Fight against Tmall, Why the e-Commerce Law Failed to Regulate the Either-Or Policy," Commercial College, June 20, 2019, available at https://t.cj.sina.com.cn/articles/view/1678512213/640c105500100gwvw?from=tech&subch=internet.

27 Yang Qian, "Galanz Fight against Tmall," China Enterpreneur, June 20, 2019, http://www.iceo.com.cn/com2013/2019/0621/306237.shtml.

28 "Galanz Sues Tmall for 'Pick 1 of 2', Lawsuit Accepted by Court," NetEase Technology, November 5, 2019, https://tech.163.com/19/1105/12/ET7GGLF0000999LD.html.

investors may decide not to enter.[29] Of course, whether the exclusives are extensive enough to cause these effects is an empirical matter.

A successful anticompetitive strategy can harm both buyers and sellers. To begin with, both lose the opportunity to multi-home on several platforms — options they would presumably have in the absence of exclusive contracts. Multi-homing intensifies competition along non-price dimensions such as service and discovery mechanisms. The exclusivity agreements can also raise prices. By limiting competition, the dominant platform can increase the commissions it charges sellers for distribution on its platform. Those sellers may pass some, or possibly all, of those increased commissions back to consumers in the form of higher prices. Depending on the jurisdiction, the competition authorities and courts may require evidence that these effects have occurred, or just that there is material risk they would occur.

B. Governance Systems and the Music Wars

The previous example concerned the possible use of exclusive contracts to harm competition by a rival platform. A governance system provides a way for a platform that provides a service on one side of the platform to harm rivals that depend on its platform to provide their services to the other side of the platform. Participants may expend resources complying with these rules. The platform could make those costs higher for a rival — that is, engage in a raising rival's cost strategy — by applying the rules more strictly with rivals or demanding costly modifications in a discriminatory way. The platform probably has rules in place that enable it to block participants from joining the platform or to kick participants off. It could therefore simply deny rivals access to its platform. Of course, the platform could simply deny rivals access without invoking its rules, but it could cloak its motives by the sham use of governance. Rivals may not know, or be able to prove, that the platform has discriminated in applying the rules to harm them.

These cases raise the usual issues involving the use of vertical restraints to harm upstream or downstream competition. The platform benefits from the participation of firms who increase the value of the platform, including driving indirect network effects, and may provide a source of revenue. It must therefore weigh the increased profits from harming competition by the rival on one side against profits lost to the platform. That calculus depends on factors such as the extent to which customers of the rival would move to other platforms, rather than switching to the platform's competing offering.

---

29 Successful anticompetitive exclusionary conduct various categories for a platform could harm overall platform competition, to the extent for example that consumers prefer platforms that give them access to multiple categories, and thereby harm competition in categories not subject to the exclusives.

There may be situations in which it is possible to establish that a platform has the financial incentives to harm a rival. The platform could be essential for providing access to a large base of customers for the rival and the rival could lack practical alternatives to bypass the platform. A specific category might constitute a relevant market and destroying rivals in that category might enable the platform to secure monopoly profits that more than offset its losses from these rivals.

Aside from the standard pro-competitive explanations for vertical restraints on rivals, however, it is possible that the platform is simply applying its governance rules neutrally to mitigate negative indirect network externalities. That is apparent in the case of egregious violations of rules. Even if the platform had financial incentives to harm a rival it would appear unexceptionable if it expelled a rival that engaged in fraud or facilitated sex trafficking. The difficult cases are where there is more room for judgment on whether the rival violated the rules, the seriousness of those violations, and whether the application was indeed neutral.

That brings us to the music wars. Apple has provided an app development platform for the iOS operating system for its iPhones since 2008. Developers can use that platform, including various tools, to write apps that make use of the operating systems and hardware features of the phone. Apple has also provided an exclusive distribution vehicle for those apps. Developers can make their apps available in the App Store and iPhone users can download apps from there. There is no other practical way for developers to distribute apps to iPhone users or for users to obtain iPhone apps. Developers also write apps for the Android operating system but that doesn't give them access to iPhone users unless those users switch platforms.

Apple has extensive guidelines for developers amounting to about 12,000 words that lay out what they must and must not do. There is a vetting process for accepting apps, or modifications of apps, for distribution through the App Store, which is based on these guidelines and Apple's judgment concerning the quality of the apps. There is also a set of rules for apps distributed in the App Store. Apple can remove apps from the App Store for violating these rules and expel their developers from the Apple Developer Program. There isn't much controversy that Apple's rules have enabled it to create a high-quality app ecosystem for the iPhone.

That doesn't mean, however, that Apple couldn't abuse these rules. Spotify claims that Apple has. Apple became the leading provider of downloadable music following its introduction of the iPod and the iTunes store in the early 2000s. Over the 2000s many people switched listening from CDs to downloads. When Apple launched the iPhone in 2007 it emphasized that the device combined an iPod, a phone, and a computer. It included an iPod app on the home screen.

Over the next decade, however, music streaming services such as Pandora, Spotify, Deezer, and others entered. Music consumption shifted to streaming and downloads declined sharply. Recognizing this, Apple launched Apple Music in 2015, which was a direct competitor to Spotify's premium service. It included Apple Music on the iPhone home screen and promoted it heavily to iPhone users.

Spotify filed a complaint with the European Commission in March 2019.[30] The following discussion is based on public statements it has made about this that relate, in particular, to the application of Apple's App Developer rules. Spotify says that Apple "introduced rules to the App Store that purposely limit choice and stifle innovation at the expense of the user experience — essentially acting as both a player and referee to deliberately disadvantage other app developers."[31] It claims that Apple "frequently decides to interpret (and reinterpret) [its rules] in ways to disadvantage rivals like us."[32] The problems worsened after Apple launched Apple Music: "Now that Apple has Apple Music, rejections of the Spotify app start becoming more and more common and they even go far as threatening to remove us from the App Store. Those rejections seem to coincide with our promotional campaign seasons."[33] Spotify says the rules apply differently to Apple which it claims sends out the same type of promotional push notifications that rivals are barred from doing.

Apple charges a commission fee for all paid apps and for digital content purchased within apps that are distributed through its App Store. Some of Spotify's complaints concern alleged efforts to avoid the commissions for its premium service.[34] For its part, Apple accuses Spotify of seeking a free ride: "After using the App Store for years to dramatically grow their business, Spotify seeks to keep all the benefits of the App Store ecosystem … without making any contributions to that ecosystem."[35] That argument, however, cuts both ways. Spotify has benefited from distribution of its free app, on which it does not pay commissions, to iPhone users. Spotify and other apps, however, have also contributed to the iPhone ecosystem, and Apple's profits, by encouraging users to get and use iPhones. In addition to the free-riding argument, Apple denies that it blocks access for Spotify's apps and updates.

---

30   Spotify, "Consumers and Innovators Win on a Level Playing Field," March 13, 2019, https://newsroom.spotify.com/2019-03-13/consumers-and-innovators-win-on-a-level-playing-field/.

31   *Id.*

32   Time to Play Fair, "A Timeline: How we got here," https://www.timetoplayfair.com/timeline/.

33   *Id.*

34   Digital apps can avoid paying commissions by having users subscribe outside of the App Store such as on a website and then using their credentials to use the app on the iPhone. Amazon, for example, does not make it possible for its app users to buy digital content, such a e-books or video, on which it would have to pay commissions, but does make it possible for its app users to buy physical goods, for which it does not have to pay commissions.

35   Apple, "Addressing Spotify's claims," March 14, 2019, https://www.apple.com/newsroom/2019/03/addressing-spotifys-claims/.

At the end of 2019, 11 years after its launch, Spotify had 100 million subscribers globally while Apple Music had 60 million, 4 years after its launch.[36] In the U.S., Apple has nudged ahead of Spotify in terms of paid subscribers. Both compete for listeners with their streaming music providers using various models. The case is particularly interesting because of the increased use of smartphones for consuming content and the battle over music listening which is a large and important category.

A successful strategy to harm competition could injure consumers who would have less choice and pay higher subscription fees and possibly music labels who would face an intermediary with greater bargaining power. An intervention into the neutral application of a governance system, that promotes platform quality and value, could also harm consumers and music labels. As a general matter, permitting the anticompetitive or prohibiting the procompetitive use of governance systems could both impose substantial harm to the platform ecosystem — the former by weaponizing the governance system to harm competition by rivals and the latter by weakening the ability of the governance system to deter bad behavior by platform participants.

C. MFNs and Price Comparison Sites

There is an extensive literature and body of caselaw involving Most Favored Nation ("MFN") clauses in contracts. Some new issues arise for digital platforms and resellers because of their widespread use of commission models. The digital intermediary charges a commission rate as a percent of the sales price, keeps the commission rate times the sales price, and pays the remainder to the seller. The commission rate is the price for distribution through the intermediary.

The contract between the digital intermediary and the seller may specify the commission rate and the price that the seller offers the product to consumers. The contract may also impose MFNs on the commission rate, to make sure it gets the highest offered fee for distribution, and the lowest price, to make sure it isn't undercut by competing intermediaries. As a general matter this does not necessarily cause any concerns.

It can, however, when the contract is with a dominant intermediary for a category. The problem arises when the MFNs apply to the price and commission rate separately. Suppose a smaller intermediary offers the seller a lower commission rate but in return for a lower price that, on net, provide the seller with a higher net margin on sales. The smaller intermediary does this to secure a competitive advantage over the dominant intermediary. It takes a lower margin but makes more sales. The seller and the smaller intermediary both find this deal profitable as it now stands.

---

36 Digital Trends, "Apple Music vs. Spotify: Which service is the streaming king?" November 11, 2019, https://www.digitaltrends.com/music/apple-music-vs-spotify/.

Given the MFN, the dominant intermediary, however, can demand the lower price without having to agree to the lower commission. Unlike a regular MFN, it isn't getting equality with the seller — it is securing a position of superiority — resulting in an "MFN-plus." This MFN can lead to a problem for the rival intermediary as well as the seller who made the offer. The seller provides the lower price to the larger platform but without getting the lower commission rate in return and thereby incurs a financial penalty for entering into the deal with the smaller intermediary. Meanwhile, since the dominant intermediary matches the smaller intermediary's price and secures a higher margin, the smaller intermediary loses the competitive advantage it sought. The dominant intermediary, however, does earn a lower margin than it did before, when it exercises the MFN, because it earns the same commission rate but on a lower price.

The MFNs by the dominant intermediary, however, could prevent the smaller intermediary from making the offer to the seller or the seller from agreeing to take it. The MFN-Plus could deter the smaller intermediary from making the offer since it could end up taking a smaller commission rate but not getting additional sales since it would not have secured a competitive advantage. And it could deter the seller from taking the offer because it could lose substantial revenue by having to extend the low price to the dominant intermediary. Of course, the extent to which these incentives not to offer the low-priced deal depend on the facts of the matter including the size of the dominant intermediary.

The UK's Competition and Markets Authority ("CMA") encountered this situation.[37] Price comparison sites provide a marketplace in which automobile insurers can sell and automobile owners can buy car insurance. Between 55 and 65 percent of new policies are sold through these sites. The insurers set a premium and the sites collect a commission rate on the premium. The large comparison sites entered into contracts with insurers that had a price MFN but not on the commission rate.

The CMA found evidence that some price comparison sites could not get insurers to agree to lower prices in exchange for lower commissions and that the inability to adopt the lower commission/low price strategy deterred entry by price comparison sites. It also found that the MFNs reduced commission competition as well as incentives to offer valuable features, such as fraud detection, in return for lower premiums. Ultimately consumers lost from the MFNs because they didn't get the benefit of lower insurance prices. Of course, these conclusions were reached following a thorough investigation into the facts.

---

37   Competition and Markets Authority, "Private Motor Insurance Market Investigation," March 2015.

IV. CONCLUSION

Vertical restraints in the digital world are an active area for competition authorities and private complainants and litigants. That is because of the rapid growth in the digital economy, the proliferation of digital platforms and resellers as intermediaries, the fact that some of these intermediaries also participate as sellers, and the tendency of large intermediaries to enter across many areas. If anything, this growth is likely to accelerate in the coming years as a result of the continued integration of the digital and physical economies, which will be further spurred by widespread deployment of 5G technologies.

Analyzing vertical restraints is seldom simple. It is no easier, and arguably more complex, in the digital world. There are opportunities for engaging in anticompetitive behavior especially in ways that, given the use of algorithms and governance systems, may be less transparent, and harder to prove, than in the physical world. But at the same time there are many compelling sources of efficiency which courts and competition authorities would not want to disturb. As noted above for governance systems, the costs of false positives and false negatives may both be high.

The digital world does not appear to be one in which presumptions are very powerful, aside from the usual one that anticompetitive behavior generally requires substantial market power in a relevant antitrust market. Determining whether vertical practices are anticompetitive, innocuous, or procompetitive on balance requires a fact-based analysis informed by sound economics, particularly the modern economic analysis of multisided platforms. Given possibly large and symmetric error costs the payoffs to methodical economic and empirical analysis are substantial.

Adapting EU Competition Law to the Digital Economy

By Thomas Kramler [1]

Abstract

EU competition rules, as well as their application by the EU courts, have proved flexible enough to address technological developments. This does not, however, mean that antitrust enforcers should be complacent about new market developments. On the contrary: in order to remain relevant, the established enforcement principles need to be applied in the context of new market realities and, where necessary, adapted in the light of these realities. The specific features of digital markets, such as the growing importance of data and network effects and the provision of "free" services to consumers in two-sided digital platform markets, can and must be factored into the assessment of conduct under EU competition law.

I. INTRODUCTION

The term "Digital Economy" is increasingly becoming a misnomer as the whole economy digitizes rapidly. Apart from the services that have been traditionally associated with the Digital Economy such as online search, e-Commerce, app stores and social networks, digitization nowadays affects diverse sectors like financial services, energy, agriculture, manufacturing, and mobility.

The digitization of the economy will further progress with the proliferation of the Internet of Things ("IoT") and 5G networks. The number of total installed IoT connected devices is projected to amount to 75.44 billion worldwide by 2025.[2] Such connected devices range from connected self-driving cars, industrial robots to household appliances such as fridges.

In view of the breadth of digitization that has already taken place and is to be expected over the coming years it would go beyond the remit of this article to

---

1   Head of Unit, Antitrust: e-Commerce and data economy, DG COMP. The author would like to thank Brice Allibert, Nicholas Banasevic, Maria Jaspers and Massimiliano Kadar for their valuable comments on an earlier version. All views expressed in this article are purely personal. Any errors are attributable to the author alone.

2   https://www.statista.com/statistics/471264/iot-number-of-connected-devices-worldwide/, visited on July 5, 2019.

try to opine on all facets of the interplay between digitization and EU competition law.

A broad reflection process is going on in many jurisdictions across the globe on whether competition laws need to be adapted to the challenges of the Digital Economy and if yes, how best to do this.

Many expert reports have been issued in the last three years, which look into these challenges.[3] On top of that, there is a vast amount of academic literature on the topic.[4]

Again, it would go beyond the remit of this article to try to summarize all the expert reports and academic literature on competition law and digitization.

The purpose of this article is much more humble. It will focus on the European Commission's (the "Commission's") decisional practice in the mandate lasting from 2014 to 2019, and the relevant case law of the European Courts in relation to digital markets in the more traditional sense, with a specific emphasis on antitrust enforcement. In doing that, it can only provide a snapshot of the "hot topics" without going into any in-depth analysis, which would be warranted for many of the topics raised.

---

3   See for example J. Cremer, Y. De Montjoye & H. Schweitzer, Competition Policy for the Digital Era, (4 April 2019), ("Special Advisor Report"), ec.europa.eu/competition/publications/reports/kd0419345enn.pdf; J. Furman ET AL., H.M. Treasury (U.K.), Unlocking digital competition report of the Digital Competition Expert Panel (March 13, 2019), assets.publishing.service.gov.uk/government/uploads/system/uploads/attachment_data/file/785547/unlocking _digital_competition_furman_review_web.pdf; Australian Competition & Consumer Commission, Digital Platforms Inquiry: Preliminary report (December 2018), www.accc.gov.au/system/files/ACCC%20Digital%20Platforms%20Inquiry%20%20 Preliminary%20Report.pdf; Japanese Ministry of Economy, Trade, & Industry, Fundamental Principles for Rule Making to Address the Rise of Platform Businesses Formulated, (December 18, 2018), www.meti.go.jp/english/press/2018/1218_002.html; H. Schweitzer ET AL., German Bundesministerium Wirtschaft und Energie, Modernising the law on abuse of market power: Report for the Federal Ministry of Economic Affairs and Energie (April 9, 2018), www.bmwi.de/Redaktion/DE/Downloads/Studien/modernisierung-der-missbrauchsaufsicht-fuermarktmaechtige-unternehmen-zusammenfassung-englisch.pdf; L'Authorité de la Concurrence, Portant sur l'exploitation des données dans le secteur de la publicité sur internet [on the exploitation of data in the internet advertising sector] (March 6, 2018), www. autoritedelaconcurrence.fr/pdf/avis/18a03.pdf, George J. Stigler Center for the Study of the Economy and the State, The University of Chicago Booth School of Business Committee for the Study of Digital Platforms, Market Structure and Antitrust Subcommittee (July 1, 2019), research.chicagobooth.edu/-/media/research/stigler/pdfs/market-structure---report-as-of-24-june-2019.pdf?la=en&hash=872E4CA6B09BAC699EEF7D259BD69AEA717DDCF9;   all visited on July 5, 2019.

4   Pars pro toto, see A. Ezrachi & M. E. Stucke, Virtual Competition. The Promise and Perils of the Algorithm-driven Economy, Harvard University Press, 2016.

II. MARKET CHARACTERISTICS AND ENFORCEMENT TOOLS

A. Characteristics of Digital Markets

In 2018, Competition Commissioner Vestager tasked three renowned experts with preparing a report on the challenges for EU competition policy in the digital era ("the Special Advisor Report"). This report was published on April 4, 2019.[5] Its authors identify three key characteristics of the digital economy:

a) **Extreme returns to scale.** The cost of production of digital services is much less than proportional to the number of customers served. While this aspect is not novel as such (bigger factories or retailers are often more efficient than smaller ones), the digital world pushes it to the extreme and this can result in a significant competitive advantage for incumbents.

b) **Network externalities**. The convenience of using a technology or a service increases with the number of users that adopt it. Consequently, it is not enough for a new entrant to offer better quality and/or a lower price than the incumbent does; it also has to convince users of the incumbent to coordinate their migration to its own services. Network effects could thus prevent a superior platform from displacing an established incumbent. The size of this 'incumbency advantage' depends on a number of factors, including the possibility of multi-homing, data portability, and data interoperability.

c) **The role of data**. The evolution of technology has made it possible for companies to collect, store, and use large amounts of data. Data is not only one of the key ingredients of Artificial Intelligence but also a crucial input to many online services, production processes, and logistics. Therefore, the ability to use data to develop new, innovative services and products is a competitive parameter whose relevance will continue to increase.

The report concludes that because of these characteristics of digital markets incumbents may have a strong competitive advantage and may be difficult to dislodge.

---

5   J. Cremer, Y. De Montjoye & H. Schweitzer, Competition Policy for the Digital Era, (April 4, 2019), ("Special Advisor Report"), ec.europa.eu/competition/publications/reports/kd0419345enn.pdf, page 2, visited on July 5, 2019.

Looking at the decisional practice of the Commission during the mandate lasting from 2014 to 2019 as regards digital markets there are two markets trends, which have also been identified in the Special Advisor Report, notably the "platformization" of the industry, that is to say the growth of online platforms, and data use, which have coined enforcement both in relation to antitrust and merger cases in digital markets.

As regards platform markets, the Commission adopted during the 2014-2019 mandate three prohibition decisions against Google[6] on the basis of Article 102 of the Treaty on the Functioning of the European Union (TFEU) and Article 7 of Regulation (EC) No 1/2003[7] and one decision pursuant to Article 9 of Regulation (EC) No 1/2003 in relation to Amazon's e-books distribution agreements.[8] The Commission also initiated proceedings against Amazon on the basis of Article 2 of Regulation (EC) No 773/2004[9], on July 17, 2019 in relation to the alleged use of marketplace seller data by Amazon's retail arm.

The use of data featured prominently in merger decisions. In *Microsoft/LinkedIn*[10] the Commission assessed whether concerns could arise from the concentration of the parties' user data that can be used for advertising purposes and concluded that this was not the case. In *Apple/Shazam*[11] the Commission concluded that the integration of Shazam's and Apple's datasets on user data would not confer a unique advantage to the merged entity in the markets on which it operates. Any concerns in that respect were dismissed because Shazam's data was not unique and Apple's competitors would still have the opportunity to access and use similar databases.

B. Intervention Logic – If and When to Intervene in Digital Markets

One of the questions that very frequently needs to be addressed by competition authorities, including the Commission, in relation to enforcement in digital markets is whether at all to intervene against anticompetitive conduct in such markets

---

6   Commission decision of June 26, 2017 in Case 39740 *Google Search (Shopping)*; Commission decision of 18 July 2018 in Case 40099 *Google Android*; Commission decision of 20 March 2019 in Case 40411 *Google Search (AdSense)*; Commission decision of January 24, 2018 in Case 40220 *Qualcomm (exclusivity payments)*; Commission decision of July 17, 2019 in Case 39711 *Qualcomm (predation)*.

7   Regulation (EC) No 1/2003 of December 16, 2002 on the implementation of the rules on competition laid down in Articles 81 and 82 of the Treaty, OJ L 1, 4.1.2003, p. 1.

8   Commission decision of May 4, 2017 in Case 40153 *E-book MFNs (Amazon)*.

9   Regulation (EC) No 773/2004 of April 7, 2004 relating to the conduct of proceedings by the Commission pursuant to Articles 81 and 82 of the Treaty, OJ L 123, 27.4.2004, p. 18.

10   Commission decision of December 6, 2016 in Case M.8124, *MICROSOFT/LINKEDIN*.

11   Commission decision of September 6, 2018 in Case M.8788 *APPLE/SHAZAM*.

given the pace of technological change and if this is answered positively, when is the right moment to intervene.

The positions on this crucial question could not be more opposed. There is one line of thinking that postulates that in digital markets competition is only "one click away" and that disruptive innovation/Schumpeterian competition will erode strong market positions very quickly, so that there is no need for intervention under competition law. A different position, which in the author's opinion, has of late emerged as the majority view, argues that the specific characteristics of digital markets, such as the strong network effects in favor of the incumbent make intervention under competition law against anticompetitive conduct more necessary in order to avoid markets irreversibly tipping towards a monopoly.

The Court of Justice already had the opportunity to pronounce itself on the question of timing in *TeliaSonera*, when asked about the relevance of the fact that the markets concerned are growing rapidly and involve new technology, which requires high levels of investment.

The Court of Justice held that taking into account the objective of the competition rules "[…] their application cannot depend on whether the market concerned has already reached a certain level of maturity. Particularly in a rapidly growing market, Article 102 TFEU requires action as quickly as possible, to prevent the formation and consolidation in that market of a competitive structure distorted by the abusive strategy of an undertaking which has a dominant position on that market or on a closely linked neighbouring market, in other words it requires action before the anticompetitive effects of that strategy are realised."[12]

In the same vein the General Court [then Court of First Instance] held in *Microsoft* that:

> "[i]f the Commission were required to wait until competitors were eliminated from the market, or until their elimination was sufficiently imminent, before being able to take action under Article 82 EC [now Article 102 TFEU], that would clearly run counter to the objective of that provision, which is to maintain undistorted competition in the common market and, in particular, to safeguard the competition that still exists on the relevant market.
>
> […] the Commission had all the more reason to apply Article 82 EC [now Article 102 TFEU] before the elimination of com-

---

12 Judgment of February 17, 2011 in Case C-52/09, *Konkurrensverket v. TeliaSonera Sverige AB*, ECLI:EU:C:2011:83, paragraph 108.

petition on the work group server operating systems market had become a reality because that market is characterised by significant network effects and because the elimination of competition would therefore be difficult to reverse."[13]

Early intervention to safeguard effective competition in digital markets has therefore been promoted by the EU Courts.

This approach is also reflected in the Special Advisor Report, which calls for rethinking the error cost framework of enforcement in digital markets.

The Special Advisors suggest "that competition law should not try to work with the error cost framework case by case, but rather should try to translate general insights in error costs into legal tests [...]. In particular, in the context of highly concentrated markets characterized by strong network effects and subsequently high barriers to entry (a setting where impediments to entry which will not be easily corrected by markets), one may want to err on the side of disallowing types of conduct that are potentially anticompetitive, and to impose the burden of proof for showing pro-competitiveness on the incumbent."[14]

While the reversal of the burden of proof is a very far-reaching suggestion, which would most likely imply changes in the law,[15] earlier intervention, which will necessarily have to come with a more prospective analysis of potential effects (see on effects analysis below) might indeed be warranted to prevent tipping in digital markets. This seems very much in line with the *TeliaSonera* and *Microsoft* case law about the need to protect effective competition and the difficulty of reversing foreclosure in markets with network effects.

What constitutes effective competition in digital markets worthy of protection is however a different, albeit equally important question.

In *Intel* the Court of Justice held that Article 102 TFEU "does not seek to ensure that competitors less efficient than the undertaking with the dominant position should remain on the market."[16]

If this guidance were literally applied to digital markets where the dominant company might have significant scale advantages and might therefore, at least from a static cost perspective, be deemed to be "more efficient" than smaller competitors such as

---

13   Judgment of September 17, 2007 in Case T-201/04, *Microsoft v. Commission*, ECLI:EU:T:2007:289, paragraphs 561 and 562.

14   Special Advisor Report, 2019, p. 51.

15   See Article 2 of Regulation (EC) No 1/2003.

16   Judgment of September 6, 2017 in Case C413/14 P, *Intel v. Commission*, ECLI:EU:C:2017:632, paragraph 133.

start-ups the "effet utile" of Article 102 TFEU, the aim of which is, *inter alia*, according to the case law to protect the structure of the market and thus competition as such[17] might be compromised. It is therefore submitted that on a proper reading of the *Intel* judgment competition by companies that can or could have (absent the abuse) exerted a competitive constraint in terms of price, choice, quality or innovation should be deemed worthy of protection under EU competition rules even if the respective competitor turns out to be less efficient or not yet "as efficient" as the dominant company in some respects.[18]

C. Enforcement Tools, Legal Tests, and Remedies

Enforcement of EU competition law in digital markets also entails challenges in terms of the legal tests to be applied and the remedies to be imposed.

Consumer Harm

In particular in the U.S., an intensive debate has started on whether the consumer welfare standard, and in particular the focus on price, which has guided the enforcement of the Sherman Act since the 1970s, needs to be revisited.[19]

In the European Union, the Court of Justice has consistently held that both Articles 101 and 102 TFEU are aimed not only "[at] those practices that directly cause harm to consumers but also practices that cause consumers harm through their impact on competition[20], and that [...] for a finding that an agreement has an anti-competitive object, it is not necessary that final consumers be deprived of the advantages of effective competition in terms of supply or price."[21]

Consequently, consumer harm has been defined widely by the European Courts. It encompasses harm to the competitive structure brought about by anticompetitive agreements or abuses of dominant positions.

This sensible (in the author's view) interpretation of consumer harm is particularly important in determining harm in digital markets. As many services in digital markets are offered free of charge to consumers, it will often be difficult to

---

17   Judgments of June 4, 2009 in Case C8/08, *T-Mobile Netherlands and Others*, EU:C:2009:343, paragraphs 38 and 39, and of March 19, 2015, in Case C286/13 P, *Dole Food and Dole Fresh Fruit Europe v. Commission*, EU:C:2015:184, paragraph 125.

18   See also Judgment of September 6, 2017 in Case C413/14 P, *Intel v. Commission*, ECLI:EU:C:2017:632, paragraph 134.

19   Special Advisor Report, 2019, p. 40.

20   Judgment of March 27, 2012 in Case C-209/10, *Post Danmark I*, EU:C:2012:172, paragraph. 20,

21   Judgment of October 6, 2009 in Joined Cases C501/06 P, C-513/06 P, C-515/06 P and C519/06 P, *GlaxoSmithKline v. Commission*, ECLI:EU:C:2008:738, paragraph 63.

establish direct harm in terms of higher prices charged to consumers. The potential consumer harm will often occur in other ways as consumers may be deprived of choices and access to innovative products because of exclusionary conduct. The consumer welfare standard that has been adopted by the European Courts, which also focusses on harm to the competitive structure, is well adapted to the potential consumer harm that may result from anticompetitive conduct in digital markets.[22]

Standard of Proof

Once it is established that the concept of consumer harm encompasses parameters such as restriction of choice and innovation it becomes important to determine the standard of proof that is required to find an infringement of EU competition law based on this concept of harm.

This is not trivial. It is about establishing the potential negative effects on price, output, choice, quality, or innovation of specific anticompetitive conduct. As pointed out above, many digital markets may be prone to tipping, but at the point in time when the relevant anticompetitive conduct takes place, the tipping might not have occurred yet, or only the first tipping trends may be discernible. If the bar for the requisite standard of proof with respect to anticompetitive conduct is set too high, this might result in under-enforcement to the detriment of consumers. If, however, the bar for the requisite standard of proof is set too low, the net may be cast too wide and conduct which will finally not result in anticompetitive effects may be outlawed prematurely.

In *Post Danmark II* the Court of Justice held that only dominant undertakings whose conduct is likely to[23] have an anticompetitive effect on the market fall within the scope of Article 102 TFEU.[24]

Similarly, in relation to Article 101 TFEU the Court of Justice held in *Asnef-Equifax* that "Article 81(1) EC [now Article 101 TFEU] does not restrict such an assessment to actual effects alone, as that assessment must also take account of the potential effects of the agreement or practice in question on competition within the common market [...]."[25] [emphasis added]

---

22 Special Advisor Report, 2019, pp. 40-41.

23 Different wording has been used in this and in other judgments, see Judgment of October 6, 2015 in Case C23/14, *Post Danmark II*, ECLI:EU:C:2015:651, paragraph 50: "is capable of having an exclusionary effect on the market; Judgment of 17 February 2011 in Case C-52/09, *Konkurrensverket v. TeliaSonera Sverige AB*, ECLI:EU:C:2011:83, paragraph 71: "the potentially anti-competitive effect of a margin squeeze is probable." [emphasis added].

24 Judgment of October 6, 2015 in Case C23/14, *Post Danmark II*, ECLI:EU:C:2015:651, paragraph 67.

25 According to the case law the anti-competitive effect of a particular practice must not be purely hypothetical. See Judgment of November 23, 2006 in Case C238/05, *Asnef-Equifax*, ECLI:EU:C:2006:734, paragraph 50.

This case law on standard of proof with regard to effects is highly important for the effective enforcement of EU competition law in digital markets. [26]

In order to avoid changes in market structure in favor of certain companies as a result of anticompetitive conduct, and as such changes may be very difficult to reverse in digital markets due to network effects and tipping, it is important that competition authorities can intervene once it is established with sufficient probability that the conduct at issue will likely lead to harm, for example through foreclosure. The point is that competition authorities should not have to wait until actual detrimental effects on the market can be shown, for example until companies have exited the market, but should be able to intervene once a clear market trend can be established which is likely going to lead to negative effects on competition.[27] This however does not discharge competition authorities from proving to the requisite legal standard that such a market trend will likely continue without intervention.[28]

Interim Measures and Restorative Remedies

In cases were early intervention by competition authorities is not feasible in order to avoid a lasting change in the market structure due to anticompetitive behavior, interim measures or restorative remedies may have to be envisioned.

Article 8 of Regulation (EC) No 1/2003 empowers the Commission in case of urgency due to the risks of serious and irreparable damage to competition to order interim measures. The Commission has however not imposed interim measures since the *IMS Health* case in 2002.[29] This has led to a debate on how this tool could effectively be "revived" in particular for digital markets. In October 2019, the Commission adopted a decision granting interim measures in a case concerning exclusivity arrangements of Broadcom.[30]

In line with the case law, the character of such interim measures should remain conservative, that is to say, indispensable for ensuring the effectiveness of any

---

26 Contrary to this case law the General Court now appears to require an analysis of actual effects to establish an infringement in the past, see Judgment of December 12, 2018 in Case T684/14, *Krka Tovarna Zdravil v. Commission*, ECLI:EU:T:2018:918, paragraphs 351 to 377. The Commission has appealed this judgment to the Court of Justice.

27 Special Advisor Report, 2019, p. 42.

28 Judgment of October 6, 2015 in Case C23/14, *Post Danmark II*, ECLI:EU:C:2015:651, paragraph 65.

29 Commission Decision of July 3, 2001 in Case 38044 — *NDC Health/IMS Health*: *Interim measures*.

30 https://ec.europa.eu/commission/presscorner/detail/en/IP_19_6109, visited on December 20, 2019.

decisions requiring undertakings to bring an end to infringements.[31] In other words, interim measures should conserve the *status quo* in the markets while the assessment of the main case is pending.

The adoption of interim measures could therefore be useful in digital markets to avoid further rapid changes in the market structure due to anticompetitive conduct.

Interim measures, while useful, cannot however be seen as the instrument which, in isolation, can ensure the effectiveness of competition law intervention.

Another possibility for ensuring effective competition in digital markets may therefore be the recourse to restorative remedies.

Article 7 Regulation (EC) No 1/2003 empowers the Commission "to [...] impose on [undertakings] any behavioral or structural remedies which are proportionate to the infringement committed and necessary to bring the infringement <u>effectively</u> to an end." [emphasis added]

Although the prevalent remedies used by the Commission are mere "cease and desist" orders, this wording empowers the Commission to impose remedies that go beyond such orders and to force companies to positively adopt certain conduct if this is necessary to bring an infringement effectively to an end, while respecting the principle of proportionality.

The question remains, however, just how far the Commission can go in ordering behavioral remedies. Can it just order remedies that bring the infringement to an end, or can it go further and order remedies that aim to restore the competitive situation?

In terms of such restorative remedies, three aims could be distinguished. The aim could be to re-establish the situation as it was before the infringement (*status quo ante*), to re-establish the situation as it would be absent the infringement (counterfactual or "but for"), or re-establish the competitive process, i.e. recreating the conditions for a competitive and contestable market to the benefit of both existing competitors and new entrants (without necessarily guaranteeing a specific outcome for any competitor, individually or taken together).

The *Ufex* judgment supports the proposition that the Commission is entitled under EU competition law to order restorative remedies.

---

31   Order of January 17, 1980 in Case 792/79 R, *Camera Care Ltd. v. Commission*, EU:C:1980:18, paragraph. 18.

In *Ufex*,[32] albeit in the context of a rejection of a complaint, the Court of Justice held that "[I]f anti-competitive effects continue after the practices which caused them have ceased, the Commission thus remains competent […] to act with a view to eliminating or neutralising them." [emphasis added]

If the Commission remains competent to intervene in order to eliminate or neutralize the persisting effects of ceased conduct, *a fortiori*, the Commission must also be able to eliminate or neutralize the effects of conduct that is still in place at the time of the adoption of a prohibition decision pursuant to Article 7 Regulation (EC) No 1/2003.

In line with the case law that EU competition law, *inter alia*, protects the competitive process, it is submitted that any restorative remedy adopted should focus on re-establishing a functioning competitive process, which has been distorted through anticompetitive conduct, that is to say a process which guarantees equality of opportunity between the various economic operators.[33]

Restorative remedies, which, by neutralizing negative effects, aim at re-establishing opportunities to compete, may be particularly relevant in digital markets in order to counter networks effects which may be fueled by anticompetitive conduct and which may lead to an incumbency advantage.

III.   MARKET DEFINITION AND MARKET POWER

A. *Market Definition*

Market definition in digital markets raises many issues. For the purposes of this article the author will focus on two topics which are of high practical relevance, notably how to define markets with regard to two or multi-sided platforms and how to define markets when services are provided free of charge.

Two or Multi-sided Platforms

As the U.S. Supreme Court put it in the *Amex* judgment, "two-sided platforms differ from traditional markets in important ways. Two-sided platforms often exhibit what economists call 'indirect network effects.' Indirect network effects exist where the value of the two-sided platform to one group of participants depends on how many members of a different group participate. The value of the services that a

---

32   Judgment of March 4, 1999 in Case C-119/97 P, *Union française de l'express (Ufex), formerly Syndicat français de l'express international (SFEI), DHL International and Service CRIE v. Commission*, EU:C:1999:116, paragraph 94.

33   Judgment of May 23, 2003 in Case C-462/99, *Connect Austria*, ECLI:EU:C:2003:297, paragraph 83.

two-sided platform provides increases as the number of participants on both sides of the platform increases."[34]

The digital economy provides many examples of two-sided platforms, such as online marketplaces which intermediate between sellers and consumers, online hotel booking platforms which intermediate between hotels and consumers, or online search engines which finance the search service, which is provided free of charge to the consumer, with online advertising. The same goes for advertising financed social networks.

In the academic literature,[35] and in the U.S. case law,[36] an attempt has been made to categorize platforms into transaction platforms and non-transaction (attention) platforms. The purported difference between the two would be that on a transaction platform an actual transaction between two user groups is initiated on/by the platform while attention platforms do not aim at intermediating a direct transaction but are in many cases financed through ads so that no direct transaction takes place through the platform.

In practice, however, it is not always that easy to distinguish platforms on which a "transaction" takes place from other platforms. Take a dating platform as an example that intermediates a transaction, which does not take place on the platform. On top of that, it might be ad-financed, and no direct transaction takes place between the user and the advertisers.

Similarly, platforms with "freemium" business models are hard to classify. These platforms offer a basic ad-financed free of charge service, and an upgrade with subscription fees.

Overall, the categorization into transaction and non-transaction platforms may raise practical difficulties.

The issue of categorization would not matter too much if this were just an academic debate on how best to explain different platform business models. This categorization has however gained relevance with the U.S. Supreme Court's judgment in *Amex*, where the Supreme Court held that "two-sided transaction platforms exhibit more pronounced indirect network effects and interconnected pricing and demand. Transaction platforms are thus better understood as 'suppl[ying] only one product'— transactions."

---

34   *U.S. Supreme Court, Ohio v. American Express Co.*, 585 U.S. (2018).

35   Pars pro toto, Filistrucchi/Geradin/van Damme/Affeldt, "Market definition in two-sided markets: Theory and practice," Journal of Competition Law and Economics 2014, 10 (2), pp. 293-339.

36   *U.S. Supreme Court, Ohio v. American Express Co.*, 585 U.S. (2018).

The Supreme Court consequently held that there is only one market to be defined for transaction platforms while this might not be the case for non-transaction platforms.[37]

This is not purely a market definition issue but also has repercussions on the definition of consumer harm. In a single relevant market, any harm must be *net* harm across the user groups. Therefore, in the *Amex* case the plaintiffs had to show not only harm on one side but also the absence of offsetting benefits to the other side of the market (merchants and cardholders).[38]

This approach to market definition in two-sided markets has not been followed in the EU, not at least because the demand and supply structure of the two sides of the market may be manifestly different and serious harm to one side of the market may be neglected if the other side benefits (low consumer prices versus high fees for sellers).

The Court of Justice follows a different approach in considering two-sided markets as separate but connected markets and only allows the offsetting of benefits between the two connected markets in limited circumstances (see below on efficiency claims in two-sided markets).[39]

Free of Charge Services

The second topic which is of high practical relevance for enforcement in digital markets is how to assess markets in which services are offered free of charge.

The Commission Notice on the definition of relevant markets for the purposes of Community competition law[40] recommends the SSNIP (small but significant non-transitory increase in price) test for assessing substitution. [41]

---

37 *U.S. Supreme Court, Ohio v. American Express Co.*, 585 U.S. (2018), majority opinion, p. 13.

38 *U.S. Supreme Court, Ohio v. American Express Co.*, 585 U.S. (2018), majority opinion, pp. 14-15.

39 Judgment of September 11, 2014, in Case C-382/12 P, *Mastercard*, ECLI:EU:C:2014:2201, paragraph 242.

40 OJ C 372, 9.12.1997, pp. 5–13, paragraphs 15 and 17: "The assessment of demand substitution entails a determination of the range of products which are viewed as substitutes by the consumer. One way of making this determination can be viewed as a speculative experiment, postulating a hypothetical small, lasting change in relative prices and evaluating the likely reactions of customers to that increase.[…] The question to be answered is whether the parties' customers would switch to readily available substitutes or to suppliers located elsewhere in response to a hypothetical small (in the range 5% to 10%) but permanent relative price increase in the products and areas being considered."

41 OJ C 372, 9.12.1997, pp. 5–13.

Evidently this test is hardly useful to determine substitution in cases where services are offered free of charge. In such cases other parameters need to be taken into account in order to determine which products constitute substitutes for the purposes of market definition.

The Commission's *Google Shopping* decision provides an illustrative example of how the Commission approaches market definition in markets where the service is offered free of charge as was the case with Google's online search service. First, the Commission established that general search services constitute an economic activity irrespective of their provision free of charge on the basis of the following arguments.

First, even though users do not pay a monetary consideration for the use of general search services, they contribute to the monetization of the service by providing data with each query. In most cases, a user entering a query enters into a contractual relationship with the operator of the general search service. For instance, Google's Terms of Service provide: "By using our Services, you agree that Google can use such data in accordance with our privacy policies." In accordance with its privacy policies, Google can store and re-use data relative to user queries. The data which users agree to allow a general search engine to store and re-use is of value to the provider of the general search service as it is used to improve the relevance of the search service and to show more relevant advertising. Second, offering a service free of charge can be an advantageous commercial strategy, in particular for two-sided platforms such as a general search engine platform that connect distinct but interdependent demands. In two-sided platforms, two distinct user groups interact. At least for one of these user groups, the value obtained from the platform depends on the number of users of the other class. General search services and online search advertising constitute the two sides of a general search engine platform. The level of advertising revenue that a general search engine can obtain is related to the number of users of its general search service: the higher the number of users of a general search service, the more the online search advertising side of the platform will appeal to advertisers. Third, even though general search services do not compete on price, there are other parameters of competition between general search services. These include the relevance of results, the speed with which results are provided, the attractiveness of the user interface, and the depth of indexing of the web.[42]

Second, the Commission distinguished other online services such as content sites, specialized search services, social networking sites and merchant platforms and excluded them as substitutes for general search services on the basis of functionality and user demand.[43]

---

42   Commission decision of June 26, 2017 in Case 39740 *Google Search (Shopping)*, paragraphs 158 to 160.

43   Commission decision of June 26, 2017 in Case 39740 *Google Search (Shopping)*, paragraphs 163 to 250.

The Commission therefore chose a functionality and user demand-based approach to establishing substitution in markets where the SNNIP test does not work. Other tests like the SSNDQ test (small but significant non-transitory decrease in quality) have also been suggested.

B. Market Power

In digital markets, as in other markets, high market shares can only be a first indicator of market power and need to be buttressed with other indicators of market power. As the General Court put it in the *Microsoft/Skype* case: "*[in a] recent and fast-growing sector which is characterized by short innovation cycles [...] large market shares may turn out to be ephemeral. In such a dynamic context, high market shares are not necessarily indicative of market power.*"[44]

On the other hand, market shares which have been stable for a long period of time might still be a strong indicator for market power, even in a fast-growing market.[45]

In addition to high market shares the Commission has in its recent decisional practice in digital markets assessed the following market features in order to establish dominance: Barriers to entry and expansion, multi-homing and the existence of brand effects, and the lack of countervailing buyer power.

As regards barriers to entry and expansion, the Commission assessed, in *Google Shopping* for example, the significant investments in terms of time and resources it requires to develop a fully-fledged general search engine and the network effects deriving from the large number of data on queries that is available to Google: "[...]a general search service uses search data to refine the relevance of its general search results pages, it needs to receive a certain volume of queries in order to compete viably. The greater the number of queries a general search service receives, the quicker it is able to detect a change in user behaviour patterns and update and improve its relevance."[46]

The assessment of multi-homing played a prominent role both in *Google Shopping* and in *Google Android* to establish dominance. In Google Shopping the Commission found that only a minority of users in the EEA that use Google's general search service as their main general search service use other general search services.[47] In *Google Android*, the Commission assessed developer multi-homing, i.e. the ques-

---

44 Judgment of December 11, 2013 in Case T-79/12, *Cisco Systems v. Commission*, ECLI:EU:T:2013:635 , paragraph 69.

45 Judgment of January 30, 2007, in Case T-340/03, *France Telecom v. Commission*, EU:T:2007:22, paragraphs 107-108.

46 Commission decision of June 26, 2017 in Case 39740 *Google Search (Shopping)*, paragraph 287.

47 Commission decision of June 26, 2017 in Case 39740 *Google Search (Shopping)*, paragraph 306.

tion of whether app developers would develop apps for multiple mobile operating systems,[48] and consumer multi-homing as regards mobile search.[49]

Generally, it can be said that market power is more likely to be established in a two-sided market if there is single homing on one side of the market, as this might induce multi-homing on the other side.

In addition, the Commission has in its decisional practice also assessed the countervailing power of customers in order to determine market power. This assessment is, however, not specific to digital markets.

In summary, the specificities of the assessment of market power in digital markets that have crystallized through the Commission's decisional practice in the 2014 to 2019 mandate are: less reliance on market shares and more reliance on other market features such as network effects and multi-homing.

IV. THEORIES OF HARM AND EFFICIENCIES

When it comes to the analysis of the "theories of harm" which have been relied on in the Commission's decisional practice during the 2014 to 2019 mandate, it is fair to say that some of them are "old wine in new bottles" while others are genuinely uncharted territory.

A. Theories of Harm

The theories of harm relied on by the Commission show the panoply of different anticompetitive conduct that may arise in digital markets. First, one finds more classical, established forms of abuses such as tying which was one of the theories of harm relied on in Google Android[50] and exclusivity payments, relied on in *Google Android and Qualcomm*,[51] or contractual exclusivity (*Google Adsense*[52]).

However, even these more established theories of harm need to be adapted to the market realities of digital markets. For example, in order prove the potential effects of tying in *Google Android* the Commission found that downloads cannot be compared in reach and effectiveness to the pre-installation of Google Chrome.[53]

Other theories of harm appear to be more specific to digital markets.

---

48 Commission decision of July 18, 2018 in Case 40099 *Google Android*, paragraphs 556 et seq.

49 Commission decision of July 18, 2018 in Case 40099 *Google Android*, paragraphs 709 et seq.

50 Commission decision of July 18, 2018 in Case 40099 *Google Android*.

51 Commission decision of January 24, 2018 in Case 40220 *Qualcomm (exclusivity payments)*.

52 Commission decision of March 20, 2019 in Case 40411 *Google Search (AdSense)*.

53 Commission decision of July 18, 2018 in Case 40099 *Google Android*, paragraphs 917 et seq.

The *Amazon e-books* case is a good example. Here, the theory of harm was that by contractually obliging its e-book suppliers to notify and offer to Amazon the same or equivalent terms for the distribution of e-books under a given business model, Amazon first reduced the incentives of its competitors to support and invest in alternative, new and innovative business models and second, deterred entry and/or expansion by e-book retailers competing with Amazon by limiting their scope to differentiate on the basis of alternative business models.[54]

Another example can be found in the *Google Shopping*[55] decision. Here the Commission took issue with the more favorable positioning and display, in Google's general search results pages, of Google's own comparison shopping service when compared to competing comparison shopping services. In order to establish that this conduct amounts to an infringement of Article 102 TFEU the Commission had recourse to a sophisticated effects analysis which sought to establish that the conduct was likely to decrease traffic from Google's general search results pages to competing comparison shopping services and likely to increase traffic from Google's general search results pages to Google's own comparison shopping service, to the detriment of competition and ultimately consumers who could be deprived of relevant comparison shopping services.

While the case can be described as a classical leveraging case where a company seeks to extend its position on the market where it is dominant into another adjacent market, one interesting aspect of the case certainly lies in the factoring in of consumer behavior into the effects analysis as it had to be established that consumers reacted to the favorable positioning of Google's comparison shopping services in terms of ranking on the general search site by clicking more on Google's service than on competing services.

In sum, the theories of harm which have been relied upon by the Commission in the decisions related to digital markets are not out of the ordinary and very well in sync with the European approach to the consumer welfare standards as outlined above, which also focusses on harm to choice and innovation. As illustrated, however, sometimes market realities require an adaptation of the "classical" theories of harm in order to better capture consumer behavior in digital markets.

B. Efficiencies

In particular in two-sided digital markets, it may sometimes be difficult to establish whether specific conduct will, on balance, result in consumer benefits or harm as very often the business model of two-sided platforms relies on offering final consumers products or services free of charge while charging the other side of the market, be it advertisers or sellers.

---

54 Commission decision of May 4, 2017 in Case 40153 *E-book MFNs* (*Amazon*), paragraphs 56 et seq.

55 Commission decision of June 26, 2017 in Case 39740 *Google Search (Shopping).*

For online platform markets the question therefore arises whether the benefits to final consumers from the provision of the free service have to be balanced against the harm that might be inflicted by anticompetitive conduct on advertisers or sellers on the platform.

In EU competition law, there is limited scope for so-called "cross-market efficiencies." The Court of Justice held in *Mastercard*,

> [...] where, as in the present case, restrictive effects have been found on only one market of a two-sided system, the advantages flowing from the restrictive measure on a separate but connected market also associated with that system cannot, in themselves, be of such a character as to compensate for the disadvantages resulting from that measure in the absence of any proof of the existence of appreciable objective advantages attributable to that measure in the relevant market, in particular [...] where the consumers on those markets are not substantially the same.[56]

This echoes the European Commission's Guidelines on Article 101(3) TFEU, which state that:

> Negative effects on consumers in one geographic market or product market cannot normally be balanced against and compensated by positive effects for consumers in another unrelated geographic market or product market. However, where two markets are related, efficiencies achieved on separate markets can be taken into account provided that the group of consumers affected by the restriction and benefiting from the efficiency gains are substantially the same.[57]

This approach avoids a situation where a Court or competition authority has to "side" with one specific consumer group and to value harm to this group as higher than harm to another group.[58]

---

56 Judgment of September 1, 2014 in Case 382/12 P *Mastercard*, ECLI:EU:C:2014:2201, paragraph 242.

57 Commission Guidelines on the application of Article 81(3) of the Treaty, OJ C 101, 27.4.2004, pp. 97–118, paragraph 43.

58 It should be recalled that the concept of consumer in EU competition law encompasses "all direct or indirect users of the products covered by the agreement, including producers that use the products as an input, wholesalers, retailers and final consumers, i.e. natural persons who are acting for purposes which can be regarded as outside their trade or profession. In other words, consumers within the meaning of Article 101(3) TFEU are the customers of the parties to the agreement and subsequent purchasers. These customers can be undertakings as in the case of buyers of industrial machinery or an input for further processing or final consumers as for instance in the case of buyers of impulse ice-cream or bicycles," see Commission Guidelines on the application of Article 81(3) of the Treaty, OJ C 101, 27.4.2004, pp. 97–118, paragraph 84.

III. CONCLUSION

The debate over whether competition law is capable of dealing with new market developments in innovative markets is as old as EU competition law enforcement. In 1958, when the competition provisions of the Treaty of Rome entered into force, the skateboard, and more importantly, microchips, which are today used in virtually every piece of electronic equipment, had just been invented. Evidently, the drafters of the Treaty of Rome could not have foreseen the technical developments that followed, such as the smartphone. However, they wisely formulated Articles 85 and 86 of the Treaty (now 101 and 102 TFEU) in a manner that allows technical developments to be taken into account and even used as a yardstick for the assessment of restrictions to competition under EU competition law.[59]

The basic tools of European competition law (Articles 101 and 102 TFEU) have been crafted in a "technology neutral" way and can be applied to "new" or "old" markets alike. The history of EU competition law enforcement since 1958 shows that the basic EU competition rules are flexible enough to address technological developments. This is well illustrated by the examples of the *IBM* abuse of dominance case on mainframe interface information in the 1980s, which was settled in 1984, and the *Microsoft* interoperability abuse of dominance case, which was decided two decades later in 2004. Both cases addressed the technological challenges of their time (mainframe and work group server interoperability) within the legal framework set out by the Treaty of Rome in 1958.

EU competition rules, as well as their application by the EU courts, have therefore proved flexible enough to address technological developments. This does not, however, mean that antitrust enforcers should be complacent about new market developments. On the contrary: in order to remain relevant, the established enforcement principles need to be applied in the context of new market realities and, where necessary, adapted in the light of these realities. The specific features of digital markets, such as the growing importance of data and network effects and the provision of "free" services to consumers in two-sided digital platform markets, can and must be factored into the assessment of conduct under EU competition law.

---

59 See the references to the "promotion of technical progress" in Article 101(3) TFEU and to "limiting the technical development to the prejudice of consumers" in Article 102(b) TFEU.

Algorithms and Competition in a Digitalized World

By Andreas Mundt[1]

Abstract

Focusing in particular on the impact of algorithms, this essay demonstrates ways in which the peculiarities of the digital economy are reflected in the practice of the Bundeskartel-lamt ("BKartA"). In light of the increasing importance of algorithms, it elaborates on the BKartA's practical experiences in this regard and points out conclusions drawn from past proceedings. These practical experiences are complemented by conceptual considerations on pricing algorithms and collusion as well as on potential interdependencies between algorithms and market power, which inform future enforcement. In view of the challenges posed by the implications of algorithms on competition, but also more broadly by the ongoing digital transformation, the essay finally points to the current discussions on adjusting the legal toolkit and highlights that digitalization, as a global phenomenon, calls for international collaboration and exchange.

I. TURNING DIGITAL

The global trend towards digitalization poses unique challenges for both competition policy and enforcement. Considering the digital economy in particular, many business models rely on positive network effects as customers often prefer services which many others use. The more a service is used – e.g. social networking websites – the more customers it attracts and the more attractive it becomes, potentially resulting in a winner-takes-all dynamic. A further important trait of many popular businesses in the digital economy is their data-driven nature, which is catalyzed by algorithms. In particular, dealing with so-called "big data," i.e. data of large volume and variety generated at high speed,[2] often requires corresponding "big analytics." However, although algorithms seem indispensable as a means for analyzing such data, it is hardly imaginable that at least more advanced machine learning algorithms could be trained or calibrated without sufficient data. For example, the German "Competition Law 4.0" Report stated that where data mining is a significant competitive factor, companies competing with "data-rich" firms would be disadvantaged, especially if self-learning

---

1   President of the German Bundeskartellamt (Federal Cartel Office).

2   For a more detailed discussion of different ways for defining (big) data, cf. *ADLC/BKartA*, Competition Law and Data, 2016, pp. 4 et seq.

algorithms were used. Training and optimizing self-learning algorithms crucially depended on regular access to large amounts of data or at least access to highly diverse data. The Commission concluded that "[i]f algorithms are trained with too little data or with data that is too uniform, this will have a negative impact on the algorithms' abilities to deal with the problems they were supposed to solve."[3]

While it is not easy to predict future technological developments both for companies and authorities, it nevertheless appears safe to say that the fundamental importance of algorithms and data is not about to change and should not be underestimated.

It falls upon competition authorities to keep markets contestable, protecting consumers and their choice options, and of course digital markets are not different in this regard. At the same time, the characteristics of digital markets make it necessary to acquire a profound understanding of their economic, technological and legal implications. The challenges of digital markets thus manifest themselves not only on a global scale, but are also of an interdisciplinary nature. In light of these considerations, the Bundeskartellamt ("BKartA") has presented several papers, *inter alia* in cooperation with the Autorité de la concurrence ("ADLC"), on the impact of big data[4] and algorithms on competition,[5] but also on other topics such as the market power of platforms and networks[6] and on innovations as challenges for competition law practice.[7] Building on previous studies, the article at hand elaborates why algorithms matter for the digital economy (II.). It contextualizes this relevance for competition authorities by discussing the practical experiences the BKartA has gathered while investigating cases involving algorithms (III.). Future cases might also draw attention to more conceptual considerations (IV.). In the end, supported by potential amendments to the legal toolkit and by exchanging experiences and expertise with each other, competition authorities are well prepared to address the challenges of the digital economy (V.).

II.   ALGORITHMS MATTER

Arguably, algorithms can be characterized as technological drivers of digitalization and there can be no doubt about their enormous positive effects. Many highly

---

3   *Schallbruch et al.*, A new competition framework for the digital economy ('Competition Law 4.0'), 2019, p. 14. Similarly, *Schweitzer et al.*, Modernising the law on abuse of market power, 2018, p. 130, argue that access to especially large amounts of data might be necessary to train algorithms.

4   *ADLC/BKartA*, Competition Law and Data, 2016.

5   *ADLC/BKartA*, Algorithms and Competition, 2019; also see the contribution by J. Moore, E. Pfister & H. Piffaut of the ADLC in the issue at hand.

6   *BKartA*, Working Paper – Market Power of Platforms and Networks, 2016.

7   *BKartA*, Innovations – challenges for competition law practice (Series of papers on "Competition and Consumer Protection in the Digital Economy"), 2017.

innovative and welfare-enhancing business models would not be imaginable without them. There is a plethora of ways in which algorithms have improved the quality of products and contributed both to innovations and lower prices. For example, many search algorithms allow for continuous improvements of their results by learning from past queries. Matching algorithms underlie numerous new services, for example within the sharing economy, but also beyond. And the use of ranking algorithms can contribute to reducing search costs, while personalization algorithms can be used to align recommendations with consumers' specific interests.

From a purely technical point of view, any kind of software consists of one or more algorithm(s). For the purposes of competition authorities, however, it appears sensible to focus on algorithms with competitive relevance. Among these are, for example,[8] pricing algorithms, which can be used by firms to monitor competitors' prices. Furthermore, such algorithms can also allow for dynamic pricing, i.e. setting prices based on a firm's own costs, capacity and demand situation, but also taking into account competitors' prices. Competitive relevance can furthermore be attributed to the use of ranking algorithms. Many services use such algorithms to sort items according to predetermined criteria, e.g. in the context of comparison websites, e-Commerce platforms or search engines. Considering, for example, the fact that a ranking created by one firm might have an effect on the visibility of and accessibility to third-party products included in said ranking, potential competitive concerns cannot be ruled out.

III. PRACTICAL EXPERIENCE

The BKartA has already encountered algorithms in its case practice on several occasions. One example is the 2018 *Lufthansa* case:[9] In the airline industry, specialized pricing algorithms, often integrated into yield management tools, are commonly used to manage and allocate inventories, contributing to a more efficient use of resources and allowing for pricing decisions to be based on a firm's current capacity as well as demand. In the 2018 case, Lufthansa held a monopoly position on some routes for a few months following the insolvency of the second largest German airline. During this time, ticket prices were on average 25-30 percent more expensive than before. The preliminary investigations showed that the airlines specified the parameters relevant for the algorithmic price adjustment separately for each flight. The airlines also actively changed these framework data and entered events unaccounted for by the system manually. However, it should not be decisive whether prices were adjusted by a pricing algorithm or an employee, because in the end the use of an algorithm naturally does not relieve a com-

---

8   For a more detailed characterization and categorization of algorithms, cf. *ADLC/BKartA*, Algorithms and Competition, 2019, pp. 3 et seq.

9   *BKartA*, Lufthansa tickets 25-30 per cent more expensive after Air Berlin insolvency, Press release of 29/05/2018.

pany of its responsibility.[10] As the BKartA did not initiate formal proceedings in the *Lufthansa* case due to subsequent market developments, this question of responsibility was, in the end, of no significance for this particular examination and its outcome.

Moreover, the BKartA has encountered matching algorithms particularly in the context of merger proceedings[11] and several of its sector inquiries. For example, the ongoing sector inquiry into online advertising touches upon "programmatic advertising," which involves algorithms that make it possible to automatically buy and optimize advertising campaigns.[12] In the area of consumer protection, the BKartA has dealt with ranking algorithms used by comparison websites.[13] In particular, it has examined the criteria on which pre-selections are based and the way in which comparison websites determine the positioning in the search results lists. Ranking algorithms and their economic effects were also relevant in proceedings concerning hotel platforms.[14] Launched in 2019, the sector inquiry into online user reviews *inter alia* involves considerations as to the ways in which algorithms support firms when dealing with potentially inauthentic user reviews.[15]

Even though the established investigative means, such as information requests, inspections and/or interviews, remain the same when obtaining relevant information on algorithms, these practical experiences have contributed to a better understanding of the peculiarities arising in algorithm-related investigations.[16] As the role and the function of certain algorithms may be unclear at the beginning of an investigation, authorities might decide that proceeding on a step-by-step basis by issuing successive requests is a viable option depending on the respective case. With regard to the relevant information that could potentially be requested, internal documentation could turn out to be particularly important. Besides technical specifications, this also applies *inter alia* to log files, user guides and documentation on data sources. Depending on the case, authorities might also decide to analyze an algorithm directly. In that situation, a decision on an appropriate method of analysis might particularly have to take into account the extent to which the algorithm in question involves machine learning methods.

---

10   In a similar vein, Commissioner *Vestager* has stated that "[…] we need to make it very clear that companies can't escape responsibility for collusion by hiding behind a computer program" (Speech at the 18th Conference on Competition, Berlin, 16/03/2017).

11   For example *BKartA*, Clearance of merger between online dating platforms (B6-57/15), Case summary of March 31, 2016.

12   *BKartA*, Bundeskartellamt launches sector inquiry into market conditions in online advertising sector, Press release of February 1, 2018.

13   *BKartA*, Sector inquiry on comparison websites, Press release of 11/04/2019.

14   For examples see *BKartA*, Decision of 20/12/2013, B9-66/10 (HRS-Hotel); *BKartA*, Decision of December 22, 2015, B9-121/13 (*Booking.com*).

15   *BKartA*, Bundeskartellamt launches sector inquiry into user reviews, Press release of 25/05/2019.

16   For a detailed discussion of the practical challenges faced when investigating algorithms, see *ADLC/BKartA*, Algorithms and Competition, 2019, pp. 61 et seq.

IV.   CONCEPTUAL CONSIDERATIONS

Algorithms relevant for competition warrant conceptual considerations especially with regard to their potential for fostering collusion (A.) and their potential interdependencies with market power (B.).

A. Pricing Algorithms and Collusion

From an economic point of view, collusion could be characterized *inter alia* as a firm causing rival firms to set supra-competitive prices by employing a reward-punishment scheme which rewards a firm for abiding by the supra-competitive outcome and punishes it for departing from it.[17] The effects of pricing algorithms on collusion appear to be ambiguous:[18] On the one hand, algorithms might increase the stability of collusion, e.g. by increasing market transparency due to price monitoring and allowing for rapid punishment after detecting deviations. On the other hand, algorithms could increase asymmetries between firms or products, e.g. through price discrimination, making collusion more difficult.

Regarding the emergence of collusion, determining (a lack of) communication is of particular importance as Art. 101 TFEU and its national counterparts distinguish between illegal explicit collusion and legal parallel behavior. In other words, without some kind of communication or sense of mutual commitment, no violation can be established. Against this background, scenarios similar to the *British poster* case,[19] in which firms explicitly agreed to not undercut each other on prices and used a pricing software for the implementation of said agreement, do not necessarily raise novel competition law issues. Assessing scenarios involving a third party – such as a software developer providing firms with similar algorithms – could be more complex. In such cases, the third party might align the competitors' behavior by having them use the same programmatically implemented pricing strategy and/or data sources. In accordance with ECJ jurisprudence, the competitors' liability could depend on whether the firms were aware of the anti-competitive objectives (or could at least have reasonably foreseen such objectives) and accepted the associated risks.[20]

A further, but so far hypothetical, scenario concerns the mere interaction of algorithms potentially causing an alignment of competitors' behavior. It currently seems to

---

17   Cf., for example, the discussion in *Harrington*, Developing Competition Law for Collusion by Autonomous Agents, Journal of Competition Law & Economics 2019, pp. 331 et seq. (334 et seq.).

18   Cf. *ADLC/BKartA*, Algorithms and Competition, 2019, pp. 15 et seq.

19   Cf. *CMA*, Decision of August 12, 2016, Case 50233 (*Poster*).

20   Cf. ECJ, Judgment of 21/01/16, Case C-74/14 (*Eturas*); ECJ, Judgment of July 21, 2016, Case C-542/14 (*VM Remonts*).

be a debatable question whether it is likely that such an alignment can arise "by chance" under real market conditions. While a convergence might be attainable in experimental settings, such experiments strongly rely, at least in part, on assumptions, such as a limited number of players, no market entries and/or stable demand.[21] Furthermore, even in experimental settings a significant number of algorithmic iterations would be required to achieve collusion. It should be noted, however, that notwithstanding this debate on the plausibility of purely algorithmic collusion, firms should always keep in mind that they "can't escape responsibility for collusion by hiding behind a computer program."[22]

B. Algorithms and Market Power

Authorities also have to pay close attention to possible relations between algorithms and the market power of companies that use them. First, the access to algorithms could in itself contribute to market power. In this context, the government memorandum accompanying the 9th amendment to the German Competition Act ("ARC/GWB") already acknowledged in 2017 that a company's capability to analyze and process data could potentially be relevant for gaining possible competitive advantages.[23] Furthermore, in the *Google Shopping* case the Commission also pointed out that the significant investments necessary for developing a competitive algorithm could potentially constitute a barrier to entry and expansion in markets in which algorithms form an integral part of the business, such as the market for general search engines.[24]

As demonstrated by the 2004 *Microsoft* case, a company's refusal to supply a competitor with information relating to its algorithms could potentially constitute exclusionary abuse. The Commission drew the conclusion that Microsoft had reached a dominant position in the work group server market.[25] In this context, refusing to provide a competitor with information necessary for the interoperability with Microsoft's system was deemed abusive. Notably, the Commission considered the disclosures in question to be indispensable to firms wishing to compete despite the existence of limited open industry standards and limited protocol licensing programs.[26]

Abusive behavior might also include pricing algorithms. First, authorities could be prompted to investigate potentially excessive pricing, i.e. whether a dominant

---

21 For more details on the debate on the plausibility/likelihood of purely algorithmic collusion, see *ADLC/BKartA*, Algorithms and Competition, 2019, pp. 45 et seq.

22 Fn. 9, *supra*.

23 Bundestagsdrucksache 18/10207, p. 51.

24 Cf. *Commission*, Decision of June 27, 2017, Case AT.39740 (*Google Search (Shopping)*), paras. 285 et seq.

25 *Commission*, Decision of February 24, 2004, Case COMP/C-3/37.792 (*Microsoft*), para. 541.

26 *Commission*, Decision of February 24, 2004, Case COMP/C-3/37.792 (*Microsoft*), paras. 666 et seq.

position has been used in such a way as to reap trading benefits which a firm would not have reaped if there had been normal and sufficiently effective competition.[27] The BKartA conducted such (preliminary) investigations *inter alia* in the 2018 *Lufthansa* case mentioned earlier. Furthermore, as pricing algorithms might allow for individual pricing and price discrimination, authorities might have to consider whether such behavior is abusive. While it might raise consumers' concern, the overall effect of such discrimination could vary on a case-by-case basis. Additionally, even though price discrimination might turn out to require a certain degree of market power, it could also reinforce competition by allowing firms to offer lower prices to customers with a strong preference for another product.[28]

Ranking algorithms could also prove relevant when investigating potentially abusive behavior. For example, in the *Google Shopping* case, the Commission had to consider whether the more favorable positioning and display of Google's own shopping service compared to competing one's constituted abusive behavior. More specifically, the Commission explained how certain dedicated algorithms reduced the ranking of some competing comparison shopping services in Google's search results pages and therefore affected their visibility in Google's general search result pages.[29] Similarly, such self-preferencing concerns are relevant in the Commission's ongoing *Amazon* case as it investigates the role of data in selecting the winners of the "Buy Box."[30] More generally, the German Commission 'Competition Law 4.0' regarded "implicit rules (e.g. those underpinning the ranking algorithms used by a platform)" as one form of platforms that set the rules governing interactions e.g. in their market places.[31]

V.   LOOKING FORWARD

As it is the task of competition authorities to keep markets contestable and protect consumers, it is only natural that authorities continuously reflect whether the established toolkit is still fit to fulfil those purposes. This holds particularly true given the challenges posed by the implications of algorithms on competition, but also more broadly with regard to the ongoing digitalization. In the past years, debates have taken place at different levels. Several circles of experts have published elaborate reports and

---

27   *ECJ*, Judgement of February 14, 1978, Case C-27/76 (*United Brands*), para. 249.

28   For a more detailed discussion, see *ADLC/BKartA*, Competition Law and Data, 2016, pp. 21 et seq.

29   Cf. Commission, Decision of June 27, 2017, Case AT.39740 (*Google Search (Shopping)*)

30   *Commission*, Commission opens investigation into possible anti-competitive conduct of Amazon, Press release of July 17, 2019.

31   *Schallbruch et al.*, A new competition framework for the digital economy ('Competition Law 4.0'), 2019, pp. 16, 51.

proposals.[32] On the enforcers' level, agencies continue working on cases and market studies backed up by conceptual work.

It is against this background of practical experiences, academic recommendations as well as the insights gathered from various reports that several legislators around the world are currently considering changes to their respective legal framework. In Germany, the draft 10th amendment to the German Competition Act intends to further improve the law, *inter alia* in the area of abuse control.33 The proposals are meant to allow for earlier, quicker and even more effective enforcement. They include provisions addressing potentially harmful conduct of undertakings of paramount significance for competition across markets. If the BKartA issues a decision declaring a company to be of such significance, it can prohibit certain kinds of behavior, including self-preferencing, certain types of (cross-market) data processing and limitations on data portability or interoperability. At least certain types of conduct addressed by the proposed provisions are likely to be connected to the use of algorithms. On the one hand, as the above considerations illustrate, algorithms could be used as a means to implement abusive practices, for example if an integrated ("hybrid") platform uses a ranking algorithm that favors its own products, possibly in a sophisticated way and as part of a potentially complex business strategy. On the other hand, remedies could also potentially include the use of algorithms, for example when facilitating data portability or interoperability via appropriate interfaces.

Authorities should also not forget that digitalization is transforming the economy on a global scale. As a global phenomenon, it continuously calls for close international collaboration and exchange. International organizations such as the ICN and the OECD work together very well to make the most of their specific strengths.[34] On the European plane, the ECN naturally is of particular importance regarding communication both between the different national agencies and also *vis-à-vis* the European Commission. At the same time, bilateral collaboration is also of great importance, in the context of conceptual work, but also with regard to enforcement.

All in all, even though the digital economy might pose novel challenges, competition agencies have been making good progress so far. At the same time, it

---

32   See for example *BRICS Competition Law and Policy Centre*, Digital Era Competition, 2019; *Crémer/de Montjoye/Schweitzer*, Competition policy for the digital era, 2019; *Furman et al.*, Unlocking digital competition, 2019; Schallbruch et al., A new competition framework for the digital economy ('Competition Law 4.0'), 2019; *Schweitzer et al.*, Modernising the law on abuse of market power, 2018.

33   The government draft ("Referentenentwurf") is available at https://www.bmwi.de/Redaktion/DE/Downloads/G/gwb-digitalisierungsgesetz-referentenentwurf.html.

34   Within international cooperation, G7 constitutes another important venue as, for example, the 2019 G7 French presidency prioritized promoting and protecting competition in digital markets.

is sensible that they continue to improve their expertise for dealing with the digital economy in close cooperation with each other.

Enforcement in European e-Commerce – The Way Forward

By Aleksandra Boutin, Xavier Boutin & Máté Fodor [1]

Abstract

A few leading platforms shape e-Commerce globally. They are able to set the conditions of competition and thereby they fall within the scope of Article 102 TFEU. Consequently, the Commission's current proposals to classify them as "gatekeepers" does not seem to fill any enforcement gap. At the same time, the new proposals intending to regulate their conduct ex ante or through the New Competition Tool, including through black lists of conduct and blanket prohibitions, carry important risks. They may discourage firms from behaviors that are pro-competitive in their market contexts. They may also unnecessarily hurt local e-Commerce platforms by constraining their ability to compete with the already much more powerful global leaders. Effective enforcement in the digital world requires building a coherent theory of harm and logically deriving dominance from it. More than ever, a more economic approach is central in this process. Instead of creating new tools, we should use the ones we already have.

I.   INTRODUCTION & SUMMARY

Google, Amazon, Facebook, Apple, and Microsoft are veritable ecosystems. The five of them together are capable of capturing virtually all digital attention. They are also able to provide solutions for almost all existing needs. These include work, communication, entertainment, shopping, and IT solutions. In many cases, their market shares reflect this ubiquity.

However, if regulators in Europe rely only on local market shares in abstractly defined markets as a first screen for enforcement, such global platforms could escape antitrust scrutiny. In this sense, Europe faces a unique challenge. National jurisdictions are fragmented, but digital markets often are not. This issue is especially apparent in e-Commerce, which may feature a peculiar disconnect between local market shares and firms' behavior.

---

1 Aleksandra Boutin and Xavier Boutin are Founding Partners at Positive Competition, Mate Fodor is an Economist at Positive Competition. We would like to thank our Partner Wojciech Dorabialski on his valuable comments on this article. Disclaimer: Positive Competition works for clients who are likely to be affected by the current European Commission proposals. This article reflects the views of Positive Competition experts only and do not represent the views of our past of current clients.

For instance, Amazon has a 47 percent share of business-to-customer ("B2C") e-Commerce turnover in the U.S.[2] This includes many vertical and closed marketplaces, which are often imperfect substitutes for merchants and buyers, such that B2C e-Commerce is likely to be too wide to constitute a relevant market. Amazon's share of B2C e-Commerce in France is much smaller, at about 20 percent, such that it is possible that its market share on a properly defined relevant market could fall below 40 percent.[3] However, Amazon's behavior seems unaffected by its local competition. For instance, on the consumers' side, Amazon bundles Prime Video with Prime Delivery in France, just like in the U.S.[4] On the merchants' side, membership in the "Fulfilment by Amazon" program is also a necessary condition to access the strategic "Buy-now" box.[5] Given the similarity between Amazon's conduct in France and its behavior in the U.S., it would appear that Amazon is able to implement its business strategy independently of local rivals.

On the other hand, there could be local e-Commerce incumbents in Europe or in the rest of the world who still represent a significant share of national B2C e-Commerce. Based on a purely formalistic assessment of market shares, competition authorities may consider them dominant. In reality, these platforms act under a very powerful competitive pressure from global players like Amazon. Their market power is in fact very limited.

Market shares are only a tool for assessing dominance and should not be mistaken for the concept of dominance itself. Local platforms in Europe, even local historical incumbents, are not capable of replicating Amazon's seamlessly integrated offer that has the potential of enveloping users – merchants and customers – on both sides of the platform. Amazon controls its entire value chain by selling its own merchandise and offering fulfilment solutions to independent sellers.[6] Amazon also provides ancillary services to customers, such as media streaming, cloud computing and AI-based solutions.[7] There is no local platform in Europe with such an integrated offer.

Against this background, higher shares of local platforms *vis-à-vis* the global players in some national jurisdictions do not necessarily mean that they have more market power. If these local platforms were to expand their presence cross-border,

---

2   For U.S. market shares, see https://fortune.com/2017/04/10/amazon-retail/.

3   e-Commerce Europe: European e-Commerce Report, July 2019 edition, p. 38.

4   See https://www.amazon.fr/b?ie=UTF8&node=12092250031.

5   See https://services.amazon.fr/services/expedie-par-amazon/outils-et-avantages.html/ref=az_fr_fba_ft?ld=AZFRFBAFooter.

6   See, for instance, https://www.statista.com/statistics/259782/third-party-seller-share-of-amazon-platform/.

7   For Amazon Web Services, see https://awsinsider.net/articles/2018/11/01/azure-fastest-but-aws-biggest.aspx. For its streaming offer, see https://www.forbes.com/sites/danafeldman/2019/08/21/netflix-is-expected-to-lose-us-share-as-rivals-gain/#3e52567566d6. For its AI-powered personal assistant devices, see https://voicebot.ai/2020/04/28/amazon-smart-speaker-market-share-falls-to-53-in-2019-with-google-the-biggest-beneficiary-rising-to-31-sonos-also-moves-up/.

Amazon would not change its conduct. On the other hand, Amazon's inexorable worldwide expansion fundamentally shapes the market conditions where Amazon is directly or indirectly present.

In this context, the economic assessment of the platforms' conduct matters more for establishing dominance than market shares. In other words, dominance is a logical consequence of the theory of harm, which directly follows from the ECJ's *Hoffmann-la-Roche* judgment.[8] A selective group of global platforms, like Amazon, clearly behaves independently of rivals and shapes the conditions under which competition develops. They are therefore dominant and cannot escape antitrust scrutiny.

In fact, the Bundeskartellamt has recently applied a somewhat conduct-based approach when establishing Amazon's dominance.[9] It concluded that Amazon's intermediation power is more telling of its dominant position than its market shares.[10] The Bundeskartellamt has also considered that absent Amazon's services for independent merchants, German e-Commerce would be much smaller than it currently is.[11]

At the same time, worried about a possible enforcement gap in the digital economy, competition authorities are seeking to designate gatekeeping platforms *"that exercise control over whole ecosystems that are essentially impossible to contest by existing or new market operators, irrespective of how efficient or innovative they may be."*[12] The European Commission's current regulatory initiatives foresee a possible *ex ante* regulation of such gatekeepers even though, defined in this way, gatekeeping platforms are clearly dominant. Article 102 TFEU applies to them and there does not seem to be an enforcement gap.

The Commission also considers introducing a New Competition Tool with an aim to allow intervening with structural remedies before markets tip.[13] Nevertheless, if a firm's conduct is able to make the market tip, it is also necessarily dominant

---

8   See judgment of February 13, 1979 in Case 85/76, paras 38- 39, available at http://curia.europa.eu/juris/showPdf.jsf;jsessionid=279E22A82EE6B7C17A1EC2FAB2F9BA56?text=&docid=89251&pageIndex=0&doclang=EN&mode=lst&dir=&occ=first&part=1&cid=2619721. See, also, Communication from the Commission - Guidance on the Commission's enforcement priorities in applying Article 82 of the EC Treaty to abusive exclusionary conduct by dominant undertakings ("the Guidance Paper"), para. 10, available at https://eur-lex.europa.eu/legal-content/EN/TXT/PDF/?uri=CELEX:52009XC0224(01)&from=EN.

9   Bundeskartellamt: Case Summary, B2 88-18, July 17, 2019, pp. 9-10.

10   *Ibidem.*

11   *Ibidem.*

12   European Commission, Inception Impact Assessment, Digital Services Act package: *Ex ante* regulatory instrument for large online platforms with significant network effects acting as gate-keepers in the European Union's internal market, June 2020.

13   *Ibidem* and European Commission, Inception Impact Assessment, Single Market – new complementary tool to strengthen competition enforcement, June 2020.

in the *Hoffmann la Roche* sense and, in our opinion, the current tools seem to apply to them as well.

At the same time, *ex ante* regulation, pre-emptive remedies and blacklists of practices have clear limitations. They ignore in particular the fact that a given conduct may be harmful or pro-competitive depending on a specific market context in which it takes place. For example, self-preferencing, which is seemingly one of the main candidates for such a black list, may be pro-competitive and actually benefit consumers. A platform with a limited first-party ("1P") offering may for instance need to promote its own sales to attract more traffic to the platform as a whole and to fill inventory gaps.

Therefore, without a theory of harm assessed in a particular market context, authorities cannot properly calibrate the scope and depth of remedies. Blanket prohibitions of market conduct may also alter the way markets develop and prevent important innovations that benefit consumers. They may also prevent smaller local platforms from being able to pursue strategies necessary for them to compete with the much more powerful global leaders.

We acknowledge that it is not the Commission's intention to regulate such local platforms. In practice, however, National Competition Agencies in EU Member States would likely use such black lists beyond the regulation in their effort to intervene in their local markets. If a practice is so intrinsically harmful that it has to be outlawed for a number of global gatekeepers in Europe, one can expect that competition agencies will, perhaps wrongly, consider such practices as object or hardcore restrictions when applied by a local incumbent as well.

In the article, we discuss the appropriate conduct-based approach to dominance in European e-Commerce, and then briefly comment on the Commission's recent proposals regarding the New Competition Tool and the *ex ante* regulation of platforms.

II.   ECONOMIC APPROACH TO DOMINANCE IN e-COMMERCE

The new business model of online marketplaces introduces a novel combination of market characteristics. These include the reliance on network effects, cross-border markets, economies of scale, access to big data and the use of algorithms. In this context, more than ever, authorities need an economic approach to delineate a relatively homogenous relevant market and the boundaries of firms. In fact, establishing a dominant position in e-Commerce should start with a thorough examination of firm's behavior.

As Glasner & Sullivan perfectly summarize it, markets are analytical tools and there is no "natural" market based on intuition, convention or observation:[14]

> *"Market definition is [...] a tool for identifying conduct and situations that have the potential to cause anticompetitive injury, and that therefore require scrutiny."*

In the context of European law, market definition is only a preliminary tool in assessing dominance. However, dominance itself is also only a tool. Its function is to assess the relevance of a theory of harm. The relevant market is therefore the one that allows assessing whether a firm has the type of market power that makes a theory of harm possible. In other words, a firm is dominant when it has the ability, or is capable, to implement a particular theory of harm. Consequently, market definition does not exist in the absence of a theory of harm.

Against this background, abstract and formalistic approaches to determining relevant markets are losing their relevance. Price-based tests to determine substitute services are insufficient in digital markets. This is especially true, for instance, in social media or web search. The zero-price transactions in these markets render the standard hypothetical monopolist test or the "small but significant non-transitory increase in prices," which was already an abstraction of limited practical interest, entirely inoperative.[15] The application of these tests in e-Commerce is also problematic: usually, at least one of the two market sides enjoys numerous services for free.

The European Commission has observed this development, which is one of the issues it considers in its April 2020 roadmap for its formal revision of the Market Definition Notice, originally published in 1997.[16] The reform's objective, among others, is to adapt the definitions of relevant product and geographical markets to the digital world.

The Commission has given a 12-week feedback period for stakeholders, academics and practitioners to respond to the roadmap. Out of the 43 responses to the call, 32 put major emphasis on the observation that the evolution of digital platforms indeed requires an update of the market definition assessment.

---

14   See Glasner, David & Sullivan, Sean, *The Logic of Market Definition*, June 2019. U. Iowa Legal Studies Research Paper No. 2018-14, page 5, available at https://ssrn.com/abstract=3223025 or http://dx.doi.org/10.2139/ssrn.3223025.

15   For further discussion on the topic, see Filistrucchi, Lapo, Damien Geradin, Eric Van Damme & Pauline Affeldt. "Market definition in two-sided markets: Theory and practice," Journal of Competition Law & Economics 10, no. 2 (2014): 293-339.

16   European Commission: Ref. Ares (2020)1911361 - 03/04/2020, pp. 1-2.

We believe that a revised Market Definition Notice may be a useful tool in understanding the reach and scope of anticompetitive harm. The Commission proposal has fostered a very high-quality debate. However, as former Commissioner Monti very correctly pointed out two decades ago, while market definition is a "*cornerstone of competition policy*," it is "*not the entire building.*"[17] Market definition can be useful to determine dominance. Nevertheless, as we discuss below, true dominance is often better assessed focusing on firm's behavior.

Similarly, in the *Hoffman La Roche* judgment, the European Court of Justice provided the following definition of dominance:[18]

> "[…] the dominant position thus referred to relates to a position of economic strength enjoyed by an undertaking which enables it to prevent effective competition being maintained on the relevant market by affording it the power to **behave to an appreciable extent independently of its competitors**, its customers and ultimately of the consumers. Such a position does not preclude some competition, which it does where there is a monopoly or a quasi-monopoly, but enables the undertaking which profits by it, **if not to determine, at least to have an appreciable influence on the conditions under which that competition will develop**, and in any case to act largely in disregard of it so long as such conduct does not operate to its detriment." (emphasis added)

While market shares are often an initial screening for dominance, they are only useful to the extent that the relevant market is correctly defined. The European Commission considers that a firm with a market share below 40 percent is very unlikely to be dominant.[19] However, dominance is generally better assessed by evaluating whether an undertaking is able to act independently of competitors and customers, and has an influence on the way competition develops. If, based on a rigorous assessment, one concludes that a firm indeed has the ability to shape the conditions under

---

17 See Professor Mario Monti Speech: "Policy Market Definition As A Cornerstone of EU Competition Policy," October 5, 2001, available at https://ec.europa.eu/commission/press-corner/detail/en/SPEECH_01_439.

18 See judgment of February 13, 1979 in Case 85/76, paras 38-39, available at http://curia.europa.eu/juris/showPdf.jsf;jsessionid=279E22A82EE6B7C17A1EC2FAB2F-9BA56?text=&docid=89251&pageIndex=0&doclang=EN&mode=lst&dir=&occ=-first&part=1&cid=2619721. See, also, *Communication from the Commission - Guidance on the Commission's enforcement priorities in applying Article 82 of the EC Treaty to abusive exclusionary conduct by dominant undertakings* ("the Guidance Paper"), para. 10, available at https://eur-lex.europa.eu/legal-content/EN/TXT/PDF/?uri=CELEX:52009XC0224(01)&from=EN.

19 Antitrust procedures in abuse of dominance (Article 102 TFEU cases), European Commission; https://ec.europa.eu/competition/antitrust/procedures_102_en.html.

which competition develops, one has to conclude that this firm is dominant. If such a firm has less than 40 percent market share, it means that the market has been poorly defined and/or that market shares miss something fundamental about market interactions and dynamics.

It is useful to revisit the example of local and historical incumbents mentioned earlier. They interact rarely with foreign users. Therefore, national e-Commerce markets may seem to be the relevant market for them in the context of certain hypothetical theories of harm.[20] The challenge is to determine whether their shares of national e-Commerce make them dominant. The key determinant here is an appropriate consideration of the real competitive constraint exerted on them by global platforms, such as Amazon, which may be disconnected from their current local market shares.

It is important to consider that European e-Commerce markets cannot be analyzed in a static way. European countries exhibit different maturity levels in customers' use of online shopping and in the prevalence of cross-border ordering.[21] The prevalence of online shopping is much higher in the U.S. than in any European country,[22] so European e-Commerce is likely to expand further.

Therefore, there is plenty of room for growth for e-Commerce in Europe. This would normally attract entry. In this context, leading international platforms benefit from a series of competitive advantages that enable them to expand, enter new markets and to fend off entry. These large marketplaces have a global reach and user bases that are large enough to attract merchants and buyers. Users, in turn, have valid expectations of finding many partners to trade with on these global platforms. This is what fuels further growth of these global platforms and reinforces their market power.

Moreover, important cross-country purchases also allow global marketplaces to gain market shares quickly. National marketplaces cannot keep up with these aggressive geographic expansion strategies by global platforms. They are almost entirely reliant on national merchants and national buyers, which limits their ability to expand internationally.

The asymmetry between what global and national players have the ability and incentives to do limits the market power of local platforms. In particular, global plat-

---

20   With the caveat that eMag, for instance, has expanded into neighboring countries, such as Hungary. However, it intermediates transactions exclusively between Hungarian merchants and buyers there.

21   e-Commerce Europe: European e-Commerce Report, July 2019 edition, p. 29.

22   Center for Retail Research: Online: UK, Europe & N. America, 2019. Available online at https://www.retailresearch.org/online-retail.html. We state the claim with the caveat that eMag has a limited offering in Poland, Bulgaria, and Hungary. See emag.pl, emag.bg and emag.hu.

forms are able to act independently of local competition, while the local ones cannot. For instance, Amazon is able to offer Fulfilment by Amazon to sellers and Amazon Prime to buyers globally, independently of local competition.

Moreover, while Amazon can envelop users on both sides of the market with its seamlessly integrated data-driven offer, other marketplaces cannot reach the scope of Amazon's activities, no matter how innovative or efficient they are. Amazon has constructed an ecosystem that allows it to be present at every level of the value chain. Half of what Amazon sells is its own merchandise.[23] For all the other sellers on the platform, it offers order fulfilment, storage, and a returns service.[24]

In addition, Amazon also has ancillary offerings that stem from its core competences. It has successfully leveraged its computing capabilities to launch Amazon Web Services, a leader in cloud computing solutions.[25] Amazon also operates one of the largest media streaming services in the world, Amazon Prime Video. In the U.S., for instance, this service has 52.9 percent market penetration.[26] Amazon also has a strong position in AI-powered personal devices that it managed to promote through its e-Commerce platform. Its share of this segment is currently 53 percent in the U.S.[27] None of the European platforms has this type of integrated offer.

With this uniquely broad offering, Amazon clearly has the ability to distort the competitive landscape. In fact, Amazon has recently come under antitrust scrutiny for various abuses in front of a number of jurisdictions. These abuses include the bundling of various services,[28] foreclosing rivals within the platform,[29] hampering data portability,[30] or imposing unfair trading conditions.[31]

---

23   See https://www.statista.com/statistics/259782/third-party-seller-share-of-amazon-platform/.

24   See for instance https://services.amazon.co.uk/services/fulfilment-by-amazon/features-benefits.html.

25   See https://awsinsider.net/articles/2018/11/01/azure-fastest-but-aws-biggest.aspx.

26   See https://www.forbes.com/sites/danafeldman/2019/08/21/netflix-is-expected-to-lose-us-share-as-rivals-gain/#3e52567566d6.

27   See https://voicebot.ai/2020/04/28/amazon-smart-speaker-market-share-falls-to-53-in-2019-with-google-the-biggest-beneficiary-rising-to-31-sonos-also-moves-up/.

28   See for instance Autorità Garante de la Concurrenza e del Mercato: Amazon: avviata istruttoria su possibile abuso di posizione dominante in marketplace e-Commerce e servizi di logistica, April 16, 2019.

29   European Commission press release: Antitrust: Commission opens investigation into possible anti-competitive conduct of Amazon, July 17, 2019.

30   Bundeskartellamt: Bundeskartellamt obtains far-reaching improvements in the terms of business for sellers on Amazon's online marketplaces, July 17, 2019.

31   *Ibidem.*

Most recently, the European Commission initiated a formal investigation of Amazon's conduct on Amazon's uses of data on independent merchants to improve the positioning of its own products and on the Amazon's behavior related to the "Buy-now."[32]

Prior to these developments, in late 2018, the German Bunderskartellamt has raised objections against a number of Amazon's practices. Amazon refused third-party ("3P") merchants the possibility to import external ratings about their products. Nevertheless, Amazon allowed this practice for its own first-party ("1P") suppliers.[33] Furthermore, Amazon has imposed additional difficulties on 3P merchants by terminating agreements at its own discretion, without prior notice or warning. As a reaction to the Bundeskartellamt's proceedings, Amazon has agreed to remedy its behavior in 2019.[34]

The Bundeskartellamt estimated Amazon's market share to be around 40 percent. Nevertheless, it argued that other economic criteria are more telling about Amazon's dominance than market shares. "[Amazon's] significance as a "gatekeeper" for customer access is high due to its large customer base, some of which use the Amazon marketplace either primarily or exclusively for their purchases."[35] Furthermore, the Bundeskartellamt argued that Amazon's market shares must be assessed in light of the fact that "smaller sellers only entered e-Commerce because of Amazon's broad range of services for merchants."[36]

The Bundeskartellamt's approach to assessing dominance and the consideration of the dynamic nature of this market show that there may actually be no enforcement gap in e-Commerce. If the only hurdle in enforcing against abusive behaviors of global e-Commerce platforms is finding them dominant in abstractly defined local market, then either the relevant market is wrong, or we should not base our assessment on market shares.

Observing firms' behavior is a straightforward way to separate market power from market shares. Accordingly, competition authorities have begun assigning significant market power to platforms that hold a "strategic market status,"[37] play the

---

32   European Commission press release: Antitrust: Commission opens investigation into possible anti-competitive conduct of Amazon, July 17, 2019.

33   Blog of the European Competition and Regulatory Law Review: Amazon cases on the move: Bundeskartellamt closes proceedings while European Commission opens formal investigation, July 19, 2019.

34   Bundeskartellamt: Bundeskartellamt obtains far-reaching improvements in the terms of business for sellers on Amazon's online marketplaces, July 17, 2019.

35   Bundeskartellamt: Case Summary, B2 88-18, July 17, 2019, pp. 9-10.

36   *Ibidem.*

37   Furman, Jason, Diane Coyle, Amelia Fletcher, Derek McAules & Philip Marsden. "Unlocking digital competition: Report of the digital competition expert panel." Report prepared for the Government of the United Kingdom, March (2019).

role of gatekeepers,[38] have bottleneck[39] or intermediation power.[40] These notions all revolve around platform's attributes that enable them to build unassailable monopoly positions. The Commission defines gatekeepers as "*large online platforms that exercise control over whole ecosystems that are essentially impossible to contest by existing or new market operators, irrespective of how efficient or innovative they may be.*"[41]

According to these definitions, if a gatekeeper is not shaping the way competition develops in a market, it is difficult to see who does. Therefore, gatekeepers directly meet the *Hoffman La Roche* standard and they are dominant.

This raises questions about the actual need for the Commission's most recent reform proposals to regulate such gatekeepers *ex ante* or through the New Competition Tools.[42]

III.   THE RISKS AND BENEFITS OF THE NEW COMPETITION TOOL AND *EX ANTE* REGULATION

There are two likely motivations for the Commission's proposals of *ex ante* regulation of gatekeeper platforms and the New Competition Tool. The Commission may worry that it would be unable to establish dominance for some of the largest global platforms in the different European jurisdictions. The Commission could also worry that it may be unable to remedy the harm that certain anticompetitive practices cause in digital markets in a timely manner.

As regards to the first possible concern, it is indeed likely that some key global platforms may not reach the market share thresholds considered as indicative of domi-

---

38   Nicolai van Gorp (e-Conomics) & Paul de Bijl (Radicand-Economics), Digital Gatekeepers: Assessing exclusionary conduct, October 2019, https://www.government.nl/documents/reports/2019/10/07/digital-gatekeepers; ARCEP, strategic note "Plateformes numériques structurantes – Eléments de réflexions relatifs à leur caractérisation," December 2019.

39   Committee for the Study of Digital Platforms (2019), Draft Report: Committee for the Study of Digital Platforms – Market Structure and Antitrust Subcommittee, George J. Stigler Center for the Study of the Economy and the State, The University of Chicago Booth School of Business, page 9 https://www.judiciary.senate.gov/imo/media/doc/market-structure-report%20-15-may-2019.pdf.

40   Draft Bill for the Reform of the German Competition Act, January 2020, Unofficial English Translation, Section 18, para. 3b, available at https://www.d-kart.de/wp-content/uploads/2020/02/GWB10-Engl-Translation-2020-02-21.pdf. The original Draft Bill can be found at https://www.bmwi.de/Redaktion/DE/Downloads/G/gwb-digitalisierungsgesetz-referentenentwurf.pdf?__blob=publicationFile&v=10.

41   European Commission, Inception Impact Assessment, Digital Services Act package: *Ex ante* regulatory instrument for large online platforms with significant network effects acting as gate-keepers in the European Union's internal market, June 2020.

42   *Ibidem* and European Commission, Inception Impact Assessment, Single Market – new complementary tool to strengthen competition enforcement, June 2020.

nance in some product markets defined abstractly and/or in some European jurisdictions. Nevertheless, a more economic and less formalistic approach to determining dominance may help alleviate this concern.

Moreover, we notice that there has been very little pushback from Courts in cases involving the application of Article 102. Consequently, there does not seem to be any reason for the Commission to exert excessive self-restraint in enforcement against platforms when it comes to dominance. If the targets of the Commission's initiatives are indeed the largest global digital platforms, they are all capable of inflicting harm to competition. Therefore, they are dominant in the sense of *Hoffmann la Roche*.

The same reasoning also questions the adequacy of the Commission's New Competition Tool. If one reaches the conclusion, after rigorous assessment, that a market can tip because of a particular firm's actions, the firm certainly has an appreciable influence on the conditions under which that competition will develop. Therefore, it is also dominant and Article 102 TFEU applies to it.

If the Commission is concerned about the adequacy of remedies, it should focus on the economic assessment of the firms' conduct in the market context in which they take place. It seems difficult to support strong remedies on the basis of a formalistic assessment of business practices, the effects of which in the particular market context have, by definition, not been analyzed. However, once the mechanisms of foreclosure have been clarified, and the precise contribution of the dominant undertaking's actions has been assessed in the given market context, it then seems much more reasonable to argue that some remedies, including interoperability, data portability, and multi-homing, are the only way to restore competition and roll-back the harm caused by the dominant undertaking.[43]

The Commission's proposals raise a number of questions from a practical standpoint as well. For instance, the criteria for designating gatekeepers are unclear. As we discuss above, platforms that control ecosystems are necessarily dominant in the sense of *Hoffmann la Roche*. However, if the Commission selects gatekeepers based on formal criteria, such as market shares or user numbers, it may erroneously capture large national platforms that are not dominant.

If this is the case, the scope of blacklisted practices becomes important. To understand a competitive impact of a given practice, we must first understand its market context and the theory of harm. Blacklisting a conduct out of context may put smaller marketplaces at a double disadvantage. One the one hand, they are unable to match the offering of true, global gatekeepers. On the other hand, they will no longer

---

43   See a longer discussion on the topic in Positive Competition's feedback to the European Commission's Roadmap on the New Competition Tool available at https://ec.europa.eu/info/law/better-regulation/have-your-say/initiatives/12416-New-competition-tool/F535710.

be free to pursue certain conduct that would otherwise be vital for their development. *Ex ante* blacklisting of certain conduct or the pre-emptive imposition of structural remedies could discourage firms from pro-competitive behaviors and thereby harm consumers.

A possible candidate for the Commission's list of prohibited practices seems to be self-preferencing. A global platform like Amazon may indeed cause harm with this type of conduct, as 50 percent of its gross merchandising value comes from its own sales.[44] However, it is unlikely that national players with very limited first-party offerings are able to cause the same damage. Their rationale for pursuing self-preferencing may be filling inventory gaps and attracting more traffic to the platform. If local platforms are discouraged from this type of conduct, which has legitimate business reasons, they may lose market shares that larger players will most likely absorb.

While establishing dominance does not seem to be a significant hurdle, the main issue, in general, and even more in the digital markets, seems to be to determine when a particular behavior in a given market context leads to consumer harm. This depends on all the market circumstances. Such an analysis cannot be shortcut by an abstract categorization of practices. This is the reason why the form-based enforcement of Article 102 has achieved so little in the last decades. In addition, such categorization is impractical: none of the behaviors of large digital platforms can be described in a non-ambiguous sentence.

Therefore, it is unclear to us how a categorization of practices in an *ex ante* regulation can be a substitute for a thorough analysis of how the current behavior of these digital platforms affects and shapes competition to the detriment of consumers.

On balance therefore, new antitrust tools are not necessary in e-Commerce and they carry important risks. The rigorous use of existing tools, however, is vital. The most important condition for adequate enforcement is building a cogent and substantiated theory of harm. Dominance and remedies logically follow from the theory of harm. More than ever, effective enforcement of Article 102 can only come from a more economic approach. In this context, we argue that true Article 102 Guidelines are more useful for effective enforcement than a necessarily narrow list of blacklisted practices for a handful of global players.

There is clearly a need for timely enforcement in e-Commerce. However, the Commission should not spend its scarce resources on introducing new tools and regulations that have dubious benefits and carry clear risks. We have learned from the CMA's experience that the leading market investigations can take up to 18 months and possibly more, depending on the firms' degree of cooperation. The Commission has recently made significant efforts to accelerate the speed of antitrust proceedings. More improvement in this direction are very welcome.

---

44   See https://www.statista.com/statistics/259782/third-party-seller-share-of-amazon-platform/.

Aleksandra Boutin, Xabier Boutin & Máté Fodor

The Australian Chapter: Competition Policy Developments and Challenges for the Digital Economy

By Andrew Low & Luke Woodward [1]

Abstract

The Australian Competition and Consumer Commission's 18-month inquiry into digital platforms was initiated to assess the impact on media and news of those platforms, principally Google and Facebook. The inquiry and the ACCC's draft and final reports promoted broad discourse on competition and digital regulatory policy; yet many of the reform recommendations are anchored in a potentially narrow "problem – solution" framework that may work against a more coherent digital policy reform agenda. This paper provides an overview of the Australian digital policy landscape and competition policy developments and the risks of relying on an inquiry emanating from a narrow set of "problems" (largely media plurality issues) to derive broad digital economy wide policy reform "solutions." We conclude that the ACCC's inquiry, while a valuable contribution, should not be seen as the road-map for digital economy reform; rather it should serve as a stepping stone for a broad and balanced policy reform process to ensure that the Australian economy can flexibly adapt, so as to accommodate and enable future digital innovation.

I. INTRODUCTION

Competition policy in Australia concerning issues associated with the digital economy has been largely driven by a substantive 18-month inquiry conducted by the Australian Competition and Consumer Commission ("ACCC") into digital platforms and their impact on media and news between December 2017 and July 2019, with a particular focus on Google and Facebook ("DPI"). As part of the DPI, the ACCC received extensive submissions and compelled the production of information and documents. The Government directed the DPI pursuant to the Competition and

---

1 Andrew Low is a Senior Lawyer in Gilbert + Tobin's Competition + Regulation group. Luke Woodward is the head of Gilbert + Tobin's Competition + Regulation group. The views expressed in this paper are the authors' views alone.

Consumer Act 2010 (Cth) ("CCA"). It did so in exchange for support for its media law reforms in 2017.[2]

The ACCC released its final report on July 26, 2019 ("Final Report") with 23 specific recommendations and on December 12, 2019, the Government released its response to each of the 23 recommendations.

The practical outcome of the DPI for digital competition policy in Australia may have been initially overstated in some respects as being "ground breaking." It is unlikely to result in substantial potential change to the current competition framework and has missed an opportunity to analyze in a more balanced and in-depth manner the broader implications of disruptive innovation on our economy beyond Google and Facebook. The Government's response to the DPI has also resulted in policy initiatives that would appear to benefit few companies outside of traditional news, media and advertising. For consumers, arguably the response has not sought to promote broader social benefits beyond a traditional consumer protection and welfare lens.

This outcome is not unexpected. In essence, digital economy competition policy in Australia is being driven by a "*problem – solution*" framework. That is, a framework of reform that arises from the specific issues the ACCC was asked to inquire into; namely the interaction between digital platform providers – such as Google and Facebook – and traditional news and media markets. While the ACCC was not limited to identifying only competition issues or proposing competition solutions – it was at its inception limited in scope with a focus on identifying specific problems arising from the particular political focus on the impact of digital platforms on media and advertising markets. The Government's approach has been to build a roadmap for digital reform by responding to the recommendations that arise from the DPI's narrow lens. This approach risks lacking the consistency and coherence to support clear guidance for businesses operating in the digital economy as to the expectations around realignment of commercial norms of conduct.

The awareness and learnings from the DPI and the following discourse arising in Australia has been overall beneficial. They have supported a general social and political consensus that clearly beneficial innovations in platform technology are not necessarily without the risk of harms and consequences, and that some of those consequences potentially extend to the fundamental operation of a liberal democracy.

For our part, we would recommend caution about driving regulatory policy for the disruptive technologies across the whole economy through the institutional lens of a competition regulator in a problem-solution directed media-based inquiry. The substan-

---

2 Jennifer Duke, "ACCC to probe Facebook, Google over media disruption," *Sydney Morning Herald* (online, December 4, 2017) https://www.smh.com.au/business/companies/facebook-google-set-for-accc-probe-over-media-disruption-20171204-gzxxow.html.

tive inquiry into these issues should not end with the Government's response to the DPI-specific issues, otherwise there will be a real potential for one-sided reform and policy without a clear and coherent agenda. The Final Report should be treated as a strong invitation for a broad policy discussion outside the problem-solution lens, and to determine how the Australian economy may fundamentally be re-structured around future digital innovation. A more complete assessment of technology, a clear expression of the values and objectives sought collectively, and consequent assessment of the laws and policies is more likely to support better outcomes in the long term for the digital economy.

II. THE AUSTRALIAN DIGITAL POLICY LANDSCAPE

On December 4, 2017 the then Treasurer (now Prime Minister), Scott Morrison, issued the Terms of Reference ("ToR") to the ACCC, directing it to conduct an 18-month long public inquiry into the impact of digital platform services on the state of competition in media and advertising services markets, pursuant to Section 95H(1) of the CCA. ACCC Chairman, Rod Sims, accurately called this a "world first" inquiry of its kind into digital platforms that goes to "the heart of their business models."[3] The Government agreed to undertake the DPI as a condition of the then Senator, Nick Xenophon's support for significant legislative changes to media control and ownership laws under the *Broadcasting and Services Act 1992*. This also occurred in the wake of growing international interest from competition regulators in digital platforms and their conduct in the use of data and advertising practices.

In this context, the ToR directed the ACCC to look at "the impact of digital search engines, social media platforms and other digital content aggregation platforms (platform services) on the state of competition in media and advertising services markets, in particular in relation to the supply of news and journalistic content, and the implications of this for media content creators, advertisers and consumers." Matters to be considered included, but were not limited to, the extent to which platform services are exercising market power in commercial dealings with the creators of journalistic content and advertisers; the impact of platform services on the level of choice and quality of news and journalistic content to consumers; the impact of platform services on media and advertising markets; the impact of longer-term trends, including innovation and technological change, on competition in media and advertising markets; and the impact of information asymmetry between platform services, advertisers and consumers and the effect on competition in media and advertising markets.

The ToR were arguably sufficiently broad to cover a wholesale review of Google's and Facebook's business practices, and to identify issues that concern adver-

---

3   John McDuling, "As Rod Sims takes on the tech giants, the world will be waiting," *Sydney Morning Herald* (online, December 7, 2017) https://www.smh.com.au/business/companies/the-whole-world-is-watching-20171206-p4yxgc.html.

tisers, content creators, and consumers. However, it is apparent and unsurprising that the ToR primarily focused on digital platforms' impact on competition in media and advertising markets.

On July 26, 2019, the ACCC's Final Report was released, outlining 23 specific recommendations for reform. There were 5 competition-specific recommendations:

The ACCC recommended reform of the merger provisions of the CCA.[4] Under Section 50 of the CCA, a merger or acquisition is prohibited if it would result in a substantial lessening of competition. The Final Report recommended that this assessment should expressly include consideration of two additional factors: "the likelihood that an acquisition would result in the removal from the market of a potential competitor"; and "the amount and nature of data which the acquirer would likely have access to as a result of the transaction."[5] These recommendations are targeted at addressing the risk of acquisition of "nascent competitors" by dominant platforms and the importance of data in merger. The ACCC recognized that this reform is intended to signal the significance of the factors and their relevance. However, this recommendation is not a substantial change to Australian merger laws under the CCA, as Section 50 likely already provides for the consideration of these factors in the overall assessment. For example, the removal of "potential" competition is at the heart of the *Vodafone v. ACCC* (2019)[6] case, and the significance of data was considered in the ACCC's 2018 review of the Transurban consortium WestConnex bid.[7]

The ACCC recommended to reach agreement with large digital platforms about an acquisition notification protocol (and absent commitment to such a protocol, the ACCC will make further recommendations to the Government).[8] The proto-

---

4 Section 50 of the CCA prohibits acquisitions of shares or assets that would, or would likely, result in a substantial lessening of competition.

5 ACCC, Digital Platforms Inquiry "Final Report" (July 26, 2019), Recommendation 1.

6 Federal Court of Australia matter number NSD818/2019. On May 24, 2019, Vodafone sought a declaration from the Federal Court challenging the ACCC's opposition to Vodafone's proposed merger with TPG. In the ACCC's opposition, it considered TPG to be "the best prospect Australia has for a new mobile network operator to enter the market": https://www.accc.gov.au/media-release/accc-opposes-tpg-vodafone-merger. This is despite TPG publicly stating it had no plans to build a mobile network absent the merger. On February 13, 2020 Middleton J ruled in favor of TPG and Vodafone finding that the proposed merger would not substantially lessen competition in any market in contravention of section 50 of the CCA: *Vodafone Hutchinson Australia Pty Ltd v Australian Competition and Consumer Commission* [2020] FCA 117.

7 In 2018, the ACCC decided to not oppose the Transurban consortium from bidding to acquire a majority in the WestConnex toll road on condition of Court enforceable undertakings to make toll road data available to competitors: https://www.accc.gov.au/media-release/accc-will-not-oppose-transurban-consortium-westconnex-bid-following-undertaking.

8 ACCC, Digital Platforms Inquiry "Final Report" (July 26, 2019), Recommendation 2.

col would specify the types of acquisitions requiring notification, including minimum transaction value and minimum advance notification period prior to completion. Such protocols would not require any legislative reform, rather it concerns how large digital platforms will engage with the informal merger process in Australia. And so, in effect creating notification thresholds for a subset of companies. However, in practice, the ACCC is not prohibited from unilaterally commencing informal reviews of mergers irrespective of whether they have been notified, nor is it prohibited from requesting notification of all mergers in certain industries. Accordingly, this recommendation is also unlikely to be a substantial change to the current practices in Australia – even if it does signal an intention to place more onus on large digital platforms to engage with the ACCC's informal review process.

The ACCC recommended that Google should provide Android users with the same options being rolled out to existing Android users in Europe, that is, the ability to choose the default search engine and internet browser on devices. Absent the introduction of this within 6 months, the ACCC will recommend the Government to consider compelling Google to offer this choice.

The ACCC recommended the creation of a new branch within the ACCC to focus on proactive investigation, monitoring and enforcement of issues in markets in which digital platforms operate as well as an inquiry into the supply of ad tech services and advertising agencies.

Another significant focus of the Final Report was consumer protection with respect to privacy and data. A significant recommendation of the Final Report include the call for an introduction of a broader and general "prohibition on certain unfair trading practices,"[9] which is in additional to the current prohibition against unconscionable conduct and misleading and deceptive conduct under the Australian Consumer Law ("ACL").[10] This recommendation to extend the current ACL prohibitions in order to address the broader unfairness observed in the digital economy.[11] A breach

---

9   Recommendation 21 of the Final Report proposes an amendment to the CCA to include a prohibition on "certain unfair trading practices." The precise scope is not defined.

10   Under Sections 20-22 of the ACL, unconscionable conduct is prohibited. Unconscionable conduct is generally understood in Australian jurisprudence to mean "conduct that is so far outside societal norms of acceptable commercial behaviour as to warrant condemnation as conduct that is offensive to conscience": *ASIC v. Kobelt* (2019) 368 ALR 1 at [92].

11   Final Report, p 498. The broader provision would be intended to capture conduct by businesses including failing to put in place appropriate security measures to protect consumer data; and businesses collecting data without express informed consent or providing insufficient time or information for consumers to properly consider contract terms.

of the ACL attracts significant penalties.[12] It also recommended a modernization of Australia's privacy laws to better protect users of digital platforms.

Other recommendations were targeted to media specific issues, namely digital platforms and their relationship with news and media businesses, the disruption of Australian media and the risk of underinvestment in journalism, and the impact of digital platforms on the consumption of news and journalism. The ACCC will also do further internal work to consider the applicability of data portability for digital platforms.

The Treasurer, the Hon. Josh Frydenberg MP's initial response to the Final Report was that the Government broadly supported the ACCC's recommendations, stating that "these companies are among the most powerful and valuable in the world. They need to be held to account and their activities need to be more transparent."[13] The Government also accepted that: "the ACCC's overriding conclusion that there is a need for reform – to better protect consumers, improve transparency, recognize power imbalances and ensure that substantial market power is not used to lessen competition in media and advertising services markets" as well as the need to develop a harmonized media regulatory framework.[14]

On December 12, 2019, the Government released what it called "a roadmap for a program of work and series of reforms to promote competition and enhance consumer protection and privacy in a digital age."[15] This "roadmap" is in essence a response to each of the 23 specific recommendations arising from the ACCC's Final Report. It is far from a comprehensive statement of policy for the digital age.

The Government has shown its support, or support in principle, for most of the 23 recommendations that the ACCC made in the Final Report, with only a small handful of recommendations not supported, but even those are not rejected outright. There is an immediate commitment to a new Digital Platforms Branch of the ACCC to monitor digital platforms and undertake specific inquiries, including an ad tech services and advertising inquiry. A voluntary code of conduct will also be negotiated between digital platforms and news media organizations. The Government has indicated overall support for and will further consult on some of the specific and

---

12   The ACL imposes a maximum penalty of $10 million per contravention or three times the benefit obtained from the breach or 10 percent of the company's annual turnover per contravention.

13   Josh Frydenberg, "Opinion: Digital giants are powerful companies and must be more accountable," *Sydney Morning Herald* (July 26, 2019, online) https://www.smh.com.au/politics/federal/digital-giants-are-powerful-companies-and-must-be-more-accountable-20190726-p52b73.html.

14   *Ibid.*

15   Treasury, "Government Response and Implementation Roadmap for the Digital Platforms Inquiry," December 12, 2019, https://treasury.gov.au/publication/p2019-41708.

substantial recommendations to reform several aspects of privacy and consumer protection laws.

The Government's response to the competition-specific recommendations were less inspiring. The merger recommendations would be consulted on in 2020, browser and search engine choice would be examined in 2021, and the ACCC would be given a new branch dedicated to monitoring digital platforms and a direction to inquire into ad tech and advertising agencies. There would also be negotiations commencing for a voluntary code of conduct between digital platforms and news media organizations. The ACCC's digital advertising services inquiry was directed on February 10, 2020, with an interim report due December 31, 2020 and a final report due August 31, 2021.[16] The focus is specifically on digital advertising technology services and digital advertising agency services (and related markets). On the same day, the ACCC was also directed to conduct a five-year inquiry into digital platform services – which includes search engine services, social media services, online private messaging services, digital content aggregation platform services, media referral services and electronic marketplace services.[17] The direction also covers digital advertising services supplied by digital platform service providers and the data practices of digital platforms and data brokers. An interim report is due September 30, 2020 and then further interim reports every six months until a final report by March 31, 2025. In September 2020, the ACCC released an issues paper for the second interim report focusing on app market places; which is due to the Treasurer by March 31, 2021.

In addition to the legislative policy response, in August 2019, the ACCC has flagged it is in the advanced stages of five separate enforcement actions against Google and Facebook under current competition, consumer, and privacy laws against digital platforms in 2020.[18] Two cases have been commenced by the ACCC – an action against Google for misleading and deceptive conduct in relation to its location tracking and data retention practices;[19] and an on July 27, 2020 the ACCC commenced action against Google alleging misleading and deceptive conduct around Google's expanded use of consumers personal data.[20] Public sources have also confirmed the

---

16   Details of the ACCC's digital advertising services inquiry can be found at https://www.accc.gov.au/focus-areas/inquiries-ongoing/digital-advertising-services-inquiry.

17   Details of the ACCC's digital platform services inquiry can be found here https://www.accc.gov.au/focus-areas/inquiries-ongoing/digital-advertising-services-inquiry.

18   Michael Fowler, "ACCC gears up for court battle with Google and Facebook," *Sydney Morning Herald* (August 13, 2019, online) https://www.smh.com.au/business/consumer-affairs/accc-gears-up-for-court-battle-with-google-and-facebook-20190813-p52gp5.html.

19   Stephen Letts, "Google sued by the ACCC over alleged misuse of personal data," *Australian Broadcasting Corporations* (October 29, 2019, online) https://www.abc.net.au/news/2019-10-29/google-faces-accc-federal-court-misleading-use-of-data/11649356.

20   ACCC Media Release, "ACCC alleged Google misled consumers about expanded use of personal data," July 27, 2020.

ACCC is in advanced stages of an investigation into Google relating to its ban of Unlockd apps from Google's platform.[21]

There have separately been other consultations in 2019 concerning the use of artificial intelligence ("AI") in Australia. On April 5, 2019 the Minister for Industry, Science and Technology released a discussion paper to encourage the conversation on "how we should design, develop, deploy and operate AI in Australia" and sought feedback on the draft AI ethics principles presented in the discussion paper.[22] A set of high-level principles were published by this discussion paper. The principles, however, are voluntary only and do not mandate or set any compulsory framework for utilizing AI.[23] Other parallel projects on AI include the Australian Human Rights Commission's project on Human Rights and Technology[24] and the Ethical AI for Defence workshop conducted in Canberra on July 30 to August 1, 2019.[25] Currently, these projects do not currently have a clear legislative agenda attached to them.

Australia is also in the process of rolling out the Consumer Data Right – a sector-by-sector data portability standard in Australia, currently implemented for the banking sector but envisaged to apply to other industries including energy and telecommunications.[26]

On April 20, 2020, the Australian Government asked the ACCC to develop a mandatory code of conduct to address bargaining power imbalances between Australian news media businesses and digital platforms, specifically Google and Facebook. On July 31, 2020 the ACCC released its draft code for public consultation ("Draft Media Bargaining Code") – responses of which were due by August 28, 2020. This draft code is the subject of significant debate in Australia. A focus of the debate is whether the code, which is directed to correcting a bargaining power imbalance be-

---

21 Paul Smith, "ACCC to sue Google over Unlockd," *Financial Review* (November 5, 2019, online) https://www.afr.com/technology/accc-to-sue-google-over-unlockd-20191030-p535u9.

22 Department of Industry, Innovation and Science, "Artificial Intelligence: Australia's Ethics Framework" (online) https://consult.industry.gov.au/strategic-policy/artificial-intelligence-ethics-framework/.

23 Department of Industry, Innovation and Science, "AI Ethics Principles" (online) https://www.industry.gov.au/data-and-publications/building-australias-artificial-intelligence-capability/ai-ethics-framework/ai-ethics-principles.

24 Australian Human Rights Commission, Human Rights & Technology (online) https://tech.humanrights.gov.au/.

25 Department of Defence, "Ethical AI for Defence: World experts gather in Canberra," (August 1, 2019) https://news.defence.gov.au/media/media-releases/ethical-ai-defence-world-experts-gather-canberra?utm_source=miragenews&utm_medium=miragenews&utm_campaign=news.

26 Treasury, "Consumer Data Right," https://treasury.gov.au/consumer-data-right.

tween digital platforms and news media companies, appropriately recognizes the significant and broader value exchange between the relationship.

While acknowledging there are a number of processes in place that concern potential digital reform, at the time of writing, Australia is largely in a position whereby the legislative policy agenda will be focused on the specific recommendations arising from a media focused DPI, and also the competition regulator's continued enforcement focus under the current laws on digital platforms and the digital economy. The ACCC appears ready to test the limits of the current competition and consumer laws and jurisprudence through its enforcement activities, including how far consumer laws can be extended to deal with privacy issues, the thresholds for unconscionable conduct prohibitions, and the issues regarding removal of potential competitors in M&A transactions.

III. LIMITATIONS OF THE PROBLEM-SOLUTION APPROACH TO DIGITAL REFORM

The problems identified in the ACCC's DPI are important issues to consider and debate, and indeed its recommendations in the Final Report have received careful consideration and are the subject of extensive submissions to Government and responses. However, as recognized in the Final Report, the ACCC was focused on three groups of users – advertisers, media content creators, and consumers – and particular regard was had to news and journalism.[27] Accordingly, the issues it identified, and hence its recommendations, were made in this context.

Focusing on specific problems will lead to identifiable solutions, but this approach does not necessarily lead to good policy design.

In a problem-solution framework, the identification of the problem for investigation is of significant importance as it drives the recommendations for solutions. Here, the problem identified was in the context of media reforms and impacts of Google and Facebook on traditional media and advertising markets. It did not arise from a broader direction or intention to rethink, review and design competition policy for the digital economy in a balanced way. Accordingly, there is a significant gap in the current policy discourse in Australia to address a number of issues beyond Google, Facebook, media and advertising.

While Google and Facebook are an important part of the "digital economy," they do not represent the full spectrum of disruptive innovation that is impacting our economy and society. This spectrum, to name a few examples, includes advances in AI, facial recognition technology, self-driving cars, private payment systems, internet of things, ride-share platforms, and pioneers of such technologies are just a starting list of technologies that will likely lead to significant disruption to existing markets.

---

27 ACCC, Digital Platforms Inquiry "Final Report" (July 26, 2019), pp 4-5.

Each of these innovations are also likely to raise their own challenges as to how we would regulate for competition, consumer rights and privacy – while at the same time challenging us to revisit our ability to direct our economy towards growth through innovation. Nonetheless, the DPI and its recommendations were not directed towards these technologies and their potential effects.

Another issue arising from the problem-solution framework of "inquiries" is that by their very nature, inquiries tend to proceed on the assumption that there is a problem that requires a solution. There will tend to be absent from the equation a broader consideration of trade-offs and why certain practices are reasonable. If one goes looking for a problem, one will usually find one – this is more so for highly experienced enforcement institutions.

To illustrate, consider the recommendations in the Final Report regarding the regulation of "data" and its use by digital platforms. The Final Report engages with data in terms of considering data portability, data enabled market power (and therefore regulation of where that market power might unilaterally or in an M&A context substantially lessen competition), existing individual consumer and privacy rights (that is, ensuring consumers have transparency and can provide fully informed consent to the use of data). The recommendations are also overall linked with the penumbra of preserving "fairness" in the online environment.[28] These solutions may arguably be justifiable when the assessment occurs in the context of considering Google and Facebook's use of data and the need to promote consumer protection, competition and privacy.

However, it is not to be assumed that such an assessment of data is complete. Data is crucial to a range of technologies and innovations outside Google and Facebook, and it also impacts policies other than consumer rights and privacy. As an illustration, in April 2018, it was reported that in Delhi facial recognition technology helped trace 3,000 missing children in 4 days.[29] It was reported in August 2016 in the UK that a new AI software can accurately predict breast cancer risk by intelligently reviewing millions of records in a short amount of time.[30] Similarly, AI such as IBM Watson for Health and Google's DeepMind Health are also working to analyze large amounts of patient data.

How did data enable these technologies and public benefits to emerge? Would the DPI's recommendations inhibit these use cases (for example, how do you get in-

---

28 ACCC, Digital Platforms Inquiry "Final Report" (July 26, 2019), Recommendation 21.

29 "Delhi: Facial recognition system helps trace 3,000 missing children in 4 days," *The Rimes of India* (April 22, 2018, online) https://timesofindia.indiatimes.com/city/delhi/delhi-facial-recognition-system-helps-trace-3000-missing-children-in-4-days/articleshow/63870129.cms.

30 Sarah Griffiths, "This AI software can tell if you're at risk from cancer before symptoms appear," *Wires* (August 26, 2016, online) https://www.wired.co.uk/article/cancer-risk-ai-mammograms.

formed consent from missing persons or from millions of deceased medical records), or adequately protect individuals from misuse in these cases? It's not clear.

Similarly, the debate over the Draft Media Bargaining Code is reflective of issues that may arise when creating policy that is specifically directed to addressing one issue (e.g. the impact of digital platform competition in terms of advertising erosion on public interest journalism) while potentially not taking into account broader aspects of commercial relationships and consumer and commercial value creation.[31]

Further, not only were the DPI's solutions specific to competition law, it was also limited to seeking to resolve disruption in traditional media and advertising markets. However, the disruptive impacts of digital innovation are much broader. In the same way Google and Facebook are not fully representative of the digital economy, media companies are not fully representative of the industries disrupted (both positively and negatively) by digital innovation. The DPI's sector specific approach to responding to technological disruption is not new. In Australia, the New South Wales and Victorian response is reflective of this. For example, the Victorian, Australia taxi industry has sought repeatedly to blame Uber for its demise, and to seek protection and compensation.[32] This approach may tend to have an incomplete view of the full breadth of trade-offs, including benefits, society is being asked to accept in exchange for technological advancement in the digital economy such as increased competitive alternatives for consumers to taxis and improved services.

It is conceivable that regulation can be crafted to achieve a prohibition of harmful conduct without necessarily trading off other values, but to assess this requires an impartial and broader review of the line between harm and reasonably necessary harm which is not focused only on the impact of one industry on another. For example, to what extent are we prepared to forego consumer rights or privacy rights in order to promote technology innovation, to facilitate lower barriers to entry into previously high-barrier industries, creation of new business markets and increased competition, better distribution and communication of peer-to-peer ideas, creating new employment and new industries, and requiring existing industries to innovate their business model and Government to innovate its regulatory approach? The pres-

---

31 See for example Google, *Mandatory News Media Bargaining Code – Response to ACCC's concepts paper*, (June 5, 2020) https://www.accc.gov.au/system/files/Google.pdf.

32 "Uber came to our 'shores, illegally, like pirates' class action lead plaintiff says," *Australian Broadcasting Corporation* (May 3, 2019, online) https://www.abc.net.au/news/2019-05-03/uber-to-face-class-action-against-taxi-and-private-drivers/11073640; Paul Smith, "Uber faces Victorian taxi industry class action over illegal operation," Financial Review (November 21, 2017, online) https://www.afr.com/technology/uber-faces-victorian-taxi-industry-class-action-over-illegal-operation-20171121-gzpuo6. New South Wales in December 2015 established a $250 million "industry adjustment package" to compensate taxi drivers; and in 2016, Victoria announced an overhaul of the taxi industry offering to buy back licenses.

ent discourse in Australia is not enabling of a nuanced value trade-off assessment between disruption that is acceptable and disruption that is not.

IV.   THE CHALLENGE FOR DIGITAL REFORM IN AUSTRALIA

The challenge in Australia is the tendency to place too much emphasis on the recommendations in a competition regulator-led inquiry to drive digital policy reform, such that they are seen as a complete and unified roadmap to regulating the digital economy. In part, this may be a tribute to the degree of trust and confidence in the ACCC as a regulator.

For example, the Australian Government's policy agenda has been focused on reviewing privacy, consumer, and competition laws, consistent with the Final Report's recommendations. This multi-disciplinary approach has merits when looking to solve specific problems, recognizing that competition law is not the panacea for all things digital. However, it is limited in terms of regulating the digital economy as a whole and we should not assume reform within these three laws will be sufficient or acceptable to drive better outcomes. The objectives of each of these laws are underpinned by specific principles and standards that may be too narrow or inflexible to cope with broader themes. For example, the consumer welfare standard has been a clear and objective framework supported by economic rigor for competition laws in Australia, however, there is criticism and at times frustration that this standard is not sufficient to achieve a total welfare for consumers.

By comparison, the European Union's ("EU") Digital Single Market strategy includes a much broader range of steps to make the EU's single market fit for the digital age including – shaping the digital single market to open up opportunities for people and businesses and enhance Europe's position as a world leader in the digital economy; boosting the European digital industry (for example, ensuring SMEs and non-tech industries benefit from digital innovations); building a European data economy; improving connectivity and access; investing in network technologies; creating a digital society; supporting media and digital culture; and strengthening trust and security.[33]

Furthermore, outside the context of solving the specific problems identified in the DPI, more often than not privacy, competition and consumer protection laws do not have consistent objectives. Privacy protection and open data can be in conflict,

---

33   See European Commission, Digital Single Market Strategy at https://ec.europa.eu/digital-single-market/. Steps forward by the European Commission include 5G digital transformation, AI, media rules for the 21st century, blockchain, cloud computing, connectivity, copyright, culture, cybersecurity, digital identity, digital skills for all Europeans, eHealth, open data, platforms, safer internet, the Internet of Things, and more https://ec.europa.eu/digital-single-market/en/news/digital-single-market-brochures.

where innovation and increased competition can come at the cost of privacy rights. Consumer laws at times can put the protection of consumers over the efficient operation of markets and consumer warranties is an example of this. In essence, our existing legislative regimes make a trade-off between these rights based on a valued judgment arrived at through a democratic process. While each of these laws can be expanded to have a multi-tiered approach to address specific problems identified in the DPI, they also tend to create ambiguity which is not conducive to creating clear commercial norms in a digital environment.

Over reliance on a policy review undertaken by a competition regulator will inevitably reflect that regulator's institutional character or specific capability in the policy solutions it proposes. For competition regulators, that capability is couched primarily in enforcement capability (that is, to investigate and seek penalties for conduct that is considered a contravention). In this way, the ACCC is an effective competition and consumer enforcement agency, and indeed the outcomes of the Final Report perhaps reflect its enforcement mindset. Around the same time the ACCC was undertaking its DPI, a similar review was being undertaken for the UK Government by a specially constituted panel of experts lead by the former Chief Economist to President Obama, Professor Jason Furman. While the "Furman Report" has much in common with the ACCC's Final Report, there are subtle but important differences in approach to the challenges of the digital economy. The Furman Report emphasized an *ex ante* co-regulatory approach to identifying permitted and non-permitted behavior:[34]

The approach should combine participation and consultation with the scope for regulatory enforcement…It should only intervene where doing so is effective and proportionate to achieve competitive aims. Where this is the case, the Panel wants to introduce a system where industry has greater clarity and confidence over what constitutes acceptable practice and the rules that apply. The best way of achieving these outcomes is through introduction of a digital platform code of conduct…developed collaboratively…with platforms and other affected parties. This will provide the opportunity to clarify what constitutes unfair or unacceptable conduct.

The ACCC's proposed approach tended to set broad requirements of unfairness and to back those with expanded enforcement powers:[35]

While the existing tools and goals of competition law and consumer law frameworks remain applicable to digital markets, the opacity and complexity of these markets make it difficult to detect issues and can limit the effectiveness of the broad principles. As a result, the ACCC considers that existing investigative tools under competition and consumer law should be supplemented with additional proactive investigation, monitoring and enforcement powers to achieve better outcomes for Australian businesses and consumers.

---

34 Digital Competition Expert Panel, "Unlocking Competition: Report of the Digital Competition Expert Panel," (March 2019), p. 58.

35 ACCC, Digital Platforms Inquiry "Final Report" (July 26, 2019), p. 13.

Understandably, from an enforcement perspective, the ACCC considers codes of conduct that are not "binding, legally enforceable and with meaningful penalties for breaching them" to be of "little use."[36] However, the use of significant penalties for the purposes of specific or general deterrence is only meaningful if there is clarity in the conduct seeking to be deterred. Absent such clarity in a dynamic digital economy, is over emphasizing the importance of penalties in order to drive business norms likely to lead to effective outcomes?

The system of assessing the areas of grey between conduct that may be seen as unacceptable or unfair in one sense, but at the same time beneficial, is not a feature unique to the digital economy. The current unconscionability test in Australia is reflective of this balance and the *ASIC v. Kobelt* case[37] in Australia is an example of grey areas which do not lend themselves well to "big stick" prosecutions.

The High Court of Australia's decision in *ASIC v. Kobelt* has been said to support of lowering the standards required for unconscionable conduct in Australia.[38] However, this case is also reflective of the challenges in assessing fairness in areas of grey in commercial conduct – the case concerned the provision of a system of credit called "book-up" by a general store in Mintabie, South Australia, where almost all of the customers were Anangu persons residing in two remote communities. The book-up system was that the general store required its customers' debit card and PIN to be linked to a store account to withdraw moneys owed. ASIC's case was that this system was unconscionable because the customers were vulnerable, and the respondent took advantage of this vulnerability to "tie" customers to its store. However, the High Court dismissed ASIC's case based on evidence that, *inter alia*, most customers considered the system as beneficial to them in many ways.[39]

V.   NEXT STEPS FOR DIGITAL POLICY IN AUSTRALIA

Competition policy and competition regulators are a logical starting place to examine the impacts of digital markets that are subject to "tipping," and to grapple with issues of market structure, including concentration of economic power and winner-takes-all markets. Competition policy has always been concerned with un-

---

36   Rod Sims, Chair ACCC, *The Digital Platforms Inquiry: Melbourne Press Club speech*, August 13, 2019 at https://www.accc.gov.au/speech/the-digital-platforms-inquiry-melbourne-press-club-speech.

37   *Australian Securities and Investment Commission v. Kobelt* (2019) 368 ALR 1 ("ASIC v. Kobelt").

38   Rod Sims, Chair ACCC, *The Digital Platforms Inquiry: Melbourne Press Club speech*, August 13, 2019 at https://www.accc.gov.au/speech/the-digital-platforms-inquiry-melbourne-press-club-speech.

39   *Australian Securities and Investment Commission v. Kobelt* (2019) 368 ALR 1.

derstanding how markets work and the primary means of regulating those markets. Consumer law policy has also been the primary tool for protecting consumers in trade or commerce, and it seems logical to apply that lens to the digital economy.

However, a competition regulator's inquiry – or even one focused on consumers – is not necessarily the most desirable end point for policy design. The imagination of competition policy is limited and not completely able to conceptualize the guard rails for the digital economy in a balanced and holistic way. Reflective of this is the current challenge to the consumer welfare standard of competition laws and advocates of a total welfare standard. Furthermore, as noted above, competition law remedies primarily involve enforcement penalties which are not well calibrated for establishing broader commercial norms in the digital environment.

In Australia, at this time, it appears there are at least two potential paths for us to take. First, our Government continues to work in accordance with the narrow path carved out by focusing on the DPI's recommendations, with an assumption that they are sufficiently broad of a roadmap for Australia's digital reform (despite the DPI only addressing specific problems). Second, and alternatively, the Government can take the broader meta theme of the DPI which is that potentially unchecked digital innovation may have unintentional and unappreciated social and economic consequences (both good and bad), and consequently conduct a broader policy design and balanced review that has a clear intention to enhance the position of all Australians in the digital economy.

Assessing Self-Preferencing by Digital Platform Operators: A Missed Opportunity by the ACCC?

By Simon Bishop & George Siolis[1]

Abstract

Do vertically integrated digital platform operators have a "special responsibility" when it comes to dealing with stand-alone businesses that rely on their platform to reach customers and which operate in another part of the supply chain (referred to as a "related market")? Can digital platform operators favor their own businesses in those related markets or do competition laws require digital platform operators to treat all firms that rely on the platform to reach customers in the same way? What are the potential risks to the competitive process if digital platform operators (in common with vertically-integrated firms in other sectors of the economy) favor their own related business (referred to as "self-preferencing")? This chapter focusses on the approach that the Australian Competition and Consumer Commission ("ACCC") took in its recent Digital Platforms Inquiry ("DPI") to answer these questions. It argues that although the ACCC was one of the first competition authorities to look at the issue of self-preferencing in the course of conducting a market inquiry, it missed an opportunity in the DPI to develop a coherent analytical framework that other agencies might have drawn on when looking at this issue.

I.   INTRODUCTION

Do vertically integrated digital platform operators have a "special responsibility" when it comes to dealing with stand-alone businesses that rely on their platform to reach customers and which operate in another part of the supply chain (referred

---

1   Simon Bishop is a Founding and now the Managing Partner of RBB Economics based in London. George Siolis is a Partner in the Melbourne office of RBB Economics. While RBB Economics has advised Google on a number of EC investigations, neither the authors nor the firm have advised Google on the ACCC's DPI inquiry.

to as a "related market")?[2] Can digital platform operators favor their own businesses in those related markets or do competition laws require digital platform operators to treat all firms that rely on the platform to reach customers in the same way? What are the potential risks to the competitive process if digital platform operators (in common with vertically-integrated firms in other sectors of the economy) favor their own related business (referred to as "self-preferencing")?

Potential concerns around vertical integration of digital platforms arise in two different, although closely related, ways.

First, businesses that provide stand-alone services, such as comparison shopping services or stand-alone mapping applications that use those platforms, often claim that they face a commercial disadvantage because digital platforms that provide their own comparison shopping services or mapping applications will favor their own related businesses at the expense of those stand-alone businesses.

Second, similar issues also arise because publishers and advertisers that rely on digital platforms to attract attention from consumers and revenues from advertising in the digital advertising market also often claim that they are disadvantaged because digital platforms can favor or preference their own ad inventory or their own advertising services, and potentially undermine competition at other stages of the digital advertising market, particularly in the open display advertising channel.

These issues are not new; rather they relate to the established debates concerning the likely pro-competitive and anti-competitive effects of vertical integration. Recently they have been considered in a number of studies undertaken in Australia, the UK, Continental Europe, and the U.S.[3] A key element of those studies has been to assess the role that vertical integration plays in promoting or harming competition in those related markets.

The pro-competitive features of vertical integration are well-understood. It can give rise to lower transaction costs or greater efficiencies including the elimination of

---

2 This paper draws a distinction between "core markets" which is the primary market in which a digital platforms operates (for example, generalized search in the case of Google and the supply of social media services in the case of Facebook,) and "related markets" which are markets that rely on digital platforms to reach customers (such as mapping or comparator shopping services).

3 The studies are: In Australia by the ACCC (2019) *Digital Platforms Inquiry – Final Report,* (referred to here as the "ACCC's DPI report"), in the UK, Furman et al. (2019) *Unlocking Digital Competition: Report of the Digital Competition Expert Panel* (referred to here as "the Furman report") and the CMA (2019) *Online platforms and digital advertising: Market study interim report, (referred to here as the "CMA's Market study interim report"),* in the European Union, Cremer et al. (2019) *Competition Policy for the Digital Era – Final Report,* (referred to here as the "Cremer report"), and in the U.S. Stigler Center (2019) *Stigler Committee on Digital Platforms – Final Report* (referred to here as the "Stigler Centre report").

double marginalization which provides a cost (and a commercial) advantage to the vertically integrated firm relative to non-vertically integrated firms that it competes with in other parts of the value chain. Those advantages may often make it harder for stand-alone businesses to compete with vertically integrated businesses, but these commercial advantages do not typically raise any competition concerns that warrant intervention.

But vertical integration can raise competition concerns in some circumstances. A firm with a substantial degree of market power in one part of the value chain might seek to leverage that power into other parts of the value chain which are currently competitive and prevent a potential competitor from one day growing to challenge its position in the part of the value chain in which it has market power.

This paper focusses on the approach that the Australian Competition and Consumer Commission ("ACCC") took in its recent Digital Platforms Inquiry ("DPI") to assess these concerns. It argues that although the ACCC was one of the first competition authorities to look at the issue of self-preferencing, it missed an opportunity in the DPI to develop a coherent analytical framework that other agencies might have drawn on when looking at this issue.

Given that self-preferencing is observed in many markets including highly competitive ones, the starting point for any competitive assessment cannot be that self-preferencing, even when practiced by firms with market power is inevitably or even mostly anti-competitive. This is true regardless of whether the concern is with third parties claiming that the digital platform is favoring its own businesses in related markets or whether the concern is that digital platforms can favor or preference their own ad inventory or their own advertising services in the digital advertising market.

The starting point must be a clear and coherent theory of harm which sets out how vertical integration will harm the competitive process in the relevant market and lead to consumer harm. But instead of setting out such a theory, undertaking a detailed fact-based, data-intensive investigation into the conduct, and recognizing that the vertical integration that gives rise to anti-competitive self-preferencing can also deliver significant benefits to consumers, businesses and advertisers, the ACCC simply asserted that firms with substantial market power, including the leading digital platforms, were likely to have the ability and incentive to leverage their market power into related markets.[4]

The deficiencies with the ACCC's approach discussed in this paper are:

It treated self-preferencing as presumptively anti-competitive, in large part because of the past history of digital platform operators of expanding into related markets.

---

4 ACCC, *DPI*, p.133.

It failed to assign sufficient weight to pro-competitive features of vertical integration, both in general as well as with regard to the alleged conduct.

It failed to set out a clear theory of harm and to test that theory of harm with observed market evidence.

The cumulative effect of these is that the ACCC is recommending increased intervention and scrutiny in this area based on very little evidence of any harm to the competitive process. As a result, the ACCC has produced a study that cannot be relied upon to deliver good outcomes for economic efficiency and consumers.

The remainder of this paper is set out as follows:

- Section 2 sets out the nature of the concerns around self-preferencing in general and then summarizes how the ACCC assessed those concerns in the DPI.

- Section 3 presents an overview of the economics vertical integration;

- Section 4 sets out some of the deficiencies with the ACCC's assessment of self-preferencing in the DPI; and

- Section 5 concludes.

II. THE ACCC'S CONCERNS IN THE DIGITAL PLATFORMS INQUIRY

This section sets out the nature of the concerns around self-preferencing in general and then summarizes how the ACCC assessed the competitive effects of these concerns.

A. Nature of Concerns Around Self-preferencing

Most of the concerns around self-preferencing identified in the recent inquiries into digital platforms have centered on the following two types of conduct:

The ability of digital platforms with market power <u>to favor their own related businesses</u> (such as comparison shopping, online travel agency services, or mapping applications); and

<u>Vertical integration in the digital advertising market affecting intermediaries,</u> particularly in the "ad tech" stack of the value chain.

This section provides a brief explanation of each of these categories of conduct.

Potential for Digital Platforms to Favor Their Related Businesses

One of the concerns with self-preferencing comes from the ability of vertically integrated digital platforms to favor their own businesses in related markets. For example, a digital platform operator who also supplies online mapping services, might be accused of diverting customers to its own mapping service instead of the mapping service provided by a third party in a way that ultimately harms consumers.

An example that the ACCC provided in the DPI was the decision by the European Commission – which has been appealed by Google – that Google had abused its dominance in the search services market by giving an illegal advantage to another Google product, its comparison shopping service, Google Shopping, in a related market.

In that case, the concern arises because the European Commission found that Google operates in two markets – the market for general search services and the market for compression shopping services. The issue in that case was that Google gave more favorable positioning in its general search results page to its own comparison shopping service compared to competing comparison shopping services.[5]

Google presented the following four arguments to contest the European Commission's allegation that it positions and displays its comparison shopping service during that investigation.

First, the positioning and display of the Product Universal[6] did not favor Google's comparison shopping service. It argued that the European Commission mischaracterized Product Universal as a separate stand-alone service that returned product offers from merchants' website and offered search tools that ate specific to product search. Google claimed that the function of Product Universal was to provide relevant responses to user queries in the same way as results on Google's general search results page. Google also claimed that the majority of links within the Product Universal led to websites of merchants and not to Google's standalone Product Search page.[7]

Second, the positioning and display of the shopping Unit did not favor Google's comparison shopping service. It argued that the Shopping Unit was not a

---

5 See paras 341 and 344 of EC *Shopping* decision.

6 Product Universal is Google's comparison shopping service, which is one of Google's specialized search services. The Product Universal comprised specialized search results from Google Product Search, accompanied by one or several images and additional information such as the price of the relevant items.

7 See para 403 of EC *Shopping* decision.

comparison shopping service but rather a better way of presenting Google's auction-based online search adverting platform (AdWords) results.[8]

Third, competing comparison shopping services can benefit from the same positioning and displays as the Shopping Unit since they are eligible to participate in Google Shopping;[9] and

Fourth, it held Product Universals to the same relevance standards that it applies to all of the generic search results on its general search results pages and it held the Shopping Unit to the same relevance standards that it applies to all of its product ads.[10]

Google has subsequently challenged the European Commission's finding that effect of the conduct was to decrease traffic from Google's general search results pages to competing comparison shopping services and increase traffic from Google's general search results pages to Google's own comparison shopping service.

In the Final Report of the DPI, the ACCC elected not to focus on the risk of digital platforms favoring their own businesses in related markets. Instead, the majority of the discussion focused on the scope for anti-competitive self-preferencing in the digital advertising market where Google operated businesses at multiple level. This is discussed in more detail in the next section.

Self-preferencing Concerns in the Digital Advertising Market

This section provides an overview of the digital advertising market and then discusses the open display advertising channel in more detail.

The Open Display Advertising Channel

Services provided by digital platform operators are usually often funded by digital advertising. The supply of general search services in the case of Google and the supply of social media services in the case of Facebook, are monetized predominantly through the selling of advertising. There is, of course, nothing novel about this aspect of the open display digital market. TV broadcasters have long been competing to provide programs that attract the most viewers in order to sell access to those viewers to advertisers during breaks in the program.

The value of the advertisements, in terms of their value to the advertisers – and consequently on the willingness of advertisers to pay platforms to place their advertisements – is higher the more attention they attract from consumer.

---

8 See para 404 of EC *Shopping* decision.

9 See para 405 of EC *Shopping* decision.

10 See para 406 of EC *Shopping* decision.

Websites, such as online newspapers and other content providers, also usually rely on digital advertising for funding. These websites are referred to as "publishers" and the space that publishers sell for advertising is referred to as "inventory."

Digital advertising is usually in the form of display advertising which enables advertisers to place ads on websites or apps in a variety of formats including banner-style advertisements, sponsored content, and video advertising. The display advertising sector is segmented into the following two channels:

The "owned and operated" channel, which is made up of large social media platforms such as Facebook, Instagram and YouTube, which sell their own advertising inventory directly to advertisers or media agencies using proprietary interfaces which uses technology to allocate inventory using real time auctions or direct deals. The digital platforms gather data from consumers which enables the advertisements to target specific audiences (which increases the willingness of advertisers to pay for the advertisements).

The open display advertising channel, which allows a wide range of publishers (online newspapers and other content providers) to sell their inventory to a wide range of advertisers through a complex chain of third-party intermediaries that run auctions on behalf of publishers and advertisers.

As concerns around self-preferencing typically arise in the open display advertising market, we consider that in more detail below.

Competition Concerns in the Open Display Advertising Channel

Publishers can use the open display advertising channel to generate revenue from advertisers in order to monetize the services that they provide. While some of their inventory is sold through direct deals between the publisher and specific advertisers (or media agencies on behalf of the advertisers), most – around 80 percent according to the CMA in its 2019 Interim Report – are sold "programmatically."[11]

Programmatic technologies enable the decisions by advertisers on whether to advertise on a publisher's website to be made in real time using information about the webpage in which the advertisement will appear as well as information about the consumer in front of whom the ad will be placed (using data collected on that consumer).

In addition to publishers and advertisers and/or their media agencies, programmatic technologies also rely on the following agents:

Demand-side platforms ("DSPs") are platforms used by advertisers and media agencies to purchase inventory from many different suppliers of inventory. DSPs rely on data about consumers in order to provide ad targeting services.

---

11 CMA *Market study interim report*, para 5.166.

Supply-side platforms ("SSPs") are platforms used by publishers to automate the sale of inventory and to help maximize the price at which inventory is sold. SSPs allow real time auctions by connecting to multiple DSPs and collecting bids from the DSPs.

Publisher ad servers manage the publisher's inventory and, based on the bids received from the different SSPs and the direct deals struck between publishers and advertisers, determine which ad to serve.

Data management platforms ("DMPs") store, manage and analyze data to allow agents across the value to chain to create audiences that can be used for targeting purposes.

The relationship between all of these agents is shown in Figure 1.

Figure 1: Overview of open display advertisement market supply chain

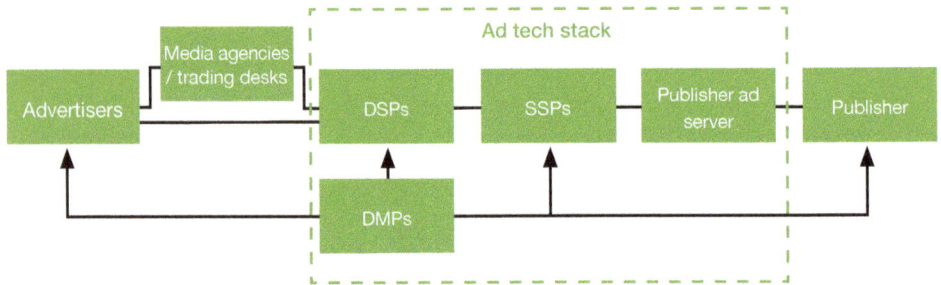

Source: CMA Interim Report, p. 194.

The agents in the light blue dotted box in Figure 1 are referred to as the "ad tech" stack and the operation of the process – which takes place in real time – can be summarized as follows:

First, a consumer opens a web page or an app (if they are using a mobile device). In either case, the next steps are the same.

Second, a number of SSPs receive ad requests for the available inventory on the website visited or the app opened by the consumer. The SSPs then send their bid requests to a number of DSPs.

Third, the DSPs respond to the bid requests depending on the objectives of their advertising campaign and any information they have on the consumer.

Fourth, SSPs rank the bids received by the DSPs and send the winning bid to the publisher. The bids can be submitted in a number of different ways including using a "header bidding" solution, or more commonly send the bids simultaneously to the publisher ad server using Google Ad Manager

Finally, the publisher ad server compares the bids receive and considers any direct deals struck between publishers and advertisers and determines which advertisement to place on the website or the app in front of the consumer.

Given the vertical integration that has recently taken place in the digital advertising market and which means that a firm such as Google is now present across the entire intermediation chain, there is the potential for digital platforms to self-preference across that value chain.[12] For example, Google's DSP, which offers advertisers the ability to place ads across a range of platforms, including its own, could preference the purchasing of ads on locations which generate the most revenue for its own business (for example, ads on YouTube or other Google websites), as opposed to acting in the best interests of the advertiser.

B. Summary of the ACCC's Assessment in the DPI

The ACCC began its assessment of self-preferencing by noting that Google and Facebook operated across a number of markets in addition to the supply of search services (in the case of Google) and the supply of social media services (in the case of Facebook). Google, for example, was active in providing mobile operating systems, web browsers, mapping applications, email, advertising, file storage, Internet of Things ("IoT") products, and payment systems. Similarly, in addition to supplying social media services, Facebook provides a platform for publishers to sell advertising through Audience Network and offers a platform for classifieds through Marketplace and Facebook Jobs.

In the DPI, the ACCC acknowledged that Google and Facebook provided advertisers with significant benefits, through an ability to specifically target relevant audiences and by providing advertisers with an additional channel to reach consumer (often at a lower cost than traditional forms of advertising), but then moved quickly to considering the potential for anti-competitive conduct by digital platforms and the risk of market failure.

Concerns about leveraging market power covered both of the categories set out in section 3 of this paper, that is, the ability to favor related businesses and the effect of vertical integration in the open display advertising channel (and in particularly in the ad tech stack of that channel). These are discussed below.

Digital Platforms Favoring Their Own Businesses in Related Markets

In terms of concerns with digital platforms favoring their related businesses, it did this mainly by listing *past* evidence of leveraging behavior undertaken by digital

---

12 Google's significant acquisitions in ad tech included DoubleClick in 2007, AdMob in 2009, Invite Media in 2010, AdMeld in 2011, and Adometry in 2014. Other examples include FreeWheel's acquisition of StickyAds in 2016, Adobe's acquisition of TubeMogul in 2017 and Amazon's launch of a header bidder solution in 2018.

platforms, arguing that the examples highlight that leveraging behavior may have previously occurred in a number of ways. The examples presented included:

The European Commission's finding in 2018 (currently under appeal) that Google had abused its dominant position by pre-installing search and browser apps on Android, which created a status quo bias towards consumers using Google Search and strengthened the dominance of Google Search.

The European Commission's finding in 2017 (also currently under appeal) that Google abused its market dominance in the search services market by giving an illegal advantage to another Google product, its comparison shopping service, Google Shopping.

Documents originating from a lawsuit filed (but not yet heard) by Six4Three against Facebook and released by the House of Commons in the UK which show how Facebook has leveraged its market power from the social media market into the online display advertising market.

Litigation that commenced (but not yet completed) in April 2019 by Dialogue Consulting Pty Ltd against Facebook alleging that it breached the misuse of market power provisions in Australia by restricting Dialogue's access to Facebook and Instagram.

Proceedings that were commenced, but discontinued, by Unlockd against Google for terminating its access to the Google Play Store and AdMob advertising service because Google viewed Unlockd as a threat to its own mobile advertising revenue.

Digital Platforms Favoring Their Own Ad Inventory or Their Own Advertising Services in the Digital Advertising Market

The ACCC then turned to examples where digital platforms might engage in leveraging behavior in the *future* and discussed concerns relating to the risk that digital platforms can favor or preference their own ad inventory or their own advertising services, and potentially undermine competition at other stages of the digital advertising market. The specific concerns were:[13]

Favoring or preferencing their own ad inventory. For example, Google's DSP could preference the purchasing of ads on locations which generate the most revenue for its own business.

Favoring their own advertising services by ranking their own advertising services higher on search results or social media feeds, or by excluding rivals from their platform. For example, by preferencing its own specialized search results (such as

---

13 *DPI*, p.135.

Google Shopping or Facebook Marketplace) instead of websites that offer competing services.

Favoring their own advertising services by excluding rival suppliers of advertising from other products. For example, by refusing rival advertising apps access to the Google Play Store, or by Facebook refusing access to rivals for its API services.

Favoring websites that are a part of Google Display Network or Facebook Audience Network. For example, for Google Search, publishers that are a part of Google Display Network could be ranked more highly in organic search results, or in sponsored or ad results, than publishers that are not a part of Google Display Network.

Favoring advertisers that use Google's or Facebook's advertising services, in the display of organic results or ordering of the news feed. For example, organic posts from advertisers with high expenditure may be displayed more prominently.

Favoring or preferencing their own ad tech services. For example, Google's DSP or SSP could preference ad inventory made available through its own ad exchange, rather than a third-party ad exchange. If this occurred, it may have flow on effects. For example, if a digital platform is able to drive additional volume to its exchange, it may decrease the viability of competing ad exchanges as they would receive less advertiser demand.

The ACCC then referred to three examples raised in an article by Geradin & Katsifis on the Social Service Research Network:[14]

DoubleClick for Publishers sheltering Google Ad Exchange from real-time competition, by allowing Google Ad Exchange to submit a real time bid to DoubleClick for Publishers but prohibiting third-party ad exchanges from doing so, resulting in a lower purchase price for Google Ad Exchange;

Google Ad Exchange having the "last look" at ad impressions, and therefore, being able to use the highest estimated price of all ad exchanges as the price floor for its own auction, making it possible for Google Ad Exchange to beat any other exchanges by submitting a slightly higher bid; and

Using information gathered by DoubleClick to favor Google Ad Exchange to cherry pick users that "happened to be at the end of the funnel stage in a purchase journey, essentially stealing attributions from other exchanges."

The claims were countered by Google who submitted in response to the ACCC's concerns in the Preliminary Report that it was not favoring its own ad in-

---

14 Damien Geradin & Dimitrios Katsifis represent News Corp. See, e.g. Damien Geradin, Geradin Partners, https://www.geradinpartners.com/team/damien-geradin/; see also Submission to the Australian Competition and Consumer Commission: Response to the Digital Platforms Inquiry Preliminary Report, News Corp Australia (Mar. 1, 2019) at 6 n. 11.

ventory in demand side platforms ("DSP") services and claimed that such a practice would undercut the value of its DSP services. It submitted that its DSP service competes against many popular DSPs and that if it favored its own ad inventory to the detriment of advertisers, it would degrade the quality of its DSP service and drive advertisers to alternative DSPs.

Google also made the following two points:

- It did not favor its own ad inventory on Google's ad exchange over inventory on other ad exchanges to the detriment of advertisers as this too would degrade the quality of its DSP service and drive advertisers to alternative DSPs; and

- It did not change the ranking or display of websites in its organic search results based on whether they buy services from Google or participate in the Google Display Network, and it has no incentive to sacrifice search quality which is its greatest source of revenue and profits in order to promote a business in which Google earns a comparatively small proportion of revenues and profits.

In terms of self-preferencing concerns related to Facebook, the ACCC noted that Facebook might also engage in anti-competitive self-preferencing because it too was present in related markets; it sold ad inventory on its owned and operated platforms but also operated in a related market through the operation of Audience Network, a service by which Facebook acts as an intermediary and sells ad inventory on third party websites.

There is no detail in the DPI on how the ACCC weighed up the competing claims or what evidence it used to test whether the conduct was cable of harming competition. The ACCC simply found that firms with substantial market power, including the leading digital platforms, were likely to have the ability and incentive to leverage their market power into related markets.[15] This failure to set out a clear and coherent theory of harm is discussed in section 4.3.

It also found specifically that given "the substantial market power of each of Google and Facebook, their presence in a significant number of related markets and the opacity of their key algorithms, there is significant potential for self-preferencing by Google and Facebook to substantially lessen competition."[16] Moreover, it found, without explaining why, that the scope for anti-competitive self-preferencing is particularly acute in the ad tech value chain where Google operates businesses at multiple levels.

---

15 ACCC, *DPI*, p.133.
16 ACCC, *DPI*, p.133.

III. THE ECONOMICS OF VERTICAL INTEGRATION

Vertical integration is a central feature of the concerns raised in the each of the inquiries regarding self-preferencing. After all, only a firm that is vertically integrated – that is, only a firm that is present in multiple parts of the value chain – can be accused of treating its own products and services in a more favorable way to those of third-party competitors that use the digital platform.

Pro-competitive Features of Vertical Integration

The pro-competitive features of vertical integration can be grouped under the following four headings:[17]

- Increasing pricing efficiency

- Increasing productive efficiency

- Preventing profit expropriation, and reducing transaction costs and the costs of incomplete contracts.

- Each of these are discussed below.

Increasing Pricing Efficiency

Although pricing efficiencies can arise from vertical integration In a number of different ways (such as by avoiding input substitution, lowering rivals' costs and by enabling pro-competitive price discrimination), the most common source of pricing efficiency is through the elimination of double marginalization. From Cournot in 1838, for example, economic theory has consistently shown that there are positive efficiency benefits from allowing vertical integration or bundling of complementary activities, most notably as a way to avoid the double marginalization effect which can cause prices to be higher and consumers to be worse off where previously integrated industry structures are performed in separate stages.[18]

These positive efficiency benefits can be illustrated by considering the hypothetical example presented in Box 1 of a firm that grows oranges and (a separate) firm that manufactures orange juice and which purchases the oranges from the firm that grows oranges.

---

17 See, for example, "The efficiency-enhancing effects of non-horizontal mergers," A report by RBB Economics for the Enterprise and Industry Directorate-General of the European Commission, 2005.

18 Augustin Cournot, Researches into the Mathematical Principles of the Theory of Wealth, 1838), August M. Kelly ed, 1971.

Box 1: Elimination of double marginalisation in the orange juice supply chain

In this example, we assume that both the firm that grows oranges and the firm that manufactures orange juice have market power, meaning that they can price their oranges and orange juice respectively at a price above marginal cost.

Because the orange grower in this example has market power, it is able to charge a mark-up above marginal cost on the oranges that it supplies to the manufacturer. As a result, the orange grower sells fewer oranges to the manufacturer than would be the case if it priced the oranges at the perfectly competitive level, but its market power means that the higher price that it receives on the lower volume of oranges sold still enables the firm growing oranges to maximise its profits.

However, as the manufacturer also has market power, it is also able to charge a mark-up on the orange juice that it supplies to retailers. The effect of the manufacturer also imposing a mark-up on the orange juice that it sells to retailers is that it sells less juice to retailers and consequently needs fewer oranges from the firm growing oranges. This means that the profits received by the orange grower will now fall below the profit-maximising level.

They key point from this example is that the demand for orange juice is ultimately suppressed because both the firm growing oranges and the manufacturer are imposing a mark-up at different levels of the value chain. Those mark-ups ultimately feed into the price paid by retailers and passed-on to consumers; the retailer has to pay two mark-ups when purchasing the juice to sell to consumers.

Both the firm growing oranges and the manufacturer would be better off if they could work together to sell more orange juice to retailers by eliminating the double marginalisation. A reduction in the margin (and price) by the firm growing oranges will benefit the manufacturer of orange juice as it can sell more juice to retailers. Similarly, a reduction in the margin (and price) of the manufacturer will mean that the firm growing oranges can sell more oranges to meet the increased demand for juice by retailers. In other words, by charging just the single profit-maximising margin, the firm growing oranges and the manufacturer can boost the sales of orange juice and then share the single pool of profits between them. This could be achieved by the firm growing oranges and the manufacturer entering into a contract that divides the additional profit between the two of them, or it could be achieved by vertical integration.

This effect described in Box 1 above can be interpreted as an "externality." An externality refers to an adverse or positive effect of one firm's action on another firm. If two producers are in a complementary relationship, it consists in a firm's gain from a price reduction by a rival. If a firm in a vertical relationship reduces its price, it has also a positive effect on other parts of the supply chain by increasing their sales. This "link" between firms in a vertical relationship is described in the economic literature and throughout this report as the "vertical externality." The externality effect is not restricted to prices. Improvements in, for example, quality, promotion or distribution will also have a positive effect on other firms in the supply chain.

Increasing Productive Efficiency

There are other compelling efficiency reasons why firms will vertically integrate. The economies of scale or scope available after integration or the improved managerial or financial efficiency, supply assurance or increased buyer power lead to an increase in productive efficiency. Vertical separation may also mean that a firm is unable to appropriate the full benefits of its investment as these benefits are partly reaped by other firms in the supply chain. In such a case, vertical integration can lead to significant efficiency gains by "internalizing" those externalities.

Preventing Profit Expropriation, and Reducing Transaction Costs and the Costs of Incomplete Contracts

Vertical integration may also reduce the transaction costs and the costs of incomplete contracts that are present when firms contract with each other across different levels of the supply chain. Under separate ownership, a party may be able to exploit contractual loopholes where contracts between parties are not fully specified. Although these issues could be overcome by implementing costly monitoring or incentive mechanisms, they could in extreme circumstances lead to the "hold-up" problem where investment may be deterred altogether.

Anti-competitive Features of Vertical Integration

Although vertical integration is typically motivated by one or more of the pro-competitive reasons outlined above it can, in some circumstances, lead to anti-competitive effects. This section discusses the evolution of some of those concerns and their applicability to the concerns raised in the ACCC's DPI.

The Starting Point – The Simple Rule that there is only One Monopoly Profit

A typical competition concern is that a vertically integrated firm that has market power in only one of the layers of the value chain in which it operates will seek to extend its market power to the layer where it faces more competition.

It might seem intuitively obvious that a monopoly problem in one part of the value chain becomes a "double monopoly problem" if the firm chooses not to supply competing operators in another part of the value chain and reserves both activities for itself.

However, the basic "Chicago School" principle of one monopoly profit has long since established that this intuition is not robust. A firm that is dominant in a particular activity (say growing oranges) has an incentive to enhance economic efficiency in a complementary area (say manufacturing orange juice). If the quality of the complementary good increases, or its price decreases, the demand for the original product would normally rise, thereby increasing the profits of the dominant firm.

Hence, in the simple Chicago School models one can leave it to the monopolist orange grower to make efficient choices about whether or not to promote competition in the orange juice manufacturing activity.

Exceptions to the Simple Rule

The main finding from the Chicago School, namely that there is only one monopoly profit and that a vertically integrated firm that is able to extract that monopoly profit in one layer of the value chain in which it operates will not be able to extend that into another, more competitive, layer of that value chain, now comes with a number of qualifications.

Some of these qualifications come from the fact that the one monopoly theory always relied on quite restrictive assumptions such as the need for the upstream input monopolist to be protected by prohibitive barriers to entry, perfect competition in downstream markets, and for the products in the two markets being used in fixed proportions.

Developing more Sophisticated "Post-Chicago School" Theories of Harm

More recently the simple Chicago School view has also been supplemented by a number of "post-Chicago" theories that have developed economic models which presented a richer analysis of vertical integration and its potential anti-competitive effects.

One of these post-Chicago theories relates to the ability of a firm with a monopoly position in one market to engage in tying in order to leverage their market power into another market (the tied market). The theory, developed by Whinston,[19] shows that this conduct may be profitable when the tied market is subject to economies of scale and is, therefore, imperfectly competitive. Under these assumptions,

---

19   Michael D. Whinston, Tying, Foreclosure and Exclusion, 80 American Economic Review n837 (1990).

the leveraging strategy either induces the exit (or deters the entry) of rivals in the tied market.[20]

Another post-Chicago theory is that the monopolist would engage in tying or bundling as a way to protect their monopoly position. Although the Chicago School view was that the monopolist in one market would make an efficient choice about whether or not to promote competition in a related market, and would benefit most if that related market was competitive, modern theories of foreclosure suggest a less benign reason for concern about the competitiveness in the related market. If there is a risk that the firm in the related or complementary market could one day grow and become a competitive threat to the monopoly supplier, than the monopolist might seek to bundle the monopoly product with the complementary product in an attempt to foreclose rivals in the complementary market and protect its position in the monopoly market.

So even though the Chicago School insight that such conduct may not be profitable in the short term for the monopolist in the short term, it may be profitable in the longer term if it delays the firm in the complementary market from developing and ultimately threatening the monopolist's position in the market where they have a monopoly.

IV. DEFICIENCIES WITH THE ACCC'S ASSESSMENT IN THE DPI

This section discusses the following issues with the ACCC's assessment of self-preferencing in the DPI:

It treated self-preferencing as presumptively anti-competitive, in large part because of the past history of digital platform operators of expanding into related markets.

It failed to assign sufficient weight to pro-competitive features of vertical integration, both in general as well as with regard to the alleged conduct.

It failed to set out a clear theory of harm and to test that theory of harm with observed market evidence.

Each of these is discussed below.

The ACCC Treated Self-preferencing as Presumptively Anti-competitive

The approach that the ACCC took to assessing the competitive effects of self-preferencing seemed to consist of the following two limbs. First, it seemed to place considerable weight on the fact that Google and Facebook both have a strong history of expanding into related markets. Second, it noted that the broad range of markets

---

20   Rivals in the tied market become less competitive because they lose sales in a market characterized by economies of scale as a result of the tying firm pricing the tied product more aggressively

that each of Google and Facebook operates in provided many opportunities for self-preferencing to occur. As a result, it concluded that "*it is likely the risk of digital platforms leveraging market power from one market to another will increase in the future.*"[21]

Such an approach raises the following two issues. First, a reliance on the "strong history" of Google and Facebook to expand into related markets implies that any expansion onto a related market is ground for concern. Yet such a concern is unfounded. Vertical integration, by definition, occurs when firms expand from one layer of the value chain to another. In the vast majority of cases, vertical integration will be pro-competitive. As discussed in section 2 of this paper, there are compelling efficiency reasons why firms will vertically integrate. As discussed above, vertical integration leads to a number of pricing and productive efficiency, reduces transaction costs and the costs of incomplete contracts, and provides incentives to boost investment.

Those widely-accepted benefits of vertical integration mean that the ACCC's concern with Google's and Facebook's history of expanding into other market – that is, with vertical integration – without developing a clearer theory of harm that explains why this is a concern is strangely incomplete.

Second, the concern that the broad range of markets that each of Google and Facebook operates in provides many opportunities for self-preferencing to occur, risks treating self-preferencing as presumptively anti-competitive. But this cannot be correct. As self-preferencing is observed in many markets including highly competitive ones, the starting point for any competitive assessment must be that self-preferencing, even when practiced by firms with market power, may be anti-competitive in some circumstances and pro-competitive in others.

A café owner, for example, who makes and sells fruit salad and juice, will put their home-made fruit salads and freshly squeezed orange juices in the more prominent shelves of its own fridge display and would also stock branded juices or fruit salads stocked by third party suppliers on lower or higher shelves of the fridge.

In this very simple example, the juices supplied by third party rivals are at a potential disadvantage compared to the freshly squeezed juices of the café owner – they are placed on less visible or less easily accessible shelves. Yet one would not seriously expect calls for increased monitoring or other forms of regulation to address the perceived inefficiency or unfairness of that commercial arrangements. The café owner benefits by having a broader range of juices to offer its customers and the third-party suppliers benefit from gaining an additional distribution channel, even if that channel does not give it access to the premium position occupied by the freshly squeezed home-made juices of the vertically integrated café owner.

---

21 ACCC, *DPI*, p. 137.

Assuming that the café owner in this example had a substantial degree of market power, meaning that they could set the prices of the food and beverages that it supplied above competitive levels, how would the ACCC have assessed the self-preferencing behavior of the café owner?

Would it have started from the presumption that the café owner should have given treatment to all the products using the fridge and expected that the more prominent shelves of the fridge be stocked with an equal assortment of home-made juices and third-party juices? Would they then have enquired into whether the café owner had placed his own juices on the more prominent shelves in the past or in other jurisdictions?

Or would it have enquired into the potential for harm in the juice market? In this scenario, it would ask how severe the hardship they faced from having their product placed on less prominent shelves in the fridge. Was it enough to drive them from the market? Would all third-party suppliers of juice be in the same position? How important was the café owner was a route to market for third party suppliers of juice? Could third party suppliers secure agreements with other retailers? And if they were successfully excluded from the café would they no longer be able to achieve scale advantages and be forced to increase their prices? Would the café owner then be able to capitalize on the cost disadvantage faced by third party suppliers and increase the price of juice above competitive levels?

The analysis presented in the DPI to assess self-preferencing suggests that the ACCC would have taken the former approach rather than the latter.

The ACCC Failed to Properly Assess the Benefits of Vertical Integration for Digital Platforms

As well as placing insufficient weight to the widely-accepted benefits of vertical integration, the ACCC completely overlooked the benefits of some of the self-preferencing behaviors identified by the ACCC.

For example, the CMA in the UK has found that vertical integration, especially between DSPs and SSPs can give rise to efficiencies, mainly relating to cookie matching and latency. The examples it gave were:[22]

DSPs and SSPs associate each consumer with a cookie ID. As cookie IDs are specific to each company, if the DSP and SSP are operated by different companies a process of cookie matching is required in order for the DSP to identify the relevant consumer information to associate to a given impression. This process is prone to failure and the inefficiency is avoided if the same company operates both the DSP and SSP.

After an SSP sends bid requests, DSPs have a time limit to submit their bids. Latency can therefore result in a bid being received too late and being excluded from

---

22 CMA Market study interim report, para 5.187.

the auction. If the same company operates both the SSP and DSP, it can locate them close by, reducing the time needed for information to travel between the two.

Failing to take these benefits into accounts is a serious omission and means that the assessment is focused only on the potential for competitive harm rather than balancing that potential for harm on the one hand and the potential for the conduct to also benefit consumers, businesses and advertisers, on the other hand. This balancing exercise is missing in the ACCC's DPI.

The ACCC Failed to Set Out a Clear Theory of Harm

Perhaps what is most striking about the ACCC's assessment of self-preferencing is the lack of a clear theory of harm around self-preferencing. Indeed, to the extent that a theory of harm can be gleaned, it seems to be related to a concern that *competitors* rather than *competition* will be harmed.

For example, the ACCC stated that it inquired into the extent that technical specifications introduced by Google or Facebook "had the potential to benefit their own products and services *to the detriment of competitors.*" The ACCC noted that some submissions claimed that Chrome did not apply certain technical restrictions to video content sites including the Google-owned YouTube, but did apply those technical restrictions to websites from other publishers.

What is noteworthy is that the ACCC chose not to investigate those claims because it did not feel that they were capable of substantial lessening competition in a relevant market, but because "the ACCC has not received evidence that this conduct has had a material adverse impact on Google's *competitors.*"

While assessing whether any conduct by a digital platform with substantial market power has a material adverse impact on a *competitor* is a part of a competitive assessment, it is not the end of the assessment. Harm to competitors is not synonymous with harm to the competitive process and the ACCC should not simply assume that any commercial difficulties encountered by firms that compete with digital platforms are the result of anti-competitive conduct.

The lack of a clear theory of harm was also apparent in the ease with which the ACCC believed that platforms with substantial market power would engage in anti-competitive leverage of that power into related markets.by assuming that digital platforms were *likely* to leverage any market power they had into related markets.

But before the ACCC finds that digital platforms are likely to leverage their market power into related markets, the ACCC needs to explain how it believes the competitive process will be harmed in each particular case. Is the concern that the vertically integrated digital platform foreclose rivals in the related markets in order to reduce the intensity of competition in those markets? Or is the concern that the stand-alone businesses could, one day, grow to threaten the digital platforms in their core markets if they were only allowed to compete on their merits today?

The absence of a clear theory of harm is a serious omission and made worse by the fact that the ACCC appeared to ignore recent developments in economic thinking that have consistently shown that it is far from trivial to show that there are robust incentives for a firm with market power in one part of the supply chain to foreclose in vertically and complementary markets. That theory shows that the starting position in any assessment of whether a firm can leverage its market power from one market into a related one is that there is only one monopoly profit for the dominant firm to capture and that a firm that is dominant in one market has a strong incentive to make efficient choices about whether or not to promote competition in the related market. Although a number of exemptions to the "one monopoly profit" theory have been developed, the current economic thinking is that the ability of firms to leverage power from one market to another is not as straightforward as the ACCC presumes in the DPI.

This more nuanced approached was adopted in the CMA's Market study interim report where the CMA expressed concern that Google may be able to leverage the market power from its "owned and operated" advertising inventory into the open display advertising market, both extending its market power and protecting its core position in search advertising and data. The CMA has not come to a final position at the time of writing this paper, but the reference to Google looking to protect its core position in search advertising and data is consistent with one of the exemptions to the "one monopoly profit" that has been developed and is more consistent with current economic theory than the approach taken by the ACCC.

V.   CONCLUSIONS

The finding in the DPI that digital platforms with substantial market power have the ability and incentive to engage in leveraging behavior which may affect competition in advertising and other markets is likely to influence the way that the newly established Digital Platforms Branch undertakes its inquiries into this issue. The new branch should put the findings in the DPI to one side and undertake a fresh assessment of the potential anti-competitive effects of self-preferencing.

That assessment should recognize that self-preferencing occurs in many markets including highly competitive ones and, as a result, cannot be treated as presumptively anti-competitive. Self-preferencing, even when practiced by platform operators with market power, may be anti-competitive in some circumstances and pro-competitive in others.

The Nexus between Innovation and Competition: Will the New Digital Technologies Change the Relationship?

By Elizabeth Webster [1]

Abstract

There has been a long and extended empirical literature examining the impact of competition on innovation. I argue that as innovation is the way firms compete, this question does not make a lot of sense and it is not surprising the empirical literature has not found stable results. We should be asking instead: what affect does (digital) innovation have on the creation of new products and better processes? And does this form of innovation accelerate the tendency toward larger firms and more concentrated markets – neither of which may not be good for income equity and civil society.

I.   INTRODUCTION

As topics for discussion, innovation and competition have long been intertwined. Will innovation produce the behemoths that choke competition and lead to the dominance of fewer and fewer firms? Does ruthless competition between near-identical firms smother the profits needed for risk taking? Will the shift from mechanical and electronic platforms towards digital ones exacerbate these trends?

In this article, I examine how the competition – innovation debate has progressed and suggest that the (voluminous) research which tests whether lack of competition holds back innovation is possibly asking the wrong question. I then look briefly at whether the recent new wave of digital innovation is creating larger firms and more concentrated markets.

II.   HOW ECONOMISTS CONCEPTUALIZE COMPETITION

Competition, between firms for customers and scarce inputs and workers for jobs, is the fundamental force allowing economists to predict the direction of economic change resulting from a given modification in conditions. By extrapolation, competi-

---

1   Swinburne University of Technology. From a conference held in April 2019 at the University of Melbourne.

tion transforms economies as changes in one market place strains on others.[2] This pivotal role of competition harks back to Adam Smith's 1776 tract, which illuminated the role prices played in guiding people's behavior. Since then, considerable attention has been given by the economics profession to defining, measuring and identifying competition.

So, what is competition? Competition is a race. For firms this largely means a race to win more customers through cheaper, better or more accessible products. Faster races make for more efficient and dynamic product offerings, or so the theory goes. Fast races depend on the internal drive of participants and external pressures. In a winner takes all race, competition is expected to be more extreme than in a race where all participants get a prize.

III.   INNOVATION AS A WAY TO COMPLETE

Innovation – i.e. change – is the route to these cheaper, better and more accessible products. The process of outmaneuvering rivals may cut prices down to the unit cost level, but beyond this, more efficient forms of production are needed to reduce prices. And, by definition, this improved efficiency depends on either new-to-the-firm or new-to-the-world innovation.

A. Measures of Competition

Economists have struggled to measure the speed of competition in a meaningful way. A logical metric would be a (weighted) count of the activities of firms to create these cheaper, better, and more accessible products. However, records of these activities are hard to obtain in a systematic and unbiased way, even in our current information-cum-big-data age.

Therefore, other, more expedient, measures of competition dominate the literature. Two common measures actually represent drivers of competition – the number of sellers in a market (or market concentration) and barriers to market entry. The logic behind the market concentration metric is that fewer market participants enable greater (tacit) collusion over prices.[3] The Herfindahl Index and CR4 metric are the prime examples here. The logic behind the barriers-to-entry measures is that an anticipation of losing customers motivates firms to act first. A third measure – the ratio of price to unit cost – is a supposed outcome of this rivalry. But price-cost margins largely assume competition is just price competition which, as discussed above, is a narrow, and uninteresting, view.[4]

B. Is there Evidence that more Vigorous Competition invokes Innovation?

There has been a multitude of studies to assess the effects of competition on innovation. In the main, these studies devolve into an estimation of the effect of mar-

---

2   Landes, D. (1969), *The Unbound Prometheus*, Cambridge University Press.

3   Smith, A., (1976) [1776], The Wealth of Nations: An inquiry into the nature and causes of the Wealth of Nations. The University of Chicago Press, Chicago.

4   It seems plausible to assume that the focus in economics on the "miracle of the price system" has subsequently led economists to narrowly define competition as merely price competition.

ket concentration, or barriers to entry, on R&D or patenting. There appear to be no studies examining the effect of price-cost margins on innovation (the closest being the effect of cash flow on R&D spending, see Cohen 2010).[5]

An argument posed by Schumpeter (1934, 1942) and subsequently explored by Mason (1951), Horowitz (1964) and later others,[6] was that by permitting higher profits, concentration (i.e. collusion) would both provide the funds for investment into innovative activities, and, lock-in future returns from executed innovations. A variant of this theory proffered by Cohen & Klepper (1996) is that large firms have an advantage performing radical innovation because they can afford to fail.[7] They are not bankrupted by a single unsuccessful innovation. However plausible these theories, the empirical results have been ambiguous.

The barriers-to-entry definition of competition has also been explored. Blair (1948),[8] Geroski (1989),[9] and Acs & Audretsch (1991)[10] were among the earliest writers to ascertain the positive effect of weak barriers to entry on innovation but with a cautious note that they are probably co-determined.

The doyen of innovation and competition, Wesley Cohen (2010), concluded after reviewing the literature that high or low R&D intensity can occur in both high and low concentrated markets, depending on third factors, and it is likely that competition and innovation are simultaneously determined.

These studies are however hampered because there are few fully satisfactory off-the-shelf measures of competition. Using market concentration as a reliable proxy for the speed of the race often flies in the face of common sense. Mobile phones, computers, microchips, automobiles are considered some of the most concentrated yet innovative markets. Similarly, the rivalry driven by weak barriers-to-entry, as found in the hospitality and retail trades, may merely play out as price-cutting activities.

---

5 Cohen, W.M. & Klepper, S., (1996), A reprise of size and R & D. The Economic Journal, 106, 925-951. There is little *a priori* reason why price-cost margins would reflect the speed of the race to improve long-term efficiency, create new products and improve market access.

6 Schumpeter, J.A. (1942), *Capitalism, Socialism and Democracy*, 3rd edition, London: George Allen & Unwin, 1976. Mason, E.S., 1951. Schumpeter on monopoly and the large firm. *The Review of Economics and Statistics*, pp.139-144. Horowitz, I., 1962. Firm size and research activity. *Southern Economic Journal*, pp.298-301.

7 Cohen, W.M. & Klepper, S., (1996), A reprise of size and R & D. *The Economic Journal*, 106, 925-951.

8 Blair, J.M., (1948), Technology and size. *The American Economic Review*, 38(2), pp. 121-152.

9 Geroski, P.A., (1989), Entry, innovation and productivity growth. *The Review of Economics and Statistics*, pp. 572-578.

10 Acs, Z. J. & Audretsch, D.B. (1991), "Innovation as a Means of Entry: An Overview," in Schwalbach, J. & Geroski, P. eds., 1991. *Entry and market contestability: an international comparison*. Basil Blackwell, Oxford.

Surprisingly, the quantity of literature questioning the reverse causation, i.e. the role innovation plays in creating concentrated markets or barriers-to-entry, is thin and even passé (i.e. see the 1940s concentration of capital literature by Paul Sweezy and colleagues). If firms vie for profits, surely a good strategy would be to invest in barriers to entry? These barriers may take the form of new products, new processes and alternative means of accessing consumers, or anything else that increases the distance between the firm and their nearest rivals.

IV.   RE-PHRASING THE QUESTION

The literature which has tried to draw a causal link from market concentration to innovation has reached the end of its natural life. If we were to be uncharitable, we would say it has been an unfortunate distraction from bigger issues.

If we accept that innovation is the only long-term way firms compete, then it does not make sense to treat competition and innovation as separate and distinct concepts. Rather than worrying about recording the effect on, or consequences of, an intractable concept such as competition, I argue that we should be focusing on the effect of innovation on our societal end-goals of, householder well-being, and the health of civil society. [11]

In the remainder of this article, I give a preliminary discussion how digital technology might affect these social goals in part by providing cheaper, better, and more accessible products. I focus on whether digital innovation represents a break from past forms of innovation and, if so, how.

V.   DIGITIZATION IS …

"…the conversion of text, pictures, or sound into a digital form that can be processed by a computer."[12] The technology was created at Bell Labs in the 1940s and involved combining transistors, which can record millions of zeros and ones, with the mathematics articulated by Shannon's Information Theory (Gertner 2013).[13] Digital technologies can store information, automate physical processes, and make calculations and pattern recognition activities hitherto beyond human ability.

Digitization has loomed large in public discourse because of its non-rivalrous and non-excludable character. Non-rivalry occurs because once the original product has been made, users can make copies, at minimal cost, that are both identical to the

---

11   Many of the problems from large anti-competitive firms arise from their power to interfere in politics, create artificial barriers to entry via political influence, restrict the flow of knowledge and information via golden handcuffs and non-compliance with tax laws.

12   See https://www.lexico.com/definition/digitization.

13   Although there were forerunners of the ideas such as Babbage's analytical engine and the telegraph. See Gertner, J. (2013), *The Idea Factory: Bell Labs and the Great Age of American Innovation*, New York: Penguin.

original and transferable between media. Non-excludability occurs because it is technically impossible, in most cases, to prevent other parties from making these copies.

However, this new technology may not be as radical as we imagine. Non-rivalrous and non-excludable goods have been with us for ever – the most basic example being knowledge. Similarly, the question of whether we should artificially curtail the use of non-rivalrous and non-excludable products has also been with us for a long time. In the case of knowledge, this took the form of the patent, copyright and publishing debates in the late 19th century.

It has become received wisdom that limiting the ability to reproduce non-rivalrous non-excludable products is the price we pay to provide an inducement to invest in their creation. Any short-term deadweight loss caused by this curtailment, is outweighed by the social gain of a (perpetual) new product. Against this view are numerous examples, illuminated by Moser, Mokyr, Mowery, Trajtenberg, Rosenberg, and Bresnahan from history, which show that early access to non-rivalrous intermediate products (in the main by not artificially restricting use via patents), is important for extracting their full social value.

It would be hard to objectively prove that non-rivalrous inputs are of greater value to the functioning of our economies than in earlier epochs, but it is easy to show that investment into digital technologies has risen dramatically since they first appeared in the 1950s (Brynjolfsson & Kahin, 2002;[14] Katz & Koutroumpis, 2013).[15]

But digitization is not just another form of knowledge in three important respects. In the past, knowledge (which is non-rivalrous and often non-excludable) had often to be embodied in physical goods, such as machinery (which are rivalrous and excludable). Digitized knowledge, on the other hand, is embodied in code which is also non-rivalrous and non-excludable. Hence, market failures associated with expropriation of its innovation profits will loom larger. Secondly, the value of many digital technologies depends on their interoperability and network externalities. Some markets are winner-takes-all, and when the winner does emerge, there is an extreme imbalance of power and a potential threat to civil society. The latter may take the form of excessive income inequality and political interference.

And thirdly, digital technologies are not just another technology. According to Bresnahan & Trajtenberg (1995), digitization is a general-purpose technology, like

---

14 Brynjolfsson, E. & Kahin, B. eds., 2002. *Understanding the digital economy: data, tools, and research.* MIT press.

15 Katz, R.L. & Koutroumpis, P., *Measuring digitization: A growth and welfare multiplier, Technovation*, Volume 33, Issues 10–11, October–November 2013, pp. 314-319.

the steam engine and electricity.[16] It enables and enhances other technologies. There is a widespread view that patents on the steam engine and electric light held back development (see the discussion in Selgin & Turner 2011).[17] However, the inhibiting factor may stem from the rules around the operation of patents rather than patents *per se*. Howells (2008), for example, examined the innovation-blocking patents in the automobile, radio, aviation, and electric lighting industries and concluded that diffusion and development was limited by the administration of patents (meaning internal patent office processes, elongated infringement cases, and inefficient licensing) rather than the existence of the patent.[18]

VI. DIGITIZATION IS THE CONDUIT FOR CHEAPER, BETTER AND MORE ACCESSIBLE PRODUCTS

The research literature on the effects of digitization, via neural network algorithms, robotics, sensors and ICT, among other things, is largely dominated by case studies and selected products and industries. Anecdotally, we all know of examples where digital technology is replacing routine service activities, such as interpreting X-rays, monitoring quality, assembling products, selecting job applicants, handling customer support phone calls, and driving cars. In addition, many old products, such as TVs, phones and cars, are shifting from electronic to digital platforms.

There are few representative studies on the effects of digitalization but one relevant study by Bessen & Righi (2019) has found that major IT investments lead, on average, to large increases in demand for the firms' products.[19] Other than this, it is difficult to find representative studies that support the proposition that these new technologies have led to lower unit costs and prices. Perhaps it is too early.

Similarly, we can all point to products that would not exist were it not for digital technologies, such as big data, mobile phones, computer games, word processors *inter alia*.

And finally, the emerging literature on global value chains and online purchasing is testament to how digitalization has extended the reach of producers into

---

16 Bresnahan, T.F. & Trajtenberg, M., 1995. General purpose technologies 'Engines of growth'?. *Journal of Econometrics*, 65, 83-108.

17 Selgin, G. & Turner, J.L., 2011. *Strong steam, weak patents, or the myth of Watt's innovation-blocking monopoly, exploded*, The Journal of Law and Economics, 54, 841-861.

18 Howells, J., 2008. Patents and Downstream Innovation Suppression—Facts or Fiction? - A Critique of the Use of Historical Sources in Support of the Thesis that Broad Patent Scope Enables the Suppression or Hindrance of Downstream Useful-Technology Development. Centre for Organizational Renewal and Evolution, Working Paper-2008–01. Available at http://www.pucsp.br/icim/ingles/downloads/pdf_proceedings_2008/11.pdf.

19 Bessen, J.E. and Righi, C., 2019. Shocking Technology: What Happens When Firms Make Large IT Investments?, *Boston Univ. School of Law, Law and Economics Research Paper*, (19-6).

new and distant markets (Athukorala, Talgaswatta & Majeed, 2017).[20] History has shown that markets widen where the costs of communication, transport and logistics fall, and the speed, quality, and reliability of communication rises. Market widening leads to reinforcing second-round effects in the form of enhanced products. This is well illustrated by Mokyr (2010), who argued that by making Britain one market, the 18th century canals and improved sea and road routes enabled the early fruits of the industrial revolution to quickly reap economies of scale.[21]

Correlation is not causation, but it can be suggestive. If the opportunity offered by digital technologies motivates firms to introduce cheaper, better and more accessible products more quickly than otherwise, then we would expect to see a positive relationship between digitization and a change in GDP per capita. We do not have this information but in Figure 1 Katz & Koutroumpis (2013) show that there is a very strong positive relationship between digitization and GDP per capita levels across countries.

Figure 1: Digitization index with log of GDP per capita in 2010.

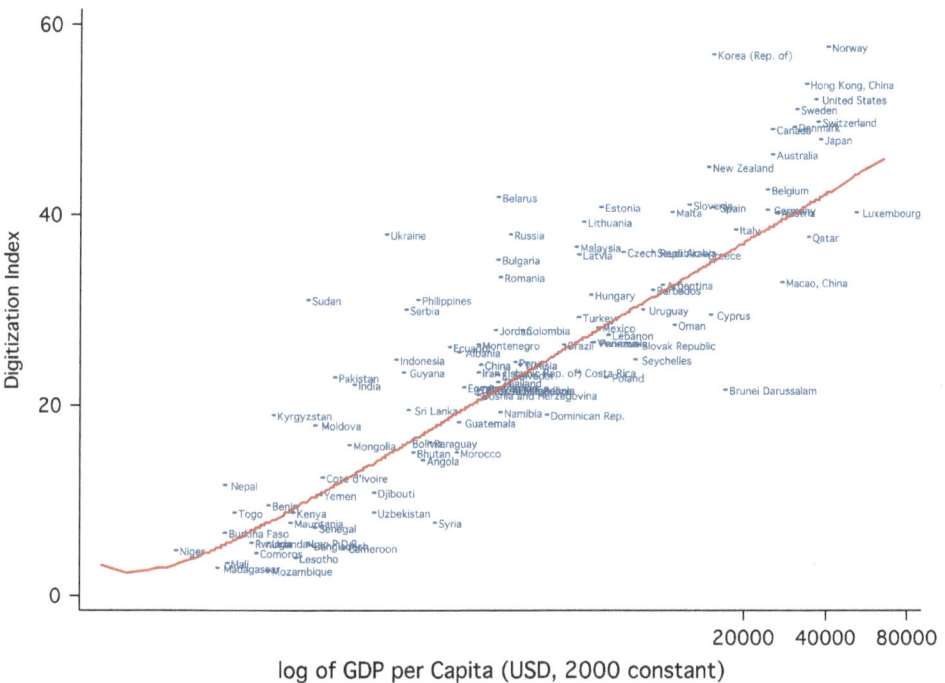

Source: Katz & Koutroumpis (2013).

---

20   Athukorala, P.C., Talgaswatta, T. & Majeed, O., (2017), Global production sharing: Exploring Australia's competitive edge, *The World Economy*, 40(10), pp. 2172-2192.

21   Mokyr, J., (2010), *The Enlightened economy an economic history of Britain* 1700-1850. Yale University Press.

VII. POLICIES TO AMELIORATE THE NEGATIVE EFFECTS

Regardless of the likely benefits from digitization, the question we must now pose is: Are the existing institutions for managing non-rivalrous and non-excludable products fit for purpose in the new digital age?

Patents and copyright, being the legal frameworks designed to increase incentives to create ideas via raising the excludability of information and knowledge, have well-known contraindications. They can generate monopoly power, and in certain circumstances, can hinder diffusion and development. Complementary policies, to ensure patents and copyright do not both strengthen market concentration and delay development and diffusion, should be reinforced. Consideration should be given to increasing the use and prevalence of licenses-of-right, standards on inter-operability, open networks, FRAND, and more transparent, faster examination systems. As an enabling technology, it is important to encourage both diffusion and the ongoing development of digital technologies.

It may be inefficient to block natural monopolies (where the size of the market only permits one firm to operate at the most efficient level). However, their ill effects may be mitigated by complementary policies to check the abuses of power such as technical inefficiency, extreme executive salaries, and monopoly pricing. Solutions need be pragmatic, and might include public ownership, regulation and *quid-pro quo* deals such as those done between the U.S. Government and AT&T (Bell Labs), IBM, and Du Pont in the 1950s.

Copyright needs a complete re-think. The most obvious reform would be to reduce the term to 20 years. With time discounting, any revenue beyond 20 years is not going to affect the incentive to be creative. It is just a payment for effort in the distant past.

The collation and dissemination of information and data is one industry to clearly benefit from the digital revolution. A growing number of organizations collate data and make it available at low cost to users. By reducing the information barriers to enter a market, it offers a marvelous service to would-be entrepreneurs. Usually however, the information industry is a natural monopoly, which makes it suitable for public ownership (e.g. national and university statistical services). However, the blooming private information sector (e.g. Google, DataStream, Connect4, LinkedIn, Bureau Van Dijk) suggests some public oversight is needed. The issue is how close are the next best substitutes and are these private providers using price to exclude small or less well-resourced customers. These questions have yet to be fully explored.

And finally, as with all economic restructuring, the value of programs to enable displaced workers to transition to new industries and occupations should be objectively evaluated and improved to minimize disruption to the digital casualties and enhance the health of civil society.

Dealing with Digital Markets in Mexico: Still more Questions than Answers

By Alejandra Palacios [1]

Abstract

The digital transformation is changing the functioning of markets and as so, it presents important challenges in terms of competition law, consumer protection and privacy. This article ponders the implications digital markets may have in the Mexican economy with respect to these three policy areas. It puts forth that since digitalization is beginning to spread into several sectors of the economy, digital businesses may represent competitive pressure to incumbents and could benefit Mexican consumers. Hence, at this point, the concerns digital markets raise in Mexico might differ from those that arise in other countries, but this may change quickly if certain digital business reach tipping points and acquire market power. Mexican authorities are in the process of understanding how to deal with this type of markets, although the set of public policies to be undertaken in the short run is not fully clear.

This contribution is comprised of six sections. After sections that introduce and define the scope of the article, Section III reviews the current international debate on the subject. It suggests that there seems to be a tacit consensus about the dynamics of digital markets, their benefits both for consumers and companies, as well as for the challenges regarding competition, consumer protection, and privacy. Section IV addresses the efforts made by several countries, international organizations and academic centers to comprehend and address these challenges. Section V dwells upon the Mexican regulatory and institutional landscape given digital markets. It also describes COFECE's most recent experiences in dealing with these types of markets and with a short description of the actions undertaken by the Commission to deal with this new context.

---

1 Chairwoman, Mexico's Federal Economic Competition Commission (COFECE). Text written on January 2020. This contribution was written in January 2020. By the time it is published, there will certainly be more academic or government initiatives that address digital markets, and some of the existing ones will have likely evolved. The survey made in this article will not reflect such developments. Likewise, actions that COFECE will take to address digital markets will be underway.

I.   INTRODUCTION

We live in a digital era that is changing every aspect of human life. Digitalization has brought about significant benefits, such as new job opportunities, cheap or free services, the customization of goods and services, easier and faster ways to be in touch with people, as well as the convergence between local and global markets.

More specifically, digitalization has transformed the functioning of the economy, namely the factors of production, business models, the ways businesses compete, the interaction between producers and consumers, consumption patterns, and the means by which consumers inform themselves about available goods and services.

Such impact is also reflected in macroeconomic terms. For instance, in 2017 the digital economy accounted for around 5 percent of global gross domestic product ("GDP") and 3 percent of global employment.[2] The study *Measuring the Digital Transformation. A roadmap for the future*, published by the Organization for Economic Cooperation and Development ("OECD") revealed that highly digital-intensive sectors were responsible for the creation of around 16 million new jobs in the OECD area between 2006 and 2016.[3]

The potential benefits of the digital economy could be particularly important for developing countries. According to the report *Latin America's missing middle: Rebooting inclusive growth*, if Latin America's economies harness the forces of digital technologies, GDP per capita in the region can increase by more than $1,000 per year, generating an incremental boost to GDP of $1 trillion by 2030.[4]

As such, Mexico is increasingly aware of the opportunities that lie in the digital economy and the importance of crafting policies that bring the benefits of digitalization to more Mexican consumers. Such an endeavor is neither clear-cut nor straightforward, since at this point there are still more questions than answers surrounding public policy related to digital markets.

This article intends to describe the recent increase in awareness of the digital economy and its implications for competition, consumer rights, and privacy by reviewing what has already been written on the subject. It also seeks to contribute to

---

2   Rumana Bukht & Richard Heeks, Defining, Conceptualizing and Measuring the Digital Economy (Centre for Development Informatics, Working Paper No. 68, 2017).

3   OECD, Measuring the Digital Transformation. A roadmap for the future (2019), OECD Publishing, Paris, https://www.oecd.org/going-digital/measurement-roadmap.pdf.

4   McKinsey Global Institute, Latin America's missing middle: Rebooting inclusive growth, (2019), https://www.mckinsey.com/~/media/McKinsey/Featured%20Insights/Americas/Latin%20Americas%20missing%20middle%20of%20midsize%20firms%20and%20middle-class%20spending%20power/MGI-Latin-Americas-missing-middle-Report-final.ashx.

the discussion by posing questions that need to be answered in order to face these new economic challenges. Sorting out these questions for the Mexican context will define the path forward for the institutional changes, and public policy design and implementation, that is needed in this digital era.

II.   SCOPE OF THE ARTICLE

The current digital transformation is overarching. At the societal level, digital technologies have transformed the way people interact by, for instance, enhancing access to information at an unprecedented speed, enabling new means of empowerment and civic participation, improving health care through tele-medicine, and broadening access to education with free online courses. Alongside such new social opportunities, some effects of digitalization raise concerns, namely perils related to cybersecurity, the dissemination of fake news, bot farms, hacked emails, the risk of human isolation by the excessive use of technologies, the immoderate use of mobile devices and its implications for our health, and a nascent digital divide between those skilled in the use of digital technologies and those who are not.[5]

The digital transformation also poses important challenges to the proper functioning of markets. This article particularly addresses the implications of digitalization in terms of competition policy, but also mentions consumer protection and privacy matters, given that these areas have become increasingly intertwined due to the dynamics of digital markets.

Companies increasingly function through digital platforms that collect enormous amounts of data that allows for the customization of goods and services to consumers' needs. However, the intricate and costly nature of building robust databases and developing algorithms to optimize the use of data divides companies between those few that get to do it, and those who do not. Especially, those who do it first enjoy an important competitive advantage that translates both into rising returns and entry barriers for other competitors. Moreover, companies may use data to generate deceptive or false information that negatively impacts consumers' purchasing decisions (e.g. a travel match maker could use consumers' data to set personalized prices on a plane ticket offering fake discounts), or mismanage online users' information at the expense of their privacy (e.g. Facebook-Cambridge Analytica scandal).

Competition and consumer protection laws share the common goal of addressing distortions in the marketplace that result in unlawful increases of sales and profitability for a business to the detriment of consumers. While competition law addresses the distortions brought about by businesses' anticompetitive conducts (e.g. avoiding anticompetitive mergers), consumer protection tackles distortions that oc-

---

5   OECD, Going Digital Toolkit (2019), https://goingdigital.oecd.org/.

cur when a company abuses its relationship with consumers through conducts like deceptive, false, or insufficient information, leading consumers to make sub-optimal purchase decisions, or through abusive contractual relations between consumers and suppliers. Regarding privacy matters, online retailers, apps, and devices harvest all possible information from users without the consumers' knowledge or expectation, as they cede almost all control over their data to be able to use certain digital services which may have become critical to their daily lives.[6] As it will be noted further, the digital age poses new challenges for these three areas of public policy.

III. A TACIT CONSENSUS ON DIGITAL MARKETS

Over the last few years, there has been an extensive discussion among academia, government agencies, international organizations, private stakeholders, and other actors around the functioning and implications of the digitalization of the economy. Such discussions agree on three traits of the digital economy: its dynamics, its benefits, and certain concerns relating to competition policy, consumer protection, and privacy.

On the dynamics of digital markets, most experts agree that these operate very differently from traditional ones. This, at least partly, is related to the prevalence of digital businesses that operate as platforms. Unlike traditional markets, which usually work as a one-sided market, digital platforms function as two- or multi-sided markets that bring together two or more actors or sides of the market that otherwise would not interact or easily connect.[7]

Economic literature addresses the characteristics that are widely accepted for digital platforms. The cost structure of these business models, which allow them to enjoy significant returns of scale and the possibility of developing economies of scope, is one of them. Thus, firms provide their services for more users at lower costs and have incentives to cater two or more different services through the same platform instead of providing them through separate ones.[8]

The presence of network effects is another important feature of digital platforms. Network effects, particularly indirect ones (by which the larger the number of participants on one side of the market, the greater the potential benefits or harms on

---

6   Rebecca Slaughter, Commissioner, Federal Trade Commission, remarks at the hearing on FTCs approach to consumer privacy (April 10, 2019) https://www.ftc.gov/system/files/documents/public_events/1418273/ftc_hearings_session_12_transcript_day_2_4-10-19.pdf.

7   Michael A Cusumano, Annabelle Gawer & David B Yoffie, The Business of Platforms: Strategy in the Age of Digital Competition, Innovation, and Power 15 (2019).

8   WEF, Competition Policy in a Globalized, Digitalized Economy, WEF White Paper, (December 2019), http://www3.weforum.org/docs/WEF_Competition_Policy_in_a_Globalized_Digitalized_Economy_Report.pdf.

the other side),[9] become more relevant when it comes to digital markets due to their implications for competition and consumer welfare. On one hand, network effects favor a "*winner takes most*" dynamics, whereby the first platform to reach a critical mass of users reduces the possibility of another platform creating a competing service. On the other hand, network effects may bring about benefits for both users and suppliers: the former enjoy the increased value of a product, and the latter have access to a greater number of users that may, in turn, generate greater revenue.[10]

Probably the most salient characteristic of digital platforms is the role of "Big Data." Data has always been essential for companies to compete. Nevertheless, when it comes to digital markets, unprecedentedly large data sets become more relevant, specifically with regard to the so called "3 Vs": volume, variety and velocity. Today, a firm's competitive advantage heavily relies on its capacity to make the most of its data. Consequently, firms or a group of firms with a large amount of data may become an obstacle for new companies (which lack this necessary input) to enter a market and compete.[11]

The second consensus relates to the benefits of digitalization to consumers and firms. As mentioned earlier, digital markets have expanded the array of products and services available for consumers, increasing the number of options at better prices, in better conditions and increasingly customized. Additionally, online markets reduce consumers' search costs, increase transparency, and facilitate their ability to compare product options simply and quickly.[12]

For companies, digitalization may imply the reduction of costs to establish global distribution channels through online markets. Moreover, digitalization has reduced transaction costs, helping firms better coordinate with their providers, and allowing them to reach out to their customers with more frequency.[13] However, even though these benefits contribute to leveling the playing field among small and medium-sized enterprises and incumbents, they may not be strong enough to offset the "*winner takes most*" dynamics mentioned earlier.

Regarding the concerns (specifically related to competition) about the implications of the digital economy in the markets, it is possible to identify at least eight points of agreement among academics and government agencies. First, that digital

---

9   There are also direct network effects, by which the more users participate in that platform, the more value the platform has for that same type of user. For example: telephone services.

10   COFECE, Rethinking Competition in the Digital Economy, (February 2018), https://www.cofece.mx/wp-content/uploads/2018/03/EC-EconomiaDigital_web_ENG_letter.pdf.

11   *Id*.

12   James Mancini, Digital antitrust: An emerging consensus?, Concurrences International N° 4-2019, (2019).

13   WEF, *supra* note 8.

platforms facilitate a *"winner takes most"* dynamics, which implies that competition for the market becomes more important than competition *in* the market.[14]

Second, as a result of changes in the cost structure and the existence of network externalities, digital platforms have the incentives to offer services at zero price to one side of the market. For competition authorities, this represents new challenges. For example, the definition of a relevant market can be problematic as the application of tests traditionally used may not be applicable when zero prices are involved.[15] In addition, we must consider that for users, such *"zero"* prices on one side of the platform may not actually be strictly zero, but may involve them providing the platform with personal information, without full awareness on their part, which the platform may then use for other profitable purposes (the Facebook model, for example, provides "free" access to content generated by other users, while using the information obtained to execute its advertising strategies).

Third, the use of algorithms fed by large data sets could increase the ability of companies to practice price fixing/collusion without human interaction.[16] In this regard, three ways of collusion put forth by Ezrachi & Stucke (2016, *Virtual Competition: The Promise and Perils of the Algorithm-Driven Economy*) are worth mentioning: (i) the use of the same price algorithm by many users to determine a market price can result in higher prices than those that would prevail under competitive circumstances; (ii) tacit collusion derived from the use of algorithms that adjust prices according to market data result in parallel price setting; and (iii) collusion derived from artificial intelligence resulting in an anticompetitive outcome without the need for the existence of an explicit or tacit agreement, but rather as a better response.[17] A challenge arises for competition agencies when a collusive arrangement occurs farther away from direct human involvement since the intentionality of the design and use of algorithms to set higher prices is more difficult to prove.

Fourth, consolidated incumbents have incentives to acquire potential or nascent competitors to hinder future competition. For merger control, these types of acquisitions can be difficult to assess since the acquired company is regularly at an early stage of development. The impact of acquisitions on innovation and other new theories of harm need to be taken into consideration by antitrust agencies to better understand these transactions.[18]

---

14 Elena Argentesi *et al.*, Ex-post Assessment of Merger Control Decisions in Digital Markets, Lear, p. 44 (May 9, 2019), https://assets.publishing.service.gov.uk/government/uploads/system/uploads/attachment_data/file/803576/CMA_past_digital_mergers_GOV.UK_version.pdf.

15 Jacques Crémer, *et al.*, Competition Policy for the Digital Era, European Commission (2019), https://ec.europa.eu/competition/publications/reports/kd0419345enn.pdf.

16 Jonathan B. Baker, The Antitrust Paradigm: Restoring a Competitive Economy 118 (2019).

17 COFECE, *supra* note 10.

18 Sai Krishna Kamepalli *et al.*, Kill Zone, University of Chicago, (November 2019), https://faculty.chicagobooth.edu/raghuram.rajan/research/papers/Kill%20zone_nov.pdf.

Fifth, digital platforms in a dominant position could exercise market power through vertical restraints and/or unilateral conducts, such as most favored nation clauses, refusal to deal, price discrimination, tying and bundling, predatory prices, among others.[19]

Sixth, market power can be reinforced by the existence of behavioral biases. Some of the behavioral biases include the tendency of consumers to prefer the *status quo* (e.g. consumers do not replace the default programs on their computers), because, in some cases, it might result more costly for consumers to migrate all their information from one platform to another (such difficulties are also known as *switching costs*); the difficulty of choosing among a lot of options or information; or the tendency of consumers to prefer immediate benefits relative to welfare gains in the future (e.g. a consumer searching for something in a browser engine will be inclined to use the first result, rather than searching on another browser or scrolling down to look for more options), among others.[20] Anticipating the existence of these biases, digital platforms will try to nudge consumers to the choice that is most profitable for the platform by exploiting users' personal data, already harvested from them or similar consumers.

Seventh, the use of Big Data generates market power that could be used to exclude current competitors or deter entry from potential ones.[21] Moreover, dominant firms can exercise market power in ways other than prices, such as exploiting data from consumers or denying the use of data to other companies.[22]

Eighth, exploitative conducts to acquire data may also result in privacy violations. Over the last decade, digital platforms have acquired an enormous mass of personal data by means which consumers are often unaware of (e.g. biometric data collected by computers, mobiles or smartwatches from daily activities). Furthermore, companies have been trading and sharing personal data in ways that could violate consumers' privacy. Although some governments have begun to enact general data protection regulations, these have not dissolved the threat.

All of the above challenges faced by the competition community in the context of the digital economy have brought about several questions. Some of the most frequently mentioned are: (i) How well equipped are competition authorities to address the digital markets of the twenty-first century?; (ii) Are current analytical and methodological tools used in competition (such as market definition and the assessment of market power) adequate?; (iii) Is the market definition of platforms so different from

---

19   Baker, *supra* note 16, at 149.

20   George J. Stigler Center for the Study of the Economy and the State, Committee on Digital Platforms Final Report, (2019), https://www.publicknowledge.org/wp-content/uploads/2019/09/Stigler-Committee-on-Digital-Platforms-Final-Report.pdf.

21   COFECE, *supra* note 10.

22   Crémer, *et al.*, *supra* note 15.

traditional markets (one-sided)?; (iv) How is market power determined in markets with products at (apparently) zero price?; (v) Should thresholds or other criteria for compulsory merger notification be modified?; (vi) What other considerations should competition authorities take into account when positioning theories of harm (for instance, data and privacy considerations)?; (vii) How must regulation be designed or modified to truly harness the advantages (and prevent the negative effects) that digital markets may bring about for consumers?; and (viii) Should a digital authority be established?

Agency heads, their teams, and international and academic organizations have made answering these questions a priority.

IV. EXPERIENCES AND PROPOSALS AROUND THE GLOBE THAT ADDRESS THE CHALLENGES OF THE DIGITAL ECONOMY

The digitalization of the economy has sparked both interest and concerns around the globe in the past few years, with some news outlets even saying that Big Tech companies are having their "antitrust moment." This "momentum" is reflected in the media: in 2015 there were around 73,000 antitrust stories around them, whereas in 2019 there were 223,000.[23] It is noteworthy that a significant amount of those stories mainly reported the probes being undertaken by the EU and the U.S. against Big Tech. [24, 25]

Aside from increased news coverage and landmark probes, 2019 also saw an effervescence in efforts to analyze the dynamics of digital markets, disentangle their implications, and suggest ways to address them.

---

23   Rani Molla, *The 14 charts that explain tech in 2019*, VOX (December 18, 2019), https://www.vox.com/recode/2019/12/18/21003145/2019-tech-charts-ipo-wework-softbank-antitrust-amazon-protests-streaming-privacy-tiktok.

24   In June 2017 the Commission fined Google with €2.42 billion for abusing its dominance as a search engine by giving an illegal advantage to Google's own comparison-shopping service. In July 2018, it fined Google €4.34 billion for illegal practices regarding Android mobile devices to strengthen the dominance of Google's search engine. In March 2019, it also fined Google €1.49 billion for breaching EU antitrust rules. In July 2019, the European Commission opened a formal antitrust investigation to assess whether Amazon's use of sensitive data from independent retailers who sell on its marketplace is in breach of EU competition rules.

25   In 2019, several enforcement actions were initiated at the federal and state levels in the US. For instance, the Department of Justice opened a broad investigation of whether major digital technology firms engage in anticompetitive practices; the Federal Trade Commission launched an investigation into Facebook's acquisitions, accusing it of buying potential rivals, and slapped a record $5 billion fine on Facebook for mishandling privacy of its users (the Cambridge Analytica scandal). At the state level, in September 2019 Texas announced an antitrust investigation of Google's search and advertising businesses. The probe includes 47 other states and three territories. In that same month, New York and seven other states and the District of Columbia announced an antitrust probe into Facebook. The probe expanded a month later to include attorneys general from 47 states and territories in total.

A. Proposals within Regional Blocs and International Organizations

For instance, the European Union (EU), a cornerstone of the efforts being made concerning the digital economy, published *Competition Policy for the Digital Era*, a report which explores how such a policy should evolve to continue to promote innovation for the sake of consumers in the digital age.[26] The report concludes that European competition law is sufficiently flexible to adjust to and face the challenges posed by the digital economy. However, it concedes it is possible to question certain methodologies and to rethink the application of some principles, namely the consumer welfare standard and market definitions.[27]

Despite its interesting insights, the report says little about how to implement the changes proposed. In December 2019, at the "Chillin' Competition Conference," the EU Competition Commissioner, Margrethe Vestager, stated that it is time to review their market definition guidelines to make sure they are accurate and up to date, and acknowledged that "… we have a whole series of interesting questions ahead of us and […] We'll need to draw on ideas and experiences that come from many different angles – from public authorities and consumer groups, businesses and individuals."[28] In a way, she addresses the necessity to explore some type of *ex ante* regulations.

Likewise, in its *Common Understanding on Competition and the Digital Economy* statement, the G7 agreed that competition policy should adapt to the challenges of the digital economy without overthrowing its guiding principles and goals.[29] Furthermore, the G7 underscores that "given the borderless nature of the digital economy, it is important to promote greater international cooperation and convergence in the application of competition laws." Though the statement emphasizes that it is important that competition authorities have the tools and means to deepen their knowledge regarding new business models and their impact on competition, it does not set a guideline on how they should converge – in law and in practice.

In its *Digital Economy Report 2019. Value Creation and Capture: Implications for Developing Countries*, the United Nations highlights that digital data and the existence of a growing number of platforms are the two main drivers of value creation

---

26 Crémer, *et al.*, *supra* note 15.

27 *Id.*

28 Margrethe Vestager, Commissioner for Competition, European Commission, Defining Markets in a New Age, remarks at the Chillin' Competition Conference (December 2019), https://ec.europa.eu/commission/commissioners/2019-2024/vestager/announcements/defining-markets-new-age_en.

29 G7, Common Understanding on Competition and the Digital Economy (2019), https://www.ftc.gov/system/files/attachments/press-releases/ftc-chairman-supports-common-understanding-g7-competition-authorities-competition-digital-economy/g7_common_understanding_7-5-19.pdf.

in the digital era. Value creation arises once the data is transformed into digital intelligence and monetized through commercial use.[30] Therefore, control over data is fundamental to be able to transform them into digital intelligence. The report goes further in arguing that "… countries (*governments*) at all levels of development risk becoming mere providers of raw data to those digital platforms while having to pay for the digital intelligence produced with those data by platforms owners."[31]

The report also addresses the kind of policies developing countries need to put in place to create and capture value in the digital economy. For instance, it suggests they ensure affordable and reliable connectivity, boost entrepreneurship in digital sectors and promote digital upgrading by enhancing capabilities to refine data.[32] At the same time, the report recognizes that "at this stage there are more questions than definitive answers about how to deal with the digital economy,"[33] thus it does not answer key policy questions such as how to assign ownership and control over data, how to build consumer trust and protect data privacy or how to regulate cross-border data flows.

More recently, the World Economic Forum ("WEF") issued the "white paper" *Competition Policy in a Globalized, Digitalized Economy*, which explores the challenges presented by digitalization for different aspects of competition law. The article, for instance, addresses issues such as the cross-border implications of competition enforcement as many digital businesses are global, and digitalization makes national boundaries less consequential. Also, the report puts forward an overview of some possible solutions, namely that when it comes to digital platforms a deeper understanding of the different business models is essential for better regulation and enforcement. Likewise, it suggests that traditional tools used to define markets or scrutinize mergers and acquisitions may need updating to remain effective. Similar to other commentary, it does not suggest *how* to revise those tools.

Given the borderless nature of the digital economy, the report also recommends the possibility of advancing an international set of competition rules that facilitates business operations in all regions of the world, but again, it does not provide hints on how to do it. In addition, the "white paper" suggests that competition enforcement and consumer protection enforcers should concentrate their powers in one institution, rather than two.[34]

---

30 UNCTAD, Digital Economy Report 2019. Value Creation and Capture: Implications for Developing Countries (2019), https://unctad.org/en/PublicationsLibrary/der2019_en.pdf.

31 *Id.*

32 *Id.*

33 *Id.*

34 WEF, *supra* note 8.

B. Proposals from Specific Countries and Academia

Besides the endeavors led by the European Union and international organizations, several jurisdictions have also taken the initiative to analyze digital markets and the path ahead. In mid-2019, the United Kingdom ("UK") published the report *Unlocking Digital Competition*, which emphasized that governments and regulators are at an enormous informational disadvantage relative to technology companies. Thus, to make competition effective, policy needs a new approach to change how digital markets work and create new opportunities for innovation and consumer choice.

Additionally, the report calls for a new digital markets' unit ("DMU") with the resources and power to set and enforce new competition-enhancing rules (some type of *ex ante* regulation).[35] So far, it is still unclear whether the report is suggesting the DMU falls within the Competition and Markets Authority's ("CMA") institutional design, or whether it would be deployed as a sectoral regulator. So, as the UK government continues working on laying out the best institutional design, the CMA has implemented a unit dealing with behavioral science and analyzing large quantities of data. This example shows that while expert recommendations are highly valuable, putting them into practice often takes time and implies thorough analysis in legal, budgetary, and institutional terms.

Building from some of the recommendations of the report, the CMA issued its Digital Markets Strategy, outlining five strategic objectives. Among these is the need to strengthen the CMA's knowledge and capacity to understand the opportunities and risks posed by digital markets, as well as the importance of adjusting the existing competition tools to the digital era.[36] It also announced it would carry out a market study into online platforms and digital markets in the UK, concentrating more specifically on Google and Facebook.

Thus, in December 2019 the agency issued the interim report on the online platforms market study proposing a set of principles and a workplan for an *ex ante* regulatory regime to apply to digital platforms in the UK as a complement to *ex post* antitrust enforcement. This makes the UK the first European nation to launch a regulatory experiment and articulate a detailed agenda on issues related to digital markets.[37] In the interim report, the CMA also makes recommendations on two major

---

35 Jason Furman, et.al., Unlocking Digital Competition, https://assets.publishing.service. gov.uk/government/uploads/system/uploads/attachment_data/file/785547/unlocking_digi-tal_competition_furman_review_web.pdf.

36 Competition Markets Authority, Digital Markets Strategy (2019), https://assets.publish-ing.service.gov.uk/government/uploads/system/uploads/attachment_data/file/814709/cma_digital_strategy_2019.pdf.

37 Cristina Caffarra, *The UK's "other" big experiment: Regulating online platforms?*, CEPR Policy Portal (January 6, 2019), https://voxeu.org/content/uk-s-other-big-experiment-regulat-ing-online-platforms.

categories: (i) devising a code of conduct for platforms to apply to digital firms designated with "strategic market status"; and (ii) various "interventions" (e.g. separation measures between portions of the vertical stack in digital adtech, measures to improve interoperability of platforms, measures to improve personal data mobility and measures to increase users' control of their data) as potential means to deal with specific problems. Both types of recommendations would be pursued by the DMU.

The Australian Competition and Consumer Commission ("ACCC") undertook a similar effort. In 2019, it released its final report on the *Digital Platforms Inquiry*, which focuses on the impact of such platforms on the choice and quality of news and journalism, and provides recommendations spanning competition law, consumer protection, media regulation, and privacy law (reflecting the intersection of these issues). The ACCC makes a set of 23 recommendations, including the establishment of a specialist digital platforms branch within the agency, focused on developing expertise in digital markets, the use of algorithms, or the need for digital platforms to implement a code of conduct to govern their relationships with users and media outlets.[38, 39]

In the United States, the Federal Trade Commission ("FTC") also embarked on the analysis of the digital economy with a two-pronged strategy. First, they led a comprehensive set of hearings on the state of competition and consumer protection law in the 21st century. Here, more than 350 panelists addressed topics like privacy, big data, the analysis of collusive, exclusionary and predatory conducts by digital and technology-based platform businesses, and the antitrust framework for evaluating acquisitions of potential or nascent competitors in digital marketplaces.[40] Second, they set up a Technology Enforcement Division dedicated to monitoring competition in U.S. technology markets, and investigating any potential anticompetitive conduct. As of now, the Technology Enforcement Division assesses *ex post* mergers in digital markets and provides technical assistance to the merger division in cases related to digital markets.

In Germany, the Federal Cartel Office ("FCO") is a "first-mover" in terms of tackling the issue of data privacy with competition law enforcement. In 2016, it initiated a proceeding against Facebook for the alleged abuse of its dominant position in

---

38 Australian Competition and Consumer Commission, Digital Platforms Inquiry (2019), https://www.accc.gov.au/publications/digital-platforms-inquiry-final-report.

39 With regards to this report, in December last year, the government of Australia released its response and implementation roadmap to the ACCC's Digital Platforms Inquiry. The creation of a specialized digital unit within the ACCC will be addressed immediately; other recommendations will need further consideration and engagement given the complexity of the issues and the potential to have economy-wide effects.

40 Bruce Hoffman, Director, Bureau of Competition, Federal Trade Commission, Antitrust in the Digital Economy: A Snapshot of FTC Issues, remarks at the GCR Live Antitrust in the Digital Economy (May 2019), https://www.ftc.gov/system/files/documents/public_statements/1522327/hoffman_-_gcr_live_san_francisco_2019_speech_5-22-19.pdf.

the market of social networks by applying unfair terms and conditions on the collection and use of users' personal data. Three years later, the FCO found Facebook guilty of inappropriately collecting, using and merging data of its users' different accounts. Moreover, Facebook's terms of service and the manner and extent to which it collected and used the data violated the European data protection rules.[41] Such conduct, according to the investigation, represents an exploitative abuse, so the FCO ordered changes to Facebook's data collection and usage practices.[42] The intersectionality of competition, consumer protection and privacy law violations in this case exemplifies the overlap often seen between these fields when dealing with digital markets.

In 2016, the FCO also launched the *Working Paper – Market Power of Platforms and Networks*, where it stated that the current antitrust tools are (almost) suitable for assessing digital platforms and networks. Nevertheless, it conceded that there is room for improvement in certain areas like merger control thresholds. When the working paper was published, merger thresholds were based on a turnover or revenue criterion. The problem with this was that when acquiring a startup, turnover or revenue values may be low enough to avoid thresholds. Hence, the FCO extended merger control to those cases where the *transaction value* of a takeover is particularly high. This will ensure that those cases where one of the parties generates no or only insignificant turnover, but where the competition potential of that party and/or the market relevance of the concentration are particularly high, will also face merger control.[43]

Consequently, in 2017 an additional threshold referring to the transaction value was introduced in Germany's competition law. Furthermore, a list of criteria, such as direct and indirect network effects, the parallel usage of multiple services, and

---

41   Peter Stauber, *Facebook's Abuse Investigation in Germany and Some Thoughts on Cooperation Between Antitrust and Data Protection Authorities*, CPI Antitrust Chronicle, (February 2019), http://noerr.com/Mailings/Kartellrecht/Brussels%20Matters%202019_04_11/CPI_Facebook%20investigation_Stauber.pdf.

42   The authority's decision covers changes in different data sources: (i) Facebook services like WhatsApp and Instagram can continue to collect data. However, assigning the data to Facebook user accounts will only be possible subject to the users' voluntary consent. Where consent is not given, the data must remain with the respective service and cannot be processed in combination with Facebook data. (ii) Collecting data from third party websites and assigning them to a Facebook user account will also only be possible if users give their voluntary consent. If consent is not given for data from Facebook-owned services and third-party websites, Facebook will have to substantially restrict its collection and combining of data. Bundeskartellamt, Press release *Bundeskartellamt prohibits Facebook from combining user data from different sources* (2019), https://www.bundeskartellamt.de/SharedDocs/Meldung/EN/Pressemitteilungen/2019/07_02_2019_Facebook.html.

43   Bundeskartellamt, Working Paper – Market Power of Platforms and Networks (2016), https://www.bundeskartellamt.de/SharedDocs/Publikation/EN/Berichte/Think-Tank-Bericht-Zusammenfassung.pdf?__blob=publicationFile&v=4.

consumer switching costs, was included in Germany's competition law to evaluate a firm's market position.[44]

At the academic front, the George J. Stigler Center for the Study of the Economy and the State issued a report on digital markets. Its principal conclusion stated that rapid self-correction in markets dominated by large digital platforms is unlikely, thus it is essential to combat big technology companies' anticompetitive conducts. Otherwise, the cost of not doing so will be very high.[45] The report suggests the creation of a specialized competition court in the U.S. dedicated to antitrust cases, and the creation of a digital authority that enacts *ex ante* regulations relevant to digital markets as a complement to competition law enforcement.[46] Yet, the report does not mention how these two new entities, particularly the digital authority, would interplay with the Federal Trade Commission and the Department of Justice, both already responsible for competition law enforcement in the U.S.

The endeavors described earlier display the issues at the core of the international debate on the digital economy. Although a few jurisdictions have obtained some clarity as to the future of competition policy in digital markets, they also leave questions open, as the full extent of the consequences of digital markets have not revealed themselves completely.

It is also important to mention that many of these analyses mainly focus on issues that come about with Google and Facebook business models, which differ from other big tech companies' monetizing models. Google and Facebook offer free services to users and primarily monetize through advertising. Given that data generation and harvesting is essential for selling digital advertising, this type of businesses have strong incentives to adopt conducts that protect their ability to exploit user data, as well as to control progressive stages of the ad-tech stack.[47] More recently, Amazon, as a marketplace, is starting to become a competition concern – "a point of consternation for competitors of all kind" as public companies mention it as a "risk factor" on their annual financial filings.[48]

In contrast, "match-making" or transaction businesses (e.g. Uber or Netflix) operate on the internet intermediating between two or more players. Their monetiz-

---

44   Justus Haucap, *et al.*, *Modernizing the law on abuse of market power in the digital age: a summary of the report for the German Ministry for Economic Affairs and Energy*, CPI Antitrust Chronicle (December 2019), https://www.competitionpolicyinternational.com/wp-content/uploads/2019/12/CPI-Haucap-Kerber-Schweitzer-Welker.pdf.

45   Stigler Center, *supra* note 20.

46   *Id.* at 79-80.

47   Cristina Caffarra, *"Follow the money"- Mapping issues with digital platforms into actionable theories of harm*, Concurrences (August 29, 2019), https://ecp.crai.com/wp-content/uploads/2019/09/e-Competitions-Special-Issue-Cristina-Caffarra.pdf.

48   The 14 charts that explain tech in 2019. Rani Molla, *supra* note 23.

ing strategy derives from taking a cut when a deal is struck. Transaction businesses raise competition concerns related to predatory prices to exclude current or potential entrants since rivals fight to attract existing demand. In addition, there are companies that function as true platforms (e.g. Amazon Web Services and Apple Store), that provide environments on which third parties can build their businesses and monetize in ways other than selling advertising. Competition agencies are paying attention to this type of platforms since some of them might have the incentive to foreclose competing apps by, for instance, self-preferencing.

Thus, when it comes to Big Tech companies operating on the internet, it is still not clear enough whether a sectoral ("tech") regulator is needed or if these are case-by-case issues.

At the Mexican antitrust agency ("COFECE") we pay special attention to the initiatives being developed by other countries and organizations to tackle the dynamics of digital markets. We are working on refining our understanding of digital markets and defining the path ahead, as we shall see in the following section.

V. DIGITAL MARKETS IN MEXICO

Mexico has an emerging economy that moves at two different speeds. Foremost, there are markets, often non-digitalized, in which lower-income households purchase basic products and services that account for a large percentage of their total expenditure. Because of their importance and impact on low income households, the Mexican competition agency cannot, and will not, be distracted from enforcing competition law in these markets.

Meanwhile, there are also markets that are immersed in a modern, global economy, that participate in worldwide production chains, and in many occasions are also part of the larger digitalization trend. As the digital economy begins to permeate the Mexican economy, we start to find some answers that will contribute to defining and implementing an effective policy vis à vis the digital economy.

A. What are the Possible Advantages of Digital Markets in the Mexican Context?

Similar to other competition agencies, COFECE is aware of the concerns raised by digital platforms in terms of competition, consumer protection and privacy. Nevertheless, given the fact that some markets in Mexico are still highly concentrated in the hands of traditional suppliers (e.g. energy, telecom, finance, retail, health), the usual concerns that stem from digital markets in more developed countries may not arise in a similar vein in the Mexican context.

So far, tech giants operating through digital platforms are an interesting source of competitive pressure for traditional incumbents with market power. For instance, Google and Facebook's activity is increasingly relevant in Mexico's advertising sector. For the first time in decades they pose a serious competitive threat to incumbent broadcasters also involved in the advertising business. Something similar happens in the retail sector with Amazon, where incumbents like Walmart have important levels of market concentration.

Therefore, the effects of tech giants in Mexican markets may not currently imply the same concerns as those identified in other geographical areas. Although COFECE is aware that digital platforms in our country may reach a tipping point which will present us with challenges similar to those faced by other jurisdictions.

The fact that digital platforms contribute to increased competition in Mexico's economy, as well as the concerns they may pose if they achieve a critical mass conferring them market power or even a dominant position, makes them a priority for the Commission going forward. Although competition law enforcement in Mexico still focuses more on traditional sectors, over the past several years COFECE has strengthened its knowledge and experience regarding digital markets.

B. What is COFECE's Experience in Digital Markets?

The Commission's experience on digital markets covers the fields of advocacy and enforcement. On the advocacy front, in 2015, as part of the global debate on whether governments should regulate Transportation Network Companies (TNCs, such as Uber, Didi, Lyft, and Cabify), COFECE issued an opinion directed at local authorities that recommended the recognition of TNCs services as a new mode of transportation. The Commission suggested that if regulation was deemed necessary by local authorities, it should be limited to the defense of public objectives such as security and user protection, prioritizing competition and free market access, and avoiding regulation which favors the incumbents of the traditional markets.

So far, thirteen states in Mexico have modified their legal framework or issued new regulations to recognize the business models under which TNCs operate. Yet, some aspects of TNC regulation remain unaddressed. For example: Is there is need for a specific federal legislation to guarantee certain consumer rights and user safety? Is it necessary to pay special attention to the price strategies used by digital platforms, or might contestability be enough to prevent potential anticompetitive behavior?

Later, in 2017, amid discussions on a draft law to regulate financial technology institutions, COFECE issued an opinion to the Mexican Senate recommending some changes to the draft law to encourage competition and innovation: (i) the stipulation of regulations that clearly establish data property and access; (ii) guaranteeing non-discrimination on behalf of larger financial institutions regarding fintechs; and (iii) eliminating infrastructure or technology restrictions that may hinder market entry. In 2018, the Fintech Law was passed attending COFECE's recommendations. Today, more than a year since the law passed, it is worth asking whether it fostered competition as it was intended, or did it instead deter the entry of new players to the Fintech sector. Will the arrival of Big Tech to the financial services market in Mexico be beneficial or harmful to our nascent Fintech ecosystem?

Regarding enforcement, COFECE opened its first investigation on a digital market in 2017. The scope of the investigation covers possible tie-in sales in e-Commerce platform services in Mexico. The investigation is still ongoing, so at the moment nothing more can be said, except that due to the nature of this investigation, COFECE faced the challenge of collecting and analyzing large volumes of information to identify possible anticompetitive behavior patterns (more than in any previous investigation at this agency).

Regarding mergers, in mid-2019, COFECE blocked the merger between Walmart, the biggest brick-and-mortar retailer in Mexico, and Cornershop, a start-up that provides home-delivery of products offered by different retailers (i.e. this would have been a vertical merger). The Commission blocked the merger because it identified the following risks: first, that Cornershop could refuse to offer its services to the retailer's competitors; second, that Walmart could refuse to offer its products on competing platforms; and third, that the new economic agent resulting from the transaction could induce Walmart's competitors to abandon Cornershop's platform due to the possible strategic use of the information produced by said competitors for retailing their products. In a nutshell, the merger meant a vertical integration where one of the merger parties had a dominant position in one of the links of the value chain.

An important lesson learned from the noted intervention is that merger analysis in digital markets must consider the effects on entrepreneurship and innovation. From this case, entrepreneurs now (should) know that, as part of their funding and exit strategies, they need to ponder that a merger review from the antitrust agency may be mandatory – something the Mexican entrepreneur community was not really aware of.

C. What Regulatory and Institutional Challenges Arise from the Digital Economy?

Existing laws in Mexico aim at regulating markets in the traditional economy. As the digital economy spreads to more sectors, two major concerns arise: (i) ensuring that sectoral laws will promote competition and protect consumer rights and privacy; and (ii) improving competition law to enhance its enforcement in digital markets.

As mentioned earlier, the Mexican Congress has passed a law to regulate fintech companies. So far, this is the only specific regulation at the national level related to digital markets. At the sub-national level, as already referred, a few states have passed laws regarding TNCs operation. The question is whether it is possible to produce a general criteria or regulation to which all innovative economic activities stemming from digital technologies should be subject to, or, as in the case of Fintech, this is a case-by-case scenario. In the Mexican case, the traditional retail sector is pushing, for example, for *ex ante* regulation (a new piece of legislation) for commercial practices for online marketplaces, including issues like prohibiting the use of sensitive data from independent retailers who sell on a marketplace if it determined as "relevant."

In terms of determining whether the Mexican competition law needs to be modified to effectively enforce competition in digital markets, COFECE, with the help of a group of outside experts, is in the process of assessing if it necessary to change Mexico's merger thresholds to avoid killer acquisitions, and other legislative modifications to facilitate the enforcement of laws to tackle digital markets. In order to make the best decisions, we are increasing our understanding of how international organizations, other jurisdictions, and experts are approaching the subject and proposing solutions.

On the institutional front, Mexico has built a robust group of agencies and a strong legal framework to oversee consumer protection, competition, and privacy issues. In 1976, Mexico established the Federal Consumer Protection Office ("PROFECO" in Spanish) to promote and protect consumer rights.

Then, in 1993, the Federal Competition Commission, COFECE's predecessor, was founded with the aim of guaranteeing competition and preventing and eliminating monopolistic practices and other restrictions to the efficient functioning of free markets.[49] Later, in 2013, two new competition authorities were established to enforce competition law: COFECE, dealing with competition matters over the entire economy, except for the telecommunications and broadcast sectors, and the Federal Institute of Telecommunications ("IFT"), a sectoral regulator, dealing exclusively with competition enforcement in these two sectors.

Privacy protection is more recent in Mexican law. The Federal Institute for Access to Information and Protection of Personal Data ("IFAI" in Spanish)[50] was created in 2002. Eight years later, the Federal Law on Protection of Personal Data Held by Private Parties was issued, followed by the Federal Law on Protection of Personal Data Held by Obliged Subjects, in force since 2017. The responsibility to monitor

---

49 Jorge Anaya, *et al.*, Evolución del derecho de la competencia en México, Boletín Mexicano de Derecho Comparado, https://revistas.juridicas.unam.mx/index.php/derecho-comparado/article/view/4574/5866.

50 In 2015, IFAI changed its name to National Institute of Transparency, Access to information and Protection of Personal Data (INAI in Spanish).

the compliance of both Laws lies with the National Institute of Transparency, Access to Information and Protection of Personal Data (IFAI's successor). Despite such advancements, privacy law remains largely unenforced and vague for tech platforms. There isn't a code of conduct for technology companies to make their privacy policies clear and transparent for users.

Although this is a robust institutional design, it is important to bear in mind that all these agencies were created to regulate their respective fields in the context of a traditional economy, where each one's sphere of action was mostly clear-cut. Nevertheless, the digitalization of the economy is giving rise to increasing hybrid cases that potentially could fall under two or more institutions.

For example, as this article is being written, COFECE and IFT (telecom and broadcast regulator) face a controversy regarding who the competition agency responsible for analyzing the merger between Uber and Cornershop (an online platform that provides home-delivery of products offered by different retailers) is. IFT argues that digital platforms in general, as well as the services they provide through them, are part of the telecom value chain, and therefore they consider themselves to be competent to review the merger. On the other hand, COFECE argues that both digital platforms at stake are match makers where several intermediations of services take place (e.g. between Uber drivers and users, between restaurants and delivery persons), and that those services are different from telecom. Additionally, neither Uber nor Cornershop require a telecom concession to run their operations in Mexico. By Mexican law, when there is a conflict of competence, the Judiciary is responsible for adjudicating the case to one of the two agencies.

This new scenario calls, in the short run, for continued close cooperation among authorities to avoid the unnecessary burdens of having parallel reviews. Yet, Mexico is obliged to assess whether this current institutional design is sustainable for addressing the challenges ahead.

With the help of a group of experts we are trying to solve the following questions: How would a forward-looking institutional landscape have to be organized? How can we eventually adjust the current institutional design to eliminate gray areas of responsibility? How can we facilitate coordination among agencies to better address the shifting dynamics of the digital economy? Would it be necessary to create a new legal framework that gives way for such an eventual institutional landscape? Or maybe, would it be possible to amalgamate competition, consumer and privacy issues under one agency?

VI.   COFECE'S ACTIONS TO DEAL WITH DIGITAL MARKETS

Like other competition agencies, COFECE has spent some time grasping the ins and outs of digital markets in general and how they operate in Mexico particularly.

We are assessing their advantages and concerns in the Mexican context while weighing possible regulatory and institutional needs.

As mentioned before, we are gathering a group of outside experts to advise on how to take on challenges arising from the current context, including a revision of the adequacy of the Mexican institutional design. The group aims to bring about a policy paper that addresses the functioning of digital markets, their advantages and perils in terms of competition, consumer protection and privacy in the Mexican context, the work done by other countries in seeking to comprehend and tackle this phenomenon, Mexico's current agency layout and possible alternatives to increase cooperation among related authorities. The need (or not) to change the competition act or other laws, or the institutional landscape will also be assessed

Likewise, COFECE will carry out a set of actions which I have somewhat previewed in previous sections, namely: (i) work on the design and creation of a multidisciplinary division to handle issues related to digital markets; (ii) implement a capacity building strategy regarding data management and economic analysis in digital markets; and (iii) bring in first-hand knowledge on digital markets to COFECE's staff directly from the global experts developing it.

This set of short-term actions will be part of a medium-term strategy under a broader public policy approach to make Mexico, its laws, and its institutional design fit for the digital transformation that lies ahead.

Data Portability: The Case of Open Banking and the Potential for Competition

By Vinicius Marques de Carvalho[1] & Marcela Mattiuzzo[2]

Abstract

This article aims to present the concept of data portability and its relevance for competition policy. It departs from the understanding that portability is a potential remedy for several issues that arise in digital markets, and therefore a very relevant aspect of the ever-growing global discussion surrounding this matter. At the same time, it calls attention for the fact that portability is a tool specifically provided for in data protection legislation, and as such must comply with data subjects' rights. It presents open banking as an example of a regulatory effort that is placed in that intersection, that has been grappling precisely with that challenge, and for that reason can help us understand and think of solutions for applying portability in other sectors.

I.   INTRODUCTION

The discussion surrounding digital markets and their dependence on data has possibly been the most debated topic in antitrust analysis worldwide for the past year. From Argentina to Zambia, authorities are constantly analyzing how to tackle the digital economy and its data-related issues. One aspect that has been greatly emphasized throughout these debates relates to the challenges of ensuring more competition, and more specifically the difficulty in designing remedies that effectively allow for competition to emerge without hindering individuals' rights, notably the right to data protection. In that context, provisions that call for data portability – set forth in data protection legislation in several jurisdictions – have gained special relevance. The goal of this article is to present some advances in data portability in the context of the financial

---

1   Professor of Commercial Law at the University of São Paulo, former President of CADE, former Secretary of Economic Law, Yale Greenberg World Fellow, and Partner at VMCA.

2   PhD Candidate at the University of São Paulo, Master of Laws (USP), Visiting Researcher at Yale Law School, former Chief of Staff and Advisor at the Office of the President at CADE, and Partner at VMCA.

sector, through so-called open banking initiatives, and what such advances could mean for a broader approach to portability in terms of its potential to stimulate competition.

To do so, we will first briefly present the concept of data portability, and the origin of this provision in connection with data protection legislation. Second, we will focus on the potential clash between competition and privacy in implementing data portability solutions. Third, we will present the case of open banking, one of the first sector-wide initiatives that has been either implemented or discussed in several jurisdictions and can provide useful inputs for the broader debate. Finally, we will point towards the main challenges we foresee for this discussion and its next steps.

II. THE CONCEPT AND ORIGIN OF DATA PORTABILITY

Discussions about the portability of data are by no means recent, but they naturally became more relevant and pervasive with the exponential growth of data gathering which took place over the past 20 years. The debate gained traction, as explained by Zanfir,[3] when portability of information gathered on the Internet started to pose a challenge for users – e.g. individuals who uploaded their pictures to one online service and later wanted to take these files somewhere else. Thus, the initial legal dimension of the discussion was focused on users' rights to control their own information, in line with one of the fundamental ideas behind data protection legislation as it is currently understood: empowering users as the rightful owners of their information.[4] However, it rapidly evolved to and embraced a competitive dimension, as portability started to be seen as a means for granting competitors access to what was being perceived as a potentially relevant asset – users' data.[5]

Data portability was first put into law by the European Union. The term appeared in the initial drafts of what we now know as the General Data Protection Regu-

---

3 Zanfir, Gabriela, The right to Data portability in the context of the EU data protection reform," International Data Privacy Law, 2012.

4 It is frequently said that this idea for its turn developed from the principle of informational self-determination. Informational self-determination was first presented in the German ruling by the Federal Constitutional Court about the 1983 census, BVerfGE, 65, 1, Available at http://sorminiserv.unibe.ch:8080/tools/ainfo.exe?Command=ShowPrintText&Name=bv065001. The term is usually defined in English as "the authority of the individual to decide himself, on the basis of the idea of self-determination, when and within what limits information about his private life should be communicated to others."

5 Janal, Ruth. Data Portability – A Tale of Two Concepts. JIPITEC 8 (2017) 1. Available at https://pdfs.semanticscholar.org/1a3d/5eb2e130b95560764e36f18576dd3186e443.pdf?_ga=2.109718790.2009351782.1579556987-99031023.1579556987.

lation ("GDPR"), and was finally sedimented in its Article 20.[6] The double function of data portability as a tool for both users and for competitors was strengthened by the GPDR. Recital 68, for instance, states that the goal of the rule is to reinforce data subject's control over his/her data, and also that data controllers "should be encouraged to develop interoperable formats that enable data portability."[7]

Given the impact the GDPR has had on data protection legislation in many other jurisdictions, it comes as no surprise that data portability was also "exported" to

---

6 It reads: "(1) The data subject shall have the right to receive the personal data concerning him or her, which he or she has provided to a controller, in a structured, commonly used and machine-readable format and have the right to transmit those data to another controller without hindrance from the controller to which the personal data have been provided, where:

A)   the processing is based on consent pursuant to point (a) of Article 6 (1) or point (a) of Article 9 (2) or on a contract pursuant to point (b) of Article 6 (1); and

B)   the processing is carried out by automated means.

(2) In exercising his or her right to data portability pursuant to paragraph 1, the data subject shall have the right to have the personal data transmitted directly from one controller to another, where technically feasible.

(3) The exercise of the right referred to in paragraph 1 of this Article shall be without prejudice to Article 17. That right shall not apply to processing necessary for the performance of a task carried out in the public interest or in the exercise of official authority vested in the controller.

(4) The right referred to in paragraph 1 shall not adversely affect the rights and freedoms of others."

7 It reads: "(68) To further strengthen the control over his or her own data, where the processing of personal data is carried out by automated means, the data subject should also be allowed to receive personal data concerning him or her which he or she has provided to a controller in a structured, commonly used, machine-readable and interoperable format, and to transmit it to another controller.

Data controllers should be encouraged to develop interoperable formats that enable data portability. That right should apply where the data subject provided the personal data on the basis of his or her consent or the processing is necessary for the performance of a contract.

It should not apply where processing is based on a legal ground other than consent or contract. By its very nature, that right should not be exercised against controllers processing personal data in the exercise of their public duties.

It should therefore not apply where the processing of the personal data is necessary for compliance with a legal obligation to which the controller is subject or for the performance of a task carried out in the public interest or in the exercise of an official authority vested in the controller. The data subject's right to transmit or receive personal data concerning him or her should not create an obligation for the controllers to adopt or maintain processing systems which are technically compatible.

Where, in a certain set of personal data, more than one data subject is concerned, the right to receive the personal data should be without prejudice to the rights and freedoms of other data subjects in accordance with this Regulation.

Furthermore, that right should not prejudice the right of the data subject to obtain the erasure of personal data and the limitations of that right as set out in this Regulation and should, in particular, not imply the erasure of personal data concerning the data subject which have been provided by him or her for the performance of a contract to the extent that and for as long as the personal data are necessary for the performance of that contract."

many countries, and added to local data protection legislation.[8] It is interesting to note that despite having reached many jurisdictions by the hands of data protection the debate surrounding data portability is today much more latent in antitrust or regulatory authorities. 2019 saw the release of several studies by authorities and experts on digital markets and competition.[9] In all of them, the topic of data portability or interoperability was discussed at length.[10] Most DPAs, on the other hand, have been focusing their enforcement and advocacy work on other topics.[11]

---

8   Even in the U.S., which is usually referred to as the opposite model of data protection legislation, for it has adopted sectorial and fragmented legislation, recent initiatives have become closer to the European model, proposing centralized enforcement and rules that apply to any company, in any economic sector.

9   The United Kingdom release a study entitled Unlocking Digital Competition, available at https://assets.publishing.service.gov.uk/government/uploads/system/uploads/attachment_data/file/785547/unlocking_digital_competition_furman_review_web.pdf, the European Commission published a report by experts regarding Competing Policy for the Digital Era: https://ec.europa.eu/competition/publications/reports/kd0419345enn.pdf, the Australian competition authority conducted an inquiry on digital platforms and later release a report to gather its findings: https://www.accc.gov.au/publications/digital-platforms-inquiry-final-report, the Stigler Center at the University of Chicago drafted a report on digital platforms as well: https://research.chicagobooth.edu/stigler/media/news/committee-on-digital-platforms-final-report, the BRICS published a report about the digital economy: http://www.cade.gov.br/acesso-a-informacao/publicacoes-institucionais/brics_report.pdf.

10   On "Unlocking Digital Competition," see the Section "Function 2a: Personal data mobility," p. 65. On "Competition Policy for the Digital Era," see the Section "Data Portability (Article 20 GDPR) and Competition," p. 81. On the "Digital Platforms Inquiry," see the Section "2.10.1 Data portability and interoperability," p. 276. On the "Stigler Committee on Digital Platforms," see Section "2. Data Control and Ownership," p. 51. At last, on the "BRICS in the digital economy: Competition Policy in Practice," see "Box 1 – Data protection legislation," p. 24. Apart from the reports referenced in the note above, see: BEIS and DCMS, Smart Data Review: terms of reference, 2018. Available at https://www.gov.uk/government/publications/smart-data-review/smart-data-review-terms-of-reference.

11   On an interview regarding the first year of GDPR, Andrea Jelinek, EDPB Chair and Director of the Austrian Data Protection Authority, stated that: "*since its creation, the EDPB has endorsed the 16 GDPR related Working Party 29 (WP29) guidelines and adopted 7 guidelines and a recommendation of its own. In addition, the EDPB completed its first major consistency exercise, which resulted in the adoption of 31 opinions on national data protection impact assessment (DPIA) lists. […] So far, the EDPB has organised 2 stakeholder events and 7 public consultations, of which 3 are still ongoing.*" Among the Guidelines, there are the Guidelines on the Criteria of the right to be forgotten in the search engines, the Guidelines on Personal Data Breach notification, as examples. ICO, by its turn, has published Guidelines on Standard Contractual Clauses and Guidelines on Law Enforcement Processing. It shows that there are a number of subjects on the DPA's agenda. The referred interview can be found at https://privacyconference2019.info/edpb-chair-andrea-jelinek-calls-for-more-global-convergence-on-data-protection-and-closer-cooperation-between-competition-data-protection-regulators/.

Many are the reasons that can explain this scenario, but two deserve further attention. First, DPAs, unlike antitrust authorities, are recent in most jurisdictions, and as such are much more focused on bringing awareness and ensuring minimal standards that should be adopted by the private sector for the treatment of individuals' data. Antitrust, on the other hand, can be said to have overcome that initial stage and is now turning to more complex issues. Second, competition authorities were not conceived in the context of digital markets, and are now grappling with the new challenges brought about by them, which has led to the questioning of its economic and legal tools, and to discussions on how to ensure more competitive digital environments in the future. The (somehow simplistic) diagnostic antitrust had to deal with saw data as "the new oil,"[12] the resource without which entry was not feasible. Because the digital environment was described as dominated by a limited number of very large companies – later nicknamed GAFA – it was imperative to find solutions that would allow for new entry. Though this simplistic description was later questioned by authorities themselves, it is in that context that data portability has flourished, as a potential remedy that would allow for more competition to emerge and consequently for more rivalry among tech companies.

Portability is not an entirely novel solution for competition challenges. As noted by Gene Kimmelman, a cornerstone of telecom regulation in the United States is precisely the interconnection of carriers.[13] The same holds true in other countries, such as Brazil, where portability is also a rule in the private healthcare system.[14] It is however undoubtedly novel to bring about to the extent that would be required in the digital environment, which also brings challenges related to potential incompatibility of competition and data protection goals, as will be explored in the next section.

III. COMPETITION vs. PRIVACY

The ultimate objective of both competition and data protection can be understood as being the same: ensuring citizens' rights and well-being. The methods by which they reach such goals, however, is very different. Data protection deals directly with individuals' rights and data holders' obligations, whereas antitrust regulation is

---

12 The Economist. "The world's most valuable resource is no longer oil, but data: The data economy demands a new approach to antitrust rules." May 6, 2017. Available at https://www.economist.com/leaders/2017/05/06/the-worlds-most-valuable-resource-is-no-longer-oil-but-data.

13 Shorenstein Center, "The Right Way to Regulate Digital Platforms," Digital Platforms & Democracy Project, 2017. Available at https://shorensteincenter.org/the-right-way-to-regulate-digital-platforms/. More of the Project can be found at https://shorensteincenter.org/about-us/areas-of-focus/platform-accountability/.

14 Agência Nacional de Saúde. Resolução Normativa – RN nº 438, December 3, 2018. Available at http://www.ans.gov.br/component/legislacao/?view=legislacao&task=TextoLei&format=raw&id=MzY1NA==.

focused on the competitive environment, on the premise that if markets are competitive, consumers will necessarily be better off.

These differences in approach can cause the policies to sometimes walk in different directions depending on the circumstances, and data portability is one such scenario in which their interests could be misaligned. As mentioned, the idea behind data portability from a data protection standpoint is ensuring users are effectively the ones who decide how and when their data flows. As such, not only should they be able to choose if their data is to be deleted from a given platform, they should also be able to decide if they want to take their information elsewhere. The focus, thus, is on the individual.

Competition law, on the other hand, is primarily concerned with ensuring economic agents are able to compete effectively in the market. If one understands data as a relevant asset for such development, then the natural conclusion is that the ideal scenario is one in which information is available broadly, to whoever is interested in having access to it.

It is easy to see why these approaches can collide. If data protection wants to empower users, it must let users decide when, if, and to whom access to their data should be granted. Competition, on the other hand, wants agents to thrive, and therefore to have broad and unlimited access to data. This tension has been identified by other authors, and even recently by companies in their attempt to develop and discuss data portability standards and programs.[15] Concretely, many layers of the debate can be visualized in social networks. By its nature, information shared on such platforms is usually linked to other individuals – a picture where someone else is tagged, a check-in alongside someone else, a post that mentions another person, etc. When implementing data portability, it is natural for companies to wonder how they should approach a request from a data subject regarding such information. If she wants to port this data to another network, how should this transfer be carried out? After all, it is not solely her information that is being transferred, but also that of her connections.

A data protection advocate would likely say that one needs to analyze the potential for anonymization for this transfer to take place, and also the technical viability of separating the data from the subject who requested the transfer from that of her

---

15 See: Diker Vanberg, A. & Ünver, MB., "The right to data portability in the GDPR and EU competition law: odd couple or dynamic duo?," in European Journal of Law and Technology, Vol 8, No 1, 2017. Available at http://data-reuse.eu/wp-content/uploads/2016/01/International-Data-Privacy-Law-2016-Custers.pdf. See also: Custers, B. & Ursˇicˇ, H., "Big data and data reuse: a taxonomy of data reuse for balancing big data benefits and personal data protection," in International Data Privacy Law, 2016. Available at https://arro.anglia.ac.uk/701565/1/Diker%20Vanberg_2017.pdf. Facebook's white paper, "Data Portability and Privacy," in turn, can be found at https://about.fb.com/wp-content/uploads/2019/09/data-portability-privacy-white-paper.pdf.

connections. Certainly, those concerns are aligned with the goal of ensuring individuals' control over their data. But from a competition standpoint, they are problematic, largely because recent research has shown that data is more valuable when it:

> contains rich information about a huge number of people. This is even more true when the rich information contains different types of data, for example, email, location, and search queries. A dataset of this type allows the provider to both learn high-level population statistics (for which it needs a large population in its dataset) and to carefully tailor its ads to each individual in its dataset (because it has very rich information about users in the dataset).[16]

Despite much of the recent debate on this topic having been carried out by antitrust authorities, the provision itself is put forward in data protection legislation, which means it cannot be implemented in a way that hinders individuals' rights. Enforcers have the burden of coming up with alternatives that balance these interests and do not eliminate or hamper data subjects' interests. As will be seen in the next section, that is the challenge Open Banking initiatives have had to address.

IV.   THE CASE OF OPEN BANKING

Among the different arrangements that can make room for data portability, one of the most discussed initiatives is Open Banking. Open Banking can be understood as a collaborative commercial model through which third unaffiliated parties can access banking data by using Application Programming Interfaces ("APIs"), following customer consent. According to the United Kingdom Treasury:

> "Application programming interfaces, or APIs, allow two pieces of software to interact with each other. In banking, APIs can be used to enable financial technology (fintech) firms to make use of customers' bank data on their behalf and with their permission in innovative and helpful ways. For instance, through external bank APIs customers can make use of applications on their smartphones which allow them to see clearly how much money they spend on food, and how their spending on food fluctuates through the course of a month or year."[17]

---

16   Stigler Center for the Study of the Economy and the State. Stigler Committee on Digital Platforms. P. 46/47. Available at https://research.chicagobooth.edu/stigler/media/news/committee-on-digital-platforms-final-report.

17   "Data sharing and open data in banking: response to the call for evidence," HM Treasury. March 2015. Available at https://assets.publishing.service.gov.uk/government/uploads/system/uploads/attachment_data/file/413766/PU1793_Open_data_response.pdf.

Different Open Banking initiatives have flourished around the globe, varying in key aspects and their regulatory approach. Apart from the more conventional models of Open Banking, it should be noted that there are other digital ecosystem initiatives that have been handling data sharing, like WeChat and Alibaba in China. Those non-bank insurgents, in the recent years, have also included financial and payment services in their portfolio.

Nonetheless, the most typical Open Banking approaches are the ones implemented in the European Union, through the Second Payment Services Directive ("PSD2"), and in the United Kingdom, through different courses of action taken by the Competition and Markets Authority ("CMA").

Since 2016,[18] the CMA has been applying considerable efforts to foster competition and innovation in payment services and retail banking. Among those efforts, the most significant and impactful remedy has been the UK's Open Banking Standard, aimed at addressing more structural problems in the British banking sector. The UK's Open Banking Standard came into force in early 2017, pushing the UK's nine largest retail banks to implement standardized banking data protocols in order to permit access by registered unaffiliated third parties. The principles that rule the UK's Open Banking Standard are also present in PSD2, administered by the European Commission.

Replacing the original 2009 Directive, PSD2 serves as a method to standardize payments regulation and consumer protection across the European Union. PSD2 was implemented in January 2016, and aimed at encouraging competition throughout the European banking sector, through innovation. It intends to promote transparency, security, quality and lower prices for costumers. PSD2 was also particularly concerned with the relevance of open banking principles to the fostering of innovation and improvement of consumer welfare. One of the most important principles of PSD2 is that, with the account holder's consent, all registered third-party providers ("TPPs") must have access to data and be able to execute the holder's instructions.

In parallel, by August 2015, the UK had already established the Open Banking Working Group ("OBWG"), to create a legal and technological framework for APIs standard in banking. In 2016, the CMA published its recommendations on the issue. Those movements resulted in what is called the Implementation Entity, responsible for creating common technical standards for open banking, that since 2017 has been applied as the UK's Open Banking Standard.

---

18   The concerns with the concentration of the banking sector and its adverse effects on competition can be found in the 2016 Retail banking market investigation. Its final report concluded that remedies must be applied in order to tackle the structural competitive problems. The main remedy proposed was Open Banking. The report is available here: https://assets. publishing.service.gov.uk/media/57ac9667e5274a0f6c00007a/retail-banking-market-investigation-full-final-report.pdf.

Reinforcing our perceptions laid out in Section 2,[19] the implementation of Open Baking in the UK followed a growing concern from the CMA with the concentration and lack of effective competition in the British banking sector. To address those competitive issues, the authority proposed a wide-reaching package of reforms, which included the requirement that banks implement Open Banking by early 2018. Different from PSD2, the Open Banking initiative in the UK set out clearer requirements related to the format of APIs, and their security and usability. The UK's nine biggest banks – HSBC, Barclays, RBS, Santander, Bank of Ireland, Allied Irish Bank, Danske, Lloyds, and Nationwide – were therefore required to share their data with TTPs in a standardized form. The data includes the location of branches and the exact details of certain banking products, including price.

The scheme is managed by Open Banking Limited, a non-profit organization created exclusively for this purpose, and monitored by the CMA itself. Owing to that reform, the UK can be considered the first country to implement a binding data sharing approach, since PSD2 was agreed in 2013, giving five years for banks to adapt in the EU, while the UK took the lead and implemented it though its own national law shortly after the publication of the report "Data sharing and open data in banking: response to the call for evidence," by the UK Treasury.[20]

As we approach the final steps of Brexit, there are obvious expectations regarding how the framework of Open Banking in Europe will change. It is important to note that many of PSD2's provisions are already implemented in national UK law, and have the support from both the government and the financial community. In addition, the British approach has had a clear influence on other jurisdictions. In the first Australian guidance on the subject, for example, there are at least 50 references to the UK Open Banking initiative.[21]

However developed and successful the UK experience has been, there are several other forms of Open Banking. In India, for example, the Open Banking efforts were adopted by regulators on two separate fronts: the first related to payments, while the other related to the sharing of financial data. Unlike PSD2 and the UK Open

---

19   Accordingly, on the "Unlocking Digital Competition" report, the United Kingdom stated, on Box 2.E (p. 69) that: "The reforms to deliver Open Banking were pursued by the CMA following a market investigation, as a remedy to boost competition and innovation in the retail banking market. The CMA used its order-making powers to require the largest banks to implement Open Banking, working with representatives from the wider industry." Available at https://assets.publishing.service.gov.uk/government/uploads/system/uploads/attachment_data/file/785547/unlocking_digital_competition_furman_review_web.pdf.

20   See Note 17 above.

21   See: "Open Banking: Customers choice, convenience, confidence. Australian Government. December 2017." Available at https://static.treasury.gov.au/uploads/sites/1/2018/02/Review-into-Open-Banking-_For-web-1.pdf

Banking Standard, there are different agents that manage the "open payments" eco-system and the "open data" ecosystem, respectively. The front addressing the payment sector was developed through the implementation of the Unified Payments Interface ("UPI"), a real-time payment ecosystem developed by the National Payments Corporation of India ("NPCI"). The other is managed by non-banking financial companies - account aggregators ("NBFC-AA").[22]

Yet another example is that of Brazil, which is currently at the initial stages of implementing Open Banking. In November, the Central Bank of Brazil released to public consultation a proposed regulatory framework.[23] It is worth noting that the authority is specifically proposing that implementation be phased, especially in terms of the institutions that will be affected by it. First, only those that are legally defined as financial institutions as per Regulation 4533/2017 will be subjected to the new rules. Only after this initial phase would payment institutions and others be affected. This is largely because regulation of this first group of companies is much more severe and follows much stricter criteria, and currently there is no clarity as to how liability would be attributed in case violations occurred owing to information shared because of the new rules.

Though not many studies have yet been carried out by official institutions to measure the impact of Open Banking initiatives, it is clear it offers a great opportunity for consumers and companies alike. Because it was implemented within a heavily regulated sector, questions such as the need for consent from users were easily addressed. Also, because the number of players subject to the rules was controlled, and patterns already to some extent existed within the market (for example, the names of tariffs in Brazil have already been standardized across banks for a while), many of the broader issues that come to light when implementing this solution in digital markets were mitigated.

V.   CONCLUDING REMARKS: THE CHALLENGES AHEAD

Initiatives that go beyond Open Banking are already being discussed today. Notably, the Data Transfer Project, launched in 2018 by Apple, Facebook, Google, Microsoft, and Twitter, aims to "create an open-source, service-to-service data por-

---

22   Account aggregators are companies aimed to connect Financial Information Providers to Financial Information Users, while making sure that the consumer's consent was given, and could be revoked at any time. The Master Directions from the Department of Non-Banking Regulation (DNBR) defined 18 classes of financial information that can be exchanged through NBFC-AA, like Insurance Policies, Equity Shares and Debentures. See Master Direction- Non-Banking Financial Company - Account Aggregator (Reserve Bank) Directions, 2016. Available at https://www.rbi.org.in/Scripts/NotificationUser.aspx?Id=10598&Mode=0.

23   The public consultation and the proposals for normative acts that provide for the implementation of Open Banking can be found on: https://www3.bcb.gov.br/audpub/DetalharAudienciaPage?0&pk=322. Proposals can be sent until 31/01/2020.

tability platform so that all individuals across the web could easily move their data between online service providers whenever they want."[24] Some concrete steps have been taken by this group, such as the transferring of photos from one application to another.[25] Moreover, many academics are turning to portability and studying the topic in greater depth to better grasp its potential for competition.

One of the conclusions so far has been that the idea of portability alone is not enough to tackle competition. Specialists have emphasized that one of the ways by which digital environments will become more competitive in the future is by ensuring users can multi-home. Though it is a natural tendency for individuals to single-home – because it indeed is much easier to find solutions for different needs within the same platform – multi-homing may ensure greater degrees of innovation and competitiveness. Therefore, it is more important to enable interoperability than portability. Users do not necessarily want to leave a platform altogether, but they may want to have the information they have shared with that platform available elsewhere as well.

Perhaps the main challenge in this debate will be defining the limits of the most basic concept in data protection debates: personal data itself. Not enough effort has been put into better understanding this concept and its extension. Though it is clear that someone's name is a piece of information that can be defined as personal data, it is much less clear when (and if) so-called "inferred" data should be considered

---

24   More details available at https://datatransferproject.dev/.

25   Andrew Rossow. "Facebook Introduces 'Data Transfer Project' Allowing for Seamless Photo Transfer," GritDaily. Dec 2, 2019. Available at https://gritdaily.com/facebook-announces-data-transfer-project-for-photo-transfer/.

personal, and what companies' claims to such data are.[26] After all, inferred data is only possible due to a combination of individuals' data and an algorithm that is capable of reading that information in a specific way, so as to find correlations. It makes sense to argue that this data only exists in its final form because of an investment made by a company in that database, and perhaps to understand that it is therefore not properly "personal." If that holds true, it is questionable whether such information should be subject to portability.

From the point of view of competition, the answer is equally tricky. As mentioned, more information is theoretically better for potential competition. But if the data in question was developed by a company, its transfer could constitute access to competitively sensitive information. It could, moreover, lead to the standardization of algorithms, something that has been pointed out as harmful to competition.

The main conclusion, therefore, is that in order to reach solutions for portability that both address data subjects' rights and competitors' interests, much cooperation will be needed. Among authorities, in order to better define their respective contributions and jurisdictions over the topic. Among experts, who will need to combine different capabilities (technical, legal, even sociological) to develop proposals. And among the public and private sectors, given that the pace of innovation in the market is tremendous, and if the regulators are always trying to catch up to companies, they will likely reach inadequate answers to obsolete questions. It is a real challenge, but similar problems have been successfully addressed before.

---

26 According to "Competition Policy for the Digital Era," referenced on Note 7 above: "Data can be categorised as volunteered, observed, and inferred data. The type of data might influence the capacity of competitors to gather or obtain the same information independently." It goes further, stating: "Data is acquired through three main channels. First, some data is volunteered, i.e. intentionally contributed by the user of a product. A name, email, image/video, calendar information, review, or a post on social media would qualify as volunteered data. Similarly, more structured data—directly generated by an individual—like a movie rating, or liking a song or post would also fall in the volunteered data category.
Second, some data is observed. In the modern era, many activities leave a digital trace, and "observed data" refers to more behavioral data obtained automatically from a user's or a machine's activity. The movement of individuals is traced by their mobile phone; telematic data records the roads taken by a vehicle and the behaviour of its driver; every click on a page web can be logged by the website and third party software monitors the way in which its visitors are behaving. In manufacturing, the development of the Internet of Things means that every machine produces reams of data on how it functions, what its sensors are recording, and what it is currently doing or producing.
Finally, some data is inferred, that is obtained by transforming in a non-trivial manner volunteered and/or observed data while still related to a specific individual or machine. This will include a shopper's or music fan's profiles, e.g. categories resulting from clustering algorithms or predictions about a person's propensity to buy a product, or credit ratings. The distinction between volunteered, observed and inferred data is not always clear. Grey zones exist, and we do not propose to turn the distinction into a legal one" (our emphasis).

Algorithmic Collusion: Fear of the Unknown or too Smart to Catch?

By Gönenç Gürkaynak, Burcu Can & Sinem Uğur[1]

Abstract

Algorithms, which businesses use more and more to set pricing strategies with each passing day, could be pro-competitive and provide significant efficiencies. Depending on how firms use them, however, they can also potentially restrict competition and harm consumers. Scholars and enforcers debate on the right scope of the theory of harm as to using algorithms in critical competition parameters, particularly in pricing strategies. Yet, one question remains open: if firms use algorithms that may tacitly collude through machine learning - particularly deep learning technologies, will that alone be sufficient to hold them liable for a competition law infringement? This article discusses the current limits of the collective knowledge on this subject and explores what guidance could still be provided to businesses. The article argues that the solution does not lie in taking premature regulatory actions without sufficient empirical evidence to justify any shift away from the traditional concepts of tacit collusion, or without proper guidance for companies to avoid the risk of legal exposure. The need is evident for further research on how self-learning algorithms operate in real-life settings, which could start defining a "red zone" for businesses to watch out and for enforcers to focus their energy and resources.

I.   INTRODUCTION

The rise of algorithms in many sectors and particularly in the digital markets has triggered a debate on whether and how these advanced tools now used increasingly by

---

1   Gönenç Gürkaynak is the founding partner of ELIG Gürkaynak Attorneys-at-Law, and a member of faculty at Bilkent University, Faculty of Law and Bilgi University, Faculty of Law. Burcu Can is a partner at ELIG Gürkaynak Attorneys-at-Law. Sinem Uğur is an associate at ELIG Gürkaynak Attorneys-at-Law.

many businesses[2] can impede competition.[3] A number of prominent scholars, with Ezrachi & Stucke on the frontline, took a first stab at laying out the theoretical framework of this thought-provoking debate.[4] Competition authorities around the world have since lined up to voice their concerns and mark their positions with respect to this new "player" in the game.[5] While this player may be relatively new, the questions at the front and center are well-known: What is the theory of harm as to using algorithms in critical competition parameters, particularly in pricing strategies? What is the standard of proof? The latter is still somewhat an uncharted territory, although we have observed some interesting – and to a certain extent, alarming – theories on how pricing algorithms can potentially lead to restrictions of competition that may harm consumers (e.g. by increasing prices).

Algorithms are not inherently good or bad - depending on how companies use them, they can be pro-competitive or anti-competitive.[6] Their potential pro-competitive effects involve both (i) supply-side efficiencies, which can be achieved by increasing transparency, improving existing products or developing new ones, reducing production costs, improving quality and resource utilization, streamlining business

---

2   European Commission's Staff Working Document reported in 2017 that "*53% of respondent retailers track the online prices of competitors, and 67% of those also use automatic software programmes for that purpose.*" (Commission Staff Working Document-*accompanying the document*-Report from the Commission to the Council and the European Parliament Final Report on the E-commerce Sector Inquiry, COM 229 (2017), p. 51, para. 149, available at https://eur-lex.europa.eu/resource.html?uri=cellar:9d1137d3-3570-11e7-a08e-01aa75ed71a1.0001.02/DOC_1&format=PDF) (last accessed Apr. 16, 2020). According to a market study by the Dresner Advisory Services in 2019, a significant number of the participating companies' sales and marketing departments were either currently using or evaluating data science and machine learning software (Louis Columbus, *State of AI and Machine Learning in 2019*, FORBES (Sept. 8, 2019), available at https://www.forbes.com/sites/louiscolumbus/2019/09/08/state-of-ai-and-machine-learning-in-2019/#c9df3331a8d0 (last accessed Apr. 16, 2020).

3   As pointed out by Thibault Schrepel, Google Scholar listed 141 academic articles that discussed "algorithmic collusion" from January 2017 to early 2020. (See Thibault Schrepel, *The Fundamental Unimportance of Algorithmic Collusion for Antitrust Law*, HARV. J.L. & TECH. (2020), fn. 4, available at https://jolt.law.harvard.edu/digest/the-fundamental-unimportance-of-algorithmic-collusion-for-antitrust-law) (last accessed Apr. 16, 2020). This number has now reached 171.

4   See, e.g. ARIEL EZRACHI & MAURICE E. STUCKE, VIRTUAL COMPETITION: THE PROMISE AND PERILS OF THE ALGORITHM-DRIVEN ECONOMY, Cambridge, Massachusetts: Harvard University Press (2016); Ashwin Ittoo & Nicolas Petit, *Algorithmic Pricing Agents and Tacit Collusion: A Technological Perspective*, L'INTELLIGENCE ARTIFICIELLE ET LE DROIT, 241, 241-256 (2017).

5   See, e.g. CMA, *Pricing Algorithms – Economic working paper on the use of algorithms to facilitate collusion and personalized pricing*, Oct. 8, 2018, available at https://assets.publishing.service.gov.uk/government/uploads/system/uploads/attachment_data/file/746353/Algorithms_econ_report.pdf (last accessed Apr. 16, 2020); Autorité de la concurrence & Bundeskartellamt, *Working Paper – Algorithms and Competition*, Nov. 2019, available at https://www.autoritedelaconcurrence.fr/sites/default/files/algorithms-and-competition.pdf (last accessed Apr. 16, 2020).

6   Ezrachi & Stucke, *supra* note 4, at 80.

processes and optimization of commercial strategies, and (ii) demand-side efficiencies, through supporting consumer decisions, enabling quick and effective access to information, providing up-to-date information on quality and individual preferences, and potentially lower and/or personalized prices for customers.[7]

Besides the operational efficiencies they offer to businesses, algorithms may also forecast changes in prices after analyzing historical data or help optimizing current prices to effectively respond to market conditions.8 Compared to the old-school business management techniques, where human employees set and implement pricing strategies without using any advanced technologies, algorithms can now provide significant benefits to many companies with their ability to process larger volumes of data, increased speed in dynamic pricing, and by offering more sophisticated methodologies to determine the willingness of customers to pay a certain price.

As regards potential anti-competitive effects, the mainstream controversy revolves around the concern that algorithms may facilitate, or even orchestrate, collusion among rival undertakings. If a competition authority is able to prove that the relevant companies have developed or used algorithms to implement an anti-competitive agreement which is already in place, or that they have employed such algorithms with intent to signal to or align their commercial strategies with their competitors, this will most probably be a clear-cut case. In these scenarios, it is easier to demonstrate that such algorithms are part of an illegal conduct. Incidentally, all algorithm-related antitrust cases around to world thus far have fallen into this category.[9]

But what if there is no evidence of any pre-existing agreement or even any communication between competitors to collude (that could be considered as a "concerted practice"), yet using algorithms has somehow resulted in high and parallel price levels? What if this is simply "tacit collusion" where competitors reach similar price levels by independently adjusting their strategies after observing their competitors, with a view to maximize their profits? Just because companies use algorithms that are able

---

7   Organisation for Economic Co-operation and Development ("OECD"), *Algorithms and Collusion: Competition Policy in the Digital Age* (2017), at 14-15, available at https://www.oecd.org/daf/competition/Algorithms-and-colllusion-competition-policy-in-the-digital-age.pdf (last accessed Apr. 16, 2020).

8   *Id.* at 11; *Algorithms and Collusion - Note by the United States*, Directorate for Financial and Enterprise Affairs Competition Committee of the OECD, DAF/COMP/WD (May 26, 2017) 41, at 2, available at https://one.oecd.org/document/DAF/COMP/WD(2017)41/en/pdf (last accessed Apr. 16, 2020).

9   See, e.g. *United States v. David Topkins*, Plea Agreement, Case No. 15-00201 WHO (N.D. Cal. Apr. 30, 2015); ECJ, Case C-74/14 – *Eturas*, judgment of January 21 2016, ECLI:EU:C:2016:42; ECJ, Case C-542/14 – *VM Remonts*, judgment of July 21 2016, ECLI:EU:C:2016:578; *Meyer v. Kalanick*, Case No. 1:2015cv09796 - Document 37 (S.D.N.Y. 2016); *Meyer v. Uber Technologies, Inc.*, Case No. 16-2750 (2d Cir. 2017).

to tacitly collude through machine learning, in particular deep learning technologies,[10] would that alone be sufficient to hold them liable for a competition law infringement?

These are undoubtedly difficult questions to answer with a simple yes or no. There are ample academic studies (some of which are based on simulation models on algorithmic pricing) and working papers from enforcers seeking these answers; yet we are still far from reaching an uncontested or even a largely accepted one. These studies and papers, however, still offer a number of potential theories of harm paving the way for a stimulating debate. Despite not being properly tested yet, these theories are worth a closer look, particularly because a number of major competition authorities, including the European Commission, appear to consider them plausible to a certain extent.

Various descriptions have been used to define the contours of this novel theory, including "collusion among black-box algorithms,"[11] "autonomous machine collusion,"[12] and "robo-sellers/robot-cartels."[13] Despite being quite catchy, these descriptions and their underlying hypotheses hardly offer sufficient guidance on how to detect and prevent a real-life algorithmic collusion scenario[14] without risking too many false-positives or premature regulatory interventions. Such excessive or unwarranted enforcement could reduce firms' incentives for investment and innovation in a way that could ultimately impede competition, which would go against the very purpose of competition law enforcement.

This article attempts to contribute to the debate by focusing on the business perspective, which appears to have been mostly neglected so far. It also explores what

---

10 *"Deep learning is a subfield of machine learning (...) that enables computer systems to learn using complex software that attempts to replicate the activity of human neurons by creating an artificial neural network."* OECD, *supra* note 7, at 11.

11 E.g. CMA, *supra* note 5, at 10; see also Autorité de la concurrence & Bundeskartellamt, *supra* note 5, at 12.

12 Ezrachi & Stucke, *supra* note 4.

13 Salil Mehra, *Antitrust and the Robo-seller; Competition in the Time of Algorithms*, 100 MINN. L. REV. 1323 – 1375 (2016); Charley Connor, *When Robots Collude*, GLOBAL COMPETITION REV. (Sept. 27, 2019); Monika Zdzieborska, *Brave New World of 'Robot' Cartels?*, Kluwer Competition Law Blog (March 7, 2017), available at http://competitionlawblog.kluwercompetitionlaw.com/2017/03/07/brave-new-world-of-robot-cartels/ (last accessed Apr. 16, 2020); Inge Graef, *Algorithmic Price Fixing Under EU Competition Law: How to Crack Robot Cartels?*, Centre for IT & IP Law (2016), available at https://www.law.kuleuven.be/citip/blog/algorithmic-price-fixing-under-eu-competition-law-how-to-crack-robot-cartels/ (last accessed Apr. 16, 2020)., available at https://www.law.kuleuven.be/citip/blog/algorithmic-price-fixing-under-eu-competition-law-how-to-crack-robot-cartels/(last accessed Apr. 16, 2020).

14 In this article, we use the term "algorithmic collusion" to refer to this algorithm-related scenario only, where hypothetically an AI-based algorithm, which is able to self-learn from data and experience by using machine learning technologies and autonomously decide on pricing strategies, tacitly colludes with other algorithms despite not being programmed to do so. This theory is explained in more detail below.

guidance could be provided to businesses in order to avoid potential legal liabilities arising from this theory of harm and potential steps enforcers may follow to address the risk associated with self-learning algorithms. This article also adds more to the already very high pile of questions on how much control companies actually have over algorithms' decision-making process. Our goal is to highlight the limits of our collective knowledge on this subject at this stage and to caution against declaring certain algorithmic pricing scenarios illegal before properly testing these theories. We particularly focus on whether the research on the theory of tacit collusion by algorithms has come far enough to take regulatory action against such algorithms, and whether potential risk scenarios recently analyzed in the literature are helpful to illuminate the thin line between legal and illegal algorithmic pricing.

II.   POTENTIAL THEORY OF HARM: UNTRACEABLE CARTELS?

Algorithms, as most technology-based mechanisms, are used in various forms, some of which are more advanced and complex than the others. In most cases, an outsider may not fully understand how these mathematical processes work or what, if any, the role of companies is in steering their algorithms towards a certain pricing strategy, in particular when artificial intelligence ("AI") is involved.[15] It is, therefore, not always an easy task to link these algorithmic processes to an illegal conduct or to hold companies liable for using algorithms in a way that leads to the restriction of competition.

Some scholars anticipate that the emergence of collusion in actual market settings would be "extremely possible in the near future, if not already occurring."[16] Sophisticated algorithms are still a mystery for competition law enforcers, but the question remains whether this mystery justifies stretching the limits of traditional antitrust concepts, or better yet, introducing a brand new legal framework for dealing with algorithms in digital markets. Is there an actual – or at least plausible – theory of harm, or is the current debate merely a reflection of the fear of the unknown related to "the rise of the machines"[17] upon the antitrust community? If there is an actual risk, how should enforcers respond to this and what guidance can they offer to businesses?

The most intriguing and controversial theory of harm has stemmed from a hypothetical case where algorithms – in particular self-learning, dynamic ones based

---

15   "In deep learning, features are created as a (possibly complex) computation over multiple features, making such algorithms' decision-making hard to explain." Avigdor Gal, *It's a Feature, not a Bug: On Learning Algorithms and What They Teach Us*, Roundtable on Algorithms and Collusion, Jun. 21-23, 2017, DAF/COMP/WD(2017)50, at 5.

16   Joseph E. Harrington, *Developing Competition Law for Collusion by Autonomous Price-Setting Agents*, (2017), available at https://papers.ssrn.com/sol3/papers.cfm?abstract_id=3037818 (last accessed Apr. 16, 2020).

17   Mehra, *supra* note 13, at 1334.

on AI – go rogue and decide to collude with other algorithms without any human intervention or instruction.[18] In this scenario, the algorithm is not programmed to collude, but instead, to find and apply the best strategy to maximize the firm's profit. By applying a highly advanced version of the game theory, the self-learning algorithm, through trial-and-error, tries first to best its competitors with discounts. But because competitors are also using algorithms that track and immediately adapt to other suppliers' pricing strategies, competitors match the first algorithm's price even before customers see this discounted price offer.[19] After playing this game repeatedly, the sophisticated algorithm is expected to realize that the best strategy to maximize the firm's profit is keeping the price high, given that it cannot get more customers through discounts anyway as competitors always match its discounted prices. The theory goes that, the price level in the market ultimately reaches a supra-competitive point (i.e. a collusive equilibrium) where all competitors are aligned, an outcome normally expected in a monopoly market. To collude on pricing strategies as such, algorithms do not need to be designed to collude, nor do they require communication among each other.[20]

According to the supporters of this theory, using self-learning algorithms may ultimately play a role in creating more durable, non-traceable cartels. These algorithms can arguably help fulfilling the criteria economists find necessary for a sustain-

---

18   This is defined as the "autonomous machine" scenario by Ezrachi & Stucke, *supra* note 4. Aside from the "messenger scenario," where an algorithm is used to implement pre-existing collusion, Ezrachi & Stucke identify three potential theories of harm for algorithmic pricing that could lead to collusion: (i) *hub and spoke*, where companies use the same algorithm in their pricing strategies, which can ultimately align and stabilize competitors' prices, (ii) *predictable agent*, where companies use their own algorithms, but they program these to swiftly react to the price changes of competitors, which ultimately results in parallel pricing, and (iii) *autonomous machine*, where companies use sophisticated, AI-based algorithms that can self-learn from experience and devise pricing strategies autonomously. See also Harrington, *supra* note 16, at 53.

19   In most of the articles explaining the game theory involving algorithms, authors emphasize algorithms' ability to play this game hundreds of times in a very short period of time, and in some cases, by changing their prices every few minutes (see, e.g. Emilio Calvano, et al., Artificial Intelligence, Algorithmic Pricing and Collusion, CEPR (2019), available at https://ssrn.com/abstract=3304991 (last accessed Apr.16, 2020); Michal S. Gal, *Algorithms as Illegal Agreements*, 34 BERKELEY TECH. L.J. 67 (2019); Harrington, *supra* note 16, at 55). Ezrachi & Stucke refer to the famous poker tournament in 2017 to illustrate this theory, where Libratus, a poker-playing algorithm, beat the world's top poker players with an unprecedented success rate. See Ariel Ezrachi & Maurice E. Stucke, *Algorithmic Collusion: Problems and Counter-Measures*, OECD Roundtable on Algorithms and Collusion, 24 (2017).

20   Calvano et al., *id.* at 35.

able collusion in oligopolistic markets[21] and even exacerbate traditional risk factors in these markets, such as transparency and frequency of interaction.[22] It is argued that, at the very least, algorithms expand the grey area between lawful conscious parallelism (i.e. tacit collusion) and unlawful explicit collusion.[23]

This hypothetical scenario is considered as a new type of coordination that could be established and implemented without actually communicating with rivals, because self-learning algorithms can "read each other's mind."[24] Allegedly, this is the end of the collusion theory as we know it in digital markets.[25] Such advanced algorithms decide on their own which data are relevant to devise the best strategy to maximize profits, how to interpret such data and how to improve themselves to solve complex problems. At the end of the day, the firm using the relevant algorithm may not know which data and parameters were used in a certain pricing strategy and whether this strategy resulted from an independent, one-sided data processing on the basis of the customer demand and market conditions, or from collusion with other competitors.[26]

---

21 The main pillars of successful collusion in an oligopolistic market (in addition to homogenous products), as defined by Stigler several decades ago, are (i) a meeting of minds upon a certain price-structure, (ii) a mechanism to detect deviations from the agreed-upon prices, and (iii) an effective punishment against deviations. (George J. Stigler, *A Theory of Oligopoly*, 72 J. Political Econ. 44, 44-61 (1964)). An additional component would be entry barriers protecting the companies against the threat of actual or potential competitive pressure (Gal, *supra* note 15, at 23). OECD Background Paper classifies the relevant factors under three groups: (i) *structural characteristics*, including the number of firms, barriers to entry, market transparency and frequency of interaction, (ii) *demand variables*, such as demand growth and fluctuations, and (iii) *supply variables*, including innovation and cost asymmetry. According to this paper, algorithms increase market transparency and frequency of interaction, but the potential impact of algorithms on the rest of the factors are either ambiguous or non-existent (OECD, *supra* note 7, at 23-24).

22 Mehra, *supra* note 13, at 1324; Gal *supra* note 15, at 24-25; OECD, *supra* note 7, at 23.

23 OECD, *supra* note 7, at 25.

24 Gal argues that self-learning algorithms do not even need to play the game several times. The algorithm can learn in a one-shot game, as it can read other algorithms' minds (Gal, *supra* note 19, at 85-87). On the ability and speed of algorithms to decode each other, as if they are "communicating," see Bruno Salcedo, *Pricing Algorithms and Tacit Collusion* (Jan. 11, 2015), available at http://brunosalcedo.com/docs/collusion.pdf (last accessed Apr. 16, 2020). Based on a simulation model in a duopolistic market and homogenous product, Salcedo claims that algorithmic pricing will "inevitably" lead to tacit collusion when algorithms are able to "respond to market conditions, are fixed in the short run, can be decoded by rivals, and can be revised over time" (Salcedo (2015), 20). For a criticism of Salcedo's argument, see Ulrich Schwalbe, *Algorithms, Machine Learning, and Tacit Collusion*, J. Competition L. & Econ. 1, 23–40 (2019); and Ittoo & Petit, *supra* note 4. Schwalbe considers Salcedo's model as an explicit collusion rather than a tacit one, given that companies are in fact communicating through decoding rival algorithms.

25 Ezrachi & Stucke, *supra* note 4, at 81.

26 CMA, *supra* note 5, at 10-11.

A number of recent studies on AI-based algorithms (in particular on independent Q-learning)[27] by computer scientists and economists have given a boost to this argument.[28] Some of these studies show that, in theory, certain algorithms are able to cooperate with other algorithms – as well as humans – for maximizing their profit.[29] Others offer simulation models which result in price coordination between competing Q-learning algorithms in a duopoly with sequential[30] or simultaneous[31] price competition.

In major competition law regimes including the U.S. and the EU, tacit collusion itself is not illegal. In these law systems, tacit collusion is merely a rational economic behavior, especially in oligopolistic markets, to track competitors' prices as well as other competition parameters and to adjust one's commercial strategies accordingly.[32] To be able to condemn parallel conduct, therefore, there must be an additional element besides the parallel conduct, a so-called "plus factor" in U.S. legal terms,[33] to establish that there could be no plausible alternative explanation for this parallel behavior other than an anti-competitive "meeting of minds" between competitors. There are ample cases in traditional markets where enforcers have rejected condemning intelligent adaptations to competitors' publicly available pricing strategies, in the absence of additional evidence of wrongdoing.[34] For most jurisdictions, therefore, there is arguably no legal basis for holding a firm liable for having programmed and/ or used an algorithm which "eventually self-learned to coordinate prices with other machines," unless there is clear evidence showing that companies aimed for this result in the first place.[35]

---

27 Q-learning is a "model-free reinforcement learning," which is able to learn to act optimally by "experiencing the consequences of actions" (Christopher J.C.H. Watkins & Peter Dayan, *Technical Note: Q-Learning*, 8 MACH. LEARNING, 279, 279-292 (1992)).

28 See, e.g. Salcedo, *supra* note 24; Harrington, *supra* note 16; Timo Klein, *Assessing Autonomous Algorithmic Collusion: Q-Learning Under Short-Run Price Commitments*, TINBERGEN INST. DISCUSSION PAPER, No. TI 2018-056/VII (2018); Calvano et al., *supra* note 19.

29 Jacob W. Crandall, et al., *Cooperating with machines*, 9 NATURE COMM. 1, 1-12 (2018).

30 Klein, *supra* note 28.

31 Calvano et al., *supra* note 19.

32 OECD, *supra* note 7, at 19.

33 According to Gal & Elkin-Koren, algorithms (or their design) could be a "plus factor" that could create competition law liability for tacit collusion (see Michal S. Gal & Niva Elkin-Koren, *Algorithmic Consumers*, 30 HARV. J.L. & TECH. 38 (2017)). "Plus factors" are defined as "economic actions and outcomes, above and beyond parallel conduct by oligopolistic firms, that are largely inconsistent with unilateral conduct but largely consistent with explicitly coordinated action" (William E. Kovacic, et al., *Plus Factors and Agreements in Antitrust Law*, 110 MICH. L. REV. 393 (2011)).

34 OECD, *Algorithms and Collusion - Note by the European Union, Directorate for Financial and Enterprise Affairs Competition Committee of the OECD*, (Jun. 14, 2017), DAF/COMP/ WD (2017)12, at 6.

35 OECD, *supra* note 7, at 35 et seq.

In the realm of algorithmic pricing, the question is whether the current approach to tacit collusion falls short of capturing illegal coordination in digital markets, in particular where pricing strategies are left in the hands of self-learning algorithms. The concern is that traditional plus factors, especially communication between competitors, are very difficult to prove in these cases, because self-learning algorithms do not even need communication in order to collude with one another. Current rules and economic models are based on certain assumptions about human incentives, but not all of these are necessarily applicable to self-learning algorithms.[36] Further, a number of academic studies suggest that AI-based algorithms could spread the risk of tacit collusion to non-oligopolistic markets.[37]

III. ENFORCERS' PERSPECTIVE: TOO SOON TO ACT, BUT STAY ON GUARD

Once policy makers decide to accept and assume the risk for algorithmic collusion, they are faced with additional and – equally difficult – questions to tackle with: To what extent should individuals/companies be held liable for the actions of algorithms? Who bears the burden of proof? What is the standard of proof for competition agencies and courts to hold companies liable for the actions of their algorithms, which were not programmed to collude in the first place? In this hypothetical scenario, the presumption is that there is no underlying agreement or a "meeting of minds" in general. Given that such a common understanding is a prerequisite for prohibiting a pricing strategy under the current antitrust laws, things get quite complicated for enforcers from this point on.

Some scholars have called for either revising the current interpretation of the law on tacit collusions[38] or adopting a brand new law[39] applicable to such slippery algorithms, which are arguably too smart and sophisticated to fall under the radar of competition authorities. In response, a number of competition enforcers have started discussing how to capture the risk for algorithmic collusion under the competition law framework. The following approaches of the competition enforcers have particularly attracted the attention of the competition law community and received commentary from different sides of the debate:

---

36 Harrington, *supra* note 16, at 48.

37 Ezrachi & Stucke, *supra* note 19, at 2; Mehra, *supra* note 13, at 1363. For a critical analysis of this approach, see Ittoo & Petit, *supra* note 4.

38 See, e.g. Gal & Elkin-Koren, *supra* note 33, at 38.

39 See, e.g. Salil K. Mehra, *De-Humanizing Antitrust: The Rise of the Machines and the Regulation of Competition* (Aug. 21, 2014), Temple University Legal Studies Research Paper No. 2014-43, at 2.

A. Using Traditional Competition Laws, but Stretching the Concept of "Human Agency"

The U.S. competition authorities have suggested that algorithms should be treated as an employee "named Bob" when they are used as a facilitator of collusion.[40] If a firm could be held liable for its employee's conduct in a particular case, then they would also be liable for the actions of their algorithms. This analogy, however, is not necessarily applicable to the theory of self-learning algorithm. The joint contribution of the Antitrust Division of the U.S. Department of Justice ("DOJ") and the U.S. Federal Trade Commission ("FTC") to the OECD roundtable acknowledges that "computers equipped with artificial intelligence (AI) or machine learning could, in theory, make decisions that were not dictated or allowed for in the programming," but finds that "these scenarios seem too speculative to consider at this time."[41] They, however, also emphasize the significant value of research in this field and indicate that, where necessary, "enforcers may need to consider stepping up [their] aggressiveness with respect to coordinated effects analysis."[42]

The European Commission appears to be keen on adopting the employee analogy also for the "autonomous machine" scenario.[43] According to the Commission, companies are expected to ensure "compliance by design," and to adopt sufficient safeguards to prevent their algorithms from colluding. The Commission further suggests that, as the algorithms are under the firms' "direction or control," firms would be liable for their actions, as would be the case in a traditional employer-employee relationship.[44] On the other hand, similar to its counterparts across the ocean, the Commission acknowledges that "there is a need to examine whether current legislation is able to address the risks of AI and can be effectively enforced, whether adaptations of the legislation are needed, or whether new legislation is needed."[45]

---

40 Maureen K. Ohlhausen, Chairman, Fed. Trade Comm'n, Keynote Address at the F.T.C: *Should We Fear the Things That Go Beep in the Night? Some Initial Thoughts on the Intersection of Antitrust Law and Algorithmic Pricing* (May 13, 2017), available at https://www.ftc.gov/system/files/documents/public_statements/1220893/ohlhausen_-_concurrences_5-23-17.pdf (last accessed Apr. 16, 2020).

41 OECD, *supra* note 8, at fn 1.

42 Terrell McSweeny, Commissioner, *Algorithms And Coordinated Effects*, (May 22, 2017) University of Oxford Center for Competition Law and Policy, Oxford, UK, available at https://www.ftc.gov/system/files/documents/public_statements/1220673/mcsweeny_-_oxford_cclp_remarks_-_algorithms_and_coordinated_effects_5-22-17.pdf (last accessed Apr. 16, 2020), at 5.

43 OECD, *Algorithms and Collusion – Note from the European Union*, OECD (2017), available at https://one.oecd.org/document/DAF/COMP/WD(2017)12/en/pdf (last accessed Apr. 16, 2020).

44 *Id*. at 9.

45 *Commission White Paper on Artificial Intelligence: A European approach to excellence and trust*, 9-10, COM (2020) 65 final (Feb. 19, 2020).

B. Risk is Likely, but Further Research is Necessary before Taking Action

A joint discussion paper recently published by the German and French competition enforcers is relatively more reluctant about distinguishing between algorithms and humans, in terms of intelligent adaptations to competitors' pricing strategies.[46] While acknowledging that it is too early to decide which types of algorithmic actions could be illegal, the relevant authorities suggest that the standard for assessing liability for algorithmic collusion could ultimately fall somewhere between holding companies liable (i) simply for developing and/or using an algorithm that ultimately engages in anti-competitive conduct, and (ii) when the firm does not comply with a reasonable standard of care and foreseeability regarding this conduct.[47]

The Portuguese competition authority (Autoridade da Concorrência, "AdC") has taken a similar approach. The AdC has signaled potential liability for firms using pricing algorithms that directly or indirectly lead to pricing collusion, but also highlighted the need to "understand the full impact of learning algorithms and of algorithms [sic] developers."[48]

C. Identifying the Highest-Risk Scenarios

In tackling this issue, the Competition and Markets Authority ("CMA")[49] in the UK opted to start with an economic analysis of algorithmic collusion, rather than jumping head-first into the legal analysis. The purpose of the CMA study was to first identify which theories of harm would raise the highest risk of collusion and under which market conditions. While the CMA acknowledged the possibility of autonomous collusion by sophisticated and complex algorithms, it identified a more immediate risk in the "hub-and-spoke" scenario, where companies in a particular market utilize the same algorithm to set their prices. The CMA considered the analysis on the likeliness of collusion risk due to self-learning algorithms to be a matter for the future, when the pricing algorithms in question will have become sufficiently widespread and technologically advanced.[50] The CMA also found that potential audit mechanisms to detect collusion depending on "whether and if a firm could know that its algorithm is implementing a collusive outcome" would be an ideal candidate as a topic for further research.[51]

---

46 Autorité de la Concurrence & Bundeskartellamt, *supra* note 5.

47 *Id*. at Section III.

48 Arezki Yaïche, *Retailers should be responsible for algorithms leading to pricing collusion, Portuguese regulator says* (Feb. 26, 2020), available at https://mlexmarketinsight.com/insights-center/editors-picks/antitrust/cross-jurisdiction/retailers-should-be-responsible-for-algorithms-leading-to-pricing-collusion-portuguese-regulator-says (last accessed Apr. 17, 2020).

49 CMA, *supra* note 5.

50 *Id*. at 31.

51 *Id*. at 52.

Similarly, the Australian Competition & Consumer Commission ("ACCC") has been taking steps that aim to "build the expertise to analyze algorithms" and to identify potential risk areas. While the ACCC considers the current case law insufficient to warrant adopting a new law against the risk of algorithmic collusion, the enforcers have also explicitly warned firms that they cannot avoid competition law liability by simply saying "[M]y robot did it."[52]

As summarized above, some of the major competition authorities around the world appear to have already started discussing potential risk areas self-learning algorithms may have created. While some authorities have issued warnings about the potential liability of firms stemming from collusions by their algorithms, their research on this field appears to be far from complete, and thus the enforcers' eventual stance on this issue remains to be seen.

IV. WHAT IS THE TAKEAWAY FOR BUSINESSES?

The debate among scholars, the simulation models constructed by economists and computer scientists, and the reactions of various enforcers to the theory of algorithmic collusion are no doubt quite thrilling to watch from the sidelines. The message to the business community is, however, somewhat ambiguous and inconsistent, which probably make these developments less than entertaining to follow from a business perspective.

Today, we have quite a voluminous set of studies indicating that the risk of algorithmic collusion may not be fictional after all, at least in theory.[53] The concerns raised on this point may have some merit, so does the call for more research on algorithmic pricing and its potential effects on competition. That said, a majority of the solutions explored thus far lack a properly defined risk area to target (which we will call the "red zone" for the sake of argument) or a road map that competition enforcers can follow to decide how to approach algorithmic pricing issues.[54]

From a business standpoint, we will focus on two issues in the rest of this article that could greatly affect the question of legal certainty. The first issue is related

---

52   ACCC, *New competition laws a protection against big data e-collusion* (Nov. 16, 2017), available   at   https://www.accc.gov.au/media-release/new-competition-laws-a-protection-against-big-data-e-collusion (last accessed Apr. 17, 2020).

53   There are also some recent commentaries arguing against the need to focus on the algorithmic collusion scenarios and that they are not a fundamentally important issue for antitrust law (see, e.g. Schrepel, *supra* note 3).

54   An exception to this is Gal's systematical analysis of a potential "rule of reason" assessment on algorithms as facilitating practices, which offers five relatively more straightforward cases that are more likely to raise competitive concerns (Gal, *supra* note 19). These "straightforward cases," however, are also based on certain assumptions that have not yet been unequivocally proven with empirical data and real-life cases. A brief commentary on this proposal is provided below.

to the eagerness to condemn all potential tacit collusion scenarios involving self-learning algorithms before properly testing the underlying theory of harm. Most of the studies on this subject are based on a limited number of experiments, which are not yet sufficient to clearly define the conditions for such conduct to harm competition beyond tolerable when compared to and balanced against the expected efficiencies. The second issue relates to the recent studies aiming to identify the relatively more "straightforward" risk scenarios, which – albeit most welcome as an attempt in the right direction for assuring legal certainty – could also lead to over-enforcement concerns. It is worth noting that the underlying assumptions of these studies have not yet been substantiated by empirical evidence either.

As regards the first issue, certain academic contributions go so far as suggesting intervention in algorithmic pricing that could lead to tacit collusion in all markets, be it oligopolistic or otherwise.[55] It is, however, not yet clear whether algorithms can actually collude autonomously, even in oligopolistic markets, which are usually considered more prone to collusion. Indeed, as explained above, all current cartel cases around the world involving algorithms are related to pre-existing collusions implemented by algorithms, but not "humanless tacit collusions."[56] In other words, there would have still been an infringement had the relevant companies not used algorithms in these cases. Further, studies so far have offered ambiguous results on whether algorithms can indeed deteriorate the market structures that were once considered competitive. While there is an often-repeated argument that algorithms may increase the market transparency and the frequency of interactions, no negative impact has been proven as to the other factors affecting the likelihood and success of collusion, such as barriers to entry, or demand and supply variables.[57] In fact, the impact of algorithms on supply conditions, such as innovation and cost asymmetry, can arguably have the opposite effect and reduce the risk of collusion.[58]

As regards the simulation models indicating that self-learning algorithms have a tendency to collude, these models were largely carried out in controlled environments and under the assumption that critical market conditions – such as the number of competitors – remain the same throughout the simulation.[59] In some models, rival firms use the same algorithm in a static duopolistic market, where it is much

---

55   See Ezrachi & Stucke, *supra* note 19, at 2; Mehra, *supra* note 13, at 1363. For a critical analysis of this approach, see Ittoo & Petit, *supra* note 4. See also OECD, *supra* note 7, at 33; Gal, *supra* note 15, at 28.

56   Ittoo & Petit, *supra* note 4, at 2-3; Schwalbe, *supra* note 24, at 5.

57   Antonio Capobianco & Pedro Gonzaga, *Algorithms and Competition: Friends or Foes?*, Cᴘɪ Aɴᴛɪᴛʀᴜsᴛ Cʜʀoɴ. 2, (2017), available at https://www.competitionpolicyinternational.com/algorithms-and-competition-friends-or-foes/ (last accessed Apr. 16, 2020).

58   *Ibid.*

59   Ittoo & Petit, *supra* note 4, at 5.

easier to monitor and align with a competitor's price.[60] Such simulations also disregard several factors that are likely to impact an algorithm's decision to adjust its prices in accordance with those of its rivals, such as the risk for potential entries, demand fluctuations and cost shocks.[61] Moreover, there is no empirical data showing that this theory can actually occur in the real world and, if so, how that can happen.[62] Most importantly, a majority of scholars and enforcers agree that not all types of algorithmic pricing facilitate collusion and that algorithms may actually have pro-competitive effects offsetting potential risks as well.[63]

In light of the above, we observe that it would be helpful to receive some guidance from enforcers to identify the circumstances in which algorithmic pricing could expose companies to legal liability, before excessively expanding the scope of enforcement and turning digital markets into a legal minefield.[64] It is, of course, not realistic to expect an exhaustive or "one-size-fits-all" set of rules applicable to all algorithmic pricing cases. First, there are still so many unknowns regarding self-learning algorithms. Second, although many researchers around the world have started working on this crucial topic, their findings show that so far we have only seen the tip of the iceberg.

Yet, it could still be possible to identify a set of factors that would be helpful in determining when the risk of legal exposure is higher, some sort of a "red zone" for companies to avoid. Needless to say, potential liability scenarios would not be limited to this zone, but it would at least provide a benchmark against which the risk level of other algorithm scenarios could be compared. This "red zone" could also serve as a focal point for enforcers to concentrate their energy and resources at this stage, rather than trying to monitor all markets where algorithmic pricing is used, the number of which has been growing exponentially in the last several years.[65]

---

60   See, e.g. Salcedo, *supra* note 24. On the shortcomings of the theory, in particular the argument that most experiments are based on one-to-one games and that the theory collapses when a third party joins, see Kai-Uwe Kühn & Steve Tadelis, *Algorithmic Collusion* (2017), available at https://www.cresse.info/uploadfiles/2017_sps5_pr2.pdf (last accessed Apr. 16, 2020).

61   See, e.g. Calvano et al., *supra* note 19, at 35-36.

62   Schwalbe, *supra* note 24, at 29; OECD, *supra* note 7, at 49; Ittoo & Petit, *supra* note 4, at 2; Kühn & Tadelis, *supra* note 60.

63   See, e.g. Ittoo & Petit, *supra* note 4, at 13; Salil L. Mehra, *Robo-Seller Prosecutions and Antitrust's Error-Cost Framework*, CPI ANTITRUST CHRON. 5 (2017), 36; Ezrachi & Stucke, *supra* note 4, at 15 et seq.; Anita Banicevic, et al., *Algorithms: Challenges and Opportunities for Antitrust Compliance*, ABA SECTION OF ANTITRUST LAW 7 et seq. (2018).

64   As regards the need for a clear guidance for the market participants, see also Gal, *supra* note 19.

65   See Schrepel, *supra* note 3.

A. The Zoning Exercise

Since there are still so many unknowns with respect to how self-learning algorithms work and under which circumstances they opt for collusion, such a zoning exercise could start with what we already know: the available research indicates that algorithms are more likely to collude (i) under particular market conditions, and (ii) when certain types of algorithms are involved.

Accordingly, a useful first step for the zoning exercise could be to identify the problematic market conditions. Based on the research so far, algorithmic collusion is more likely to occur, *inter alia*, in concentrated markets with high barriers to entry, a limited number of players, a homogenous product, a high degree of transparency, effective deterrence and retaliation mechanisms, and no significant buyer power.[66] In other words, factors restraining humans' ability to tacitly collude are also applicable to self-learning algorithms.[67] If enforcers provide guidance on such factors, companies would realize that the risk for their algorithms to collude and for them to be held liable for such collusion could be higher in certain markets. The more we move away from these problematic markets, the more it will be likely for the market dynamics themselves to eliminate the risk for algorithms to successfully coordinate and/or sustain such coordination, in the absence of explicit collusion among the relevant firms. Enforcers would then be expected to offer more evidence on why and how a certain algorithmic pricing strategy could restrict competition in other markets and, more importantly, could be illegal.

Another critical point to consider at this juncture is that a concentrated (in particular, oligopolistic) market that satisfies some or all of the conditions above is already an alarming market setting, regardless of the pricing method to be used. A differentiating factor here could be whether the relevant market is already prone to tacit collusion – meaning a purely human-controlled and independent pricing strategy in this market could also lead to the same result – or whether price-setting algorithms are the actual reason for the market to become more conducive to collusion.[68]

While we consider this analysis as a helpful starting point, it should not lead to an assumption that algorithmic pricing will inevitably result in collusion in certain markets every single time, and thus should be *per se* illegal when used in such markets.[69] If that were the case, the message to the business community would be to "avoid algorithmic-pricing in these markets altogether." There is no sufficient empirical data

---

66 See, e.g. Ezrachi & Stucke, *supra* note 19, at 3-4; Schwalbe, *supra* note 24, at 25; Ittoo & Petit, *supra* note 4, at 11-13.

67 See Ittoo & Petit, *supra* note 4, at 5.

68 *Id.* at 3.

69 Mehra, *supra* note 13, at 1371.

indicating that algorithmic pricing in certain markets will always restrict competition.[70] Assuming otherwise and deviating from the mainstream approach towards tacit collusion, which currently allows such conduct, would not be justified at this stage. Nor would it meet the standard of proof currently applied to price-fixing collusions.[71]

A second step could be, as also discussed to a certain extent in the literature,[72] determining the characteristics of algorithms which could make collusion more likely. Simulation models mentioned above mostly assume that all competitors would use a specific – and often the same – type of algorithm and employ a pre-determined pricing method in controlled, static market conditions.[73] In real life, however, there are a vast number of algorithm options that companies can choose from.[74] Further, the way these algorithms behave significantly differs depending on the market dynamics and due to the complexity of their pricing and learning mechanisms.[75] Starting the analysis with a presumption that all algorithms have the ability and incentive to collude (and

---

70 "Oxera reported that "The degree to which such collusion among algorithms is likely to happen in practice is not yet clear." (Oxera, When Algorithms Set Prices: Winners and Losers, 2 (June 19, 2017), available at https://www.oxera.com/publications/when-algorithms-set-prices-winners-and-losers/ (last accessed Apr, 16, 2020). Furthermore, in some of these models, collusion would be more difficult to sustain as the profitability decreases (see, e.g. Calvano et al., *supra* note 19, at 27). Accordingly, "algorithmic collusive behavior is not as likely or even unavoidable as some legal scholars seem to suspect." (Schwalbe, *supra* note 24, at 32).

71 According to the U.S. law, in order to prove collusions on price-fixing (i.e. a cartel), the courts and enforcers must evince the existence of such collusion "beyond a reasonable doubt." To be able to meet this standard of proof, the case law suggests that, in addition to parallel conduct, there must be a plus factor proving that this is not the result of oligopolistic interdependence, but a coordination among competitors. (See, e.g. Monsanto Co. v. Spray-Rite Service Corp., 465 US 752, 768 (1984); Matsushita Electrical Industrial Co. v. Zenith Radio Corp, 475 US 574 (1986); In re Flat Glass Antitrust Litigation, 385 F 3d 350, 359-60 (3d Cir. 2004). See also Kovacic et al., *supra* note 33, at 395 et seq.) As regards the EU law, while the standard of proof is not defined as clearly as their counterparts did across the Atlantic, a similar approach has also been adopted by the EU courts regarding whether parallel conduct alone would be sufficient to prove a price-fixing cartel. The EU case law indicates that parallel conduct would not be sufficient to prove collusion unless "concentration constitutes the only plausible explanation for such conduct," which rules out oligopolistic interdependence (see, e.g. Cases 48, 49, 51-7/69, ICI v. Commission (Dyestuffs) [1972] ECR 619, [1972] CMLR 557; Ahlström Osakeyhtiö and Others v. Commission (Woodpulp II), [1993] 4 CMLR 407.

72 See, e.g. Harrington, *supra* note 16, at 64 et seq.; Gal, *supra* note 19, at 113 et seq.; Schwalbe, *supra* note 24, at 24.

73 Schwalbe, *supra* note 24, at 24.

74 Schwalbe exemplifies the types of algorithm models used in real life as "*bandit-type models, customer choice models, econometric regression models, machine learning models, and greedy ad-hoc approaches*" (*supra* note 24, at 24).

75 Van de Geer et al., *Dynamic Pricing and Learning with Competition: Insights from the Dynamic Pricing Challenge*, in INFORMS RM & Pricing Conference, at 1 (2018), available at https://arxiv.org/pdf/1804.03219.pdf (last accessed Apr. 16, 2020).

extending this presumption to all types of algorithms in every market setting) would lead to a significant over-enforcement.

Which types of algorithms, then, could land businesses in the "red zone"? When could enforcers conclude that tacit collusion was "a conscious, avoidable act"[76] for the firm using the algorithm? The lack of real-life examples limits one's ability to make an educated guess on this point.[77] Yet, the literature suggests a few suspicious cases to focus on. This brings us to the second potential concern for businesses with respect to their need for legal certainty.

The most frequently discussed "red zone" scenario is the case where all competitors use the same or similar algorithms and the result is parallel price levels in the relevant marketplace.[78] Unless there is a plausible justification for using the same or very similar algorithms (e.g. there is no better or equally efficient algorithm available) which had similar outcomes for all competitors, this could be an indication for the firms' "intent" to coordinate their pricing strategies when the market dynamics allow it. If this scenario is to be included in the red zone, however, enforcers should again leave room for firms to rebut this allegation.[79]

For all algorithmic pricing scenarios, including the one above, one of the critical questions that come to mind is whether the algorithm's programmer (and ultimately the firm) could have been perceived to have control over the algorithm's pricing decisions. While certain scholars respond to this question in the affirmative,[80] the research available on this subject – albeit not yet very extensive – suggests that the response may in fact not be that straightforward, given our limited understanding of how self-learning algorithms work.[81]

Scholars have pointed out that certain algorithms, in particular those with deep-learning capabilities, comprise many layers of neurons to process the data received from various sources (including publicly available content, customer feedback and the

---

76   Gal, *supra* note 19, at 108.

77   Harrington proposes that certain types of pricing algorithms (such as estimation-optimization algorithms) could be considered illegal by distinguishing between properties of algorithms that generate efficiencies and those promoting collusion (Harrington, *supra* note 16, at 49 et seq). This may not be an easy task in practice, as we have not yet seen any real-life examples to guide enforcers through such distinctive properties of algorithms.

78   Dylan I. Ballard & Amar S. Naik, *Algorithms, Artificial Intelligence and Joint Conduct*, CPI ANTITRUST CHRON., 32 (2017); Calvano et al., *supra* note 19, at 36.

79   Using the same or similar algorithms may not always lead to the same price levels, given the differences between competitors' cost and demand structures. Therefore, the similarity in the algorithm alone would not be sufficient to prove an underlying collusion (Gal, *supra* note 19, at 113).

80   Gal, *supra* note 19, at 108 et seq.

81   Oxera, *supra* note 70, at 19; Schwalbe, *supra* note 24, at fn. 30.

firm itself) and to find the optimal pricing level in order to maximize the firm's profit.[82] These numerous layers could create a so-called "black box," which might be difficult to understand, even by the firms using such algorithms, let alone by the competition law enforcers.[83] If we are to follow these scholars' approach, businesses should either choose not to use sophisticated algorithms that they do not understand,[84] or be prepared for the legal repercussions, as it could be argued by enforcers that the firms must have foreseen (and accepted) the risk of collusion if they are using complex algorithms.

This line of reasoning appears to comply with the standard of "reasonable foreseeability" the Franco/German Study explores and the "compliance by design" system the European Commission calls for. But when it comes to application of this standard, we once again hit the brick wall of unfounded presumptions problem. Indeed, unless we are committed to presuming that all deep-learning algorithms are capable of tacitly colluding at some point and in any market when the stars align, all external conditions to facilitate collusion fall into place and collusion inevitably becomes the "optimal" choice for all algorithms involved; businesses will need some proper guidance on what exactly "reasonability" entails. Are there specific safeguards they can adopt to ensure that collusion will never ever be the optimal pricing strategy? Is it realistic to expect firms to be able to program sophisticated algorithms "not to collude,"[85] without risking excessive intervention in their algorithms to the detriment of the efficiencies they expect to derive from these algorithms? What if a firm took all precautions technologically available to prevent its algorithm from tacitly colluding with others, but its prices are still parallel with other competitors – could this still be an infringement? Where do we draw the line? There are arguments both in favor of and against firms' ability to control their self-learning algorithms, which clearly indicates that further research and empirical evidence will be needed to resolve this issue.

When firms use different algorithms, another critical point to consider would be whether certain algorithms are able to communicate with one another. The answer to this question would be particularly important to meet the standard of proof for anti-competitive agreements, at least within the current legal framework. A number of scholars have argued that self-learning algorithms can communicate by decoding the

---

82 CMA, *supra* note 5, at 14.

83 *Ibid.*

84 Francisco Beneke & Mark-Oliver Mackenrodt, *Artificial Intelligence and Collusion*, 50 IIC 109, 125-134 (2019). The authors suggest that firms may, in fact, not prefer using black-box algorithms as "they have an incentive to know what drives the prediction in order to obtain better market insights" (see p. 129). There is, however, insufficient information on whether we can assume that this is the business reality and there is in fact no such thing as a black-box algorithm that even the programmer himself cannot completely comprehend (see Gal, *supra* note 19, at 108, for an argument that treating algorithms as a black box is "fallacious").

85 For an argument that an algorithm's goals are set and can be revised by their programmers in a way not to collude, see Harrington, *supra* note 16, at 65; see also Gal, *supra* note 19, at 108.

decisional parameters of each other.[86] Such decoding would then serve as an exchange of information between competing algorithms. That said; decoding sophisticated algorithms by other algorithms may not be an easy task in real life. This is because some algorithms include millions of lines of code which could include the firm's proprietary information and software besides the elements other algorithms can access.[87] Unless firms take some additional actions to make these codes and the underlying information transparent to their competitors, other algorithms may not be able to decode these by simply observing their behavior on the market.

Even scholars favoring a conservative approach suggest that, additional actions from firms would be needed for a certain algorithmic pricing to fall in the red zone, at least based upon the limited information we currently have on self-learning algorithms. These additional actions could include, *inter alia*, (i) feeding the same or similar datasets to algorithms although better or more reliable alternatives are available, in a way that enables the pricing strategies of all algorithms to align, and (ii) designing algorithms in a way that only competitors will be able to monitor their potential reactions to market conditions and future strategies.[88] Once again, we should caution against taking a *per se* approach to these scenarios, as companies may be able to offer objective justifications for these actions. Lowering the standard of proof and applying a presumption of illegality without any evidence of additional facilitating actions or intent would be dangerous and unwarranted. Such a presumption should only be built upon a well-established understanding of a certain practice as being so inherently harmful that such a practice should always be illegal, and certainly not without an elaborate analysis of its potential effects or underlying objective justifications.[89] The current state of the research clearly shows that we are not there yet.

In light of the above, the third step in the zoning exercise appears to be less controversial: policy makers should expand their research on how self-learning algorithms work in real-life settings, investigate the conditions under which they are more likely to collude and explore whether these algorithms can indeed autonomously collude without the assistance of their firms' additional facilitating actions. The existing literature offers some options for the methodology of this research, such as devising "an algorithmic pricing incubator" by the authorities to analyze whether a certain price level is competitive or a result of an algorithmic collusion.[90] The starting point of

---

86 See, e.g. Salcedo, *supra* note 24, at 4 et seq., and Gal, *supra* note 19, at 109.

87 Oxera, *supra* note 70, at 19; Schwalbe, *supra* note 24, at 22. See also Kühn & Tadelis, *supra* note 59, for a criticism of the theory that algorithms can communicate without the assistance of firms/humans.

88 Gal, *supra* note 19, at 114.

89 *Northern Pacific R. Co. v. United States*, 356 U.S. 1, 5, 78 S. Ct. 514, 518, 2 L.Ed.2d 545 (1958).

90 Ezrachi & Stucke, *supra* note 19, at 28.

this research could be the red-zone scenarios discussed above, as these are considered more likely to restrict competition.

Once the policy makers obtain sufficient empirical data to form a reliable view on this issue, a fourth step could be to analyze whether the current legal framework is able to capture any potential competition risks these scenarios may generate. If the answer to this question is a clear "no," only then the fifth and final step should be considered, i.e. exploring the validity of either a novel approach to the concept of tacit collusion or designing a brand new legal framework to address such concerns.

V. CONCLUSION

The competition law enforcers should acknowledge and closely watch the technological developments redefining market dynamics in the modern global economy. They, however, should also be wary of too much – and too soon – intervention as that could lead to false-positives, remove legal certainty for businesses, and reduce the incentive to innovate and invest. The theory of self-learning algorithms rebelling against humans and colluding outside the control of companies, which once sounded like a good sci-fi, appears to be no longer a myth. Nevertheless, blindly venturing into this new territory and taking drastic actions could turn enforcement efforts in this area into a horror movie for the business community. Enforcers should be cautious against over-enforcement without sufficient empirical evidence to justify any shift in the approach to the traditional concepts of collusion, or a proper guidance for companies to enable them to avoid the risk of legal exposure.

Assurance of some foreseeability would be beneficial before the competition enforcers start to take action against tacit collusion by algorithms. Admittedly, it could be too soon to lay out a full-fledged action plan. Yet, for the sake of legal certainty, enforcers could first define the boarders of the battlefield rather than starting a random gun fire. In this regard, when defining the red-zone risk scenarios, one should always mind the dangers of acting on the basis of unfounded presumptions. Setting the zone too widely to render all tacit collusion scenarios illegal, or assuming that all self-learning algorithms can communicate under all circumstances, would defeat the purpose of the whole exercise. The need is evident for conducting comprehensive research on how self-learning algorithms work in actual market settings and thereby determining when they are more likely to raise material competition law risks.

Despite some early research signaling potential liability for companies simply because of their choice to use certain algorithms, enforcers appear to have taken, at least for the moment, the sensible approach outlined above. Indeed, it is somewhat comforting for businesses to observe that the leading antitrust enforcers are conducting market studies one after another to gain a better understanding of what the use of algorithms may entail for competition, rather than hastily condemning such algorithms for collusion purely on theoretical grounds. Given that the voices warning against potential risks are getting louder, the time appears to be ripe for enforcers to delve into a comprehensive research plan on the potential risk scenarios and to test how effective the current legal framework is to capture and mitigate such risks.

Consumers, Digital Platforms, and Abuse of Superior Bargaining Position

By Reiko Aoki[1] & Tetsuya Kanda [2]

Abstract

Individuals are able to access and interact in the digital world with ease. Digital platforms have offered new opportunities to individuals with business models to accommodate the new role of the individual in the market. Nature of individual as consumer or worker has changed and existing laws, such as labor laws and consumer protection laws need to change or expand. Similarly, application of competition law needs to be re-examined for a market with individuals and digital platforms.

We argue that one way to guarantee individual's ability to compete in the market is to recognize the superior bargaining position that platforms have over individuals. To be precise, platforms are able to make "take-it-or-leave-it" offers to individuals, implying that it is in a position to appropriate all the gains (surplus generated) from trade. The concept of "abuse of a superior bargaining position" in the Japanese competition law may well capture those phenomena.

We then turn to the question of whether consumer surplus also be appropriated by the platforms through price discrimination using information the platform has accumulated. Recent works in mechanism design have shown the relationship between information structure and what kind of price discrimination can be implemented. This suggests understanding and incorporating information structures into policy, including competition enforcement, may be effective.

I. INTRODUCTION

The objective of the Japanese antimonopoly law is to "promote the democratic and wholesome development of the national economy as well as secure the interests of general consumers" by promoting "fair and free competition." Though most of the law concerns firms' behavior, the application of the rule prohibiting the

---

1 Japan Fair Trade Commission. Opinions expressed here are those of the authors and do not represent those of the Japan Fair Trade Commission or the Consumer Affairs Agency of Japan.

2 Consumer Affairs Agency of Japan.

abuse of a superior bargaining position ("ASBP") protects not only "firms." Any party engaged in trade can be the instigator or victim of such an abuse, including individual consumers.

We first argue that the fact that consumers trade information for goods and services by accepting a take-it-or-leave-it offer from a platform implies that the platform is in a superior bargaining position. We then review the recently released "Guidelines Concerning Abuse of a Superior Bargaining Position in Transactions between Digital Platform Operators and Consumers that Provide Personal Information" by the Japan Fair Trade Commission ("JFTC"), which focuses on abusive behavior concerning the use of consumer information and data. We discuss the possibility of consumer surplus erosion through price discrimination as a result of consumer information gathered using take-it-or-leave-it offers by platforms.

II.   ROLE OF THE INDIVIDUAL IN DIGITAL MARKETS

Access to the Internet has changed the role of the individual in the economy. Consumers are considered to be atomic agents in the economy, where the behavior of each individual consumer has no effect on the market. Firms are atomistic in this sense only in a perfectly competitive market. Consumers, however, have always been atomistic in economic analysis.

Individuals are protected in the consumer goods market by consumer protection laws, and by labor laws when they sell labor. The emergence of digital markets or platforms[3] has changed how individuals buy and sell in the market. Individuals can barter information about themselves for goods and services. Individuals can also sell labor or services without traditional employment relationships. In these cases, the individual may not qualify as a traditional consumer or worker (employee), and not be protected by traditional laws.[4]

---

3   When we say digital platforms, we include digital markets in most cases. One can argue that retailers are platforms, bringing products and consumers together, and there is always some direct network effect. Perhaps more important is the word digital. Digital interface makes identifying individuals and obtaining information from individuals easy. Information will not be as useful if the individuals were not identified when they visited the platform again.

4   There are many laws that protect consumers in Japan. Consumers are protected against "multilevel sales" and "chain sales," i.e. pyramid schemes by Specified Commercial Transaction Law by requiring a cooling off period for contracts. The Act against Unjustifiable Premiums and Misleading Representations guarantees truth in advertising and labeling. https://www.caa.go.jp/en/law/. See https://www.jil.go.jp/english/laws/index.html for Japanese labor laws.

One solution is to expand the definition of "employee" to include new workers, as in California Assembly Bill 5.[5] Another possible alternative is to apply competition law to protect an individual that trades on the labor market for artistic and athletic performance or digital content procurement. Their contracts may have anticompetitive elements (such as exclusivity and noncompete obligations), and forcing such contracts may constitute an ASBP. The publication of the Report of Study Group on Human Resources and Competition Policy (JFTC 2018) has led to a reexamination of contract terms by some sports associations and talent agencies.[6]

Similarly, individuals trading on digital markets and platforms could be protected from incurring economic loss by competition law (Furman, J., D. Coyle, A.Fletcher, D.McAuley & P.Marsden,2019[7]). This is a natural approach when one considers consumers participating in social networks or using search engines are trading information for services.[8] Consumer protection laws may not be well suited to grapple with the issues, because they basically focus on correcting asymmetric information problems, protecting consumers from false advertising and fraud. Ripping consumers off by misrepresenting products does not represent the business model of digital platforms. However, there may be cases where individuals are not compensated as they should be for information they trade, due to the superior bargaining position that platforms hold over consumers.[9] Although it is often considered to be unique, the Japanese ASBP concept can shed a spotlight on certain conduct, which consumer protection laws cannot, on the business models of those platforms accumulating data, which they turn into competitive advantages over their competitors and, eventually, consumers.[10] It is not surprising that the idea of ASBP has been applied in other jurisdictions recently (Sugimoto, 2020).[11]

---

5   More precisely, the bill has redefined the definition of "employee" for purposes of unemployment insurance provisions and also put the burden of proof on the hiring entity, to claim that a certain individual be an independent contractor, rather than an employee for purpose of a few labor-related laws.

6   Japan Fair Trade Commission Competition Policy Research Center (CPRC), 2018. *Report of Study Group on Human Resources and Competition Policy.* Japan Fair Trade Commission. https://www.jftc.go.jp/en/pressreleases/yearly-2018/February/180215_files/180215_3.pdf.

7   Furman, J., D. Coyle, A. Fletcher, D. McAuley & P. Marsden, (2019). *Unlocking Digital Competition - Report of the Digital Competition Expert Panel.* Crown.

8   Equivalently paying for service with information or bartering information for service.

9   There is an argument that "when the alleged violator has a "superior bargaining position" in the sense of the guidelines, it has a dominant position (or at least a quasi-dominant position) in an appropriately defined relevant market." (Shiraishi 2017). Shiraishi, T., (2017), "The Exploitative Abuse Prohibition: Activated by Modern Issues." *The Antitrust Bulletin* Vol 62(4):737-751.

10   This might pose a provocative question over the definition of "unfair" or "unjust," in the context of competition law, which is beyond scope of this paper.

11   Sugimoto, K. (2020), "Developments and Prospects for the Discussion and Regulation of `Abuse of Superior Bargaining Position' in the Digital Age" in David Anderson & Paul Lugard eds., *ICN at Twenty,* forthcoming.

III. TAKE-IT-OR-LEAVE-IT OFFERS

The problem is that individuals face take-it-or-leave-it offers when trading. They can only accept or reject offers, with no opportunity for counteroffers or bargaining (Osborne and Rubinstein 1999).[12] When two sides negotiate in a take-it-or-leave-it situation, the side that makes the offer (the proposer) is able to extract almost all the surplus the responder obtains from the trade. This is because if the responder rejects the offer, the responder must walk away with nothing. Therefore, the proposer needs only to offer a little to make the responder better off than not trading, and therefore accept the offer. The ability to make a take-it-or-leave-it offer means the proposer is in a very powerful bargaining position. Take it or leave it offers are explained in Box 1 below:

Box 1: Take it or leave it offers

When A is in a superior bargaining position relative to B, A is able to dictate terms of trade unilaterally. This is because B does not, from a practical perspective, have the opportunity to find alternative business partners to make up for the expected loss on short notice, especially when B is highly dependent on A in terms of business continuity and trapped in loss aversion. In other words, A may give B a choice of either accept or reject the terms. In bargaining theory jargon, A is able to make a "take-it-or-leave-it offer" to B and B is unable to make a counteroffer.

B has a component that it can sell for 100 (reserve value) to another buyer. A can combine this with its own component and sell the new product for 300. B's component is very important: A will only get 100 for a product without B's component. How much should A offer B for the component?

If A can make a take-it-or-leave-it offer, then it should offer 101. B is able to get 100 on its own. So, it will be better off taking the 101. A gets 300 − 101 = 199 and B gets 101.

What if B is able to make a counteroffer to A if it rejects A's offer? The reasonable outcome then is for A to offer 199 to B and B will accept the offer. A gets 300 − 199 = 101 and B gets 199. (One could argue that B should reject A's offer but then B offers A 101 because A will otherwise reject and both end up with 100.)

The point of the example is that together A and B can realize a value of 300. However, how the surplus 300 − (100 + 100) = 100 is shared depends on the rule of bargaining. In particular, if A can make a take-it-or-leave-it offer, it appropriates (almost) all the surplus. The second part of the example illustrates

---

12 Osborne, M. J. & A. Rubinstein, (1990), *Bargaining and Markets*. Academic Press.

that the tables are turned if B can make a counteroffer and A is unable to make a counteroffer after it rejects. Knowing this, if the traders could decide on rules of bargaining, one would like to be the one that makes the last take-it-or-leave-it offer. One predictor to such a bargaining situation is the Nash Bargaining Solution, which predicts $150 = 100 + ½ 100$.

Consumers are offered take-it-or-leave-it terms of trade by digital platforms. If they reject, they must be satisfied with the second option. Whatever the value of the second option, the digital platform will be appropriating almost all the gains from the transaction. When the terms of trade are for the consumer to offer information, private and nonprivate, in return for a service, the digital platform is offering the minimum service that the consumer is willing to accept if it is a take-it-or-leave-it offer. Giving the consumer the option of agreeing or not agreeing to a contract is a take-it-or-leave-it offer. There is no room to negotiate, i.e. make counteroffers.

Consumers are always faced with a take-it-or-leave-it offer in the market. At the supermarket, a consumer sees the price for a carton of milk and decides whether to buy it or not. This, in fact, is a take-it-or-leave-it offer. The consumer decides to buy the carton of milk or not and does not negotiate over the price.

At the supermarket, the price of a particular brand and carton of milk is the same for all consumers. A 200 yen carton of milk may actually be worth 215 or 250 for some consumers. Those consumers actually are ahead by 15 or 50 yen, i.e. they appropriate surplus from the trade.

What could happen on a digital platform where the platform has very detailed information about the consumer, in particular, if it has a good idea about how much a particular service is worth to a particular consumer? A digital platform is able to make a take-it-or-leave-it offer to all consumers, appropriating all the gains from the trade. This is equivalent to a supermarket charging exactly 215 or 250 according to how much the consumer values the carton of milk. This is called perfect price discrimination.

The ability of digital platforms to price discriminate perfectly means that consumers are not a mass that trades, but rather each consumer trades individually with the platform.

Note that for the proposer to extract all the surplus, they must know the responder's surplus, i.e. exactly what the responder gets from the trade. In traditional markets, the proposer usually does not have access to such exact information. In fact, the usual framework is that the proposer only knows the demand curve that represents the surplus of all consumers and is unable to identify which responder corresponds to which surplus (consumer) on the demand curve. So, the proposer offers the same price (uniform price) to all consumers. Then, all consumers whose surplus from the trade is greater than the price will accept the offer (price). Almost all consumers get a positive surplus by accepting. This is how it works in the traditional market, where each consumer's value is unknown to the firm because it is private information.

However, contrary to the case in such traditional markets, digital platforms may find themselves in a strong bargaining position, which is the result of several factors such as superior information and lack of credible alternatives for the responder. Individuals facing a particular platform will find it very difficult to find a comparable alternative. When the platform has accumulated information about a particular individual, it is able to customize its services in a manner that is superior to other platforms that do not have the same transaction history and thus information about the consumer. And the information is customized — it is not just information that makes the service, but information that makes the service attractive to the particular individual. In other words, the platform is in a superior bargaining position.

It is true that all individuals in the market constantly face take-it-or-leave-it offers. They are quoted a price at which they can buy or not buy. But the seller cannot differentiate among consumers. The difference between consumers buying in a traditional market and individual trading on a digital platform is that platforms can differentiate among consumers and set personalized prices to price discriminate.

IV. ABUSE OF SUPERIOR BARGAINING POSITION ("ASBP") IN THE JAPANESE ANTIMONOPOLY ACT

The current concept of ASBP was introduced in 1982 by the establishment of the Fair Trade Commission Public Notice under the Antimonopoly Act ("AMA") and refers to one of five refinements of "unfair trade practices" listed in Article 2 of the AMA where a business behaves "unjustly in light of normal business practices by making use of one's superior position over the other party,"

(1) Causing the said party in regular transactions (including a party with whom one intends to have regular transactions newly; the same shall apply in (2) below) to purchase goods or services other than the one pertaining to the said transactions;

(2) Causing the said party in regular transactions to provide for oneself money, services, or other economic benefits;

(3) Refusing to receive goods pertaining to transactions from the said party, causing the said party to take back the goods pertaining to the transactions after receiving the said goods from the said party, delaying the payment of the transactions to the said party, or reducing the amount of the said payment, or otherwise establishing or <u>changing trade terms or executing transactions in a way disadvantageous to the said party.</u>

We note that the transacting party does not have to be a firm. An individual trading with a business (which again is not necessarily a legally incorporated firm) with a superior bargaining position can fall victim to abusive behavior. A consumer that first agrees to a take-it-or-leave-it offer and then <u>has terms of trade changed or transactions executed in a way that disadvantages them</u> should be protected by the AMA.[13]

As we noted previously, a superior bargaining position is the result of the ability to make take-it-or-leave-it offers and information. A superior bargaining position does not always require dominance in the relevant market. It is precisely because the individual trades information under take-it-or-leave-it terms with a platform that the platform is put in a superior bargaining position. This approach differs, for instance, from looking at the behavior of platforms as the dominant suppliers in social networking services or advertising (Australian Competition and Consumer Commission 2019).[14]

Superior information is often a result of the accumulation of information over time. This implies that incumbents or well-established firms may have acquired their superior position, while entrants would not have. So, an incumbent is prone to ASBP while an entrant is unlikely to perform such abuse.

V.   THE NEW JFTC GUIDELINES

The JFTC released "Guidelines Concerning Abuse of a Superior Bargaining Position in Transactions between Digital Platform Operators and Consumers that Provide Personal Information, etc." in December 2019 (the "Guidelines").[15] Superior

---

13   Recent court rulings in the U.S., EU and Japan regarding standard essential patents with FRAND commitments also focus on the bargaining process and the strong bargaining position of a take-it-or-leave-it offer. The EU Communication is "Setting out the EU approach to Standard Essential Patents" (November 29, 2017). In *Imation v. One-Blue LLC*, the Tokyo District Court found that seeking an injunction for infringement of FRAND encumbered SEP against a willing licensee an abuse (February 18, 2015). In *Samsung v. Apple*, the District Court of The Hague found Samsung's injunction was an abuse of rights because it initiated the proceedings before making the first license offer and it failed to respond substantively to counteroffers (June 20, 2012). In *Apple v. Samsung*, the Japanese IP High Court denied an injunction to Samsung as long as Apple was a willing licensee (May 16, 2014).

14   Australian Competition and Consumer Commission, 2019. *Digital Platforms Inquiry – Final Report*. Commonwealth of Australia.

15   Japan Fair Trade Commission 2019. *Guidelines Concerning Abuse of a Superior Bargaining Position in Transactions between Digital Platform Operators and Consumers that Provide Personal Information, etc. Tentative translation* https://www.jftc.go.jp/en/pressreleases/yearly-2019/December/191217DPconsumerGL.pdf.

bargaining position takes market dominance into account along with other factors, such as ease of switching buyers.

As we discussed earlier, consumers cannot but accept "take-it-or-leave-it" offers by platforms due to the lack of reasonable alternatives. Such "acceptance" allows platforms to collect and accumulate data on each consumer, which eventually enables nearly perfect price discrimination and other manipulative measures. At the same time, giving up their own data to the platforms might enhance the quality of service that consumers will receive in return. In this sense, the consent would not be problematic as long as it is made on well-informed basis for the usage and scope of data. The Guidelines are intended to ensure that the transaction of data will be done in such an appropriate manner, and that data would be employed to cater to consumers' needs and wants.

The Guidelines also cover unintended and insufficiently advised changes in terms of trade. Such changes could be coerced after consumers have (unintentionally) allowed the platform to accumulate data. There always might be a take-it-or-leave-it offer on the table for consumers to leave, but consumers have no choice but to stay given the switching cost or ignorance (asymmetric information) about what is at stake.

The Guidelines state that "A digital platform operator has a superior bargaining position over consumers who provide personal information, etc. when the consumers, even if they suffer detrimental treatment from the digital platform operator, are compelled to accept this treatment in order to use the services provided by the digital platform operator." Specifically, (1) Unjustifiable acquisition of personal information, etc.; and (2) Unjustifiable use of personal information, etc. which unjustifiably causes a disadvantage for consumers in light of normal business practices, may constitute abusive behavior. The Guidelines present the following six examples, in two categories.

(1) Unjustifiable acquisition of personal information, etc.

a. Acquiring personal information without stating the purpose of use to consumers [Assumed Example] Digital Platform Operator A acquires personal information from consumers without stating the purposes of use on its webpage or in any other ways when acquiring personal information.

b. Acquiring personal information against consumers' intention beyond the scope necessary to achieve the purpose of use. [Assumed Example] When acquiring personal information Digital Platform Operator B stated to consumers that the purpose of use was the sale of goods, but acquired from the consumers information on gender and occupation beyond the scope necessary for the sale of goods without obtaining the consent of consumers.

c. Acquiring personal data without taking the appropriate and necessary precautions for safe management of personal information [Assumed Example] Digital Platform Operator C caused consumers to use their services and to provide personal data without taking the appropriate and necessary precautions for safe management of consumers' personal information.

d. Causing consumers in continuous use of services to provide other economic interests like personal information, etc. in addition to the consideration provided in exchange for the use of services. [Assumed Example] Digital Platform Operator D caused consumers in continuous use of services to provide personal information, etc. in addition to the personal information, etc. provided in exchange for the use of services.

(2) Unjustifiable use of personal information, etc.

 a. Using personal information against the intention of consumers beyond the scope necessary to achieve the purpose of use. [Assumed Example] Digital Platform Operator E stated that the purpose of use was the sale of goods and used the personal information acquired from the consumers by indicating the purpose of use as targeted advertising without obtaining the consumers' consent.

b. Using personal data without taking the appropriate and necessary precautions for the safe management of personal information. [Assumed Example] Digital Platform Operator G caused consumers to use their services and used personal data without taking the appropriate and necessary precautions for the safe management of the personal information.

VI.   IMPLICATIONS FOR CONSUMER AND SOCIAL WELFARE

Platforms collect data on individuals, which could be of much use especially when they are combined with other data they have collected themselves, or with those collected by others. In this sense, it is also useful to focus on how the data are used. Individual-level data can be used for matching or pricing (Loertscher & Marx 2019).[16]

---

16   Loertscher, S. & L. M. Marx, (2019), "Digital Monopolies: Privacy Protection or Price Regulation?," Mimeo.

Matching leads to a higher surplus from the transaction, all or a fraction of which can potentially be captured by the consumer. Pricing is a question of how the surplus is divided between the consumer and the platform. In other words, platforms can use information and engage in price discrimination, charging different prices to a group of consumers or individual consumers for the same or similar products.

Could platforms hurt consumers by using data to price discriminate, and would it be ASBP (Guidelines (2a) Using personal information against the intention of consumers beyond the scope necessary to achieve the purpose of use)? The welfare implications of price discrimination are not straightforward. This is because when different groups of consumers are charged different prices, one group of consumers benefits from the lower price relative to a single or uniform monopoly price, while the other group is worse off. (A monopolist increases profit beyond uniform monopoly pricing by lowering the price and increasing sales for one group and raising the price and decreasing sales for another group.) The need for antitrust or other policy intervention is ambiguous (Armstrong 2006).[17]

A firm can charge each consumer a different price and thus achieve perfect price discrimination when the seller knows the value of a good or service for each individual. Then, the seller can charge exactly that value to each individual.[18] It will be a perfect match (and thus social surplus would be maximized), but consumers pay the exact value so there is no surplus left on their side. The platform, by accumulating very good information about each consumer's preference, can do this, hypothetically (Bourreau, M. & A. de Streel, 2018[19]).

An essential condition for implementing perfect price discrimination is that there is no resale. When Amazon charged returning customers a higher price because they were locked in and at the same time charged first-time customers a lower price

---

17   Armstrong, M. (2006)," Recent Developments in the Economics of Price Discriminationm." R. Blundell, W. K. Newey & T. Persson, eds. *Advances in Economics and Econometrics: Theory and Applications: Ninth World Congress*, Cambridge University Press.

18   It is possible to achieve the same social welfare outcome as perfect price discrimination but with different allocation of social surplus: monopolist gets only the monopoly profit and consumers gets rest of the surplus (Bergemann, Brooks and Morris 2015). Bergemann, D., B. Brooks & S. Morris (2015), "The Limits of Price Discrimination," *American Economic Review*, 105(3), 921–957. This is achieved by charging different prices to different groups where groups are organized with the right mix of high- and low-valuation consumers, possible with particular information structure. If a monopolist has the incentive to do this a separate issue. However, it does lead to the question of how data brokers strategically deciding what to include and level of aggregation (information structure) to maximized information value (Elliot and Gallotti, 2019) and there may be public policy concerns.

19   Bourreau, M. and A. de Streel, (2018). "The Regulation of Personalised Pricing in the Digital Era – Note by Marc Bourreau and Alexandre de Streel," OECD Directorate for Financial and Enterprise Affairs Competition Committee

so they would come back, people were outraged.[20] Amazon quickly discontinued the practice. Had Amazon continued the practice, first-time customers could have bought the product and resold it to regular customers for a profit. Digital markets make identifying such opportunities for arbitrage and resale very easy. From a policy point of view, restricting resale may be more relevant (Woodcock 2019).[21] Just as Coase conjectured (Coase 1972),[22] consumers can act strategically or non-myopically and undo whatever damage caused when someone attempts to exercise market power. This is the case with dynamic price discrimination, which could be another problem that Amazon might have faced.[23]

A more straightforward countermeasure to having surplus extracted is to hide your preferences by having the information, such as past purchases, eliminated. Giving individuals the opportunity to have personal information eliminated has been a focus for policy. If consumers have an option to be forgotten, it might be welfare reducing. This is because when the choice of whether to refrain from providing information is left to consumers, consumers that choose to do so are those with high value (i.e. those that have most to lose from price discrimination). Unable to extract a surplus from high-value consumers, the platform will raise its prices, and extract more from those consumers it can reach (the worse off), while charging a uniform price to consumers for whose valuation the platform has no information (the better off), compared with the situation where consumers are unable to hide information. Total welfare may be reduced by giving consumers the option to hide personal information (their product valuation). A "policy" that would increase welfare would be to have consumers that hide information be uniformly distributed among different categories, so there will be just as many "low-value" consumers as high- and medium-value consumers with hidden information. Thus, consumers that get price discriminated are not hurt as much by consumers that hide information (Belleframme & Vergote 2016).[24]

Competition (duopoly) between platforms is good (welfare improving) when there is price discrimination using data, although who in fact has the data matters. If both firms have information to discriminate, competition makes consumers better off than uniform pricing. If only one of the firms has information, the informed firm must price discriminate (as a monopoly) while competing for the marginal consumers

---

20 https://www.bizjournals.com/seattle/stories/2000/09/25/daily21.html.

21 Woodcock, R.A., (2019), "Personalized Pricing as Monopolization," *Connecticut Law Review* 51(2):311-373.

22 Coase R. (1972), "Durability and Monopoly," *Journal of Law and Economics*, Vol. 15(1), 143-149.

23 In this sense, the example here must be sellers of goods like Amazon, instead of other digital platforms mainly offering digital services that are not resalable.

24 Belleflamme, P. & W. Vergote, (2016), "Monopoly price discrimination and privacy: The hidden cost of hiding, *Economic Letters* 149:141-144.

with a firm that charges only a uniform price. So, some consumers are better off while some are worse off when one firm is informed and the other is not (Armstrong 2006, Montes et al. 2019).[25] Thus, not so surprisingly, data must be accessible to both firms in order to have effective competition.

Is it possible to remedy one-sided data access by giving consumers the opportunity to hide (erase), or by neutralizing data advantage? Montes, R., W. Sand-Zantman & T. Valletti (2019) show that such an option for consumers actually makes things worse.[26] The principle is similar to that of the monopoly case. If the high-valuation consumers choose to hide, they benefit from competition, but lower-valuation consumers are left with a low surplus. Montes et al. point out that among two possible policies, access to data by platforms and consumers being able to hide information, access is the more effective for improving welfare.[27]

VII. OTHER LAWS AND REGULATIONS ABOUT CONSUMERS AND INFORMATION

There are other laws and regulations, both new and old, that protect individuals or consumers who are at a disadvantage with information. Consumer protection laws are designed to protect consumers from harm including that of asymmetric information. In Japan, the "Act against Unjustifiable Premiums and Misleading Representations" (the "Premiums and Representations Act," or PRA"), protects consumers from fraudulent products and advertising.[28] The Consumer Affairs Agency conducts investigations and issues cease and desist orders. The focus is on asymmetric information. If a product results in bodily harm, there will be a criminal investigation. The PRA's function is separate from safety regulations such as food safety and financial regulation, violation of which is a criminal offense. Words such as data and information mean different things in different contexts.

The PRA does not cover the use of data or information *per se*. Data can be at an individual or aggregate level, and it can be personal or nonpersonal (Cremer, de

---

25 Armstrong, M. (2006), "Recent Developments in the Economics of Price Discriminationm." R. Blundell, W. K. Newey & T. Persson, eds. *Advances in Economics and Econometrics: Theory and Applications: Ninth World Congress*, Cambridge University Press; Montes, R., W. Sand-Zantman & T. Valletti, (2019). "The value of personal information in markets with endogenous privacy," *Management Science*, 65(3):955-1453.

26 Montes, R., W. Sand-Zantman & T. Valletti, (2019), "The value of personal information in markets with endogenous privacy," *Management Science*, 65(3):955-1453.

27 Montes, R., W. Sand-Zantman & T. Valletti, (2019). "The value of personal information in markets with endogenous privacy," *Management Science*, 65(3):955-1453.

28 Consumer protection laws and ASBP regulation may overlap for some consumer transactions. For example, one might argue that the changes in terms of trade could constitute either ASBP when the changes are explicit, or misrepresentation when the changes are made inexplicitly.

Montjoye & Schweitzer 2019).[29] The Japanese Personal Data Protection Law defines what personal data is and sets boundaries on its use. Personal information is any data that can identify an individual. Aggregate-level data are not only the aggregation of individual data collected by a platform, but such data combined with information from other websites and sources (ACCC 2019). Similarly, combining data may result in making it possible to identify personal data. This is an example of a violation of the Personal Information Protection Law.

In the case of the "Rikunabi," the Personal Information Protection Commission issued a warning against Recruit Career Co. Ltd., the firm that operates the Rikunabi website, because the Protection Law was violated. Rikunabi is a platform that matches job applicants to firms. Instead of providing application information directly to each firm, an applicant can provide information to Rikunabi, which will forward the information to the firms under instruction from the applicant. Rikunabi also provided the firms with an analysis[30] about the job applicant (for a fee), using information that the applicant had provided to Rikunabi. Such information is good for the firm, while it may harm the applicant. Rikunabi therefore mishandled and misused personal information. It can also be inferred that Rikunabi used the data in a way that was different from the original intention of data collection and therefore injured applicants. Although Rikunabi was sanctioned by the Personal Information Protection Commission, it could have been found to be engaging in an ASBP.

VIII. CONCLUDING REMARKS

We focused on the new role of the consumer in digital markets — no longer a passive individual in the market but lacking protection. When traditional consumer protection is not enough, initiating protection from a trading partner in a superior bargaining position is one possibility.

There are two ways in which consumers can be victims when they trade with digital platforms. First, where consumers trade information for services without any

---

29 Cremer, J., Y-A. de Montjoye & H. Schweitzer, (2019), *Competition Policy for the Digital Era*. Luxembourg: Publications Office of the European Union.

30 The exact analysis and information Rikunabi provided is very particular to the Japanese job market for new graduates. The market is active only once a year to match graduates of that year to firms. Firms give job offers to graduates which graduates are not obliged to honor. (It is very similar to offers from Ph.D. programs in the U.S.) Firms do not know exactly how many of the graduates that they gave offers to will actually show up to work for them. (Exactly like graduate programs that may end up with a small incoming class.) Because Japan is currently experiencing a labor shortage, a firm may not have enough workers if they did not guess correctly. Rikunabi provided an estimate of probability that a particular graduate will honor the job offer. (Graduate directors will probably agree this is useful information.) https://www.japantimes.co.jp/news/2019/08/14/business/corporate-business/toyota-honda-bought-data-based-job-hunters-browsing-activity/#.XhrDh8j7R9M.

discretion on how the data they offered are handled and used, since the is a "take-it-or-leave-it" proposition.[31] The finality of "take-it-or-leave-it" offers affect both the original terms of trade and possible subsequent unilateral changes in the terms of trade. Second, the data and information accumulated can be employed by digital platforms for price discrimination to extract all or part of the consumer surplus, although the impact on social surplus is still ambiguous, as we argued.

One important topic we have not considered is how platforms can use information to signal product quality or consumer preference (Armstrong & Zhou 2019) and other literature that focuses on the structure of information.[32] The literature examines how information can be designed to maximize profit (see also footnote 9). This profit can accrue to information brokers or firms that buy from them (Bergman & Morris 2019).[33] Of course, firm profit is related to information broker profit, but will differ if the firm is a monopoly or in a duopoly, and thus requires detailed analysis. Neural networks and auction theory were thought to be theoretical but technology made them practical. It is probably a matter of time before designed information structures (Elliot & Galeotti, 2019) are put into practice by data brokers.[34] Then, data policy intended to restrict or promote particular groupings of consumers with different product valuations (Belleflamme & Vergote, 2016) may be realistic.[35]

---

31 The compelling nature of "take-it-or-leave-it" offer might lead to negligent consumer attitude towards how the data be used, since there is no point thinking about it when there are no other options.

32 Armstrong, M. & J. Zhou, (2019), "Consumer Information and the Limits to Competition," Department of Economics Discussion Paper Series No.888. University of Oxford.

33 Bergemann, D., & S. Morris (2019), "Information Design: A Unified Perspective," *Journal of Economic Literature*, 57(1), 44–95.

34 Elliott, M. & A. Galeotti, (2019), "Market Segmentation through Information."

35 Belleflamme, P. & W. Vergote, (2016), "Monopoly price discrimination and privacy: The hidden cost of hiding, *Economic Letters* 149:141-144.

The Role of Competition Law and Policy in Supporting ASEAN e-Commerce

By Burton Ong, Celestine Song & Hi-Lin Tan [1]

Abstract

E-Commerce plays an increasingly significant role in the way ASEAN consumers purchase goods and services and will continue to be a key front for ASEAN economic integration, especially in the face of the COVID-19 pandemic. Against a backdrop of multiple measures taken by ASEAN leaders to promote intra-ASEAN e-Commerce trade, digital trade in the region might be simultaneously facilitated and impeded by regional market developments that impact the competitive landscape in which online merchants operate. For instance, super apps that make it easier for individuals to transact in a range of different products and services through a common digital platform have brought about tangible benefits to ASEAN consumers, who stand to reap further benefits down the road as cross-border e-Commerce expands across ASEAN. However, the sheer size and scale of some of these super apps invites antitrust scrutiny in relation to the degree of market power they wield and their impact on competition. Antitrust concerns may arise because of the impact of such platforms on the contestability of these markets and interoperability with competitors. E-Commerce platforms that engage in misleading price practices could prevent consumers from making informed purchasing decisions, which might then impede the ability of honest rival businesses to compete with such errant market players on a level playing field and retard the development of e-Commerce markets. Competition authorities can play a role in addressing these concerns. They can deploy competition law and policy as a regulatory tool against conduct that has an adverse effect on market contestability, interoperability, transparency, and the development of a vibrant digital ecosystem. Examples of such measures include the CCCS's enforcement against the Grab/Uber merger in 2018 and investigation into the food delivery sector in 2016 to safeguard market contestability. CCCS also worked with a payment service provider to remove restrictions that prevented

---

1   Associate Professor Burton Ong, Head of Competition Law Research at the EW Barker Centre for Law and Business, National University of Singapore. Celestine Song, Assistant Director of the Policy and Markets division of the Competition and Consumer Commission of Singapore. Dr. Hi-Lin Tan, Director of the Policy and Markets division of the Competition and Consumer Commission of Singapore.

merchants from accepting other payment cards on common payment terminals and has developed a set of guidelines on price transparency to educate suppliers on when pricing practices may be potentially misleading, so that such practices can be reduced over time, thereby enabling consumers to shop confidently online. ASEAN competition authorities have also cooperated among themselves to achieve effective competition enforcement in their respective jurisdictions. For example, CCCS cooperated with competition authorities in Malaysia, Philippines and Vietnam on the Grab/Uber merger, where agencies shared non-confidential information and worked with other ASEAN competition authorities to develop a competition assessment framework for the e-Commerce sector. As nurturing a regional ecosystem that is conducive to ASEAN e-Commerce growth requires Member States to understand the impact of their respective governmental actions on competition and market access, national competition authorities can also play the advisory role to other government agencies in evaluating the impact of their policies on e-Commerce to avoid any unintended negative consequences on competition. Recognizing how empowering consumers with greater control over their data can support the growth of digital economy and trade, CCCS partnered with Singapore's Personal Data Protection Commission to study how data portability might be facilitated to support the digital economy.

I.   e-Commerce IN ASEAN

ASEAN[2] consumers are increasingly turning to their smart phones and mobile apps to engage in e-Commerce transactions, whether for transport, food delivery, e-payments or shopping. In Southeast Asia, the tremendous growth of cross-border e-Commerce has the potential to facilitate regional economic integration and economic growth within the ASEAN Economic Community ("AEC"). ASEAN has the third largest population in the world with 650 million people, and a Gross Domestic Product that is the fifth largest in the world at US$3.0 trillion in 2018.[3] The region which has a large and growing middle class with over 360 million internet users,[4] has seen its internet economy grow to US$100 billion in 2019 and is expected to reach US$300 billion in 2025.[5]

For all ASEAN economies, the digital economy can unlock the potential of SMEs across the region as it affords an unprecedented opportunity for even the smallest enterprises to access consumers in many markets throughout the AEC, allowing them to expand their reach across national boundaries to offer their goods and services

---

2   The Association of Southeast Asian Nations (ASEAN), which was established in 1967, is comprised of ten Member States, namely Brunei Darussalam, Cambodia, Indonesia, Lao People's Democratic Republic, Malaysia, Myanmar, Philippines, Singapore, Thailand, and Viet Nam.

3   The ASEAN Secretariat: "ASEAN Key Figures 2019," October 2019.

4   Google, Temasek, Bain & Company: "e-Conomy SEA 2019," October 2019.

5   Google, Temasek, Bain & Company: "e-Conomy SEA 2019," October 2019.

in neighboring territories. For example, businesses hoping to sell to consumers outside of their home markets to consumers in other parts of ASEAN no longer need to set up physical retail stores in these markets. This enables businesses to expand into foreign markets more quickly to tap on business growth opportunities. The cost savings could then be passed on to ASEAN consumers that could also benefit from having access to a wider range of products and services from vendors in the region with greater convenience. The COVID-19 pandemic has further highlighted the strategic commercial importance of cross-border e-Commerce. As many traditional brick-and-mortar businesses have been greatly affected by the COVID-19 related restrictions on business operations and physical activities, e-Commerce has helped retailers diversify their sales channels and revenue streams. For example, businesses that list their products on multiple e-marketplaces to sell to consumers overseas may be able to make up for the loss of domestic sales. Even when the COVID-19 pandemic abates and restrictions are eased, the role of e-Commerce in strengthening business resilience and supporting economic recovery across ASEAN is likely to stay. Therefore, if ASEAN governments continue to support and harness digital connectivity, and ASEAN businesses continue to move towards greater levels of digitalization in their operations, the pay-offs will be significant.[6]

Recognizing the importance of cross-border e-Commerce, ASEAN has taken various significant steps to realize the potential of ASEAN e-Commerce trade, including the e-ASEAN Framework Agreement7 adopted by the ASEAN leaders in 2000. These efforts have resulted in encouraging signs such as the entry of, and investments by, large and sophisticated foreign e-Commerce players such as Amazon and Alibaba into the region. Successful e-Commerce platforms operating across ASEAN today include Tokopedia[8] from Indonesia and Lazada[9] from Singapore. These online marketplaces have provided businesses the means to reach new consumers, both within their home countries and beyond. ASEAN Member States ("AMSs") have continued to step up their efforts quickly to facilitate the creation of a more conducive regulatory environment for the growth of e-Commerce. Singapore, for instance, pushed for the roll-out of an e-Commerce agreement between the AMSs to develop an innovation

---

6 Channel NewsAsia (CNA) article dated March 2, 2018: Singapore to push for ASEAN e-Commerce agreement, innovation network.

7 The objectives of the e-ASEAN Framework Agreement are to: (a) promote cooperation to develop, strengthen and enhance the competitiveness of the information and communications technology (ICT) sector in ASEAN; (b) promote cooperation to reduce the digital divide within individual ASEAN Member States and among ASEAN Member States; (c) promote cooperation between the public and private sectors in realizing e-ASEAN; and (d) promote the liberalization of trade in ICT products, ICT services and investments to support the e-ASEAN initiative. More information about the agreement can be accessed via https://asean.org/?static_post=e-asean-framework-agreement.

8 Please refer to www.tokopedia.com.

9 Please refer to Lazada.sg.

network to benefit businesses[10] when they expand across Southeast Asia, building on the e-ASEAN Framework Agreement to develop an ASEAN Agreement on e-Commerce[11] that had sought to advance e-Commerce trade rules, lower barriers to entry and build greater digital connectivity to facilitate e-Commerce flows in the region.[12] AMSs have also committed to the AEC Blueprint 2025, which has called for strategic measures such as harmonized consumer rights and the establishment of protection laws and a comprehensive framework on personal data protection to be put in place.[13] One of the objectives of the AEC Blueprint, set out in [27](iv), is for the AMSs to "[e]stablish regional cooperation arrangements on competition policy and law by establishing competition enforcement cooperation agreements to effectively deal with cross-border commercial transactions."

While some progress has been made in developing the ASEAN e-Commerce landscape in recent years, there is still substantial potential for greater e-Commerce adoption in the region. Obstacles to foreign market access,[14] as well as the lack of

---

10   The agreement encourages paperless trading between businesses and governments, which can generate more rapid and efficient transactions in ASEAN. In addition, businesses can access and move data across borders more easily, subject to appropriate safeguards. The agreement also helps to bolster the trust and confidence of ASEAN consumers in e-Commerce and drive adoption, which will enable ASEAN businesses to grow domestically, regionally and globally.

11   The ASEAN Agreement on e-Commerce was signed by economic ministers from ASEAN on November 12, 2018. Apart from aiming to facilitate cross-border e-Commerce transactions, the pact will look to foster an environment of trust and confidence in the use of e-Commerce and aims to deepen cooperation among ASEAN Member States so as to spur the use of e-Commerce as a way of driving regional economic growth. More information of the ASEAN Agreement on e-Commerce can be accessed via https://www.channelnewsasia.com/news/business/asean-economic-ministers-ink-first-e-commerce-agreement-10920610.

12   Description of the ASEAN Agreement on e-Commerce taken from the keynote address by the Minister for Trade and Industry, at the Asia Business First Forum 2018 on March 28, 2018. Keynote address can be accessed via https://www.mti.gov.sg/te-IN/Newsroom/Speeches/2018/03/Speech-by-Minister-Iswaran-at-the-Asia-Business-First-Forum-2018.

13   Two of the strategic measures to be included in the ASEAN Agreement on e-Commerce described in the ASEAN Economic Community Blueprint 2025 (refer to page 24, para 53 of the blueprint) is to put in place an "Harmonised consumer rights and protection laws" and "Coherent and comprehensive framework for personal data protection. The Blueprint can be accessed via https://www.asean.org/storage/2016/03/AECBP_2025r_FINAL.pdf.

14   Lack of foreign market access was cited as a cross border challenge for e-Commerce in ASEAN the EDB report titled "e-Commerce in ASEAN: Seizing opportunities and navigating challenges." Report can be accessed via https://www.edb.gov.sg/en/news-and-events/insights/innovation/e-commerce-in-asean-seizing-opportunities-and-navigating-challenges.html.

interoperable payment[15] and digital services,[16] can be a challenge for firms looking to capitalize on cross-border e-Commerce opportunities. In addition, the evolution of e-Commerce platforms has led to the emergence of interconnections between previously unrelated markets and industries. For example, the rise of multi-market e-Commerce applications ("super" apps) that make it easier for consumers to transact in different product and service markets through a common digital platform have the potential to simultaneously impede and to facilitate cross-border e-Commerce transactions. The sheer size and scale of some of these super apps invites antitrust scrutiny in relation to the degree of market power they wield over the different participants they interact with in the multi-sided markets they operate. Antitrust concerns might also arise in relation to the impact of such entities on the contestability of these markets to existing or potential competitors.

II.   POTENTIAL OPPORTUNITIES AND CHALLENGES FOR ASEAN e-Commerce

Super apps first emerged in China and took the country by storm, with Chinese companies such as Meituan, Alipay and WeChat leveraging on the high recurring usage of their platforms to consolidate many types of services onto a common application platform. Meituan grew from a F&B group buying app to a super app that offers many different services such as catering, on-demand delivery, car-hailing, hotel and travel booking and movie ticketing.[17] Alipay leveraged on its high volume of payment transactions to incentivize the use of other services within the app itself. The most prominent example is perhaps WeChat, which started as a mobile messaging app but has branched out into building infrastructures for other apps to build on top of their app to facilitate e-Commerce transactions. Once in the WeChat eco-system, one can make cashless payments in stores, hail a cab, order food and pay utility bills, among other functions using WeChat's payment service – WeChat Pay.

---

15   Keynote by Jacqueline Loh of the Monetary Authority of Singapore at the June 26, 2018 Central Bank Payments Conference mentioned how it is important to aim for interoperability and efficiency beyond domestic systems as "more businesses find ways to deliver goods and services overseas, payments will also need to keep up." It also noted that although cross-border linkages offer huge benefits in important areas such as trade and tourism, implementing them is an up-hill task. This suggests that interoperability of payment services across borders is an existing challenge. Keynote speech can be accessed via https://www.mas.gov.sg/news/speeches/2018/epayments-in-asia.

16   One of the strategic action plans under the ASEAN Economic Community Blueprint 2025 (refer to page 24, para 53 of the blueprint) is to put in place a "inter-operable, mutually recognised, secure, reliable and user friendly e-identification and authorisation scheme." This suggests that interoperability of digital services is still an existing challenge which ASEAN is trying to resolve. The Blueprint can be accessed via https://www.asean.org/storage/2016/03/AECBP_2025r_FINAL.pdf.

17   Please refer to https://about.meituan.com/en/about for more information.

We see similar promising developments in Southeast Asia with specific on-demand service providers leveraging on the user data they have accumulated to expand their presence across various verticals. Both Indonesia's GoJek[18] and Singapore-based Grab[19] started as ride-hailing platforms, but swiftly expanded to offer other services including their respective payment services, with the latter recently announcing its collaboration with the SingTel Group (a provider of infocomm technology services) to bid for a digital banking license in Singapore. While GoJek's digital payment service, Go-Pay,[20] and Grab's equivalent of that, GrabPay,[21] do not currently allow cross-border payment transactions, there is potential for these super apps to allow for such developments and facilitate cross-border e-Commerce moving forward. A partnership between Grab and Fave[22] allows Fave to use GrabPay credits in Singapore and Ma-

---

18   GoJek was founded in 2010 with providing solutions to Jakarta's ever-present traffic problems in mind, GoJek started as a call center with a fleet of only 20 motorcycle-taxi drivers. With the principle of using technology to improve the lives of users, the GoJek app was launched in January 2015 for users in Indonesia to provide motorbike ride-sharing (GoRide), delivery (GoSend), and shopping (GoMart) services. Today, GoJek has transformed into a "super app": a one-stop platform with more than 20 services, connecting users with over 2 million registered driver-partners, 400,000 GoFood merchants, and 60,000 GoLife service providers – with a total of more than 130 million total downloads across the region. More information about GoJek can be accessed via https://www.gojek.com/sg/about/.

19   Grab began as a taxi-hailing app in 2012 and is now Southeast Asia's leading super app, which provides highly-used daily services such as ride-hailing, food delivery, payments, and more. In Singapore, Grab provides hotel booking, movie tickets booking, trip planning and video streaming services among others. An overview of the services provided by Grab can be accessed via https://engineering.grab.com/grab-everyday-super-app.

20   Go-Pay was officially launched in April 2016 as an e-wallet service in Indonesia. According to an article by Financial Times dated December 2019 titled "Fintech: the rise of the Asian 'super app'," Go-Pay is used in 370 cities across Indonesia. Go-Pay is a mobile wallet to pay for both in-store purchases and services on the GoJek app such as GoJek rides and deliveries. Users can also use Go-Pay for peer-to-peer fund transfers. More information on Go-Pay can be accessed via https://blog.gojekengineering.com/easier-payments-with-gopay-2de099aabeb0 and https://kr-asia.com/features-and-functions-of-go-pay-vs-ovo-side-by-side.

21   GrabPay is a mobile wallet to pay both for in-store purchases and services on the Grab app such as Grab rides and GrabFood deliveries. Users can also use Grabpay for instant and free peer-to-peer fund transfers. More information on GrabPay can be accessed via https://www.grab.com/sg/pay/.

22   Fave - formerly Groupon Singapore, is a deals platform which provides discounted offers in Singapore, Malaysia and Indonesia in a single, convenient mobile app. More information about Fave can be accessed via https://www.myfave.com/.

laysia.[23] In 2018, Grab announced plans to offer instant remittance service to allow Grab users to send money instantly and securely to other countries.[24] The potential to develop interoperable ASEAN e-wallets could significantly reduce payment friction related to intra-ASEAN tourism and business travel. Currently, GrabPay Wallet users in Singapore are already able to send money from their Singapore GrabPay Wallet to another GrabPay Wallet in the Philippines without incurring transfer fees.[25] Such interoperable real-time regional payment systems will expand and enhance cross border e-Commerce opportunities for consumers, especially the large segment of unbanked citizens and small businesses in ASEAN,[26] to access products and services across ASEAN. An example of interoperability of payment services is the linkage be-

---

23   Under the tie-up which started in October 2018, GrabPay mobile wallet was added to Fave's platform, enabling Fave's customers to spend their GrabPay credits at restaurants and retailers on the Fave network. Users can spend their credits across multiple Fave categories - from food and beverage to beauty, massage, fitness, travel and attractions - and get discounts and cashback. More information on the strategic tie-up between Fave and Grab can be accessed via   https://www.straitstimes.com/business/companies-markets/grab-fave-in-strategic-tie-up-to-boost-growth-across-asean.

24   More information on Grab's plans to offer instant remittance services for Grab users can be accessed via https://www.straitstimes.com/business/banking/grabpay-wallets-to-offer-instant-remittance-overseas-from-early-2019.

25   More information about the Grab remittance services for Singapore and Philippines users can be accessed via https://www.grab.com/sg/pay/remittance/.

26   According to an article titled "How Grab is transforming finance and payments in Southeast Asia" by TECHINASIA published in August 2019, 73 percent of the ASEAN population remains unbanked. More information on the article can be accessed here https://www.techinasia.com/grab-transforming-finance-payments-southeast-asia.

tween Singapore's PayNow[27] and Thailand's PromptPay.[28] This linkage allows someone in Singapore to send money to another person in Thailand, and vice versa, using just their contact numbers at any time of the day. Businesses and consumers clearly benefit from the availability of this cross-border cashless payment service.

Interoperable regional payment services for unbanked consumers and businesses benefit both brick-and-mortar retailers and e-Commerce retailers. While consumers are already able to make e-Commerce transactions via credit cards and online payment systems such as PayPal, transactions using these payment methods require e-Commerce retailers to integrate and maintain the necessary electronic payment infrastructure that can support such payment methods in their online business platforms and may incur additional transaction fees for offering these payment methods. However, setting up such an online store with a functional payment gateway can be challenging, time-consuming and expensive for small retailers that do not have the expertise. Even with e-Commerce website builders that offer online retailers a suite of services including payments, marketing, shipping and customer engagement tools to simplify the process of running an online store for small retailers, these retailers would still need to pay for these services and spend time on copywriting and go through a se-

---

27　PayNow is a peer-to-peer funds transfer service available to retail customers of nine participating banks in Singapore – Bank of China Singapore branch, Citibank Singapore Limited, DBS Bank Limited/Post Office Savings Bank, Hongkong and Shanghai Banking Corporation Limited, Industrial and Commercial Bank of China Limited, Maybank Singapore Ltd, Oversea-Chinese Banking Corporation Limited, Standard Chartered Bank (Singapore) Limited and United Overseas Bank Ltd. PayNow offers an enhanced funds transfer experience that enables retail customers of the nine participating banks to send and receive Singapore Dollar funds from one bank to another in Singapore by using just their mobile number or Singapore national registration identity card number or foreign identification number, almost instantly. The sender no longer needs to know the recipient's bank and account number when transferring money via PayNow. PayNow, launched on July 10, 2017 is provided free to retail customers and is available 24/7, 365 days. PayNow has also been extended beyond retail customers to corporates, businesses, Singapore Government agencies, associations and societies through PayNow Corporate of participating banks. More information about PayNow can be accessed via https://www.abs.org.sg/consumer-banking/pay-now.

28　Thailand's national money transfer and e-payment system PromptPay, is a service that enables Thai citizens to easily receive and transfer funds, using their Citizen ID or mobile phone number instead of a bank account number, via electronic channels – namely internet banking, mobile banking and automated teller machines. Foreigners can use their passport as an identification document and register for PromptPay, connecting only to their mobile phone number with their preferred account. PromptPay was launched in January 2017. More information on PromptPay can be accessed via https://www.bangkokbank.com/en/Personal/Digital-Banking/PromptPay and https://www.bangkokpost.com/learning/learning-news/1261237/promptpay-a-big-success.

ries of processes to link the payment systems to their online store.[29] While retailers can outsource such work to web companies, the costs involved may not be an amount that small retailers with very thin profit margins are willing or able to pay. With interoperable payment services that connect national money transfer systems, small retailers can showcase their products on any online platform, such as internet forum pages and social media sites that may not offer payment system integration, and transact with customers separately without the hassle of building an online store and incurring additional transaction fees.

The speed at which super apps have expanded their offerings has brought about benefits to our society and there remains potential for them to do more, especially with respect to cross-border e-Commerce. It could thus be difficult to imagine a day when the very super apps that have provided us with these benefits could produce harmful outcomes instead. However, lessons should always be drawn from the plethora of examples of similarly innovative offline businesses abusing their respective dominant market positions by preventing rivals from competing on the merits and offering consumers competing products previously not available on the market. Just like their non-digital counterparts, businesses that operate super apps are, in principle, capable of leveraging on a dominant market position to harm competition in various different markets if they engage in exclusionary conduct, such as by preventing merchants from using other apps, platforms or payment systems.

III. THE ROLE OF COMPETITION LAW AND POLICY

While super apps may, at present, have been received with enthusiasm by consumers who benefit from their wide array of features, should we nevertheless be concerned that they might eventually dominate the e-Commerce landscape to such an extent that they might impair competition in the digital marketplace? For example, a super app that has a dominant position in one market may offer its consumers bundled discounts (discounts for using the same app for more than one type of service) in order to encourage its users in this market to also use its app for other services in different markets. If the super app successfully attracts a large enough number of such consumers to use the super app for services in other markets due to the bundled

---

29 For example, online business owners who wish to link their PayPal account to their bank account would have to wait for PayPal to send two small deposits to their bank account and subsequently check the bank account statement and enter the two amounts of the deposits on their PayPal account. For online business owners who wish to link their PayPal accounts to their credit card accounts would have to wait for PayPal to charge 3 Singapore Dollars to their bank account and send a 4-digit PayPal code to them. Subsequently, the user would have to check his or her card statement for the code and enter it on their PayPal account. These steps do not include those that an online business owner may need to undertake to ensure that the relevant coding or necessary steps are taken to integrate the PayPal payment facility with the e-Commerce website to process online orders and/or refunds.

discounts, the resultant "network effects" may compel businesses in other markets to use that super app to access their consumers. If other apps without the market power are unable to replicate such strategies, would businesses ultimately be forced to list on these dominant platforms or to use their payment services exclusively? Should competition law regard a business's pursuit of strategic measures to magnify the indirect network effects associated with the multi-sided markets they operate within as abusive conduct? For example, super apps that utilize such exclusionary conduct to sustain their dominance after driving out competitors may, subsequently be able to charge higher fees from businesses and consumers that transact on their platforms, raising the cost of cross-border trade for everyone. Without facing robust competition, owners of super apps may not be incentivized to engage in continuous product innovation unless the legal and regulatory environment ensures market remains contestable, systems remain open and interoperable, and pricing practices remain transparent. The absence of new competitors could also deprive the market of a pool of innovators that could have been able to provide innovative solutions that address challenges of regional e-Commerce development, such as in the area of cross-border payment and cross-border logistics. The resulting harm to competition and the welfare of society might end up outweighing the benefits that such services have bestowed upon us thus far. Fortunately, we are not entirely defenseless against these scenarios, though there may be some debate over whether pre-emptive measures should be taken or if actions can be taken only after harm has actually materialized. Legal and regulatory mechanisms can be deployed to facilitate market contestability, interoperability and transparency.

This is where competition law and policy can play a role. Competition policy and law can deter and rectify anticompetitive behavior that might jeopardize market contestability. In 2018, the acquisition of Uber by Grab showed how quickly a merger of online players could be completed and made irreversible. On March 26, 2018, Grab and Uber announced and completed the sale of Uber's Southeast Asia business to Grab in consideration of Uber holding a 27.5 percent stake in Grab, and began the transfer of the acquired assets immediately. On March 27, 2018, the Competition and Consumer Commission of Singapore ("CCCS") commenced an investigation into the transaction which constitutes a merger under the Competition Act and found that the merger had led to a substantial lessening of competition in the provision of ride-hailing platform services in Singapore. Specifically, CCCS's investigation[30] found that the merger had removed Grab's closest competitor in ride-hailing platform services, allowing Grab to increase its prices after removing its closest competitor, the effects of which were reinforced by the imposition of exclusivity arrangements that hampered potential competitors from achieving an operational scale necessary to compete

---

30   CCCS issued its infringement decision against Grab and Uber in relation to the sale of Uber's Southeast Asian business to Grab for a 27.5 percent stake in Grab on September 24, 2018.

effectively against Grab.[31] Besides penalizing the merger parties for the irreversible harm[32] to competition between ride-hailing platforms, the CCCS also imposed directions on the parties to restore market contestability. These directions included stopping exclusive arrangements to keep the market open and encourage new entry.[33] The market saw the entry of GoJek a few months later.[34] In another example to safeguard market contestability, the CCCS investigated an online food ordering and delivery services provider for its exclusive arrangements with restaurants which prevented the restaurants from using other providers' services in 2016. Although CCCS did not take enforcement action[35] as competition has not been harmed in that case and the online food delivery industry was found to be vibrant with new entrants competing aggressively with market shares changing significantly, it cautioned market players that exclusive arrangement could be problematic in the future if competition was harmed after dominance was achieved; businesses were encouraged to compete on merit so as to achieve a more vibrant market with more choices for restaurants and consumers, instead of relying on exclusive dealing practices.[36] The industry has since grown tremendously. In addition, CCCS launched an investigation in September 2019 to look into concerns over the practice of online delivery providers in relation to the rental of kitchens to F&B outlets, including the use of exclusive agreements by online delivery providers (which also operate shared kitchen premises that they lease out to food and beverage operators) to prevent tenants of their shared kitchens from using the online food delivery services of their landlords' rivals, as well as the refusal of delivery service providers to offer their services to F&B outlets that were tenants of shared kitchens

---

31 Grab had imposed exclusivity obligations on taxi companies, car rental partners, and some of its drivers.

32 More information on CCCS's investigation can be accessed via https://www.cccs.gov. sg/public-register-and-consultation/public-consultation-items/uber-grab-merger?type=public_register.

33 More information on the directions and financial penalties imposed by CCCS on Grab and Uber can be accessed via https://www.cccs.gov.sg/media-and-consultation/newsroom/media-releases/grab-uber-id-24-sept-18.

34 More information on GoJek's entry can be accessed via https://www.gojek.com/sg/blog/gojek-extends-beta-phase-to-all-consumers-in-singapore/.

35 While competition law in Singapore does not *per se* prohibit businesses from achieving market power or striving towards it, businesses with a dominant market position are prohibited from preventing their competitors from competing effectively or shutting them out of the market through exclusive business practices such as exclusive agreements with their suppliers or customers. If such conduct is found to harm competition, CCCS can take enforcement action.

36 More information on CCCS's investigation into the online food delivery industry in 2016 can be accessed via https://www.cccs.gov.sg/media-and-consultation/newsroom/media-releases/investigation-of-online-food-delivery-industry.

run or owned by their competitors. [37] While no enforcement action was taken by CCCS, it should be noted that these online food delivery providers who also operated shared kitchen premises started supplying their online food delivery services to tenants of competing shared kitchens after the commencement of CCCS's investigations. As a result, food and beverage operators operating out of non-affiliated virtual kitchens now have access to multiple online food delivery service providers, thereby expanding their pool of potential customers and increasing competition among affiliated and non-affiliated virtual kitchens. With greater competition in the virtual kitchen sector, consumers who use food delivery apps will have a greater range of food options to choose from, while affiliated and non-affiliated virtual kitchens will be incentivized to innovate when they have to compete against each other.[38]

In an earlier case involving interoperability, CCCS worked with a payment service provider to remove restrictions that prevented merchants from accepting other payment cards on common payment terminals. With these restrictions, merchants that wished to accept different payment methods would have had to install different terminals, when otherwise a common terminal could have been used. CCCS found that the restriction by the payment service provider prevented competitors from offering their services to merchants, thus limiting competition from competitors and undermined the interoperability of payment terminals.

The ability of consumers to easily and accurately compare and choose between alternatives is important for e-Commerce growth. Yet, consumers may be discouraged from participating in e-Commerce due to a lack of trust in online transactions caused by low levels of transparency and consumer safeguards against the associated harm. The emergence and rapid growth of online platforms such as marketplaces and price comparison websites ("PWCs") have made price comparison significantly easier for consumers, which reduces search costs for consumers. This increase in price transparency has also intensified price competition. Online reviews and ratings on various platforms such as marketplaces and PWCs help consumers make more informed choices. Unfortunately, consumer reservations about false and misleading information can affect the development of e-Commerce despite some progress made on this front. For example, the way prices are displayed can influence consumers' decisions. Consumers make fully informed purchasing decisions when accurate prices are displayed fully and clearly upfront. However, e-Commerce platforms sometimes engage in misleading price practices such as drip pricing, false time-limited discounts and "free" offers to entice customers. These misleading pricing practices thwart consum-

---

37 More information on CCCS's probe into the online food delivery sector in October 2019 can be accessed via https://www.straitstimes.com/singapore/probe-into-online-food-delivery-sector.

38 https://www.cccs.gov.sg/media-and-consultation/newsroom/media-releases/online-food-delivery-and-virtual-kitchen-sector-5-aug-20.

ers' ability and efforts to make informed purchasing decisions, which then impedes the ability of honest rival businesses to compete with such errant market players on a level playing field.

Recognizing the importance of the digital economy and the growth of e-Commerce, the CCCS recently conducted a study on the online provision of bookings for flight tickets and hotel accommodation to Singapore consumers. The study examined various business practices adopted by the industry players, and the associated competition and consumer issues, including misleading prices[39] displayed by suppliers.[40] Following on from this study, CCCS is developing a set of guidelines on price transparency which will address various questionable pricing practices such as "drip pricing" and "pre-ticked boxes," discounts, use of the term "free" and price comparisons (with other suppliers).[41] By educating suppliers on when pricing practices may be potentially misleading, such practices can be reduced over time, thereby enabling consumers to shop confidently online.

IV. COOPERATION AMONG COMPETITION AUTHORITIES IN ASEAN

While competition authorities are able to take enforcement action against anti-competitive activities, the cross-border nature of e-Commerce platforms may pose enforcement challenges. Antitrust jurisdiction is based on the impugned conduct having adverse effects on competition within the territorial jurisdiction over the national competition authority, but the businesses involved in the anticompetitive conduct may be located overseas. For example, some e-Commerce websites may target domestic consumers but have limited physical presence domestically. This highlights the importance of regional cooperation among competition authorities to achieve effective competition enforcement. Competition authorities in ASEAN have already begun to work together on common challenges. For example, CCCS cooperated with competition authorities in Malaysia, Philippines and Vietnam on the *Grab/Uber* merger, sharing non-confidential information. Memorandums of understanding ("MOUs") between ASEAN competition authorities can help to facilitate enforcement cooperation, which is particularly relevant to tackling cross-border issues and common challenges. CCCS has signed an MOU with the Indonesia Competition Commission in 2018 to encourage notification of enforcement activities that potentially affect one

---

39   CCCS has statutory powers to gather evidence against retailers who engage in such practices, file injunction applications against them and enforce compliance with injunction orders issued by the courts.

40   CCCS's market study into the Online Travel Booking Sector in Singapore can be accessed via https://www.cccs.gov.sg/resources/publications/market-studies.

41   More information on the CCCS's proposed guidelines on price transparency can be accessed via https://www.cccs.gov.sg/media-and-consultation/newsroom/media-releases/otb-and-price-transparency-guidelines-30-sept-19.

authority's interests, facilitate exchange of information between the two authorities, and support enforcement coordination for cases of mutual interest.[42] The MOU will also contribute towards more consistent and effective outcomes and remedies, which will, in turn, provide businesses with greater regulatory certainty.

Alongside enforcement cooperation, ASEAN competition authorities have come together to build and strengthen their capabilities to identify and address anti-competitive activities in the e-Commerce sector. This has been done, for example, through the development of a competition assessment framework for competition issues in e-Commerce sector, training programs and educational materials such as the Handbook on e-Commerce and Competition in ASEAN,[43] which was developed by the CCCS. ASEAN Member States are also taking important steps to bridge digital divides through the ASEAN Digital Integration Framework[44] which enables ASEAN Member States to prioritize[45] existing policy actions, including facilitating digital trade and innovation, while enabling seamless digital payments.

Similar attention has been paid to the development of consumer protection regimes as the part of the AEC Blueprint. The first publication on consumer protection regimes in ASEAN – the Handbook on ASEAN Consumer Protection Laws and Regulations[46] is part of the important process of providing consumers access to information and building awareness.

The aim of establishing a regional trade bloc requires a competitive ASEAN region as a whole, achievable only through deep cooperation across every ASEAN member on various fronts, including competition and consumer protection.

---

42 More information in relation to the MOU and a copy of the MOU can be accessed via https://www.cccs.gov.sg/media-and-consultation/newsroom/media-releases/kp-pu-cccs-mou-enforcement-coorperation-30-aug-18.

43 The Handbook on e-commerce and Competition in ASEAN can be accessed via https://cccs.gov.sg/resources/publications/other-publications/asean-ecommerce-handbook.

44 More information on the ASEAN Digital Integration Framework can be accessed via https://asean.org/storage/2019/01/ASEAN-Digital-Integration-Framework.pdf.

45 The ASEAN Digital Integration Framework enables ASEAN Member States to prioritize existing policy actions that will deliver the full potential of digital integration. Facilitating seamless trade, protecting data while supporting digital trade and innovation, enabling seamless digital payments, broadening digital talent base, fostering entrepreneurship and coordinating different actions of the ASEAN Digital Integration Framework have been identified as priority areas in the immediate term address the critical barriers and accelerate existing ASEAN platforms and plans to realize digital integration.

46 The Handbook on ASEAN Consumer Protection Laws and Regulations can be accessed via https://asean.org/wp-content/uploads/2018/05/Handbook-on-ASEAN-Consumer-Protection-Laws-and-Regulation.pdf.

V. ENSURING THAT GOVERNMENT POLICIES AND REGULATIONS ALSO SUPPORT MARKET ACCESS

As competition can also be affected by government policies and regulations, government agencies should ensure that their policies and regulations provide a conducive environment for businesses to grow and expand into new markets. Nurturing a regional ecosystem that is friendly and conducive to ASEAN e-Commerce growth requires the authorities to understand the impact of their actions on competition and market access, which plays a critical role in developing the AEC's e-Commerce landscape. National competition authorities can play the advisory roles to other government agencies in evaluating the impact of their policies on e-Commerce so as to avoid any unintended negative consequences on competition.

For example, in developing the physical infrastructure necessary to support e-Commerce in Singapore, the government-initiated Locker Alliance[47] piloted by the Infocomm and Media Development Authority ("IMDA")[48] in end 2018 adopted an open access delivery network comprising of parcel lockers and collection points to enable consumers to collect parcels at their convenience. The Locker Alliance brought together industry players from different segments of the e-Commerce supply chain, including locker operators, logistics service providers and e-marketplaces onto one interoperable platform. In Singapore, lockers are used as convenient delivery pickup points given their functional contribution to the "last mile" segment of the delivery process. With parcels being sent to a conveniently located locker, consumers will never have to miss a delivery to their homes and are able to retrieve their items easily by entering an authentication code.[49] This extensive network ensures that consumers will have easy access to the locker stations that are near their homes, or along the routes of their daily commute on the public transport network. With the growth of e-Commerce in Singapore, open access to the "last mile" delivery infrastructure has become a key component to building and retaining a solid customer base. The coordinated policy efforts which have given consumers timely and convenient access to their e-Commerce purchases have also given logistic service providers and online merchants the ability to deploy cost-efficient strategies to meet the demands of an ever-growing customer base. In addition, this initiative has the potential to reduce the distance travelled by delivery drivers and increase the number of parcels that can be delivered a day. This, in turn, will support the exponential growth in e-Commerce locally and regionally. In developing this initiative, the government was mindful of the need to

---

47   More information about the Locker Alliance can be accessed via https://www.lockeralliance.net/.

48   The IMDA is a statutory board in the Singapore government. It develops and regulates the infocomm and media sectors.

49   More information on the pilot can be accessed via https://www.opengovasia.com/imda-launches-pilot-for-singapores-federated-locker-initiative/.

ensure that the system was open and interoperable, thereby preventing any market player from excluding their rivals from using this national infrastructure. For example, the platform is designed to allow different locker operator networks to function alongside each other. Using a standardized data interchange, it creates a transparent, secure and consistent user experience across the delivery process. Through the platform, each operator will utilize a standardized service mediation layer to orchestrate the "last mile" delivery segment. Currently, individual locker operators may be using different unique proprietary programs but the Locker Alliance allows any operator to join the Alliance easily by simply switching to the standards prescribed in the application programming interface it has adopted. This makes it easier for new market players to scale up their operations and reach multiple locations.[50]

Competition authorities can also work with other government agencies to address emerging issues that affect e-Commerce, especially when they cut across competition and other domains, such as balancing the benefits to consumers and businesses of data portability with its compliance costs for businesses. Recognizing how empowering consumers with greater control over their data can support the growth of digital economy and trade, CCCS also partnered with the Personal Data Protection Commission ("PDPC")[51] to study data portability and how it can be introduced to support a digital economy.[52] For example, online shoppers can have their shopping history at one e-Commerce provider transferred to another platform, allowing the latter to extend more tailored offers from the get-go with data portability. These ongoing discussions with different regulators ensure that various issues that could affect e-Commerce development can be concurrently monitored, and hopefully, addressed.

E-Commerce will continue to play an increasingly significant role in the way the ASEAN nationals consume goods and services, and will continue to be a key front for ASEAN economic integration. For ASEAN to fulfil its e-Commerce growth potential, competition law and policy can be deployed as a regulatory tool to facilitate development of a vibrant digital ecosystem for the benefit of both businesses and consumers across the region.

---

50 More information on the launch of the Locker Alliance pilot and the steps taken to ensure interoperability between parcel locker networks operated by various operators can be accessed via https://www.opengovasia.com/imda-launches-pilot-for-singapores-federated-locker-initiative/.

51 The PDPC was established on January 2, 2013 to administer and enforce the Personal Data Protection Act 2012 (PDPA). More information of the PDPC can be accessed via https://www.pdpc.gov.sg/About-Us/Who-We-Are.

52 More information on the discussion paper on data portability and a copy of the discussion paper can be accessed via https://www.cccs.gov.sg/resources/publications/occasional-research-papers/pdpc-cccs-data-portability.

Competition Law Enforcement in Digital Markets - Emerging Issues and Evolving Responses in India

By Payal Malik, Sayanti Chakrabarti & Maria Khan [1]

Abstract

While digitalization has led to myriads of benefits for the consumers and created a new structure of dependencies and complementaries, at the same time it has also raised concerns on multiple fronts - effect on competition being one of them. The approach of the antitrust authorities, world over, has witnessed a shift in the enforcement pendulum when it comes to digital market. The earlier notion that market power in digital market is ephemeral and hence may not raise competition concern has changed. It is being widely held now that the digital markets are not characterized by gale of creative destruction but by entrenched and unchecked dominance. The Indian antitrust authority too has gradu-ated from almost a non-interventionist approach to a nuanced case-by-case assessment. In recent years, India has ordered investigations in many cases involving digital markets and has conducted in depth market studies. It has adopted a cautious but flexible approach while assessing the cases in the digital markets. The paper discusses the analytical frame-work employed by the Indian antitrust authority in dealing with such cases, the challenges involved therein and the drift of the rulings.

I. INTRODUCTION

Digitalization is aiding innovation in products, business processes, and business models across industry sectors. Often these advancements are proving to be disruptive, causing a rapid and fundamental shift in the way demand and supply decisions are made, communications are done, and transactions are carried out. A combination of exponential increase in digitally generated data, a multi-fold increase in computational power and advanced artificial intelligence algorithms underpins most of these developments, which on the one hand promise myriad benefits for consumers and

---

1 The authors work for the Competition Commission of India ("CCI"). The opinions and arguments presented herein are those of the authors and do not reflect the official views of the CCI. E-mail address of the corresponding author: payal.malik@gmail.com;payalmalik@cci.gov.in.

economic growth, but on the other hand raise concerns on multiple fronts – impact on competition being one of them. One of the most prominent issues in the competition policy discourse in this context is to delineate the role of competition regulators and the limits on their ability to bring about desired outcomes.

India too has witnessed the emergence of a new class of entrepreneurs and innovators, who are revolutionizing industries and business landscapes piggybacking on the new technologies and the opportunities they offer. Some statistics are in order to understand the importance of the digital economy to the Indian growth story. Fueled by rapid expansion in mobile and internet penetration,[2] government policies promoting digitization, digitization of payment options, digital identification and e governance initiatives, India's digital economy generates about $200 billion of economic value annually. This is expected to increase fivefold to $1 trillion by 2025.[3] India ranked fourth in terms of value added by the ICT sector to its own GDP between 2010 and 2017.[4] At present, the Indian e-Commerce sector is the 9th largest in the world (UNCTAD, 2019)[5] and by 2034 it is expected to become the second largest in the world and is expected to reach US$ 200 billion by 2026.[6]

Against this background, the attention of the policymakers and the competition regulator is shifting to the dynamic platform configurations that characterize the new economy, so that the intermediaries do not operate in the absence of public oversight. The technologies defining these markets indeed have a revolutionary impact on the economy, as they impose a new structure of dependencies and complementarities. It may also not be wrong to conceptualize these platform-centric technologies as General Purpose Technologies ("GPTs") that are "characterised by the potential for pervasive use in a wide range of sectors and for their technological dynamism."[7] The application of competition law to disruptive technologies is challenging, and the role of the competition authority in the entire regulatory architecture is extremely important as they seek to discover the sweet spot on the fabled inverted U shaped curve relating to competition innovation trade-offs.

---

2   The mobile phone subscriber base in India has increased from 904.51 million in March 2017 to 1173.75 million in September 2019. The number of internet users has increased from 445.96 million in 2017 to 665.31 million in 2019 and is expected to increase to 829 million in 2021 (TRAI, 2019 and IBEF.

3   Ministry of Electronic and Information Technology (2019). *India's Trillion Dollar Digital Opportunity.*

4   UNCTAD. (2019). *Digital Economy Report: Value Creation and Capture: Implications for Developing Countries.* United Nations Publications

5   *Ibid.*

6   Indian Brand Equity Fund (2019). *E-commerce Industry in India.*

7   Bresnahan, T. & Trajtenberg, M. (1995), General purpose technologies "Engines of growth?" *Journal of Econometrics* 65(1), 83–108.

In this chapter we outline these challenges in Section 2. Section 3 discusses the Indian experience in the enforcement of competition law in these markets by discussing some important issues such as the definition of the relevant market, assessment of market power and assessment of conduct, by illustrating some examples of the cases dealt with by the Indian competition authority. Section 4 briefly summarizes the findings of an e-Commerce market study undertaken by the Commission under its advocacy mandate to better understand these markets. Section 5 discusses the recent recommendations of the Competition Law Review Committee set up by the government to suggest amendments to the law including to meet the challenges of the new age markets and big data. We conclude in Section 6.

II. CHALLENGES FOR COMPETITION ENFORCEMENT IN DIGITAL MARKETS

The competition concerns in digital markets identified by antitrust authorities, discussed in the antitrust literature, and those raised by market participants span across a wide range of issues. One may categorize them into three broad, inter-linked sets - one consisting of concerns emanating from dislodgement of traditional modes of business due to the advent of digital technology, the second relating to the emergence of platform-centric configurations in many markets and its impact on markets and, the third set comprising issues surrounding the collection, use and sharing of data generated in digital transactions, and their implications for competition. These issues have given rise to challenges for competition enforcers both in terms of deciding the appropriate scope of competition law enforcement as well as in terms of gauging the adequacy of the legislative provisions and the traditional toolkit in tackling these issues in view of the specificities of digital markets.

Globally, there has been a sea change in how antitrust authorities and scholars are viewing these digital markets from a competition perspective. Perhaps the impact of these concentrated markets took some time to unfold, and after the European Commission initiated a series of investigations and imposed stiff penalties for anticompetitive conduct, the pendulum has indeed shifted. The role of BRICS countries also became important, as under the aegis of this cooperation they forged a partnership to address the competition issues being posed by digital capitalism. In a recent BRICS report it was pointed "the prevailing policy responses to the challenges posed by the digital economy often fall into "a mechanistic trap," leading to a fragmented and disconnected legal regimes for each of the digital economy phenomena (i.e. big data, digital platforms, social networks and AI). This 'mechanistic" approach establishes a status quo without instituting strong, transnational, countervailing regulatory regime(s) for the digital giants, invoking BRICS partners to have a common, perhaps a bit more aggressive competition law enforcement regime. (BRICS Competition Law and Policy Centre Report, 2019).[8]

---

8 BRICS Competition Law and Policy Centre. (2019). *Digital Era Competition: A BRICS* View.

Not so long ago, it was widely contented that market power in such markets is rare and fleeting,[9] and that intervention would entail a prohibitively high risk of chilling innovation (Geoffrey et al, 2011).[10] High demand elasticity due to low switching costs makes market power transient. Innovation rivalry would help market correction. This dynamic competition would lead to creative destruction, as monopoly profits would attract disruptive upstarts and replace dominant incumbents. Reverse network effects can also lead to exponential decline, as each lost consumer induces other consumers to leave as well (Evans & Schmalensee, 2018), leading to reduction in the incumbency advantage.[11] Thus, these markets are characterized by competition for the market rather than competition in the market, making the digital players in continuous threat of disruption (EC, 2018).[12]

However, critiques of this Schumpeterian notion of digital markets pointed out that these markets are not characterized by the "gale" of creative destruction, but by entrenched and unchecked dominance (Newmann, 2018).[13] It is argued that certain features of digital markets result not in ephemeral market power but one that is durable and hence susceptible to non-erodible concentration. Technology now allows firms to compile and refine information into a more useful finished product and that allows the firms to protect their positions by creating an ecosystem comprising multiple portals among which users can easily switch. The building of such ecosystems intensifies the likelihood of increased entry barriers, market concentration and reduced innovation.

The presence of network effects further reduces the likelihood of meaningful entry. New entrants need to provide a product which is not only better, but is able to outweigh the incumbent's network advantage. The size of the incumbency advantage in turn depends on the possibility of multi-homing, data portability and data interoperability (European Commission, 2019).[14] Access to huge amounts of data, user feedback loops and monetization feedback loops further strengthen market power, make markets prone to tipping, and create barriers to entry. Additional barriers to entry are reinforced by consumers' status quo behavioral biases when they single-home on one platform, do not alter default settings, or do not scroll down while searching (U.S. Stigler Center, 2019).[15]

---

9 European Commission decision of October 3 2014 in *Facebook/WhatsApp* (Case M.7217).

10 Manne, A.G. & Wright, J. D. (2011). Google and the Limits of Antitrust: The Case Against Google. *Harvard Journal of Law and Public Policy*, Vol. 34, No. 1.

11 Evans, D.S & Schmalensee, R. (2017). Debunking the 'Network Effects' Bogeyman. *Regulation*, Vol. 40, No 4

12 Copenhagen Economics. (2019). Digital Platforms Market Power. *Shaping Compeition policy in the era of digitisation.*

13 Newman, J.M. (2018). Antitrust in Digital Markets. *Vanderbilt Law Review*, Vol.72.

14 European Commission. (2019). *Competition Policy for the Digital Era*. European Union.

15 Stigler Center For the Study of Economy and the State. (2019). *Stigler Committee on Digital Platforms.*

Sometimes, the mere presence of digital giants in a given market can hinder entry and stifle innovation. Dominant digital firms are in a unique position to copy small start-ups' features (Obear, 2018),[16] thus dis-incentivizing entry and investment, creating "kill zones"[17] in the market. Kamepalli et al. (2019) also argues that digital platforms create a kill zone around the area of their activity by acquiring any potential competitors, dissuading others from entering, and thus preventing innovation from serving as a competitive threat.[18]

Platforms' superior data analytics ability nudge users with suggested matches that suit their tastes, charge personalized prices based on their observed willingness to pay and help them in recoupment. The whole combination of below-cost pricing, recoupment, elimination of competition, and domination by one or two firms, makes this scenario seem like predatory pricing (Bhattacharjea, 2018).[19] Dominance of an incumbent digital platform also allows it to impose restrictive terms of service and loose privacy terms leading to reduction in quality which may in turn result in both exclusionary and exploitative practices (Valletti, 2019).[20]

Such characteristics of digital markets also make them peculiar in their anti-trust assessment. For instance, it is often observed that the market boundaries in the digital space may often change quickly and may not be rigid, as in case of traditional markets. The interdependence of the sides in multi-sided platforms also has to be taken into consideration for defining the relevant markets. Similarly, in case of market power assessment, its approximation by market shares doesn't make much sense, as in the presence of network effects, prices do not necessarily represent the value of goods and services (European Commission, 2019).[21]

In the next section(s), we will see this shift in the enforcement pendulum in India as well. The Indian competition authority has graduated from almost a non-interventionist approach to a nuanced case-by-case approach ordering investigations in many cases involving digital markets and also conducting in depth market studies.

---

16   Obear, J. (2018). Move Fast and Take Things: Facebook and Predatory Copying. *Columbia Business Law Review*, Vol. 3.

17   Schecter, A. (2018). Google and Facebook's 'Kill Zone': 'We've Taken the Focus Off of Rewarding Genius and Innovation to Rewarding Capital and Scale'. *Promarket*.

18   Kamepalli, S. K., Rajan, R., & Zingales, L. (2019). Kill Zone. *Stigler Center for the Study of the Economy and the State*.

19   Bhattacharjea, A. (2018). Predatory Pricing in Platform Competition: Economic Theory and Indian Cases. In Bharadwaj A., Devaiah V., Gupta I. (eds)., *Multi-dimensional Approaches Towards New Technology*. Springer.

20   Valletti, T. (2019). Online Platforms and Market Power Part 3: The Role of Data and Privacy in Competition. (Oral Submissions at theHouse Judiciary Committee Subcommittee on Antitrust).

21   *Supra* note 14.

III. COMPETITION LAW ENFORCEMENT IN DIGITAL MARKETS: THE INDIAN EXPERIENCE THUS FAR

The prominence of digital markets in India, one may say, coincided with the first decade of antitrust enforcement by the Competition Commission of India (the "Commission"). The antitrust provisions of the competition law in India, i.e. the Competition Act, 2002 (the "Act"), came into force in May 2009. It was in the immediately subsequent years that many a digital product/service, including e-Commerce, app-based ride hailing services, digital payments, app-based instant messaging applications, either forayed into the Indian market or started gaining popularity in the country. Concomitantly, cases from these spaces also started coming to the Commission. The Commission, thus, had to gear up to examine digital market issues early on in its journey and evolve its regulatory approach in digital markets at a time when jurisprudence in many important areas in traditional markets was yet to settle.

A review of the Commission's decisional practice in digital markets suggests that the Commission has taken a cautious, case-by-case approach and has exercised the flexibility allowed by the statutory framework while assessing these cases. In the following paragraphs we intend to focus on the analytical framework employed by the Commission in dealing with such cases, the challenges involved therein and the drift of the rulings.

A. Definition of Relevant Market

As per the provisions of the Act, defining the boundaries of relevant market within which the market power of an enterprise is to be assessed and eventually the competitive assessment of the impugned conduct would be undertaken, is the necessary first step in unilateral conduct cases. The exercise must also precede competitive assessment of combinations (M&A). The three key questions that the Commission has to address while defining relevant markets in digital markets are – (i) whether digital/online markets and traditional/offline markets together constitute a single relevant product market? (ii) Whether separate relevant markets should be defined for each side of a multi-sided platform, or a single relevant market be defined encompassing all sides? (iii) Can an antitrust relevant product market be defined for a zero-priced product?

i) Whether digital/online markets and traditional/offline markets together constitute a single relevant product market?

This question has emerged as a key point of inquiry mostly in the e-Commerce cases. Addressing this issue essentially entailed an assessment of substitutability between offline and online markets. The widely cited case in this context is *Ahuja v. Snapdeal* (2014), where the characteristic differences between online and offline modes of transaction notwithstanding, the Commission ruled that online was only a "different channel of distribution" and not a separate relevant market different from offline markets. As per Section 2(t) of the Act, a "relevant product market means a market comprising all those products or services which are regarded as interchangeable or substitutable by the consumer, by reason of characteristics of the products or services, their prices and intended use." The Commission's view was premised on the rationale that the buyers weighed the options available in both markets while choosing between the channels and that any significant increase in price in one would drive consumers to the other.[22]

The relevant market delineation, however, needs to be interpreted in light of the facts of the case. The allegation in *Ahuja v. Snapdeal* (2014) was primarily against a manufacturer of portable storage devices (USB pen drives etc.), which allegedly restricted the sale of its products only to its authorized distributors, and insisted that products sold through online portals should also be bought from such distributors only. While an online portal's refusal to deal with unauthorized sellers, at the behest of the manufacturer, was also under scrutiny in the case, the impugned conduct, i.e. the sales restriction, was imposed by the manufacturer. Thus, the relevant market was defined to assess the market power of the manufacturer in this particular case, which was closed at the *prima facie* stage. It is also important to note that while briefly alluding to the kind of competition that the online portal faced, the Commission noted the presence of other significant online portals, without making any reference to the offline segment.

It was in *AIOVA v. Flipkart* (2018)[23] that the Commission categorically referred to the uniqueness of marketplace platforms emanating from network effects, and the relevant product market was defined as "services provided by online marketplace platforms." Recently the Commission demarcated online intermediation services as a relevant product market, in its *prima facie* order directing investigation in a case filed against an Online Travel Agency ("OTA").[24] The Commission observed that given the growing importance of online platforms for discoverability of hotels, it was unlikely that in case of a small but significant increase in the commission rates by all platforms, such a significant proportion of hotels would move completely offline or to direct supply so as to make such an increase in commission unprofitable for a hypothetical monopolist. The relevant market was accordingly defined as the "market for online intermediation services for booking of hotels in India." In a merger review of two OTAs[25] in early 2017 the Commission's competitive assessment carried out in

---

22   Para. 16 of *Ashish Ahuja v. Snapdeal*, Case No. 17 of 2014 (CCI, 2014).

23   *All India Online Vendors Association v. Flipkart India Ltd.*, Case No 20 of 2018 (CCI, 2018).

24   *FHRAI v. MakeMyTrip India Pvt. Ltd. & Others*, Case No. 14 of 2019 (CCI, 2019).

25   *MIH Internet SEA Pte Limited, Singapore and MakeMyTrip (MMT) Limited*, Case No-C-2016/10/451 (CCI, 2017).

the broader market encompassing online and offline and the combining OTAs' market shares were found to be insignificant. This was cited by the accused OTA in the antitrust case. The Commission opined that delineation of relevant market had to be based on market realities as they existed at the time of assessment and that in rapidly changing markets in particular, market assessment could not have a static approach. Referring to the changes in the intervening period, the Commission acknowledged the hotels' current perception of OTAs as a distinct mode of distribution and restricted the market to online intermediation in its *prima facie* order. This suggests that the Commission's market delineation exercise is not restricted by legal precedents, but can evolve in tandem with the changes in market circumstances.

ii) Whether separate relevant markets should be defined for each side of a multi-sided platform, or a single relevant market be defined encompassing all sides?

A characteristic feature of digital multi-sided platforms is the close linkages between different sides. Market definition by competition authorities should necessarily reflect these linkages. However, platforms are not a homogeneous group. There are important differences between different types of multi-sided platforms, which must also be accounted for in defining relevant markets. Platforms such as ride-hailing apps, where each interaction between the different sides, i.e. riders and drivers, is characterized by an observable and verifiable transaction, are transaction platforms. On the other hand, an online search platform, where there is no direct or verifiable transaction between the two sides, i.e. advertisers and users of search engine, is a non-transaction platform. In *Bharat Matrimony.com v. Google LLC* (2018),[26] the Commission defined separate relevant markets for each side, i.e. online general search and online search advertising, while appropriately accounting for the cross-side effects. Collapsing all users, i.e. advertisers and users of search engine, into a single product market would have ignored the fundamental differences between online general search and online search advertisement and would thus fail to provide the right framework for assessing competition issues in either. On the other hand, in *Fast Track v. Ola* (2017),[27] taking into account the single transaction that takes place on the app provider's platform and keeping in view the end consumer's perception of OLA as the radio taxi service provider which made the identity of the driver inconsequential, a single relevant market for 'radio taxi services' was defined. Likewise, in *FHRAI v. MMT* (2019),[28] a single market encompassing both sides, i.e. online intermediation services, was defined, though given the facts of the case, the substitutability assessment was undertaken from the standpoint of hotels as consumers of the intermediation services provided by the OTAs.

---

26 *Matrimony.com Limited v. Google LLC & Others*, Case Nos. 07& 30 of 2012 (CCI, 2018).

27 *Fast-Track Call Cabs and Anr. v. ANI Technologies Pvt. Ltd.*, Case No. 6 & 74 of 2015 (CCI, 2017).

28 *Supra* note 24.

iii) Can an antitrust relevant product market be defined for a zero-price product?

In the digital space, ostensibly zero-price markets exist with their own unique characteristics. Such markets for digital services, where consumers do not have to pay any monetary consideration, have given rise to questions regarding the nature of transaction and whether such "free-of-charge" markets should be considered stand-alone relevant markets for the purpose of competitive assessment.

In *Bharat Matrimony.com v. Google LLC* (2018), Google contended that search services offered by it were free and so there was no purchase or sale of goods or services and hence applicability of Section 4 of the Act (abuse of dominance) did not arise.[29] This contention was rejected by the Commission on the grounds that although users were not providing any consideration for availing themselves of the services, they did provide personal data as well as "eyeballs" to the search engine as consideration. Thus, there existed a commercial relationship and the conduct of the participants in such commercial relationships could be examined under the Act. The Commission observed, "The revenue earned by search platforms through provision of search based ad services bears testimony to not only to the potential of ad services offered by them but also negates the view that search services offered by such platforms are free." The definition of "price" as set out under Section 2(o) of the Act is inclusive and therefore includes non-monetary consideration such as data. This enabling legal provision allowed the Commission to make this first-of-its-kind determination that products that are provided for "free" can constitute a relevant antitrust "market."

B. Assessment of Market Power

The fast-changing nature of many digital markets often renders the standard toolkit and static framework for assessing dominance less effective. Moreover, the source of market power of digital players may lie in factors such as network effects, data etc., which are not commonly considered to be relevant in traditional markets. However, the strength of the network effects, the replicability of data, its economic value etc. may at times be nebulous and hence in the absence of a metric, reliance on market shares may give erroneous conclusions about market power. The Act lays down an inclusive framework for assessment of dominance, enumerating a host of factors, market share being only one of them. Further, it allows the Commission to consider any factor that it may deem relevant in a particular market context.

We see the Commission acknowledging the characteristics of digital markets and making explicit emphasis on the limitation of a static market share-centric approach in the *Fast Track v. Ola* case (2017).[30] The case dealt with alleged predatory

---

29 *Supra* note 26.

30 *Supra* note 27.

pricing, through discounts to the riders and commissions to the drivers, by the largest (in terms of market share) incumbent app-based taxi service provider Ola in the city market of Bengaluru. The Commission had to ascertain whether Ola enjoyed a dominant position in the relevant market for radio taxi services in Bengaluru before delving into the assessment of the impugned conduct. The Commission observed that the relevant market was in a state of flux throughout the period of investigation.

Despite having the highest market share, Ola had been witnessing a decline in its share, matched by a commensurate increase in Uber's market share, which reflected the competitive constraint posed by Uber and the fragility of a leadership position in a dynamic business environment. The strength of network effects was considered to be a key factor in the determination of dominance in this case. However, the ease of multi-homing both by drivers and riders, and the absence of switching costs acted as a countervailing force to such effects, which in this case was demonstrated by the entry and rapid gain in market share by Uber. In view of the still unfolding competitive landscape, the Commission held that "any interference at this stage will not only disturb the market dynamics, but also pose risk of prescribing sub-optimal solution to a nascent market situation."

The Commission's market power assessment has been subject to judicial review in another case in the same relevant product market albeit in a different city.[31] This case, dealing with alleged predatory pricing by Uber, was closed at the *prima facie* stage (unlike the previous case against Ola which was closed after investigation) since the Commission did not find Uber to be a dominant player in the relevant market of Delhi, in view of the presence of another formidable competitor Ola, who at that time were both found to be fiercely competing for the market.[32]

The Supreme Court, in its judgement, however relied upon the conduct of Uber to infer its dominance.[33] The apex court's judgement brings into focus the definition of dominance as provided in Explanation (a) of Section 4 of the Act. As per the Explanation, a "dominant position" means a position of strength, enjoyed by an enterprise, in the relevant market, in India, which enables it to — (i) operate independently

---

31 *Meru Travel Solutions Private Limited v. Uber India Systems Pvt. Ltd.*, Case No 81 of 2015 (CCI, 2015).

32 In *AIOVA v. Flipkart* (2018), the Commission did not find Flipkart's dominance on similar grounds. The Commission held that "*No doubt, the size and resources of Flipkart are largest, it cannot be disputed that the closest competitor to Flipkart is Amazon which has a valuation of around 700 billion dollars and has a global presence.*"

33 The Supreme Court, through this judgement, disposed of Appeal No.31/2016 filed by Uber India against the order of the erstwhile Competition Appellate Tribunal ('COMPAT'). The COMPAT's judgement overturned the CCI's decision and directed the DG to commence an investigation in Uber's case as it found issues in the definition of relevant market and evidence for dominance. The COMPAT further held that dominance is not only a question of market shares and had to be informed by various other factors.

of competitive forces prevailing in the relevant market; or (ii) affect its competitors or consumers or the relevant market in its favor.

The Commission's conclusion as to the non-dominance of Uber was premised on Explanation (a) (i), i.e. in view of the presence of Ola, with considerable market share and a comparable competitive position in the market, Uber could not operate independent of competitive forces. The Supreme Court observed, however, that if a loss was incurred on the trips by Uber, then Explanation (a) (ii) would *prima facie* be attracted as this would certainly affect Uber's competitors in its favor.[34]

While this may lead to a hasty conclusion that the two clauses cannot coexist since the first one sets a high and the second a relatively low threshold for dominance, one must interpret the clauses in light of the factors of dominance enumerated in the Act. Inferring dominance only from the conduct of a business enterprise can bring about anomalies in the assessment of abuse of dominance. New entrants may engage in practices such as introductory pricing, loyalty discounts, exclusive tie-ups etc., to gain a toehold in a market and holding them dominant based on simple observation of conduct could have the undesirable result of chilling competition. This had been earlier observed by the Commission in *Fast Track v. Ola*, where the Commission opined that in most markets, every enterprise would have some degree of market power, by virtue of which they could affect consumers or competitors to its favor to some extent. A narrow interpretation of the explanation of dominance would mean even a new entrant that challenges the status quo in a market and shifts a large consumer base in its favor would have to be erroneously held dominant.[35]

An investigation has been opened in the Uber case[36] following the Supreme Court judgement. It remains to be seen whether the Commission will alter its analytical framework for assessing market power in digital markets. If the conduct of Uber led to an inference of dominance, similar discounting practices by its competitor Ola should suggest its dominance as well. Arguably, many real estate firms in India were indulging in practices that would classify them as dominant according to Explanation (a) (ii) of the term dominant position provided in Section 4 of the Act, resulting in all participants in the industry as dominant.

C. Assessment of Conduct

Assessment of conduct in digital markets is not straightforward. First, owing to the unique characteristics of these markets, the source of competitive harm and

---

34 *Uber India Systems Pvt. Ltd. v. Competition Commission of India & Others*, Civil Appeal No. 641 of 2017 (SC, 2019)

35 Para 97 of *Fast-Track Call Cabs and Anr. v. ANI Technologies Pvt. Ltd.*, Case No. 6 & 74 of 201 (CCI, 2017)

36 *Supra* note 31.

consumer benefits may often coincide warranting a fine balancing act in the competitive assessment. Second, some issues are unprecedented and peculiar to the new age industries which may require retooling of the analytical framework.

The platform configuration of these markets implies that the strategies that yield demand-side scale economies could foreclose the market for potential new entrants. The platform that grows first can accelerate further with feedback effects between sides. So, it can have irreversible effects on the market structure resulting in the near monopolization of the market in question. This form-based approach is overly simplistic and overlooks the competitive ambiguity in platform strategies. The strategies that generate market power also help achieve demand side efficiencies that increase value to consumers. Moreover, competition between several platforms may not be necessarily be beneficial to the consumer when compared to monopolistic market structures.

The application of competition rules in the presence of such ambiguities might generate false positives. A counterintuitive result in these markets is that judging these markets by a counterfactual notional competitive benchmark that informs regulation may lead to a decline in welfare. Thus, the assessment of conduct becomes an extensive fact-finding exercise unravelling the minutiae of the market and the innovation system governing a particular technology. Competition authorities and regulators, in making reliable assessments, should account for the complexities of price and non-price decisions in platform markets before coming to conclusions on "observed behavior" of these firms.[37]

Second, the very edifice on which modern antitrust enforcement stands i.e. its focus on consumer welfare (i.e. judging whether a merger or commercial practice is permissible, based on whether it makes consumers better or worse off) has been questioned by commentators. Critiques of the consumer welfare standard argue that antitrust law is fundamentally flawed as it is not able to effectively address the new-fangled problems of industry concentration and corporate power (Steinbaum & Stucke 2018).[38] The errors in the consumer welfare standard can be visibly observed in digital markets ((Evans & Schmalensee 2017).[39] Platform based firms are likely to support aggressive low-price strategies, leverage across multiple lines of businesses, discriminate against digital complements, and engage in predatory start up acquisitions and M&A (Khan 2017).[40] A view which is gaining traction is that the consumer welfare standard should be forsaken, and a host of new factors should be considered

---

37 Jakhu, G. & Malik, P. (2017). Dilemma in antitrust enforcement: how use of economics can guide enforcement rules in multi-sided markets. *Journal of Antitrust Enforcement*, Volume 5, Issue 2, pages 260–275.

38 Steinbaum, M., & Stucke, M. (2018). *The effective competition standard—A new standard for antitrust*. New York: Roosevelt Institute.

39 Evans, D., & Schmalensee, R. (2017). Why the claim that markets with two-sided platforms become one-sided when they mature is wrong. *Amicus Brief*.

40 Khan, L. (2017). Amazon's Antitrust Paradox. *The Yale Law Journal*, 126, 710.

by antitrust authorities, especially in the context of digital markets. According to this, consumer welfare overlooks other values, including vibrant small businesses, innovation, privacy, worker interests, and healthy democratic processes.

The jurisprudential history of the Commission shows that the Commission has steered away from multiple and often conflicting objectives in the application of competition law and has adopted a consumer welfare standard. We believe that the consumer welfare standard, properly defined, protects all counterparties from anti-competitive behavior or transactions. It incorporates non-price harm to consumers, such as lower quality, reduced variety, or slower innovation. It allows regulators and courts to focus on long-term changes. Pure static price effect metrics for the assessment of a given type of conduct or combination is now passé, and various considerations are incorporated in a sound competition assessment. But redistributive concerns still do not enter these considerations. In our view, it is important that antitrust policy remains focused on market activity and be backed by a clear economic analysis of likely effects.

In India, the issues in digital market cases have centered on the disruption caused by digital technology-enabled business models and the conduct of online platforms in terms of extending their dominance into related markets as also with respect to their agreements with the business users. The cases relating to digital disruption were raised mostly by affected traditional players when digital players had just entered the market and the new competitive dynamic was still unfolding. Most of such cases have been closed by the Commission, since markets were found to be in flux, and dominance by any one enterprise could not be established. The cases concerning conduct of online platforms have been examined by the Commission under the provisions of the Act relating to abuse of dominance, and recently also under the provisions relating to vertical agreements. The most important among them pertained to online search and search intermediation, smart mobile device operating systems and e-Commerce. Some of the major issues dealt by the Commission are discussed in the ensuing paragraphs.

In Bharat Matrimony.com v. Google (2018), the Commission found Google's conduct in online general search and online search intermediation markets to be an abuse of its dominant position, in contravention of Section 4 of the Act.[41] The breach related to search bias in presenting search results on Google's online general search platform, and Google's exclusive agreements with certain web publishers for providing online search intermediation service.

The discussion in the Commission's order of its regulatory approach towards digital markets merits a mention here. The Commission opined that public intervention in digital markets should be targeted and proportionate, so that intervention

---

41   *Supra* note 26.

remained effective and it did not restrain innovation. In the context of search bias, it was further noted that product design was an important dimension of competition, and that any undue intervention in designs might affect legitimate product improvements, resulting in consumer harm. However, it was clarified that such regulatory forbearance was only by way of self-imposed restraint, and that if in a given case the Commission found the conduct to be egregious, appropriate remedies and directions would be issued to correct such a distortion.

What was found egregious in this case was the prominent placement of Google's commercial flight units and the disproportionate real estate allotted to it on Google's Search Engine Result Page ("SERP"). The Commission observed two anti-competitive implications of this practice – first, the diversion of traffic by Google Flights that may not allow equally efficient third-party travel verticals to acquire sufficient volume of business; and second, capturing of user data by Google which would not allow competing vertical search pages the same benefit, and deteriorate their ability to further innovate their products. Such a search design, according to the Commission, resulted in restriction of additional choice for consumers, thus amounting to an unfair imposition on the users of Google's online search platform. Google's pre-2010 practice of displaying its Universal Results[42] on fixed positions was also found to be unfair to users as it created a misleading façade that such search results were algorithmically determined on the basis of relevance. Finally, by having an exclusivity clause in Google's negotiated search intermediation agreements with web-publishers, Google was found to be denying its competitors access to the search business, endangering their viability while strengthening its own position.

The Commission's decision in the *Google* case was not unanimous, with a two-member dissent pointing out inadequacies in the evidence and anomalies in the analytical framework relied upon. In both the majority decision and the dissenting opinion, the conduct of Google was viewed from the competitors' perspective as well as from the vantage point of consumers. The key point of difference was regarding whether only the form of the conduct and a likelihood of it causing competition or consumer harm should be sufficient to conclude its unfairness/anti-competitiveness in digital markets characterized by entrenched market power, or whether the competitive assessment should still account for empirical evidence on user preferences/behavior as also the actual effect of the impugned practice. The case is not yet final, as the majority decision of the Commission has been challenged by Google. The decision of the appellate authority will be critical in guiding the analytical approach and providing the normative basis for future cases.

The Commission has recently opened three major investigations in digital markets. The Commission's 2019 *prima facie* order directing the Director General

---

42   Universal Results are groups of search results for a specific category of information, such as news, images, or local businesses.

to probe Google's conduct in the market for licensable smart mobile device operating systems pertains to the issue of Google allegedly leveraging its dominance in the application-store market to perpetuate its dominant position in other relevant markets such as online general search.[43] The compulsory tying of a bouquet of Google apps in order to be able to license the Google Play Store, was *inter alia* found to be *prima facie* anti-competitive. The outcome of the case will depend on the market insights and evidence unearthed in the investigation. It will be interesting to see if the market realities in India and, accordingly, the effect of Google's conduct here, are similar to or different from what was observed in the EU, where Google has been penalized by the European Commission for breaching the antitrust rules for largely similar conduct.[44]

The Commission has also issued investigation orders in two e-Commerce cases.[45] The issues of contention in these cases largely centered on the vertical arrangements between online e-Commerce platforms and their business users. In a case against MakemyTrip-Goibibo (2019), the largest OTA in the online intermediation market for hotel booking in India. The concerns, *inter alia*, include room and price parity restrictions imposed by the OTA on hotels, exclusive listing of a particular hotel chain and delisting of its competitors from the OTA's platform, and deep discounting practices and exorbitant commissions charged by the OTA. The OTA was found to be *prima facie* dominant in the relevant market for online intermediation services for booking of hotels in India, and the Commission found it fit to open an investigation into its practices. In goods e-Commerce, the Commission has closed a case of alleged abuse of dominant position by Flipkart, a major e-Commerce platform in India, at the *prima facie* stage, as Flipkart was not found to be occupying a dominant position in the presence of Amazon, a significant competitor in the same relevant market.

However, in January 2020, an investigation has been ordered by the Commission into the conduct of both Flipkart and Amazon for *prima facie* violation of Section 3(4) of the Act, that deals with vertical agreements. The Commission noted that the exclusive launch of select mobile phones on certain e-Commerce platforms, coupled with preferential treatment for select sellers, and the discounting practices of platforms, taken in conjunction, could create an ecosystem that might have an adverse effect on competition.

The issues of data protection and user privacy came up in Gupta v. WhatsApp (2017),[46] where the informant alleged that WhatsApp was abusing its dominant position in the relevant market for instant messaging services using consumer

---

43   *Umar Javed & Others v. Google LLC & Others*, Case No 39 of 2018 (CCI, 2019).

44   *Google Android*, CASE AT.40099 (EC, 2019).

45   *FHRAI v. MakeMyTrip India Pvt. Ltd. & Others*, Case No. 14 of 2019 (CCI, 2019) & *Delhi Vyapar Mahasangh v. Flipkart and Others*, Case No 40 of 2019 (CCI, 2019).

46   *Vinod Kumar Gupta v. WhatsApp Inc.*, Case No: 99 of 2016 (CCI, 2017).

communication apps through smartphones in India, by changing its terms of service and privacy policy and compelling the users to share their account details and other information with Facebook for the purpose of targeted advertisements. The Commission closed the case on the grounds that WhatsApp provided the option for its users to 'opt out' of sharing user account information with Facebook within 30 days of agreeing to the updated terms of service and privacy policy. However, the manner in which the change was effected appears to have made the choice of "opting out" ineffective in practice, as it was not made available upfront, and the complete absence of an 'opt out' policy thereafter appears questionable. Despite having exploitative conduct of dominant enterprises within its ambit, the Commission's decision to close the case without investigation indicates its reluctance in bringing pure privacy or data protection issues in the fold of antitrust. However, while lower data protection can lead to exploitation, it can also have an exclusionary effect, as incumbents, due to their data advantage, would be able to further entrench their dominant positions and leverage into neighboring markets, resulting in entry barriers (Valletti, 2019).[47] Thus, how to deal with the data use policies of dominant players is a challenge facing all competition authorities, including India, in the absence of a counterfactual competitive benchmark.

IV. MARKET STUDY

Besides enforcement, a major initiative of the Commission in the digital space has been the recently conducted market study in e-Commerce. Lack of platform neutrality, unfair platform-to-business contract terms, exclusive contracts, platform price parity restrictions and deep discounts were among the competition issues that emerged from the study. The study report[48] mentions that many of these issues would lend themselves to a case-by-case examination by the Commission under the relevant provisions of the Act. It further notes that given the economics of platform markets, where the winner takes all or most, any potentially anti-competitive unilateral conduct of platforms or platforms' vertical arrangements with business users would receive enforcement attention.

The common thread that connects most issues discussed in the report is the bargaining power imbalance and information asymmetry between e-Ccommerce marketplace platforms and their business users. Many platform-to-business issues are arising even with platforms which are not technically dominant. In absence of provisions relating to abuse of superior bargaining position, the competition law in India cannot address such issues, which do not have any exclusionary implications. In view of the

---

47 *Supra* note 20.

48 Market Study on E-Commerce in India: Key Findings and Observations is available at https://www.cci.gov.in/sites/default/files/whats_newdocument/Market-study-on-e-Commerce-in-India.pdf.

same, certain stakeholder groups were expecting the Commission to recommend *ex ante* platform-to-business ("P-2-B") regulation. At a time when India is in the process of framing its e-Commerce policy, such a recommendation could have triggered the necessary stakeholder consultation for a detailed review of the necessity, potential impact and mechanics of bringing in a P-2-B regulatory framework as part of a comprehensive policy. The report instead enumerates certain areas for self-regulation by the e-Commerce marketplace platforms, such as search ranking criteria, collection, use and sharing of data, user review and rating mechanisms, revision of contract terms and discount policies, with a view to reducing information asymmetries, promoting competition on the merits and to foster a sustainable e-Commerce ecosystem in India. These are all very pertinent measures, nevertheless, in absence of any legal backing, whether such recommendations would actually lead to any tangible change in the platforms' behavior remains to be seen.

V.   COMPETITION LAW REVIEW COMMITTEE AND DIGITAL MARKETS

The Indian competition law recently completed ten years of its journey. The Government constituted a Competition Law Review Committee ("CLRC") in 2018, with one of its objectives being to review the adequacy of the existing statutory architecture to address anti-competitive behavior arising out of digital markets. The moot question before the CLRC was whether digital markets demand a different antitrust dispensation or whether the existing set of antitrust rules have the flexibility and bandwidth to envisage and regulate these markets.

While the CLRC confirmed the robustness of the existing provisions of the Act in meeting the challenges posed by digital platforms, it has recommended some additions to the existing provisions. The Committee has recommended covering "hubs" in the assessment of "hub and spoke" cartels and imputing liability to such hubs based on the existing rebuttable presumption rule in the Act. The Committee also recommended widening the scope of anti-competitive agreements to cover all kind of agreements which do not fall within the categories of either a horizontal or vertical arrangement. Further, to make the factors in the determination of relevant markets comprehensive, the Committee has recommended widening the scope to accommodate factors that may apply to the new economy.

The Committee recognized that merger tools maybe the most appropriate to deal with competition concerns on account of data monopolies and in fact the *ex post* tools on abuses of dominance may be counterproductive, as consumers may be too entrenched in a particular technology. An amendment to Combination threshold provision, which is currently based on assets and turnover, has been suggested – to incorporate an enabling provision empowering the government to introduce necessary thresholds, including a 'deal value threshold' for notification. Further, in the interest of speedier resolution of cases, which is particularly critical in the context of fast changing digital markets, the Committee has recommended additional enforcement mechanisms in the form of Settlements and Commitments.[49]

VI. CONCLUSION

In order to understand the development of antitrust enforcement in the digital markets in India, it is important to understand the genesis of the law. The enforcement of the Act and the establishment of the Commission was a clear signal to the corporate world that the state is relinquishing the allocation of resources to the market. The Preamble of the Act affirms the role envisaged for the Commission as an instrument for engendering and protecting competition in the market. It makes an unambiguous assertion of the focus of the Act being on "competition" and not on survival or welfare of individual "competitors."

In that sense the law is 'purist' and the legislative history does not confirm that it was meant to be an instrument to address larger 'public interest' needs. Protecting small businesses, promoting domestic firms and other public interest considerations are neither mentioned in the Act for the Commission to consider, nor have been pursued by the Commission in either antitrust or merger review. Furthermore, the recent debates in the Competition Law Review Committee have argued for a continuation of a competition assessment based on economic factors that include quality, investment and innovation (in addition to price). This does not imply that the Commission is re-defining the welfare standard; it is just an extension of the consumer welfare standard and the endeavor is to adopt a correct welfare standard, which is multidimensional and is in service of the larger goals of economic development. However, any determination of anticompetitive conduct or of the impact of a given merger will be inextricably linked with outcomes, and outcomes can be related to the narrow goals of economic efficiency. We believe that competition on the merits is quite consistent with the consumer welfare standard, as it prohibits conduct that creates, or is likely to create, market power for reasons that are unrelated to economic efficiency. A staple result in regulation literature is that a regulator has to strike a trade-off between reducing a firm's rent and ensuring that the firm's incentive compatibility condition is satisfied. It forces the regulator to optimally compromise between these twin objectives, leaving leaving some rents for the regulated firm. This canonical result could not be more true for digital markets, and calls for a cautious approach to antitrust enforcement, backed by evidence of harm.

Thus, in the initial years the Commission summarily dismissed cases received by aggrieved competitors in the traditional economy who could not face the onslaught

---

49   Competition Law Review Committee (2019). Report of the Competition Law Review Committee. *Government of India*. Available at http://www.mca.gov.in/Ministry/pdf/Report-CLRC_14082019.pdf

of the new technology and the new markets that were spawning as a consequence of disruption. This was quite evident in the decisions of the Commission, be it in online retail or in the app-based taxi market. However, certain egregious conduct by platforms that were clearly identifiable as causing competitive harm such as search bias, exclusive agreements and prominent placement of firm's own product; imposition of unfair conditions and compulsory tying, platform parity restrictions etc. came under the competition scanner.

While the Commission has made an oblique reference to abuse of market power through gaining an "unsurmountable" data advantage in the *Google Search* bias case, it has steered away from privacy as an antitrust issue. However, there is an increasing acceptance of the view that data is emerging as a key (intangible) asset that can drive certain acquisitions in the digital space. The CLRC has recommended an amendment to the merger notification thresholds to include a "transaction value" threshold to exercise greater control over deals in the digital economy. The idea that is gaining currency in India is that these deals should not escape enforcers' scrutiny just because a company's revenue does not reach a prescribed level.

A Data Protection Law and Data Protection Authority are currently on the anvil in India, and a bill has been introduced in the lower house of the parliament. The authorities responsible for data protection in the digital sector and the Commission will need to follow a consultative process to ensure a harmonized regulatory framework to promote efficient digital markets.

The Competition Commission of India's Approach Towards Digital Markets: The Shift Towards Interventionism

By Naval Satarawala Chopra, Yaman Verma & Aman Singh Sethi [1]

Abstract

The Competition Commission of India ("CCI") joins an increasing number of regulators embracing enhanced intervention in digital markets. The CCI initially exercised a "self-imposed restraint," adopting a light-touch, hands-off approach. Its traditional enforcement in digital markets focused on cases where dominance was evident, and the CCI avoided investigating markets witnessing fierce competition between disruptors, as well as where there was ease of switching or multi-homing. However, traditional businesses, or those unable to keep pace with innovation, saw these digital disruptors as a threat and called for intervention. Entering its second decade of competition law enforcement, the CCI seems to have heard this call.

The CCI's recently concluded market study on e-Commerce in India was a watershed moment. Following the study, they appear to have adopted the position that interference only in "egregious" cases was not sufficient to protect competition. They have demonstrated interest in creating an equitable environment for businesses dependent on platforms where it is suggested that competition between platforms is insufficient to protect the interests of these businesses. This is evidenced by new investigations into markets previously examined and blessed, commencing shortly after the study. In this article, we track the evolution of the CCI's ideology in relation to digital markets.

I.   INTRODUCTION

The regulation of conduct in digital markets by competition authorities across the world is a mixed bag. While several authorities leave markets free to correct themselves through the competitive process, others tend to prefer greater engage-

---

1   Naval Satarawala Chopra (Equity Partner), Yaman Verma (Partner) and Aman Singh Sethi (Principal Associate), Shardul Amarchand Mangaldas & Co. The firm has advised on several cases discussed in this chapter. The views expressed here are personal.

ment. India's competition regulator, the Competition Commission of India ("CCI"), initially adopted a light-touch, hands-off approach, but has now embraced increased intervention.

Over the years, the CCI has recognized the fast pace of innovation cycles and the merits of limited, targeted and proportionate intervention. It has noted that "intervention in technology markets has to be carefully crafted lest it stifles innovation and denies consumers the benefits that such innovation can offer. This can have a detrimental effect on economic welfare and economic growth, particularly in countries relying on high growth such as India."[2] Therefore, it has intervened in cases where it believed the conduct to be "egregious."[3] However, that approach has undergone a change.

In late 2018 and early 2019, there was immense pressure and growing calls, from traditional players in the retail and hospitality sectors, for the regulation of competition from technology enabled disruptors by the CCI.[4] Sectors of the Government of India too echoed similar sentiments. In response, the CCI launched a market study into the e-Commerce sector ("Market Study"). While the stated objective of the Market Study was for the CCI to gain greater clarity on the market developments and impediments to competition and ascertain its enforcement and advocacy priorities, the Market Study marked the shift to a more interventionist approach. The CCI has since shown a greater inclination towards using a wide range of tools to examine concerns of anti-competitive conduct in digital markets. It is no longer only focused on whether a defendant is dominant, but also looks at vertical agreements that the defendant has entered into and the effect of such agreements on competition in the market.

This article identifies trends in the CCI's approach towards digital markets, including the use of newer, more flexible means for greater regulation, and explores the possible effects of this change on various players in digital markets.

II. THE PREVAILING REGIME

The Competition Act, 2002 ("Competition Act") governs anti-competitive agreements (under Section 3), abuse of dominance (under Section 4), and combinations (mergers and acquisitions) (under Sections 5 and 6) in India.

---

2 *Matrimony.com Limited v. Google LLC*, CCI Case Nos. 07 and 30 of 2012 ("*Matrimony.com v. Google*"), at paragraph 203.

3 *Id.* at paragraph 205.

4 At this stage, while the CCI had looked into the e-Commerce sector, it did not direct any investigation into allegations of capital dumping, predatory price, etc. raised by these players. Relevant cases are discussed subsequently.

A. Anti-Competitive Agreements

Section 3(1) of the Competition Act prohibits anti-competitive agreements that cause, or are likely to cause, an appreciable adverse effect on competition ("AAEC") in India. In determining whether an agreement causes an AAEC in India, the CCI is required to consider a number of "negative" and "positive" factors listed under Section 19(3) of the Competition Act. The "negative" factors are: (a) the creation of barriers to entry; (b) driving existing competitors out of the market; and (c) foreclosing competition by hindering entry into the market. The "positive" factors are: (a) accrual of benefits to customers; (b) improvement in production or distribution; and (c) promotion of technical, scientific and economic development.[5] The Competition Act broadly discusses two forms of agreements, i.e. horizontal and vertical.

1. Horizontal anti-competitive agreements

Horizontal agreements are agreements between enterprises at the same level of the production chain (i.e. agreements between competitors). Section 3(3) of the Competition Act deals with horizontal agreements which: (a) directly or indirectly determine prices; or (b) limit or control production, supply, markets, technical development, investment or provision of services; or (c) share the market/source of production/provision of services, by way of allocation of geographical area/type of goods and services/number of customers; or (d) directly or indirectly result in bid rigging or collusive bidding. Further, horizontal agreements are presumed to cause an AAEC, however such a presumption is rebuttable.

2. Vertical anti-competitive agreements

Vertical agreements are agreements between enterprises at different levels of the production chain (for instance, a manufacturer and distributor). Section 3(4) of the Competition Act deals with certain vertical agreements, including: (a) tie-in arrangements; (b) exclusive supply and distribution agreements; (c) refusal to deal; and (d) resale price maintenance, where such agreements cause or are likely to cause an AAEC in India. Unlike horizontal agreements, vertical agreements do not carry the presumption of causing an AAEC, and a "rule of reason" (effects based) approach is adopted in assessing them.

B. Abuse of Dominance

Section 4 of the Competition Act prohibits the abuse of a dominant position by an enterprise or a group. A "dominant position" is defined as a position of strength

---

5   The CCI has not issued any guidance on how these factors are prioritized and weighed. The standard applied by the CCI in deciding whether an agreement causes an AAEC is the civil standard of preponderance of probabilities.

enjoyed by an enterprise in the relevant market in India, which enables it to operate independently of competitive forces prevailing in the relevant market, or affect its competitors or consumers or the relevant market in its favour.[6]

A dominant enterprise or group is seen as abusing its dominant position if it either: (a) imposes unfair prices (including predatory pricing) or unfair conditions on sale or purchase; or (b) limits or restricts production/ technical development so as to detrimentally affect consumers; or (c) denies market access to other players in the market; or (d) makes conclusion of contracts subject to acceptance of supplementary obligations which have no connection with the subject of such contracts; or (e) uses its dominant position in one relevant market to enter into or protect another relevant market, i.e. the leveraging abuse.

C. Merger Control Regime

Under Sections 5 and 6 of the Competition Act, an acquisition of assets which meets the prescribed jurisdictional, asset and turnover thresholds has to be pre-notified to the CCI. The thresholds are provided on a "parties" and "group" basis and if either of the tests are met, the transaction cannot be consummated unless it has received prior approval of the CCI.

The Government of India, has exempted the notification requirement for transactions where the target enterprise (i.e. enterprise whose control, shares, voting rights or assets are being acquired, taken control of, merged or amalgamated) has either Indian assets of not more than INR 350 crores (approx. USD 49 million), or turnover of not more than INR 1,000 crores (approx. USD 140 million) in India ("Target Exemption"). The CCI has clarified that while assessing thresholds under the Target Exemption, only the value of assets being transferred and turnover attributable to such transferred assets shall be considered as the relevant assets/turnover. This has had a substantial impact on the number of transactions that are required to be notified to the CCI, and a greater number of transactions can avoid merger control review.

III. THE CCI'S OUTLOOK ON DIGITAL MARKETS BEFORE THE MARKET STUDY

An analysis of the CCI's decisional practice before 2019 shows that it was concerned about the detrimental effect of unnecessary intervention in technology markets on innovation, consumer welfare and economic growth. Statements reiterating the dangers of an interventionist approach were included in a number of its decisions. For instance, the CCI held that it is, "hesitant to interfere in a market, which is yet to fully evolve" while examining cases related to taxi aggregators since interference, in its opinion would, "not only disturb the market dynamics, but also pose a

---

6   Explanation (a) to Section 4, Competition Act.

risk of prescribing sub-optimal solution to a nascent market situation."[7] Accordingly, the CCI made it clear that such "regulatory forbearance from interfering ... is only by way of self-imposed restraint but if in any given case, the Commission finds the conduct to be egregious, appropriate remedies and directions shall be issued to correct such a distortion."[8] In another matter, relating to an e-Commerce platform, the CCI observed that, "the marketplace based e-commerce model is a relatively nascent and evolving model of retail distribution...recognizing the growth potential as well as the efficiencies and consumer benefits that such markets can provide ... any intervention in such markets needs to be carefully crafted lest it stifles innovation."[9]

We explore whether the CCI's stated positions have been applied in practice through an assessment of its decisions during this period. In order to better understand the CCI's decisional practice, the following section discusses: (a) cases where CCI closed the investigation at the threshold stage itself, declining to interfere in evolving and innovative markets; (b) cases where CCI did order an investigation but eventually did not find any contravention of the Competition Act; (c) cases where CCI found a contravention of the Competition Act and decided to intervene; and (d) ongoing investigations.

A. Instances Where CCI Closed a Case at the Threshold Stage

1. WhatsApp

In 2017, the CCI considered whether a change in privacy terms of messaging platform WhatsApp would amount to an abuse of dominant position. The CCI adopted a pragmatic approach in examining these allegations.

At the time, WhatsApp was found to have a very high market share (90 percent as per the evidence before the CCI), and it was *prima facie* found to be dominant in the market for instant messaging apps in India. However, the CCI appreciated the nature of the instant messaging industry, the standard practice of competitors to offer services free, and evidence of multi-homing by users and low switching costs.[10] It noted that:

> ... there are no significant costs preventing users to switch from one consumer communication app to another. It may be due to

---

7   *Fast Track Call Cab and Meru Travel Solutions* ("*Meru*") *v. ANI Technologies* ("*Ola*"), CCI Case Nos. 6 and 74 of 2015 ("*Ola Bangalore*"), at paragraph 123.

8   *Matrimony.com v. Google,* at paragraph 205.

9   *All India Online Vendors Association v. Flipkart*, CCI Case No. 20 of 2018 ("*AIOVA v. Flipkart*"), at paragraph 34.

10   *Vinod Kumar Gupta v. WhatsApp Inc.*, CCI Case No. 99 of 2016 ("*WhatsApp*").

the following reasons: (i) all consumer communication apps are offered for free of cost or at a very low price (mostly free), (ii) all consumer communication apps are easily downloadable on smartphones and can co-exist on the same handset (also called 'multi homing') without taking much capacity along with other apps, (iii) once consumer communication apps are installed on a device, users can pass on from one app to its competitor apps in no-time, (iv) consumer communication apps are normally characterized by simple user interfaces so that costs of switching to a new app are minimal for consumers, and (v) information about new apps is easily accessible given the ever increasing number of reviews of consumer communication apps on apps store like google play store etc.[11]

Taking this into account, along with the observation that there are no significant barriers to entry into the relevant market (as well as the rise of competitor, Hike, at the time) the CCI finally concluded that WhatsApp's conduct would not amount to abuse.

2. AIOVA v. Flipkart

In 2018, the CCI dismissed at the threshold stage a complaint against Flipkart, an operator of a marketplace-based e-Commerce platform. The complaint alleged that Flipkart had abused its dominant position by facilitating discounts and leveraging its position to enter another market of manufacturing products through private labels.

While holding that Flipkart had not abused its dominant position, the CCI noted the distinct nature of online marketplace platforms, including network effects, and observed that digital markets offer greater welfare for all stakeholders, in particular allowing sellers to save costs involved with setting up a physical store, and customers to buy from the comfort of their homes, saving time and money. As mentioned previously, recognising the growth potential and efficiencies of the e-Commerce model, the CCI was conscious of the fact that interference could hamper further innovation.[12]

Further, while the allegations in the case were against Flipkart alone, the CCI invited Amazon to participate in its deliberations. In light of the presence of Amazon

---

11 *Id.*

12 *AIOVA v. Flipkart.* Note, this decision has subsequently been reversed by the National Company Law Appellate Tribunal ("NCLAT") which has directed the CCI to investigate into the allegations against Flipkart. This does not amount to any final determination and only directs the commencement of an investigation. *All India Online Vendors Association v. CCI*, NCLAT Appeal No. 16 of 2019.

– a strong competitor to Flipkart, the CCI concluded that at the current stage of evolution of the market, no one player commanded a dominant position. Since Flipkart was not dominant, the CCI decided that the question of abuse did not arise.

3. Cases relating to the taxi aggregation market

With the rise of taxi aggregators such as Uber and Ola, the CCI received a number of complaints from competing traditional players in India alleging anti-competitive conduct. Seven of these cases were closed at the threshold stage itself as the CCI considered the existence of the "other" aggregator as a competitive constraint on Uber or Ola.[13]

In the latest case against both Uber and Ola, Meru a competitor, alleged that Uber and Ola, entered into anti-competitive exclusivity agreements with their respective drivers foreclosing this input, and had abused their dominance by engaging in predatory pricing. The CCI dismissed the allegations on anti-competitive vertical restraints, noting that there was no evidence of any such agreement. In particular, it observed that:

> … both drivers and riders can have applications developed by multiple service providers and can 'multi-home'. The drivers/ fleet owners connected to various aggregators through apps, can easily switch between different aggregators depending on the incentive scheme etc. by simply switching off or switching on their mobile handsets. Moreover, there is no reason to believe that there are supply constraints in the market for drivers such that these alleged agreements can cause lock-ins and, hence, barriers to entry in the radio taxi services market.[14]

Further, while assessing the allegations of abuse, the CCI considered the market share data furnished by Meru and noted that in the radio taxi market, "market shares were neither an indicator of lack of competitive constraints nor depicted the real competition that existed in the market. Though market share is theoretically an important indicator for lack of competitive constraints, it is not a conclusive indicator of dominance."[15] Accordingly, the CCI did not find a case of dominance let alone abuse by these players.

4. OYO

In July 2019, the CCI rejected at the threshold stage a complaint against Oravel Stays ("OYO"), which provides budget accommodation in a franchise model. The complainant, a budget hotel operator alleged that OYO had abused its dominant

---

13 *Meru v. Uber*, CCI Case No. 96 of 2015, *Meru v. Uber*, CCI Case No. 81 of 2015, *Mega Cabs v. Ola*, CCI Case No. 82 of 2015, *Meru v. Ola and Uber*, CCI Case Nos. 25 – 28 of 2017.

14 *Meru v. Ola and Uber*, Case Nos. 25 – 28 of 2017, at paragraph 37.

15 *Id.* at paragraph 41.

position by imposing one-sided, unfair and discriminatory terms in a marketing and operational agreement, and would revise rates unilaterally.

The CCI held that even though OYO appeared to have the largest budget hotel network, and was a significant player in the "market for franchising services for budget hotels in India," it could not be "unambiguously concluded" that it was dominant.[16] In reaching its conclusion, the CCI noted that franchising was one of many business models for operating hotels, and counted for only a small percentage of the total rooms in the budget segment. Further, there was a large untapped number of hotels which could be accessed by existing and potential competitors of OYO, including online travel agencies/ aggregators.

Departing from its usual forbearance from assessing allegations of abuse where it finds no dominance, the CCI additionally considered the conduct of OYO. It considered that certain provisions in the agreement, including the requirement for commission on gross revenue and a prohibition on dealing with aggregators, were inherent to franchising arrangements and hence justified. The CCI also found justification for branding and benchmarking requirements, for the charging of taxation and platform fees and for the use of a quality evaluation tool to affect hotel rankings. Based on the above, the CCI concluded that the terms and conditions of the agreement were not unfair.

B. Where CCI Ordered an Investigation but did not Find a Violation: Ola Bangalore

A separate case against Ola was initiated by competitors, Fast Track and Meru, who alleged that Ola held a dominant position in the provision of "radio-taxi" services in the city of Bangalore and abused such dominant position through predatory pricing.

This case preceded the cases in the taxi aggregation market discussed previously. Here, the CCI initiated an in-depth investigation by its independent investigative wing, the Office of the Director General ("DG"). Following a detailed investigation, the CCI held that Ola was not dominant as its conduct was constrained by Uber, and could therefore not be guilty of any abuse. The CCI further stated that Ola's penetrative pricing strategy facilitated network development and interference was not required before a market develops.[17]

C. Where CCI Found a Violation: Matrimony.com v. Google

The CCI's first case against Google was triggered by two complaints filed in 2012 by Matrimony.com (an online matrimonial website) and The Consumer Unity & Trust Society, (a non-profit organisation focusing on consumer related issues).

---

16 *RKG Hospitalities v. Oravel Stays*, CCI Case No. 3 of 2019 ("*RKG v. OYO*").

17 *Ola Bangalore.*

Google was alleged to have engaged in running its core businesses of search and advertising in a discriminatory and anti-competitive manner which had caused harm to the advertisers, Google's competitors and users.

The CCI found Google to be visibly dominant in the markets of *"online general web search"* and *"online web search advertising."* The CCI noted that Google had the highest market share in both markets, which was exponentially greater than of its nearest competitor, Microsoft. Further, that as innovation was key in technology markets, it would be fair to expect that market shares in such markets should be transient. However, Google's market shares had been consistently high, which indicated that it benefitted from advantages beyond mere technical ones, which buttressed Google's position in the market. Further, the CCI was of the opinion that Google would not lose market share even if it were to reduce innovation given the high barriers to entry and Google's insurmountable scale advantage, which reduced effective competition.

The CCI agreed with the allegations that Google engaged in search manipulation, ensured undue prominence to its own commercial units and leveraged its dominance in the market for online general web search to strengthen its position in other markets. Having said this, not all of the allegations against Google stuck and the CCI, following an analysis of market conditions, accepted some of Google's justifications for the alleged abusive conduct.

Google's conduct that the CCI did find to be abusive related to *"traditional"* competition law abuses, i.e. discrimination, unfairness and leveraging. Such conduct has been held to be abusive in a number on non-technology market cases previously and demonstrates that the CCI does not require any additional tools for an assessment in the digital sector. Even then, as discussed earlier, the CCI admitted to exercising a *"self-imposed restraint"* and only interfered where it felt that Google's conduct was *"egregious."*[18]

D. Ongoing Investigations

In addition to the cases above, investigations into allegations of abuse of dominance have been ordered by the CCI in a few other cases.

1. Cases against Intel

In November 2018, the CCI directed an investigation into allegations of Intel's non-discriminatory access to information required to design server boards compatible with its processors. The CCI noted that Intel had a market share of 80-90 percent, and coupled with customer's preference for Intel and the consequent depen-

---

18 *Matrimony.com v. Google*, at paragraph 205.

dence of the complainant on it, the CCI *prima facie* held that Intel was in a dominant position and that an investigation into its conduct was warranted.[19]

The CCI separately considered a complaint against Intel by a parallel importer of microprocessors, alleging that Intel had abused its dominant position by refusing to provide warranty services within India to boxed microprocessors which had not been sourced from authorized Indian distributors. Here too, Intel was *prima facie* found to be dominant, in the market for boxed microprocessors for desktop and laptop PCs in India, by virtue of its market share, high barriers to entry, lack of countervailing buyer power and the dependence of consumers on Intel. While the complainant had also alleged that Intel had entered into anti-competitive exclusivity agreements with its dealers, and engaged in resale price maintenance in contravention of Section 3(4) of the Competition Act, the CCI declined to interfere on this ground for the lack of any supporting evidence.[20]

2. Google Android Investigation

In April 2019, the CCI *prima facie* found Google to be abusing its dominant position in the market for "licensable smart mobile device operating systems in India," and ordered an investigation into conduct surrounding the Android operating system. On the basis of evidence suggesting that Google's Android had approximately 90 percent of the relevant market, as well as drawing from its past investigation into Google's conduct in Matrimony.com v. Google, the CCI found that Google was *prima facie* dominant. The CCI found that Google's requirement to adhere to a compatibility standard for Android, by device manufacturers wishing to pre-install its proprietary apps (including Google Play Store), could reduce the ability and incentive of these device manufacturers to develop and sell devices operating on alternative versions of Android. The CCI held, *prima facie*, that Google imposed an unfair condition on the device manufacturers and limited technical and scientific development to the prejudice of consumers. The CCI also noted that Google's conduct amounted to leveraging of its dominance in crucial apps such as Play Store to protect markets such as online general search and resulted in denial of market access for competing search apps. Accordingly, the CCI directed an investigation against Google.[21]

E. Reflection on the CCI's Assessment Thus Far

While the CCI was assessing questions of anti-competitive conduct in digital markets so far, its decisional practice shows that it was restrained in its interference. Where clear evidence of dominance and abuse was available, the CCI did step in. For

---

19 *Velankani Electronics v. Intel Corporation*, CCI Case No. 16 of 2018.

20 *Matrix Info Systems v. Intel*, Case No. 5 of 2019.

21 *Umar Javeed v. Google LLC*, CCI Case No. 39 of 2018.

example, in cases against Google and Intel, there was evidence to show consistent high market shares, combined with consumer dependence, high barriers to entry, etc. However, at the same time, the CCI generally followed a hands-off approach, in line with its statements regarding the merits of non-intervention in technology markets. The large number of cases closed, particularly at the threshold stage are indicative of the CCI's view that high technology digital markets were nascent, fast moving, and evolving; therefore, undue intervention could cause more harm than any perceived benefit.

IV.   THE WATERSHED MOMENT: THE e-COMMERCE MARKET STUDY

The landmark shift in the CCI's approach came with the launch of the CCI's market study into e-Commerce (the Market Study). The aim of the Market Study was to allow the CCI to develop, a "better understanding of the functioning of e-commerce in the country and its implications for markets and competition."[22] In particular, the Market Study focussed on examining emerging trends in market structure, business models and practices, including contractual provisions and vertical restraints. The CCI utilized desk research, market surveys, as well as extensive consultation with the stakeholders across the country to achieve its aims.

The Market Study focused on the three broad categories of e-Commerce, namely, consumer goods, accommodation services and food services. During the stakeholders' consultations, and discussion on the CCI's interim findings in August 2019, several players including restaurant owners, hotels, online travel agencies, e-Commerce vendors, etc. highlighted and discussed practices such as deep discounting, and issues with algorithmic search ranking on digital platforms.[23]

These concerns were examined in detail, and the CCI's observations were finally published in January 2020.[24] The CCI identified a number of issues which in its view restrict competition in digital markets. For instance, in relation to platforms acting as both marketplaces as well as participants, the CCI noted that there may be incentives to provide preferential treatment to owned/ related businesses. The CCI also recognized a need for platforms to improve transparency on certain key issues such as the collection, use and sharing of data, and their review and rating mechanisms.

---

22   Press Release, CCI, "*CCI Market Study in E-commerce in India: Interim findings to be presented at a workshop*," available at https://www.cci.gov.in/sites/default/files/press_release/ ccipress.pdf, last accessed on April 30, 2020.

23   *CCI initiates market study on e-commerce*, Economic Times, August 30, 2019.

24   CCI, *Market Study on E-Commerce in India: Key Findings and Observations*, January 8, 2020.

Another key observation was in relation to contractual terms between platforms and the participants on them. In earlier cases, such as *WhatsApp*, the CCI had factored in the prevalence of multi-homing as a competitive constraint on the dominance of platforms. However, in the Market Study, the CCI noted that multi-homing was not an effective competitive constraint in cases where major platforms engaged in similar business practices. It was also observed that the asymmetry of bargaining power in favor of the platforms on account of fragmented supply, and the presence of only a few platforms, allowed them to impose unfair contract terms as well as unilaterally revise them. This could lead to both exploitative and exclusionary abuses (to be determined on a case-by-case basis). The CCI thus recognized the potential for anti-competitive conduct which can affect a market even where there was no one clear dominant player. The CCI expressed a need to protect the interest of all contracting parties in such cases.

Accordingly, the Market Study highlighted that the CCI needed to examine conduct using other tools at its disposal including assessing conduct under Section 3(4) of the Competition Act. The CCI observed that certain conduct, while not *per se* abusive, could be used as an exclusionary tactic to foreclose competition or impede entry, particularly in markets where there was already insufficient competition. Analysing such conduct under the provisions relating to vertical restraints allows the CCI to intervene at an earlier stage, if required, than in cases involving a high threshold of "*dominance*." Further, this approach also allows CCI to deal with situations where there may be more than one significant player whose conduct needs to be checked. This could otherwise not be dealt with as the concept of "collective" or "joint" dominance is alien to the Competition Act.

The Market Study nudged players in the e-Commerce markets to undertake self-regulatory measures to reduce information asymmetry, promote competition on the merits and foster a sustainable e-Commerce ecosystem in India. It also set a background for the CCI's enforcement actions that followed.

V.   CURRENT OUTLOOK ON DIGITAL MARKETS

A. Enforcement Action

Recent decisions of the CCI relating to digital markets evidence the shift in their approach towards greater interventionism.

1. MakeMyTrip - OYO

Following the publication of the CCI's interim findings from its Market Study, the CCI considered alleged abuse of dominant position and vertical restrictions in the hotel booking and franchise sectors. The complainant, the Federation of Hotel and Restaurant Associations of India, alleged that MakeMyTrip India ("MMT"), Ibibo Group ("GoIbibo") (collectively, "MMTGo")[25] and OYO had abused their dominant positions, cartelized and entered into restrictive vertical agreements with each other. The CCI defined separate relevant markets for MMTGo and OYO. It adopted its earlier market definition for OYO[26] and reiterated that there was no dominance in that market. Separately, the CCI found that MMTGo was *prima facie* dominant in the market for online intermediation services for booking of hotels in India. The CCI considered allegations of imposing room and price parity requirements, denial of market access, predatory pricing, misrepresentation of information and the charging of hotel service fees against MMTGo, and concluded that there was a *prima facie* case for investigating its conduct. The CCI also directed an investigation into an alleged agreement between MMTGo and OYO which raised *prima facie* concerns of exclusive dealing.

This decision came shortly after the CCI's closure of allegations against OYO in the other case discussed earlier. While in the previous case, the CCI assessed OYO's conduct from the lens of dominance, in this case the CCI reasoned that the vertical agreement between OYO and MMTGo could, *prima facie*, have an AAEC on the market and therefore, should be investigated.[27]

2. Flipkart – Amazon

Immediately following the release of the Market Study, the CCI directed an investigation into allegations of anti-competitive agreements between e-Commerce marketplaces Amazon and Flipkart, on the one hand, and sellers on these marketplaces, on the other. A Delhi based traders' body alleged that Amazon and Flipkart offered deep discounts through select preferred sellers who also benefited from preferential listings and exclusive tie-ups (such as with OEMs to be the exclusive seller for newly released phones), resulting in other retailers being excluded from the market. It was also alleged that Amazon and Flipkart were jointly dominant and were abusing their dominance.

In a marked shift from previous dismissals of allegations against these marketplaces, the CCI noted *prima facie* that competition between Amazon and Flipkart did not reduce the potential effect on competition as they followed the same practices. It also noted, in light of linkages between these preferred sellers and the marketplaces coupled with the allegations above, that the effect on other retailers also needed to be investigated. However, keeping with past practice, the CCI declined to address allegations of joint dominance.[28]

---

25 MMT had acquired GoIbibo in 2017, with these companies forming part of the same group, MMTGo.

26 *RKG v. OYO.*

27 *Federation of Hotel & Restaurant Associations of India v. MakeMyTrip India and OYO*, CCI Case No. 14 of 2019.

28 *Delhi Vyapar Mahasangh v. Flipkart and Amazon*, CCI Case No. 40 of 2019. This was challenged before the High Court of Karnataka which has since stayed the CCI's investigation.

B. Other Developments

The CCI's renewed focus on dealing with competition issues in digital markets was also reflected in the work of the Competition Law Review Committee ("CLRC"), which was set up in late 2018 to review the Competition Act. The CLRC was tasked to assess the existing competition regime, taking into account the inputs of key stakeholders, and to suggest changes in the substantive and procedural aspects of the law. The CLRC constituted "working groups," one of which was dedicated to examining the challenges posed by "New Age Markets and Big Data."

CLRC finalized its report in July 2019 ("CLRC Report").[29] While deliberating on challenges posed by posed by "New Age Markets and Big Data," CLRC examined the prevailing competition regime, and concluded that the tools available with the CCI were, by and large, broad enough to tackle the characteristics of digital markets.

However, the CLRC noted that high value transactions in digital markets might escape merger review in jurisdictions, such as India, that relied primarily on asset / turnover review thresholds. The CLRC Report recommended that the Government formulate new thresholds based on broad parameters including a "*size of transaction*" or "*size of deal*" to supplement the existing merger control framework of the Competition Act. Subsequently, the Government published draft amendments to the Competition Act which included a provision for introducing such "deal value" based thresholds.[30]

VI. CONCLUSION

It can be seen that the CCI has shifted its position from one of non-interference and demonstrated its desire to increase its involvement in digital markets. The shift is on account of a growing realization that its regulatory forbearance may not be sufficient to protect competition in the market.

The CCI previously focused its examination on practices such as predatory pricing, deep discounting, etc. under the provision relating to abuse of dominance. However, proving dominance in a rapidly changing digital space has proved to be difficult. In contrast, analysing such conduct under the provision relating to vertical restraint allows the CCI to interfere at an earlier stage, if required, and deal with a situation where more than one player held market power.

---

29 The CLRC Report published on the website of the Ministry of Corporate Affairs, Government of India ("MCA") is available at http://www.mca.gov.in/Ministry/pdf/ReportCLRC_14082019.pdf, last accessed on April 30, 2020.

30 The Draft Competition Amendment Bill, 2020 is published on the website of the MCA and is available at http://feedapp.mca.gov.in//pdf/Draft-Competition-Amendment-Bill-2020.pdf, last accessed on April 30, 2020.

The CLRC Report also recommended wider assessment of mergers in the digital space with the possibility of using "deal value" based thresholds as a tool to review transactions currently below the jurisdictional thresholds.

With all of this in the background, we have also observed an increased willingness on the part of competitors, consumers and associations to raise allegations of anti-competitive conduct in the digital ecosystem, particularly in relation to platforms. Some of these complainants have been unable to adapt to digital markets or have been slow to innovate, others are armchair lawyers and economists, and still others, appear to be proxies for big players who want to fight from the shadows. India is going to see a lot of activity in this space and provided the CCI intervenes in a targeted and proportionate manner, our competition law jurisprudence has a safe future.

Editors' bios

David S. Evans' academic work has focused on industrial organization, including antitrust economics, with a particular expertise in multisided platforms, digital economy, information technology, and payment systems. He has authored eight books, including two award winners, and more than one hundred articles in these areas. He has developed and taught courses related to antitrust economics, primarily for graduate students, judges and officials, and practitioners, and have authored handbook chapters on various antitrust subjects.

David's expert work has focused on competition policy and regulation. He has served as a testifying or consulting expert on many significant antitrust matters in the United States, European Union, and China. He has also made submissions to, and appearances before, competition and regulatory authorities with respect to mergers and investigations in those and other jurisdictions. David has worked on litigation matters for defendants and plaintiffs, on mergers for merging parties and intervenors, and for and in opposition to competition authorities.

Allan Fels AO graduated in economics (first class honors) and law from the University of Western Australia in 1965. He has a PhD in Economics from Duke University and was a research fellow in the Department of Applied Economics at the University of Cambridge from 1986-1972, where he wrote The British Prices and Incomes Board (Cambridge University Press, 1972).

On his return to Australia Professor Fels joined the Economics Department of Monash University as a Senior Lecturer, before becoming Professor of Administration and Director of the Graduate School of Management from 1984 until 1991.

The career of Professor Fels in Australia falls into two parts. He was generally regarded as the nation's leading regulator, serving as inaugural Chair of the Australian

Competition and Consumer Commission (and its predecessor bodies) from 1989 until 2003. The Australian Competition and Consumer Commission is the country's regulator of competition law and consumer law; it also regulates public utilities in the telecommunications and energy industries (in a similar manner to industry-specific bodies such as Ofcom in the UK and FCC in the US). He has had numerous other regulatory roles (for example, in insurance, agriculture, telecommunications, and aviation).

Professor Fels remains a leading figure globally in competition policy. He co-chaired the OECD Trade and Competition Committee from 1996 to 2003 and continues regularly to be a keynote speaker at major global competition events including the world's two peak events, the International Competition Network Annual Conference and the OECD Global Competition Forum.

He was a participant in the 15-year process of drafting the Chinese Antimonopoly Law 2008 and currently advises the Chinese government on the law's implementation. Academically, he is co-director of the Competition Research Centre at the Chinese Academy of Science, a prestigious position, and an international adviser to the Chinese Academy of Social Science.

The second part of Professor Fels' career has been academic. He was appointed Foundation Dean of the Australia and New Zealand School of Government and served in that position from 2003 until 2012. The predominant activity of the School has been the provision of management development programs to senior public servants in the two countries. There is also a substantial research program and other professional and outreach activities.

Catherine Tucker is the Sloan Distinguished Professor of Management and a Professor of Marketing at MIT Sloan. She is also Chair of the MIT Sloan PhD Program.

Her research interests lie in how technology allows firms to use digital data and machine learning to improve performance, and in the challenges this poses for regulation. Tucker has particular expertise in online advertising, digital health, social media, and electronic privacy. Her research studies the interface between marketing, the economics of technology, and law.

She has received an NSF CAREER Award for her work on digital privacy, the Erin Anderson Award for an Emerging Female Marketing Scholar and Mentor, the Garfield Economic Impact Award for her work on electronic medical records, the Paul E. Green Award for contributions to the practice of Marketing Research, the William F. O'Dell

Award for most significant, long-term contribution to Marketing, and the INFORMS Society for Marketing Science Long Term Impact Award for long-run impact on marketing.

She is a cofounder of the MIT Cryptoeconomics Lab which studies the applications of blockchain and also a co-organizer of the Economics of Artificial Intelligence initiative sponsored by the Alfred P. Sloan Foundation. She has been a Visiting Fellow at All Souls College, Oxford. She has testified to Congress regarding her work on digital privacy and algorithms, and presented her research to the OECD and the ECJ.

Catherine Tucker is coeditor at Quantitative Marketing and Economics, associate editor at Management Science, Marketing Science, and the Journal of Marketing Research and a research associate at the National Bureau of Economic Research. She teaches MIT Sloan's course on Pricing and the EMBA course "Marketing Management for the Senior Executive." She has received the Jamieson Prize for Excellence in Teaching as well as being voted "Teacher of the Year" at MIT Sloan.

She holds a PhD in economics from Stanford University and a BA from the University of Oxford.

Authors' Bios

Reiko Aoki has been Commissioner of the Japan Fair Trade Commission since 2016. She has conducted research and published on the economics of patents, patent pools, standards, innovation and intergenerational political economy in academic positions at the Ohio State University, SUNY Stony Brook, University of Auckland and Hitotsubashi University. She is Professor Emeritus of Hitotsubashi University. She has served as Executive Member of the Council for Science and Technology Policy, Japanese Cabinet Office 2009-2014, Member of the Information and Communication Council 2014-2016 and Member of Science Council of Japan 2014-2016. Prior to joining the JFTC, she was Executive Vice-President (International, Gender Equality, and Intellectual Property) at Kyushu University. She received her B.S. in mathematics from University of Tokyo, M.A. in economics from University of Tsukuba, and PhD in economics and MS in statistics from Stanford University. She is currently President of the Japanese Law and Economic Association, and Executive Board Member of the Japanese Economic Association.

Robert D. Atkinson is founder and president of the Information Technology and Innovation Foundation ("ITIF"), the world's leading think tank for science and technology policy. He is an internationally recognized scholar, a widely published author, and a trusted adviser to policymakers around the world, with expertise in the broad economics of innovation and specific policy and regulatory questions around new and emerging technologies. Rob's most recent book, co-authored with Michael Lind, is Big Is Beautiful: Debunking the Myth of Small Business.

Before founding ITIF, Atkinson was Vice President of the Progressive Policy Institute and Director of PPI's Technology & New Economy Project. He received his Masters in Urban and Regional Planning from the University of Oregon and was named a distinguished alumnus in 2014. He received his Ph.D. in City and Regional Planning from the University of North Carolina at Chapel Hill in 1989.

Simon Bishop is co-founder and Partner at RBB Economics. He has over 20 years' experience of providing expert economic advice in competition law matters and has advised on several hundred cases before competition authorities and courts around the world. Clients for whom Simon has acted as lead economist on several occasions include GE, British Airways, FA Premier League, Bertelsmann, Sony, and BHP Billiton.

Simon has published widely including reports and articles on market definition, non-horizontal mergers, bidding markets, loyalty rebates and vertical restraints. He is the co-author of The Economics of EC Competition Law (3rd edition, Sweet & Maxwell, 2009), a leading textbook on the application of economics to European competition law, and is co-editor of the European Competition Journal.

Aleksandra Boutin is a Founding Partner of Positive Competition. She is featured in the Who's Who Legal: Thought Leaders - Competition, a ranking listing the world's leading competition professionals. She has more than fifteen years of experience in competition policy as an enforcer, consultant and academic. She is a member of the Scientific Council of the GCLC and a Non-Governmental Advisor for Poland in the ICN.

Aleksandra advises clients on a wide range of competition issues in the context of competition proceedings in front of the European Commission, National Competition Authorities and Courts. Her recent experiences involve cartel overcharge analysis, vertical and horizontal mergers, exclusionary and exploitative abuses, state aid and information exchanges. She has also advised clients in antitrust cases involving digital platforms in e-commerce and in the software industry.

On the policy front, she was the lead author of the European Commission's Guidelines on Horizontal Cooperation Agreements and Block Exemption Regulations, she participated in preparing the communication of the Commission on quantifying harm in antitrust damage actions and in the Commission's IP Guidelines.

Aleksandra holds a Master in Theoretical Economics and Econometrics from Toulouse School of Economics, and a Master in European Law and Economic Analysis from the College of Europe. She completed her PhD studies at the Université Libre de Bruxelles.

Xavier Boutin is a founding partner at Positive Competition and an adjunct professor of economics at the Université libre de Bruxelles. He holds a PhD in Economics from EHESS (Paris School of Economics). He is featured in the Who's Who Legal Thought Leader: Competition, a ranking listing the world's leading competition professionals. Xavier is also a founding and board member of l'Entente, the association of French speaking antitrust practitioners in Brussels.

Xavier leads a team of consultants advising clients in the context of merger, State Aid and antitrust proceedings in front of the European Commission and national competition authorities. Prior to founding Positive Competition, Xavier was an expert in an international consultancy. Before joining the private sector, he spent almost eight years in the Chief Economist Team of the European Commission's DG Competition.

Xavier made a major contribution to the EU Commission's Article 102 guidance paper, its Article 101 horizontal guidelines and the accompanying Block Exemption Regulation ("BER"). He also contributed to the State Aid Modernization, in particular, in the areas of R&D&I and Regional Aid.

Xavier's most recent work includes the assessment of vertical and horizontal mergers. In addition, Xavier has led many investigations involving exclusionary and exploitative abuses in the digital platform sector. These include the assessment of vertical restraints and self-preferencing in e-commerce, as well as Article 102 cases in the software industry.

Burcu Can graduated from Ankara University, Faculty of Law in 2008. Over five years of her close to 10 years of career in competition law was devoted to the Turkish Competition Authority as a competition expert case handler. Burcu has obtained her LL.M. degree from Harvard Law School and worked for many years at the Brussels office of one of the top international law firms as a competition lawyer. During her years at the Turkish Competition Authority, Burcu took part in leading antitrust and merger cases concerning banking, finance, motor vehicle and transportation sectors, contributed to the preparation of secondary legislation for competition law and several International Competition Network projects. In addition to her LL.M. degree from Harvard Law School, Burcu also has a master's degree in commercial law from Gazi University in Turkey. Burcu is a member of the New York Bar and the Istanbul Bar.

Sayanti Chakrabarti is the Joint Director in the Economics Division of the Competition Commission of India, where she is responsible for carrying out economic analysis of antitrust and merger cases. She has also contributed to several research outputs of the Division on competition law and policy. Prior to joining the CCI in 2010, Sayanti worked with the Economic Affairs Team of the Federation of Indian Chambers of Commerce and Industry, where she contributed to a number of surveys and studies on issues of importance to the Indian business and economy. She holds an MSc in Economics from Calcutta University.

Naval Satarawala Chopra is a partner at Shardul Amarchand Mangaldas and has been practicing competition law since its inception in India. He is the first Indian lawyer in GCR's top "40 under 40" competition lawyers in the world (2015);

listed as a global "thought leader" (Who'sWhoLegal); and recognized regularly as a leading advisor in Chambers & Partners.

Naval has been involved in some of the most prominent abuse of dominance cases in India. He is particularly skilled in advising on antitrust aspects of technology related matters, having successfully defended WhatsApp in relation to its privacy policy and separately digital payments services, Microsoft Corporation in relation to software licensing terms and Uber in relation alleged predatory pricing, before the Competition Commission of India ("CCI").

Naval has recently advised Facebook in its acquisition of minority share-holding in India's fastest growing telecom company. He has also advised in Avago's acquisition of Broadcom, Ctrip's investment in MakeMyTrip, the failed merger of Publicis and Omnicom as well as the conditional approval for Bayer AG's acquisition of Monsanto Company.

Naval also advises a number of clients in cartel cases and is involved in challenges on account of due process and natural justice issues before the Supreme Court of India.

David S. Evans' academic work has focused on industrial organization, including antitrust economics, with a particular expertise in multisided platforms, digital economy, information technology, and payment systems. He has authored eight books, including two award winners, and more than one hundred articles in these areas. He has developed and taught courses related to antitrust economics, primarily for graduate students, judges and officials, and practitioners, and have authored handbook chapters on various antitrust subjects.

David's expert work has focused on competition policy and regulation. He has served as a testifying or consulting expert on many significant antitrust matters in the United States, European Union, and China. He has also made submissions to, and appearances before, competition and regulatory authorities with respect to mergers and investigations in those and other jurisdictions. David has worked on litigation matters for defendants and plaintiffs, on mergers for merging parties and intervenors, and for and in opposition to competition authorities.

Máté Fodor is an Economist at Positive Competition. Prior to joining the company, he was an assistant professor of Econometrics and Game Theory at the International School of Economics, a University of London affiliate institution. Máté holds a MSc. in Economics from Trinity College Dublin, where he was the recipient of the Terrence Gorman Prize for valedictorian. After consulting missions for the public sector authorities, he joined ECARES at the Université libre de Bruxelles to obtain his PhD in Economics. He has secured research funding from several prestigious grants, such as the Marie Curie Framework and FNRS. His research profile is diverse with peer-reviewed publications in political economy, labor, energy, development, and media economics.

Since joining Positive Competition, Máté has worked on abuse of dominance cases involving digital platforms in the e-commerce and software industries. Máté has also been involved in overcharge and damages estimations in the construction and primary resources industries. He has also contributed to the economic assessment of mergers.

Gönenç Gürkaynak is a founding partner of ELIG Gürkaynak Attorneys-at-Law, a leading law firm of 90 lawyers based in Istanbul, Turkey. Mr. Gürkaynak graduated from Ankara University, Faculty of Law in 1997, and was called to the Istanbul Bar in 1998. Mr. Gürkaynak received his LL.M. degree from Harvard Law School in 2001, and is qualified to practice in Istanbul, New York, Brussels, and England and Wales. Before founding ELIG Gürkaynak Attorneys-at-Law in 2005, Mr. Gürkaynak worked as an attorney at the Istanbul, New York, and Brussels offices of a global law firm for more than eight years of his total of 23 years of career in private practice so far. Mr. Gürkaynak heads the competition law and regulatory department of ELIG Gürkaynak Attorneys-at-Law, which currently consists of 45 lawyers. He has unparalleled experience in Turkish competition law counselling issues with more than 23 years of competition law experience, starting with the establishment of the Turkish Competition Authority. Mr. Gürkaynak frequently speaks at local and international conferences and symposia on competition law matters. He has published more than 200 articles in English and Turkish by various international and local publishers, and he has published three books. Mr. Gürkaynak also holds teaching positions at undergraduate and graduate levels at two universities, and gives lectures in other universities.

Peter K. Huston is a partner in the San Francisco office of Baker Botts. He has 30 years of experience in high-stakes civil and criminal antitrust litigation, trials, government investigations, class actions and merger clearance work, both in and out of government. In 2020 he was recognized in the 27th Edition of Best Lawyers in America. Prior to joining Baker Botts, Peter served as Assistant Chief in the San Francisco Office of the Antitrust Division of the United States Department of Justice where he led and supervised both criminal price-fixing matters and civil merger matters. For his government service, Peter was awarded the Attorney General's Distinguished Service Award and was twice awarded the Antitrust Division's Award of Distinction. He also received the California Lawyer Attorney of the Year Award in 2013 and was named to the Daily Journal Top 100 Lawyers in 2012. Peter currently serves on the Executive Committee of the California Lawyers Association Antitrust, Unfair Competition and Privacy Law Section and the ABA International Cartel Task Force.

Tetsuya Kanda has been a Senior Planning Officer in Legal System Planning Division, Consumer Affairs Agency ("CAA") of Japan, since July 2019. In the current capacity, he is in charge of an initiative to reinforce the Whistleblower Protection Act.

Prior to the current position, he held various positions in the Japan Fair Trade Commission ("JFTC"), in both fields of investigation and policymaking. Mostly recently, he was a Senior Planning Officer for Investigation from 2017 to 2019, where he dealt with procedural and substantive issues of investigations against major technology firms. His past responsibility in the JFTC includes drafting of law amendments strengthening public enforcement of the Japanese Antimonopoly Act and its "monopoly" guidelines.

He was seconded to the Directorate-General for Competition of the European Commission from 2012 to 2013.

He holds a Master of Public Policy from the University of Michigan and a Bachelor of Laws from the University of Tokyo. He also teaches the Japanese competition law at the Graduate School of Law, Meiji University in Tokyo.

Joe Kennedy is a senior fellow at ITIF. For almost 30 years he has worked as an attorney and economist on a wide variety of public policy issues. His previous positions include chief economist with the U.S. Department of Commerce and general counsel for the U.S. Senate Permanent Subcommittee on Investigations. He is president of Kennedy Research, LLC, and the author of Ending Poverty: Changing Behavior, Guaranteeing Income, and Transforming Government (Rowman & Littlefield, 2008). Kennedy has a law degree and a master's degree in agricultural and applied economics from the University of Minnesota and a Ph.D. in economics from George Washington University.

Maria Khan is a Research Associate in the Economics Division of the Competition Commission of India. She has over five years of work experience in the field of Competition Law and Policy. She is responsible for carrying out economic assessment of antitrust conduct cases and mergers and acquisitions, competition advocacy and research related to competition law and policy. Maria is an Economist by qualification and holds an M.Phil. in Economics degree from Jawaharlal Nehru University, New Delhi and a Post Graduate degree in Economics from Jamia Millia Islamia, New Delhi.

Thomas Kramler is head of the unit dealing with e-Commerce and the data economy in the European Commission's Directorate General for Competition. Before that, he was Head of the Digital Single Market Task Force responsible for the e-commerce sector inquiry. Mr. Kramler holds a law degree and a PhD from the University of Vienna, Austria. He has graduated with a Master's degree in European Community Law from the College of Europe (Bruges).

Previously Mr. Kramler was deputy head of the unit responsible for antitrust cases in the information industries, internet and consumer electronics sectors. Before joining the European Commission, Mr. Kramler worked as agent representing the Austrian government before the European Courts in Luxemburg.

Andrew Low is a senior lawyer in Gilbert + Tobin's competition and regulation group. Andrew's practice is directed to providing complex advice and advocacy for clients in complex and high-profile matters across each core area of the Competition and Consumer Act (including complex merger clearance, enforcement investigations, industry inquiries, and dispute resolution).

Andrew has a particular expertise and interest in, and has contributed significant thought leadership to, digital issues for competition policy and regulation. This includes chairing sessions including with the ACCC Chairman and international experts Maurice Stucke and Ariel Ezrachi on reflections on the Digital Platforms Inquiry and whether Robots Can Collude?. He has authored a number of papers including Decoding the Data Lifecycle, ACCC signals a changing approach to digital M&A, Digital Reform unfolds, and Impact of competition policy on data access and management, and the soon to be published Digital Competition Australia 2021 (Lexology/GTDT). He has spoken at the Law Council of Australia's Rising Stars 2019 Conference on digital competition policy.

Such thought leadership is supported by in-depth commercial experience advising large tech companies. He is widely recognised by key clients as a rising star competition lawyer and is sought after by clients for his digital economy expertise.

Payal Malik is Adviser, Economics and Head of the Economics Division at the Competition Commission of India. She is on secondment from PGDAV College,

University of Delhi, where she is an Associate Professor of Economics. Her areas of expertise are competition law, policy and regulation. She has several years of research and economic consulting experience in network Industries such as power and tele-communication, ICTs, Innovation systems, and Infrastructure.

Her research and professional collaborations have been with NCAER, Delhi, OECD, Orbicom, IDEI, University of Toulouse, University Of Québec at Montreal, CEPR, JRC, European Commission, IPTS Seville, ICEGEC, Hungary, Department of Information Technology, TRAI, Ministry of Power, Ministry of Information and Broadcasting, Planning Commission of India, CSO, India, WSP-SA, World Bank and AFD, Paris. She was on the team that drafted the Electricity Act of India ushering competition into the sector.

She has a BA (Hons.) in Economics from Lady Shri Ram College, University of Delhi and an MA and MPhil in Economics from the Delhi School of Economics. She also has an MBA in finance from University of Cincinnati, Ohio.

Vinicius Marques de Carvalho is Partner at VMCA Advogados and Professor of Commercial Law at the University of São Paulo. He holds a PhD in Com-mercial Law from the University of São Paulo and a PhD from the University Paris I (Pantheon-Sorbonne) in Public Comparative Law. He was a Yale Greenberg World Fel-low (2016), President of the Administrative Council for Economic Defense ("CADE") (2012-2016), Vice-President of the International Competition Network (2013-2016), Secretary of Economic Law (2011-2012) and Commissioner at CADE (2008-2011).

Marcela Mattiuzzo is Partner at VMCA Advogados and PhD Candidate in Commercial Law at the University of São Paulo. She holds a Masters in Constitu-tional Law from the same institution and was Visiting Researcher at Yale Law School. She was Advisor and Chief of Staff at the Office of the President at the Administrative Council for Economic Defense ("CADE"), Commissioner at the Federal Fund for the Defense of Collective Rights and CADE's representative before the National Strategy for the Fight Against Corruption and Money Laundering.

Andreas Mundt has been President of the Bundeskartellamt since 2009, member of the Bureau of the OECD Competition Committee since 2010 and the Steering Group Chair of the International Competition Network since 2013.

After qualifying as a lawyer, Andreas Mundt entered the Federal Ministry of Economics in 1991. In 1993 he joined the staff of the Free Democratic Party in the

German Parliament. In 2000 he joined the Bundeskartellamt as rapporteur and later acted as Head of the International Unit and Director of General Policy.

Maureen K. Ohlhausen chairs the antitrust group at Baker Botts LLP, where she focuses on competition, privacy and regulatory issues and frequently represents clients in the tech, life sciences, energy, and retail industries. She served as Acting FTC Chairman from January 2017 to May 2018 and as a Commissioner starting in 2012. She directed all FTC competition and consumer protection work, with a particular emphasis on privacy and technology issues. Ms. Ohlhausen has published dozens of articles on antitrust, privacy, regulation, FTC litigation, and telecommunications law issues and has testified over a dozen times before Congress. She has received numerous awards, including the FTC's Robert Pitofsky Lifetime Achievement Award. Prior to serving as a Commissioner, Ms. Ohlhausen led the FTC's Internet Access Task Force and headed the FTC practice group at a leading communications law firm. Ms. Ohlhausen clerked at the U.S. Court of Appeals for the D.C. Circuit and received her J.D. with distinction from the George Mason University School of Law and her B.A. with honors from the University of Virginia.

Dr. Burton Ong, LLB (NUS); LLM (Harv); BCL/DPhil (Oxon) is an Associate Professor at the Faculty of Law, National University of Singapore ("NUS"), where he teaches and researches in the fields of competition law, intellectual property and contract law. He is an Advocate and Solicitor of the Supreme Court of Singapore, as well as an Attorney and Counsellor-at-Law in New York State. He is a member of the Ministry of Trade and Industry's Competition Appeal Board, an IP Adjudicator with the Intellectual Property Office of Singapore and sits on the dispute resolution panel of the Casino Regulatory Authority. He is a Director (Competition Law) at the EW Barker Centre for Law and Business at the National University of Singapore. He is the editor of "The Regionalisation of Competition Law and Policy Within the ASEAN Economic Community" (2018), published by Cambridge University Press.

Alejandra Palacios, Chair of Mexico's Federal Economic Competition Commission (Comisión Federal de Competencia Económica; "COFECE") is the first woman to head the Mexican antitrust authority. Following a major constitutional reform that set forth a new framework for competition in Mexico, Alejandra was appointed by Congress in 2013 to head the COFECE. She was reelected in 2017 for a second four-year tenure that will end in September 2021.

Before her current role at COFECE, Alejandra worked as Project Director at the Mexican Institute of Competitiveness (the Instituto Mexicano para la Competitividad; "IMCO") for research projects focused on economic regulation, telecom, public procurement and other issues related to competition.

Since June 2016, she is Vice-President for the International Competition Network ("ICN"), the most prominent international network on competition, composed of 138 competition authorities around the world, and as of 2017, Member of the Bureau of the Competition Committee of the Organisation for Economic Cooperation and Development ("OECD"). Alejandra is also a member of the International Women's Forum, Mexico chapter. In 2019 the Women@Competition organization included her in its list of "40 in their 40s" as one of the 40 most notable women in competition in the Americas, Asia and Europe.

Alejandra holds a bachelor's degree in Economics, as well as an MBA from the Instituto Tecnológico Autónomo de México ("ITAM"). She completed a second master's degree in public policy at the Centro de Investigación y Docencia Económicas ("CIDE").

Her academic work includes teaching as well as serving as the Academic Coordinator for the ITAM Economics faculty.

Aman Singh Sethi is a Principal Associate at Shardul Amarchand Mangaldas. He has a diverse work experience, and has been closely involved on matters pertaining to anti-competitive agreements and abuse of dominance before the CCI, the National Company Law Appellate Tribunal as well as the Supreme Court of India. He has also been involved in a number of challenges seeking due process and the preservation of natural justice rights for clients against the CCI before the High Court of Delhi.

Aman has worked for several clients in the high-tech/disruptive industry, agrochemicals and agricultural traits, cement, petrochemicals, and telecommunication sectors in contentious cases. He also writes, and advises clients, on issues related to the interplay of competition law and intellectual property.

Along with co-authors Naval Satarawala Chopra and Yaman Verma, he successfully represented Matrimony.com in an abuse of dominance case against Google. Aman has also represented Uber and Indian hospitality disruptor OYO in wins against abuse of dominance claims before the CCI.

George Siolis joined the Melbourne office as a Partner when RBB Economics was established in Australia in 2009, and since then he has advised clients on a number of contentious mergers before the ACCC as well as a variety of behavioral matters involving the alleged misuse of market power. He is a member of the Consumer and Competition Committee of the Business Law Section of the Australian Law Council and is listed in Who's Who Legal of Competition Lawyers and Economists. George has worked as a micro-economist for 20 years. Prior to joining RBB Economics George worked with Telstra and was an economic consultant based in the UK for eight years where he developed and led the communications practice at Europe Economics.

Celestine Song is an Assistant Director at the Competition and Consumer Commission of Singapore, where she leads teams working across a wide range of competition enforcement, policy formulation, outreach and advocacy work, including providing competition advice to government agencies. Prior to joining CCCS in 2014, Celestine worked on manpower and productivity policy formulation matters in the Ministry of Manpower. Celestine holds a bachelor's degree in Economics from the Nanyang Technological University of Singapore and a masters' degree in Public Policy from Peking University.

Hi-Lin Tan is the director of the policy and markets division and a member of the senior management at the Competition and Consumer Commission of Singapore, where he is involved in engaging and advising other government agencies on competition matters, and conducting market studies, investigations, and other competition law enforcement activities. Among the cases he has supervised include a market study on online travel booking, and abuse of dominance investigations into online food delivery and payment terminals.

Prior to joining CCCS in 2007, he was a teaching fellow at Boston College, a trading member of the Singapore Exchange, and an economist at the Monetary Authority of Singapore. He holds a PhD in economics from Boston College and master's and bachelor's degrees from the London School of Economics.

Sinem Ugur is a senior associate at ELIG Gürkaynak Attorneys-at-Law. She graduated from Istanbul Commerce University, Faculty of Law in 2011. She is admitted to the Istanbul Bar and has experience close to 10 years in competition law in a variety of industries. She provides legal consultancy to global and domestic clients in all areas of competition law including vertical agreements, abuse of dominance, cartel cases, concentrations, joint ventures, and compliance programs. Sinem Ugur has co-authored numerous articles relating to competition law and international trade matters in English and Turkish. She is also fluent in German.

Yaman Verma is a Partner at Shardul Amarchand Mangaldas with over 10 years' experience practicing competition law. He is recognized as a "future leader" (Who'sWhoLegal, 2017-20); a "rising star" (Competition/Antitrust, Expert Guides, 2018-20) and included in the list of "next generation lawyers" for India (Legal 500, 2017-20).

Yaman has successfully defended WhatsApp against abuse of dominance allegations in relation to its privacy policy, Microsoft Corporation against allegations of unfair and discriminatory software licensing terms, and e-tailer Flipkart against allegations of preferential treatment and discrimination.

Yaman has recently advised on Facebook's acquisition of minority shareholding in India's fastest growing telecom company. Previously, he helped obtain unconditional approvals for Vodafone India's merger with Idea Cellular Limited, the capital alliance between Suzuki Motor Corporation and Toyota Motor Corporation, the Fiat/Peugeot merger, Walmart's acquisition of Flipkart (and successfully defended the approval in follow on litigation), and Microsoft's acquisition of Nokia's mobile telephony business. He has also advised on obtaining conditional approvals for several major global transactions, including Dow/DuPont, Agrium/PotashCorp, and Linde/Praxair.

Yaman has represented Globecast Asia in their leniency application before the Commission, and was successful in obtaining a 100 percent reduction in penalty for Globecast and its officials. He advises several trade associations in relation to compliance with competition laws.

Beth Webster is Director of the Centre for Transformative Innovation at Swinburne University of Technology. She is also Pro Vice-Chancellor for Research Impact and Policy. Her expertise centers on the economics of the way knowledge is created and diffused through the economy. She has a PhD in economics from the University of Cambridge and an M.Ec and B.Ec (hons) from Monash University. She is a fellow of the Academy of Social Sciences Australia.

Professor Webster is responsible for providing advice and leadership on policies relating to the economic and social impact of research, public industry and innovation policies. She is also responsible for measuring university research engagement and impact.

Professor Webster has authored over 100 articles on the economics of innovation and firm performance and has been published in RAND Journal of Economics, Review of Economics and Statistics, Oxford Economic Papers, Journal of Law & Economics, the Journal of International Economics and Research Policy. She has been appointed to a number of committees including the Bracks' review of the automotive industry, Lomax-Smith Base funding Review, CEDA Advisory Council, and the Advisory Council for Intellectual Property. She is a past President of the European Policy for Intellectual Property Association and is the current General Secretary of the Asia Pacific Innovation Network.

Luke Woodward heads Gilbert + Tobin's Competition and Regulation group, advising and representing clients on competition and consumer law investigations and prosecutions, ACCC acquisition and merger clearances and infrastructure regulation, including in the digital, telecommunications, gas, electricity, water, airports, sea ports and rail industries in Australia.

He has over 30 years competition and consumer law enforcement experience, both on the enforcement side with the former Trade Practices Commission ("TPC") and Australian Competition and Consumer Commission ("ACCC"), and in private practice. Prior to joining the firm in 2000, Luke held senior positions at the ACCC as General Counsel, Executive General Manager, Compliance Division (responsible for enforcement) and Senior Assistant Commissioner, responsible for mergers and asset sales.

Luke was awarded "Competition Lawyer of the Year" in Best Lawyers 2021 and is recognized as "the ultimate strategist" by a client who notes: "He knows the law, knows the ACCC inside and out and knows the best way to approach a matter from a strategic perspective; it's a real value-add." (Chambers Asia-Pacific 2020).